Accommodating the Republic

KIRSTEN E. WOOD

Accommodating the Republic
Taverns in the Early United States

The University of North Carolina Press *Chapel Hill*

*This book was published with the assistance of the Thornton H. Brooks Fund
of the University of North Carolina Press.*

Set in Arno Pro by Westchester Publishing Services
Manufactured in the United States of America

Library of Congress Cataloging-in-Publication Data
Names: Wood, Kirsten E., author.
Title: Accommodating the Republic : taverns in the early United States / Kirsten E. Wood.
Other titles: Taverns in the early United States
Description: Chapel Hill : The University of North Carolina Press, 2023. |
    Includes bibliographical references and index.
Identifiers: LCCN 2023025312 | ISBN 9781469675534 (cloth ; alk. paper) |
    ISBN 9781469675541 (paperback ; alk. paper) | ISBN 9781469675558 (ebook)
Subjects: LCSH: Bars (Drinking establishments)—United States—History—19th century. |
    Bars (Drinking establishments)—Economic aspects—United States—History—
    19th century. | Infrastructure (Economics)—United States. | United States—Social life
    and customs—19th century. | BISAC: HISTORY / United States / Colonial Period
    (1600–1775) | SOCIAL SCIENCE / Sociology / Urban
Classification: LCC TX950.56 .W66 2023 | DDC 647.9573—dc23/eng/20230608
LC record available at https://lccn.loc.gov/2023025312

Cover illustration: Drawing of tavern, ca. 1852, by Augustus Kollner.
Courtesy of the Library Company of Philadelphia.

For Tom, who knows all the reasons why

Contents

Illustrations

Acknowledgments

Like any historian, I owe a great debt to librarians and archivists, without whom we could not work. I want particularly to thank the archivists and staff at the Library Company of Philadelphia, especially Connie King and Sarah Weatherwax, the Historical Society of Pennsylvania, the American Philosophical Society, the New-York Historical Society, the New York Public Library, the New York State Archives, the Southern Historical Collection at the University of North Carolina, the David M. Rubenstein Library at Duke University, and Baker Library at the Harvard Business School. Special thanks also to the reproductions and the permissions departments at the New York Public Library, the American Antiquarian Society, the Library Company, the Toledo Museum of Art, the Saint Louis Museum of Art, and Hargrett Library at the University of Georgia, especially Brianne Barrett, Emily Smith, Julia Hayes, Jason Gray, and Mary Palmer Linnemann. I do not know how often they and their colleagues receive requests from headless chickens in human shape, but I am grateful for their calm efficiency. Sophie Labys and Bryant Keith Barnes did some archival legwork for me as I looked for appropriate images. Immediately after finishing work on a demanding show, Christa Kelly created new drawings for me, which turned out even better than I had hoped.

As with many research projects, money shaped this book's contours. Early funding from a Gilder-Lehrman Institute fellowship at the New-York Historical Society, an Isaac Comly Martindale Library Research Fellowship from the American Philosophical Society, a Society for Historians of the Early American Republic Fellowship at the Library Company of Philadelphia, and a Faculty Research Award from the College of Arts and Sciences at Florida International University (FIU) helped me launch the project. At the same time, these funding sources also helped ensure this project's mid-Atlantic evidentiary slant. That orientation is, happily, true to the region's significance in the period and the dynamics I explore. A different early influence on this book's geographic scope came from learning that a graduate student, Adam Criblez, was already researching taverns in the Midwest. Although he ended up moving in another direction, at the time I resolved not to crowd a junior scholar's turf. For these and other reasons, this book does not fully represent the vast early republic. I hope my readers will agree that there is both room and need for additional work on the early republic's taverns.

The opportunity to lay down a thick foundation of archival and library research guided my later research in digitized primary collections. I drew many of my published primary sources from Accessible Archives, Readex's America's Historical Newspapers, HathiTrust Digital Library, HeinOnline, Sabin Americana, LexisNexis, the Library of Congress's Chronicling America, the University of North Carolina's Documenting the American South, the Internet Archive, Google Books, and Newspapers by Ancestry. I also relied on A New Nation Votes, the National Historic GIS data sets at IPUMS, the Atlas of Historical County Boundaries at the Newberry Library, and several other digital history projects, as well as Ancestry, FamilySearch, JSTOR, Project MUSE, and the indispensable services of interlibrary loan. Some of these resources are free to the public, many I reached courtesy of my university library's institutional subscriptions, and for a few I invested in personal subscriptions. For better or worse, this wealth of digitized materials made it possible for me not to make long research trips once I had a young family. At the same time, having reveled in (and struggled with) the ever-expanding trove of digitized primary sources, I have come to appreciate all over again the critical importance of having begun this project with funded time in the archives.

Foundational intellectual support and guidance came in the form of summer seminars, which provided opportunities to engage deeply in my own work and with other scholars. I spent a happy month in Philadelphia at a National Endowment for the Humanities seminar run by John Larson and Mike Morrison and hosted at the Library Company and the Historical Society of Pennsylvania. I spent a shorter but also formative period at the American Antiquarian Society for a seminar on newspapers and the culture of print, headed by John Nerone and David Paul Nord.

At the University of North Carolina Press, Chuck Grench encouraged me to believe in my project and ensured a smooth transition to Debbie Gershenowitz when he retired. Debbie supported me in taking the time I needed to rewrite the book after the first round of readers' reports. JessieAnne D'Amico helped me navigate the ins and outs of permissions with great good humor. For their help in the publishing process, I also thank Kristen Bettcher, Mary Carley Caviness, Madge Duffey, Iris Levesque, Joyce Li, Lindsay Starr, and Dylan White. My thanks as well to Susan Certo for creating the index and to Jessica Ryan for providing expert proofreading assistance. The anonymous peer reviewers provided supportive, challenging feedback about my arguments, structure, and writing, without which I would never have imagined this book into the shape it has finally taken. I was touched when John Larson unmasked himself since he saw the project at its inception.

At FIU, my longtime department chairs Ken Lipartito and Victor Uribe supported me with course releases and reminders to move forward, not in circles. Ken also helped me understand how business history's insights could inform my work; he may not approve of what I did with his suggestions, but I appreciate them all the same. Bianca Premo and Rebecca Friedman supported me as I began to write, reading multiple early iterations of my first chapters. Our conversations about space, time, suffering, and nostalgia have stuck with me over the years. I also owe special thanks to Jessica Adler, Jenna Gibbs, April Merleaux, and Okezi Otovo for their friendship and support. Watching my undergraduate and graduate students light up as they wrestle with old sources and fresh scholarship continues to inspire me to return to my own work. It is an honor to accompany them in doing the hard work of history.

Looking beyond my department, I also have many people to thank. Rosanne Adderley, Ed Baptist, Mark Cheathem, Niki Eustace, Drew Faust, Craig Friend, Patrice Gammon, Bonnie Gordon, Joshua Greenberg, Sally Hadden, Tom Humphrey, Kate Jewell, Catherine Kelly, Daniel Kilbride, Sarah Knott, Lara Kriegel, Anya Jabour, Kirsten Meisinger, Christopher Olsen, Dominique Reill, Keith Revell, Jennifer Ritterhouse, Seth Rockman, Honor Sachs, Renée Silverman, Abby Schrader, Allison Sneider, Amy Torbert, and Natalie Zacek all helped me at different points and varied ways; some of them may not even remember how, but I appreciate them all. Right before the pandemic altered our lives, I was lucky enough to present a chapter at the McNeil Center for Early American Studies: many thanks to Dan Richter and the generous members of that community for their incisive feedback. I owe a special debt to Cindy Kierner and Lorri Glover for reading the whole manuscript on short notice before I first sent it to the University of North Carolina Press. I am grateful for their friendship and academic generosity. Ashli White has been an insightful reader, a good friend and neighbor, a guide through the thicket of image permissions, and a moral support in the war against backyard iguanas. For mentorship, guidance, and opportunities at critical junctures, my thanks to Glenda Gilmore, Caroline Simpson, and especially Suzanna Rose. Karen Dainer-Best helps me see the humane possibilities between impossible success and abject failure.

My sister Karin understands the highs and lows of this journey as well as any nonhistorian could. At least she should, given the time I have spent talking her ears off. I am a lucky duck to have her in my life. I have also been very lucky in my parents, who are still happy to see us—and hear about taverns and life in academia—even after the unusually prolonged visits that travel in COVID-19 times required. I apologize for all the times my anxiety prompted me to give curt or snarky answers to sincere questions. For their friendship, fellowship, wisdom, and good humor, I thank Laura Leigh Rampey and Ron Cox, Julian and Pam Edward, and Willie Allen-Faiella and my cheering squad at Saint Stephen's Episcopal Church. I am grateful, too, for my in-laws, the Leness-Boudreau-Southworth family, for their kindness over the years as well as their patient curiosity about this book. I wish I had finished it in time for my father-in-law Tim to see it.

Even with all those wonderful people in my life, finishing this book became a surprisingly hard and lonely journey. I started the archival research at the same time my husband and I decided that we would embark on the wild journey of parenthood. I had no idea then that this book would become a similar leap of faith. I once believed that finishing my first book and getting tenure would cure impostor syndrome and anxiety's other manifestations. Ha. As my children were born and began to grow up, I wrote hundreds of pages that seemed to go nowhere and spent rather a lot of time in the bleak corners of my mind. Yet, while thinking about this book's gestation period can still make me flinch, I have gained two important insights. First, I gave myself a bigger challenge than I initially realized when I crafted a project that drew me into questions, literatures, and sources so different from those of my first book. Tenure gives you that freedom, but I did not realize what that freedom might mean until I was years into this book.

The second insight is more personal. For well over a decade, I felt torn in two, and I believed that this feeling meant that my "mom side" and my "historian side" were at war. And yes, being a parent and being a historian could each be a full-time vocation. Yet the kids have truly been a reason to finish this book. Now young adults, my children have grown up watching their mother working hard on something that no one else needed her to do and no one else cared all that much if she ever finished. Watching my children invest time, effort, and even pain in projects of their own choosing has helped me realize that the deep conflict I felt stemmed not just from some work-parenthood dilemma but from my attempts to suppress ambitions and hopes I thought I had lost the right to feel. I dedicate this book not to George and Anne, however, but to my husband Tom, who neither gave up on me nor suggested that I might let my research agenda go.

Although I started thinking about this book in 2005, it finally came together in the shadow of environmental dangers, medical catastrophes, and political challenges the likes of which I had naively hoped to encounter only in works of history or speculative fiction. Against that backdrop, I have sometimes wondered why taverns were worth bothering with at all. My understanding of taverns came into focus when I began to think again about how people try to use, change, and conserve institutions from the inside, whether in conjunction with or in reaction against wider social patterns. As for my temporally broad construction of the early republic, my efforts to span gender, cultural, social, economic, and political history, and my struggle to account for commonalities and contrasts across regions: they all owe something to my amazing graduate cohort and to historiographical currents swirling in and after the early 2000s. Any number of waves have crested since then, so I hope to claim the mantle of fashionable lateness—a hope that ought to make my family and friends laugh, given my tendency to be unfashionably early to airports and performances.

Accommodating the Republic

Introduction

In the fall of 1833, newspaper editors in eastern Massachusetts printed a letter in which "a subscriber" pointed out that "temperance taverns are now in successful operation in many of our large towns." Thanks to "a great change" in American drinking habits, the author continued, it should now be possible to establish a "public house of this character" in Salem. A temperance tavern "would be well sustained and lucrative to its proprietor" because "strangers with their ladies or families" who preferred to avoid "the noise and bustle" common in conventional taverns "might pass a few days or weeks" there. Such a tavern would "undoubtedly induce" many people to visit "our ancient town, who now merely pass through it." A temperance tavern would also benefit "many persons from the adjacent towns, who visit us daily or weekly on business or for amusement." The author concluded by suggesting that the "enterprising keeper of the Lafayette Coffee House" could benefit himself and his town by adding a temperance tavern to his portfolio.[1]

To someone versed in the drinking history of the early United States, a temperance tavern might sound like a contradiction in terms or possibly a punch line.[2] According to the best available estimates, the nation's average per capita alcohol consumption peaked in the early 1830s. At that point, when the hypothetical average man drank six ounces of distilled spirits daily, roughly half of the nation's men probably consumed only two ounces a day, while "'regular topers'" drank twelve ounces and "'confirmed drunkards'" up to a quart. The notion that a tavern without alcohol might be a profitable business reflected growing discontent with the individual, familial, and social consequences of all this drinking. Thanks to an increasingly powerful temperance movement that promoted first moderation and later total abstinence, Americans' average intake declined to nearly 25 percent of its peak levels by 1845. Even this dramatic change did not, however, explain the logic of *taverns* without alcohol.[3]

As the temperance advocate from Salem implied, the case for a new type of tavern rested not only on people with temperate habits but also on the multiple ways such people might still patronize taverns. Across the country, thousands of small-town and village tavern keepers sold many goods besides alcohol: fodder for livestock, locally produced foodstuffs in bulk, and often an array of manufactured goods. In addition to helping neighbors provision their households and stock their workplaces, tavern keepers accommodated travelers over long and short distances, facilitated other people's commercial ventures, promoted formal and informal sociability, and hosted officially mandated gatherings such as courts, town meetings, and elections. In part because of these activities, people also gathered in taverns to seek out, discuss, and sometimes act on oral and written news from near or far.

Tavern spaces and behaviors created powerful vernaculars of citizenship. In both their mundane and exceptional forms, Americans' tavern encounters did more than reflect the norms of the local society in which each tavern was enmeshed. Rather, tavern encounters helped shape those norms and that society because taverns were both vectors and theaters for American pursuits of mobility, economic opportunity, and republican self-rule. As such, taverns contributed to the young nation's territorial expansion, migration (forced and free), infrastructural investment, developments in agriculture, manufacturing, finance, and consumption, and the growth of republican institutions and expansive political participation.[4] At the same time, taverns were places of significant contestation. White men who shared norms for manly behavior often vied with each other for precedence. Genteel men came into covert and open conflict with men who adopted alternative constructs of masculinity. Middling and wealthy white men made respectable women their allies in shaping taverns to their tastes, and the same women staked their own claims to tavern spaces. As workers and patrons, people of color launched still other claims. Together, these dynamics had implications far beyond Americans' differential access to space and belonging in taverns. From individual pursuits of happiness to collective efforts to promote the general welfare, tavern encounters helped shape Americans' relationship to the republic itself.[5]

So what was a tavern? In Great Britain, a public house that accommodated travelers was known as an inn rather than a tavern, but in much of the early United States, the commonplace and legal definition of taverns implied a public accommodation with two overlapping clienteles: drinkers and travelers. As Noah Webster indicated in his 1828 dictionary of American English, a tavern was "a house licensed to sell liquors in small quantities, to be drank on the spot." He continued, "In some of the United States, *tavern* is synonymous with *inn* or *hotel*, and denotes a house for the entertainment of travelers, as well as for the sale of liquors, licensed for that purpose." The linkage between drinking and travelers' accommodations was no accident. Many tavern keepers sought licenses because they hoped to profit from selling alcohol in "small quantities," mostly to their neighbors. Almost everywhere in the young republic, tavern licenses allowed licensees to sell by the drink and required them to furnish lodgings for travelers, a combination that helped ensure travelers would find the accommodations they needed.[6]

As Webster's definition implied, Americans had several terms for public accommodations. Which terms a person used was in part a function of geography. At the turn of the century, for example, some Virginians still clung to the older word, "ordinary." Legal writers who drew on English precedent and vocabulary often preferred the word "inn" when considering keepers' obligations to travelers. If a tavern stand consisted of several buildings, people sometimes used the word "tavern" for the whole establishment and sometimes just for the building that housed the bar. Further complicating the picture were changing fashions in public accommodations. By the late 1820s, the word "hotel" had entered general usage in at least three ways—as an alternative word for, a categorical alternative to, and a particular type of tavern— but it did not refer to a legally distinct form of public accommodations. Unmentioned in Webster's definition and most tavern licensing laws but implied in popular parlance were activities only loosely connected to drinking or travel. Also missing from Webster's definition was the significance of tavern transactions, which depended on who participated in them and who was judging.[7]

Even the most basic elements of Webster's definition contained multiple possibilities. For starters, not all tavern drinking looked alike. Many people stopped in once a week or less and drank moderately, while others lingered for hours and drank to inebriation. Many drinkers preferred strong spirits, but some chose equally cheap, low-alcohol beer or cider, while still others dabbled in costly punch, sling, toddy, and imported wines as their means and the occasion allowed. Perhaps the most consistent pattern was simply to judge the drinking of anyone who either looked different or drank differently than oneself.[8] Travel likewise had many different implications in the expanding republic. People traveled short and long distances to chase opportunity, meet or evade obligations, visit family and friends, recover their health, and see new sights. Americans did not measure all travelers, let alone all tavern-goers, with a single yardstick. Instead of trying to define what kinds and proportions of travel, drinking, and other sorts of commerce made a tavern, therefore, I take a broad lens, focusing on how patrons and keepers used the places they called by that name, how they made meaning from those uses, and how those meanings advanced competing visions of the republic and its citizens.[9]

Historians of colonial British America have long understood that a variety of needs and interests brought people to taverns. In meeting them, taverns could reinforce or elide existing divisions within the wider society. In the seventeenth century, one historian argues, colonial taverns "preserved traditional culture" rather than incubating transformation. Scholarly work on eighteenth-century taverns has highlighted their role in the political transformations that produced the revolution. In Massachusetts, taverns became entrenched in community life only through a lengthy process of contestation between ordinary colonists and their leaders in Boston, who feared taverns' tendency to promote resistance to authority. In Philadelphia, urban taverns also helped foment change to the extent that men came to expect important insights about politics from listening to and observing each other in heterogeneous taverns. During the long imperial crisis, urban and rural taverns alike incubated political mobilization and helped produce independence and a republican frame of government.[10]

Taverns' potential to incubate change and division in the early republic owed much to the ways that they reflected and encouraged differences within their neighborhoods. By the mid-eighteenth century, a small number of large and well-furnished taverns in each urban American seaport catered to the local elite. Often located on a main street or central square, such taverns attracted merchants, country gentlemen, and well-heeled travelers. Taverns in more working-class and residential areas were usually smaller and saw comparatively few strangers but might be orderly or rowdy depending on the needs and tastes of their usual denizens. Waterside taverns tended to attract sailors, transients, local laborers, and a larger than usual number of women. Such taverns had a reputation, not totally unearned, for being among the most disorderly. A similar if truncated spectrum existed beyond the colonial seaboard.[11]

By the mid-nineteenth century, the spectrum of taverns had widened considerably. At one end were "tippling-houses," "dram shops," and "groggeries," often operated by keepers who either ignored bothersome licensing provisions or had no license at all.[12] People who never visited such establishments often saw them as boils on the body politic because they supposedly made laboring people drunk, idle, rowdy, and violent. Outsiders believed that such places neither served travelers, nor hosted formal political gatherings, nor encouraged legal commerce but instead harbored counterfeiters, fences, prostitutes, and fugitives from justice or labor. Taverns where working men drank heavily in fact served important economic and political purposes for their patrons, but few middle-class observers or city officials appreciated this fact. Although temperance advocates found taverns of this sort nearly everywhere they looked, public officials thought they were particularly a problem in the nation's cities.[13]

At the opposite end of the mid-nineteenth-century spectrum of public accommodations, we find the first-class or luxury hotel, which built on and surpassed the previous century's urban elite taverns. First-class hotels were usually urban but also emerged in more rural areas, where they served as tourist destinations. At three, four, or even more stories, they were usually among the tallest buildings in their setting. They boasted dozens if not hundreds of bedrooms, as well as many rooms dedicated to specific activities or subsets of guests, such as smoking and reading rooms for men. Lushly furnished and decorated, the leading hotels also featured whatever was newest in domestic technology, such as washing machines or gaslights. Throughout the country, boosters hoped that such large, refined, and complex public accommodations would bring people, trade, and credit to their neighborhood, town, or city. Not accidentally, these hotels raised significant questions about what it meant to accommodate the public: not everyone was welcome in the most luxurious of these public palaces.[14]

Luxury hotels and the taverns frequented by hard drinkers from the laboring classes each represented important developments in the early United States. However, the conclusions that both Americans and foreign visitors drew about this spectrum of accommodations were unstable and often mutually contradictory. Some travelers complained that a state, region, or even the entire country had no taverns worthy of the name, while others noted that they had found both lousy and excellent accommodations in a single day's travel. In the first third of the nineteenth century, commentators did not routinely distinguish between taverns, presumed to be bad, and hotels, presumed to be good. Instead, they described establishments, or certain aspects of them, as dreadful, poor, tolerable, fair, decent, good, or excellent. They also used the word "hotel" to denote multiple things: a massive, luxurious establishment, a tavern that was better than others in the area, or even a keeper's aspirations. Americans increasingly used the term "hotel" in contexts that implied change, progress, or modernity, but they did not universally conclude that taverns were backward, stagnant, or alien to improvement, as temperance taverns and other innovations demonstrated.[15]

In the towns, villages, and rural areas where most Americans lived in the first half of the nineteenth century, low population densities did not allow most public accommodations under any name to become as large and elaborate as the biggest city or rural resort hotels.[16] However, many keepers improved their taverns' capacity and complexity in ways that paralleled and even anticipated changes usually identified with leading urban hotels. That cosmopolitan elites often failed to recognize such changes demonstrated not stasis beyond the urban seaboard but improvement's high stakes in the early republic.[17] And it is these dynamics, not terminology or location, that define the taverns I study here. Most of them were in towns and villages, although I consider urban and rural examples as well. Many of them fell somewhere in the broad middle of the public accommodations spectrum. Within this broad middle were some important distinctions and changes over time. Whereas rural taverns usually depended on their local customers, some wayside country taverns became more defined by their traveling than their local trade. In market towns, county seats, and state capitals, one, two, or more taverns, usually found on the main street or near government buildings, became hubs for business, politics, civic activism, and fashionable society. Although these distinctions mattered, it would be equally true to say that any given tavern occupied multiple points on the spectrum, according to the perspectives of the people who lived and worked there, patronized it regularly, passed through, observed it from the outside, or tried to regulate it.[18]

From the 1780s through at least the 1840s and across the spectrums of architectural form, location, and clientele, town and village keepers and their taverns provided material support to the geographic, social, cultural, economic, and political transformations of the early republic.[19] The many types of commerce, interpersonal interactions, and assemblies that brought people to town and village taverns made these institutions into small engines of expansion and development. As Americans subordinated millions of acres to private ownership and the plow, they also built out the transportation, commercial, and republican infrastructures needed to absorb both people and lands into the nation.[20] Taverns contributed to each of these infrastructures, facilitating the movement of people, goods, credit, and information, while providing space for sociability, politics, and government. As taverns accommodated the public in all these ways, they participated in its contested definition. Depending on time, place, and perspective, the tavern public might mean everyone who worked in or passed through public accommodations, only the travelers whom keepers were legally obliged to serve, the enfranchised citizenry, tavern regulars, respectable middle-class consumers, or members of voluntary associations. Each of these tavern publics made claims on taverns' space and disputed other claimants' access. In the process, these tavern publics tested and contested what Barbara Anne Welke calls the "borders of belonging" in the emerging nation.[21]

How taverns fostered competing vernacular understandings of citizenship is most easily understood with regard to travel and mobility. Histori-

FIGURE I.1 Buck Horn Tavern, 22nd St Broadway, 1812 (1881). This spacious two-story tavern sat on the outskirts of New York City, a reminder that the dense urban conditions of lower Manhattan did not extend far up the island in the early nineteenth century. As pictured, the tavern is well equipped to handle travelers entering and leaving the city, having ample room for guests' carriages and horses. The scene also suggests how a tavern porch could be a convenient vantage point for keeping an eye on passers-by, other guests, and tavern workers. The tavern's many windows provide both light and additional opportunities to survey the surroundings. Courtesy of the Miriam and Ira D. Wallach Division of Art, Prints and Photographs: Picture Collection, New York Public Library.

ans and other scholars have long understood the links between the freedom to move or stay and the ability to act and be treated as citizens in the United States.[22] In a period of aggressive territorial conquest, national expansion, and coerced movement, the importance of voluntary mobility can hardly be overstated. Throughout the early republic, white men of means could move around more or less as they chose. Financial exigencies compelled many other white men to move, but they usually had considerable discretion over whether and where, as fewer and fewer white men were bound by indentures or similar legal constraints. Husbands, parents, guardians, and occasionally employers or masters both compelled and constrained the mobility of white women and minors.[23] Enslaved and Indigenous peoples experienced brutal forms of coerced mobility at the hands of private citizens and government agents. Through self-willed and sometimes illegal movement, however, subordinated people also laid claim to mobility and

FIGURE I.2 Spread Eagle Tavern, Strafford, Pennsylvania, from Isaac Weld, *Travels through the States of North America* (1799). Isaac Weld found much to criticize in the new republic and its taverns, yet this finely rendered image does not compel a dire reading of tavern conditions in this rural neighborhood. Instead, the stagecoach suggests both commercial and interpersonal connections to areas of denser settlement, while the tavern itself, sitting at the edge of the forest with recently cleared and fenced fields stretching away in front of it, evokes future agricultural prosperity. Although contemporaries often represented taverns as masculine space, this image includes two women, one looking out through the tavern window and another seated on the steps outside. Courtesy of the Library Company of Philadelphia.

self-determination.[24] Access to taverns was never an absolute prerequisite to any of these forms of mobility, but tavern goods and services under-girded many people's movements over both short and long distances. As a result, tavern stops became dynamic occasions to affirm, question, or violate other people's freedom to move.

A second component of the vernacular citizenship of tavern-going involved economic opportunity, which like mobility had legal, cultural, political, and material dimensions. The men who wrote the early republic's laws presumed that only a portion of the adult population—sometimes men with property, sometimes explicitly white men—could be allowed to pursue economic goals of their own choosing. In practice, married women bound by coverture women had more discretion over their daily work and more ability to accumulate property than the strict letter of the law implied.[25] Even enslaved people sometimes had opportunities to work for their own benefit, although those opportunities were most resilient when they articulated with enslavers' own interests.[26] In the decades following the American Revolution, however, the burden and freedom of economic agency became associated with white masculinity starting in late boyhood. The decline of legal dependence among white men rested on new opportunities to acquire land, find wage labor, or start businesses of their own, in conjunction with the nation's growing population, borders, and markets for manufactured and agricultural goods.[27] Through these changes, economic and geographic mobility became ever more mutually entangled, heightening the stakes of tavern access. People passed through taverns as they migrated and traveled on business, but they also came to taverns to buy and sell goods, secure credit, disseminate new technology, and recruit capital for speculative ventures. White men were not the only people who used taverns in these ways. However, the nexus of mobility and opportunity both implied and reinforced the political prerogatives to which they had the greatest claim.[28]

At the dawn of the nineteenth century, formal electoral politics had both democratic and antidemocratic features. Many white men had enjoyed suffrage before independence, and the republic's new states tended to impose the same or lesser tax-paying or property-owning requirements. Because of the comparatively wide distribution of wealth, in turn, most white American men could vote throughout their adult lives. As a result, they could move from state to state without worrying that they would lose their political rights, although voters still complained of being comparatively underrepresented and underserved if they lived far from their state capital or county seat. As property and tax-paying thresholds fell for white men, however, Black men faced new barriers to voting: several states either increased race-specific property requirements or made disfranchisement based on race and gender newly explicit. The spread of universal white manhood suffrage encoded the emerging assumption that white men "could be trusted to preserve property and liberty," but Black men and all women could not. Even so, white manhood remained an incomplete basis for political rights. After 1828, in reaction against the democratic claims of Andrew Jackson and his common men, multiple states disfranchised white men for being paupers. In addition, property, residency, age, and other qualifications continued to limit eligibility for officeholding in many states and the federal government.[29]

While the lack of voting rights marked most Americans as second-class citizens at best, suffrage was never an absolute prerequisite for meaningful involvement in early republican politics. A small number of white women wielded more political influence than most voters thanks to their connection to powerful husbands or fathers. The rapid growth of print culture and voluntary associations enabled both nonvoters and voters to work collectively to accomplish their ends, sometimes influencing laws and policies in the process.[30] In this realm, too, participation was not equally distributed. Literate people who controlled their own time and money and those who lived in towns or cities often had the greatest opportunities.[31]

This complex political landscape implicated taverns in direct and indirect ways. Men in positions of power summoned others to taverns to engage in political activities mandated by the federal and state constitutions, including elections and jury trials. Voluntary associations and political parties relied on taverns as appropriate places in which to gather and mobilize. For white men, tavern-going manifested their linked rights to drink, move around, make material choices about their property and livelihoods, and govern themselves, and sometimes others, as they chose. Despite and because of the controversy around tavern-going, the freedom to use taverns in multiple ways became a concrete expression and practice of white male citizenship in the early republic. Even for white men, however, factors that were not always within their control conditioned their access, including business cycles, geography, familial resources, domestic responsibilities, and cultural norms. As a result, patrons' uses of taverns in pursuit of individual and collective goals constituted multiple, often contradictory, versions of citizenship.[32]

Disputes over white men's conduct had implications for the ways that white women and people of color used taverns. Two diverging understandings of whom taverns should serve, and how, emerged over the course of the early nineteenth century, both tied to contemporary debates over improvements. In the first half century after independence, Americans from many walks of life embraced the idea of improvements, but they did not always mean the same things. The most familiar use of the word to modern students of the period concerned internal improvements, or the development of transportation infrastructure. For many Americans, improvements also meant the imperative to privatize land, clear trees, build fences, plant particular crops, and erect buildings. As any struggling farmer, enslaved Black American, or displaced Indigenous person might have observed, however, one man's improvements could be another's crisis.[33] In part as a result, many Americans believed that to effect any real improvement in their fortunes, they had to speculate. In short order, land speculation became a prime driver of the volatile business cycle and much business travel, both of which brought white men—and many slaves—to taverns.[34]

Beginning in the late eighteenth century and accelerating in and after the 1820s, a growing slice of American men endorsed another understanding of improvement, which included ambitious and often divisive ideas about the relationship between manners, self-advancement, morality, and the role of government. For some American men, improvement in this sense included mastering as many of the behaviors and acquiring as many of the goods associated with refinement and respectability as they could afford. Many hardworking wage earners decided that their path to manly respect and independence required new degrees of reserve and self-restraint, even if some of them had endorsed boisterous masculinity as youths. Improvement in this sense often came to require either alcoholic moderation or total abstinence. To varying degrees, improvers of this sort saw self-restraint, refined manners, domestic attachments, piety, and industriousness as evidence not of weakness but true masculine strength. These ambitious self- and other-improvers often joined the Federalist, National Republican, or Whig parties, which regarded the federal and state governments as important partners in their efforts.[35]

Yet white masculinity was not entirely a partisan affair. In the 1790s and 1800s, Republicans rejected Federalist pro-British policies and elitism, but that stance did not mean that all Republicans forswore the British-inflected culture of refinement.[36] A generation and more later, Democrats were usually more at ease than their Whig counterparts with sporting culture and the behavior of "jolly fellows" who drank heavily, swore, gambled, and fought. Democrats resisted Whiggish societies and laws that sought to restrain white men's moral conduct. Yet wealthy Republicans and Democrats often joined their Federalist and Whiggish peers in preferring the amenities of an improved tavern, especially when traveling with their wives and daughters. Although political affinities shaped men's understanding of manhood and taverngoing, in short, those differences were not absolute or even stable. In addition, many well-to-do men across much of the political spectrum relished the occasional opportunity to modulate between more and less self-restrained modes of conduct, an important prerogative that taverns' multiple publics facilitated.[37]

Efforts to shape taverns and tavern-going in the early nineteenth century thus formed part of a protracted struggle on multiple fronts. From the perspective of taverns' mostly white male users, improvement could be a reason to avoid taverns altogether or a reason and a way to use them. Working toward refinement, domesticity, respectability, and temperance fueled a struggle for control *within* taverns as well as a campaign against them. Equally, tavern improvements tended as much to strengthen as unravel public accommodations' entanglement with white men's mobility, economic agency, and political self-representation.

Capturing these dynamics requires attention to how different historical actors made tavern spaces, encounters, and meanings from a variety of vantage points. I illuminate contests over and within taverns using travel journals, letters, memoirs, account books and financial papers, occasional census records, published travel narratives, tourist guides, newspapers, almanacs, geographic gazetteers, maps, city directories, laws and ordinances, judicial decisions, and county and town histories. These sources both illuminate distinct aspects of tavern-going and support different kinds of storytelling. I have selected my sources chiefly from parts of the country where taverns were relatively frequent early in the nineteenth century, which generally meant to the east of the Mississippi River. Even though that informal dividing line excludes much of the early republic, it allows ample scope for considering differences between cities, towns, villages, and the countryside, between old and new settlements, and between regions.[38]

Some of my sources played a direct role in shaping the tavern dynamics I analyze. Well-off travelers often used reading and writing to distance themselves from disconcerting tavern encounters. Tavern keepers' accounts of their daily sales documented the activities of people who rarely left papers of their own; their account books also sustained networks of obligation. Likewise, printed materials did not just comment on tavern publics but also helped create them. Newspapers drew people to taverns and connected them to larger regional and national communities. A small but important proportion of what appeared in newspapers reflected local tavern happenings. The print and oral aspects of tavern culture intersected in firsthand local and imagined regional and national communities. In short, these sources did more than document taverns: they situated individuals within taverns, taverns within neighborhoods, and neighborhoods within the nation.[39]

To better capture these developments and keep the stakes of tavern-going in view, three pairs of chapters highlight different components of vernacular citizenship. Part I explores how the movement of people, goods, and ideas shaped taverns. It also introduces two overlapping types of taverns: the wayside tavern, much patronized by travelers from beyond the immediate neighborhood, and the improving tavern in which people's movements and manners, as much as the physical space itself, expressed keepers' and patrons' commitment to ideals of refinement and comfort.[40] Chapter 1 argues that wayside taverns shaped the logistics and meanings of human travel on the early republic's emergent national transportation network. As the nation more than doubled in size, new technologies helped people travel farther and faster, yet travel remained closely tied to taverns. Access to wayside taverns helped make hundreds of road, water, and rail segments into a patchy but functional national transportation network. While wayside taverns shaped long- and short-distance travel, so too did travel shape taverns. Patrons' heterogeneity raised the stakes of chance interactions, as strangers assessed others' likelihood of providing information, diversion, obstruction, or danger. Compounding the difficulty of rubbing shoulders with strangers in unfamiliar and sometimes cramped surroundings were mobility's many meanings, including self-advancement, leisure, obligation, and exploitation. As travelers of varying conditions mingled and reflected on their tavern encounters, they helped create the emerging American tendency to associate the fullest measure of citizenship with the freedom to travel and visit taverns in the process.[41]

Chapter 2 examines the diffusion of gentility into small-town and village taverns, both as an ideal and as a set of behavioral, material, and spatial practices. The middling and elite travelers whose opinions saturate the archives often complained of taverns' inadequate accommodations. Many such travelers mobilized national, regional, ethnic, or cosmopolitan prejudices to set themselves apart in places where spatial distancing was difficult or impossible. Read alongside tavern advertisements, however, travelers' writings document the substantial material and linguistic investments that some keepers made in refinement and comfort. Genteel and comfortable improvements marketed to families and ladies suggested a modest feminization of early republican taverns. Yet even improving taverns remained equivocal in their welcome to female patrons, as town and village keepers continued to serve men who wanted different things from their taverns, including basic, affordable accommodations and the sometimes riotous sociability that accompanied heavy drinking. Dividing taverns into distinct spatial zones produced an uneasy coexistence between the quasi-democratic norms of white masculine drinking culture, middle-class respectability, and the most elite forms of gentility. In this complicated and contentious environment, even Black travelers sometimes managed to use improving taverns to their own ends.[42]

In part II, the focus shifts from mobility to economic opportunity, illustrating how Americans used tavern spaces and networks to pursue economic as well as social ends. Chapter 3 uses account books from small-town and rural taverns to explore keepers' transactions with their patrons across a variety of settings. The accounts also situate patrons' drinking, and tavern-going more broadly, within networks of local economic activity. Tavern keepers who offered generous credit, accepted multiple forms of payment, and offered a variety of goods beyond the standard tavern fare linked their customers to each other and their own neighborhoods to distant markets. The social dynamics of drinking and other aspects of tavern commerce, meanwhile, extended the tension over whether and how taverns were white men's space. As places for conducting both sociability and business, taverns became an important front in the long struggle over the meanings and borders of economic activity in the early republic.[43]

Chapter 4 pivots to the ways that patrons used taverns as venues for their own enterprises. As "trading spaces" associated with mobility and gathering, taverns fostered private ventures and innovations throughout the early republican economy.[44] People involved in everything from land speculation, agriculture, and manufacturing to genteel entertainments and even crime found tavern spaces and networks useful in meeting one or more business needs. Solo operators, informal networks, and firms of various sorts encountered difficulties in researching potential markets and sources of supply, conducting negotiations, and finalizing bargains, among other tasks known to economists as transaction costs. These tasks would become easier and more efficient over time thanks to steam power's transformation of transportation and printing, to say nothing of telegraphy. Yet in the first half of the nineteenth century, in the many places where even short-distance communications remained effortful and costly, taverns and their keepers helped individuals, partnerships, and corporations do business. Since rural, village, and small-town people came to taverns for news and novelty, using taverns as a place of business also helped local and itinerant entrepreneurs market innovative services, technologies, and other goods. While white men made the fullest and easiest use of taverns in these ways, tavern keepers' improvements created opportunities as well as barriers for entrepreneurial white women and people of color. The norms that shaped these tavern uses never represented a simple projection of rigid hierarchical ideals around gender or race; instead, they also reflected and influenced complex, dynamic relationships that shaped particular neighborhoods.[45]

Part III explores how taverns' links to mobility and economic agency informed the evolving work of republican self-governance in both "formal political institutions" and "the activities of ordinary people."[46] Chapter 5 examines how men in federal, state, and local office made public accommodations into objects and tools of regulation, agents of state power, and constituents of local networks of influence and opportunity. From the waning days of the revolution through at least the 1830s, state and territorial legislatures attempted to use licensing laws to shape taverns into orderly public institutions that affirmed hierarchical relationships, restrained public drinking, and met travelers' needs. State and local authorities also acknowledged taverns' use for activities beyond the narrow ambit of tavern licenses and even mandated their use for public and government business. As more men in power subscribed to temperance, legislators and jurists contested the place of alcohol in taverns in new ways without forgetting the need for public accommodations in an increasingly mobile and commercial nation. As a result, anti-alcohol laws in the 1830s, 1840s, and 1850s sought not to eliminate taverns outright but to force them to work better for temperate locals and respectable travelers.[47]

Chapter 6 argues that tavern-going habits helped legitimate and foster organized collective politics in both democratic and antidemocratic ways. At the turn of the nineteenth century, the parameters of acceptable political activity under the new constitution remained subject to debate. Although white men had possessed broad voting rights even before the revolution, many of the new nation's early leaders did not at first believe that ordinary citizens should play a robust role either in deciding who should stand for office or in shaping policy through their representatives. Similarly, although gentlemen had formed voluntary associations long before the revolution, the Constitution included no right to associate. Over time, however, the prospect of shaping government through partisan politics motivated intense engagement among many voters, while voluntary associations provided alternative means to pursue collective ends. Because many partisan and nonpartisan voluntary societies assembled in taverns, tavern spaces and networks became material assets for collective work within local communities. As both parties and societies coalesced into national organizations, local tavern meetings lost some of their power, but public accommodations took on new importance in political travel to regional, state, and national conventions. Although most of this political work involved white men, the temperance and antislavery movements created new opportunities for middle-class white women and people of color to use and shape taverns for their collective ends.[48]

Advocates for reform and respectability did not, of course, win full control of taverns in the early republic, but they made more headway than most historians have realized. A capacious understanding of improvements helps illuminate how this happened and why it mattered. Taverns contributed in material and conceptual ways to the diffusion of infrastructural, economic, cultural, political, and other improvements beyond the urban seaboard. Far from being neutral conduits for these developments, taverns became peculiarly important trying grounds for citizenship. At some level, every interaction in a public house raised defining questions: who was a member of the republic and for what purposes? In the early history of the United States, the answers to these questions usually favored white men, yet we must not ignore either the socioeconomic and political divisions among them or the spectrum of competing answers that white women and people of color offered. The early twenty-first century bears witness to two important continuities with this formative period. As anyone seeking to provide or enjoy commercial public spaces might tell you, the business of accommodating the republic continues to shift in both small and dramatic ways. At the same time, the relationship between commercial hospitality and the ability to move around freely, pursue economic opportunity, and participate in collective self-determination continues both to sustain and to qualify Americans' exercise of citizenship in their own country.[49]

Part I
Mobility

CHAPTER ONE

Wayside Taverns

The Transportation Revolution and
American Self-Fashioning

At the beginning of an 1835 business trip that took him from Connecticut through South Carolina and Georgia, a young man marveled at the changes in transportation during his lifetime: with the rise of the railroad, a person could now travel at thirty miles per hour! Had anyone predicted such speeds a century before, John Wight Bill mused, "he would have been persecuted or set down as a madman." Bill speculated that "it may not be hazzarding to much" to predict that "by the year 1935, a traveller may take Breakfast and leave Portland ME the same day dine at St. Louis or the foot of the Rocky Mts, and sup in the eve at the mouth of the Columbia River, on the Pacifick Ocean."[1] Even as he fantasized about transcontinental travel, Bill presumed that long trips would still entail a repeated sequence of movement and stasis, often involving meals. Throughout the early republic, tourists, migrants, and business travelers organized each day's onward movement to include stops for food, drink, rest, or shelter for themselves and sometimes for their animals. Many of these pauses took travelers to wayside taverns that shaped both the logistics and the meanings of human travel on the early republic's emergent national transportation network.

Travelers' continued recourse to taverns in the early republic overlaid dramatic changes in both technology and geography. As the nation more than doubled in size, improved roads, canals, and steam engines made travel in some parts of the country faster and cheaper than ever before. The combined promise of transportation and land set people in motion and multiplied opportunities for commerce. Territorial and population growth spawned dozens of counties and hundreds of villages. In each, settlers built taverns that served new waves of people on the move. In the same period, infrastructural improvements also made leisure jaunts a pleasurable reality not only for elite but also for middling and even some working-class Americans. As John Wight Bill's fantasy implied, however, new technologies sped people across the landscape without severing their ties to taverns. On so vast a continent, no technology available to the nineteenth century could wholly eliminate travel by road, which guaranteed a regular schedule of tavern stops in any region settled enough to support them. Although people who arranged their own transportation relied most on wayside taverns, commercial travelers also visited, while transportation companies looked to taverns and their keepers for passenger services and help with company equipment and personnel. East and west, north and south, wayside taverns helped a thicket of road, water, and rail routes function as a network.[2]

While taverns helped make both long- and short-distance travel possible, travel in its turn shaped wayside taverns. In much-traveled districts, taverns assembled people from all walks of life. As Irish immigrant Fortescue Cuming noted, men "trucking their wares" rubbed elbows with drovers conducting herds of livestock, farmers going to market, hopeful migrants heading west, judges and lawyers "attending the courts," and members of "the better class" traveling for pleasure. This heterogeneity sometimes made it difficult to predict how one might be received in a wayside tavern.[3] Compounding the difficulty of encountering strangers in unfamiliar and sometimes cramped surroundings were the varied meanings of mobility itself. Although licensing laws required tavern keepers to serve travelers, not every person on the move was considered a bona fide traveler. State and territorial tavern regulations suggested that indentured servants and most people of color had no right to patronize taverns of their own accord.[4] These restrictions meshed with a host of old and new legal restrictions on movement. State manumission laws, the federal Fugitive Slave Acts of 1793 and 1850, and other codes governing enslaved and free people of color defined their movements as presumptively suspect or even criminal. Multiple midwestern state constitutions prohibited Black immigration and settlement. By 1844, Maryland had stipulated that a Black resident who left the state for thirty days needed the state's permission to return home.[5] State and federal laws also sought to regulate Indigenous people's movements, sometimes by restricting when and how they could move around and sometimes by forced removal with no right of return. Laws, ordinances, and labor contracts constrained some white people's geographic mobility as well: indirectly in the case of married women's coverture and explicitly in anti-vagrancy laws, indentures, and apprenticeships. Yet as indentured servitude gave way to self-employment and wage labor for most white men, the early republic increasingly associated the full measure of white manhood with the freedom to move.[6]

Of course, law represented only one factor shaping people's freedom to move around. Whenever travelers entered wayside taverns, they negotiated their access to the nation's evolving transportation network through their interactions with keepers, local patrons, and other travelers like and unlike themselves. Depending on their race, gender, legal status, economic position, means of transportation, and reasons for being on the move, they jockeyed for position in more and less overt ways. This chapter focuses most on the people who reached for their pens to reframe their tavern encounters, either in the moment or after the fact; these were usually but not always travelers with considerable privilege. Whether as a complement or an alternative to drinking and informal sociability, writing in taverns created a temporary buffer between the writer and other tavern denizens. Both in their persons and on paper, these travelers testified to the importance of tavern services and interactions in shaping the possibilities and meanings of movement. In the process, they contributed to the emerging American tendency to associate the freedom of both traveling and tavern-going with citizenship.[7]

From Travel Stages to a Transportation Network

Between the 1780s and the 1850s, Americans gained access to a network of improved roads, waterways, and railroads, as well as a host of printed materials that helped them imagine and plan travel on that network. In the late eighteenth century, only prosperous Americans owned well-rendered maps for domestic display or for use on the road.[8] By the 1850s, free people contemplating a trip faced a nearly overwhelming volume of travel-related information, including tourist guides, geographic gazetteers, train and steamboat schedules, and descriptions of journeys into all corners of the nation. Taverns' importance in travel print diminished as commercial passenger carriers proliferated, but through the mid-nineteenth century, personal accounts documented taverns' persistent role in sustaining travelers and coordinating their movements.[9]

One of the most widespread forms of print in the eighteenth century was the annual almanac. Better known for their planting calendars, zodiac charts, and conversion tables, many almanacs also helped readers plan or imagine travel. Pages listing the "Roads to the principal Towns" identified the towns, villages, and "Houses of Entertainment" a traveler would encounter on the way to various destinations. In long- and densely settled parts of the country, almanacs informed readers that travelers did not need to pack provisions because taverns were so frequent. For those contemplating travel in the area around Boston, for example, Bickerstaff's 1774 almanac identified taverns that were two, three, or four miles apart. Readers of *Poor Will's Almanack* learned that anyone heading west out of Philadelphia could stop at the Prince of Wales, the Buck, the Sorrel-horse, or the Plough on their way out of the city, at the Admiral Warren, the White Horse, or Downing's tavern the next day, and at the Duke of Cumberland, the Red-Lyon, or the Lancaster Court House tavern a day or two later.[10] Perhaps less well informed, some almanac compilers contented themselves with printing only the names of post towns, but their accompanying mileage lists provided at least some reassurance that travelers could get between listed towns in a day or less. Newspaper editors complemented almanac readers' geographic knowledge by printing lists of the nation's post roads, which sometimes mentioned post office taverns as well as post towns.[11]

Travelers created their own lists of taverns along particular routes. On a trip from Baltimore to Kentucky in 1809, George Hunter consulted a list of "the best Taverns on the rode." Fragmentary lists tracing "Routes to & from Charleston, 1815 & 1816" or the "Road from Philad. to Pittsburg recd from the Chief Justice, Sep 27 1824" survived to be archived because they were useful and easy to consult. Echoing almanacs' lists of towns, taverns, and mileage, personal lists sometimes added terse evaluations. On the road to Charleston, for example, one anonymous traveler memorialized one tavern as "bad," another as "tole[rable]," and a third as "good." As planning tools, both manuscript and almanac lists were most useful to people who knew the area or had maps at hand since they provided no directional cues or compass bearings to guide travelers from stage to stage. Another option was to consult a tavern keeper such as Martin Browne of northern Virginia, who maintained a list of taverns along the road and could explain directions and distances to passing travelers.[12]

Published travel narratives likewise emphasized tavern stops. Inspired in part by the American market for European travel writing and in part by curiosity about the new republic, Europeans produced numerous American travelogues at the turn of the century. Many of these works reconstructed their authors' progress through the country stage by stage. Among the first was François-Jean de Beauvoir, better known today as the Marquis de Chastellux, who narrated his experiences in the last months of the Revolutionary War as an officer in the French expeditionary force. From the first pages of his memoir, Beauvoir described his movements from town to town and from tavern to tavern. On a typical day, he "alighted at a good inn"—this one happened to be in Warren, Massachusetts—where he baited his horse and took shelter from the frosty November weather. Other days, he paused at taverns for meals, to rest his horse, or because nightfall "obliged me to stop." Irishman Isaac Weld did not recapitulate his daily stages with such precision, but he maintained that a traveler could identify key features of a region from its taverns, which many long-distance travelers entered more often than private homes.[13]

Early in the nineteenth century, the emergent genre of American tourist guides took taverns' role in travel for granted.[14] One of the earliest was George Temple's 1812 *American Tourist's Pocket Companion*. Formatted to fit in a coat pocket or a travel bag, the *Companion* began with general advice and ended with blank pages for recording tavern bills and travel memoranda. In addition, Temple provided brief descriptions of many towns, while his detailed list of the route from Albany to Niagara directed the traveler from Albany to Woodsworth's (five miles) to M'Lellan's (two miles) to Truaxes' (five miles), and so on for over three hundred miles, with only two intervals of more than ten miles between taverns. More explicit than any almanac, he also pointed out the rare neighborhoods inadequately served by taverns, such as the area around Lake George, New York, where travelers should "provide themselves with cold tongues, bologna sausages, crackers and liquids, to supply themselves for at least two days." As Temple's concern for travelers' hunger suggests, he focused on the man who traveled "either on horseback or in his one-horse chaise," not by stagecoach.[15]

Travelers who arranged their own transportation had to solve the problems of food, water, and shelter every day. In 1776, the Reverend Doctor James Clitherall traveled from Charleston to Philadelphia as escort to Mary Izard Middleton and Henrietta Middleton Rutledge, both married to delegates to the Second Continental Congress. In detailed diary entries, Clitherall confirmed the centrality of taverns to overland travel. Intent on making good time, "the ladies [were] in the carriage at six" one morning, and they rode thirteen miles before stopping at a tavern for breakfast. Over the next month, the party stopped at taverns once or twice each day for meals and again for their night's rest.[16] Thirty years later, Philadelphia's James Gibbons made a similar record of stops on a speculative trip to and from Ohio. On a typical day, Gibbons recorded that he, his father-in-law, and some chance companions rode eight miles to breakfast and another twenty miles to dinner, before they finally "put up at the Green tree tavern" in Chambersburg, "making in all forty miles." Pleasure seekers and tourists usually maintained a more relaxed pace but made their share of tavern visits. During an 1818 pleasure tour from New York City to Niagara Falls with her family, Sarah Howland noted at least seventy-five such tavern stops.[17]

As stagecoach lines, canals, steamboats, and trains proliferated, however, many travelers became less overtly reliant on taverns. Commercial carriers decided for their passengers what routes to take and whether and where to stop. The greater speed of overland travel thanks to improved roads, better carriages, and especially steam-powered railroads also meant fewer tavern stops per mile. Some transportation promoters even predicted that American travelers would soon enjoy a great reduction in their tavern expenses thanks to train travel, as the English were said to have done.[18]

Travel publications in and after the 1830s reflected the attenuated importance of taverns for tourists planning to rely on commercial travel by land or water. In his 1830 *The Tourist, or Pocket Manual for Travellers on the Hudson River, the Western Canal, and Stage Road, to Niagara Falls*, Robert Vandewater assumed that tourists would use commercial transportation and thus had no need for lists of conveniently spaced public accommodations between the destinations he recommended. Samuel Augustus Mitchell's pocket-sized 1832 *Travelers Guide through the United States* gave the impression that one could travel the country with no forethought about accommodations. Mitchell's guide included more than thirty different steamboat routes across the country and listed the towns in the order a traveler would encounter them. None of these routes mentioned taverns as intermediate points at or between major destinations, even those that relied on stagecoach legs of a hundred miles or more between waterways. Later publications such as *Benjamin's New Map of the Hudson River* (1845) likewise drew attention to steamboat schedules and railroad connections, ignoring accommodations except for a passing reference to the "principal Hotels" near the railroad and the steamboat landings. *Appleton's Companion Hand-Book of Travel*, a series of travel guides that first appeared in 1847, paid somewhat more attention to accommodations. Hotels the editors deemed worthy were identified by name, while the listing for a sizable town might mention the presence of "upwards of 30 hotels and taverns." Entries for many small towns and villages offered no description of their public accommodations.[19]

As any experienced traveler knew, however, taverns continued to matter even for people using commercial transportation. Passengers consigned many decisions to operators, but they could not have failed to notice that wherever they joined or left a commercial line, taverns proliferated, sometimes serving as passenger depots as well. Stagecoach lines retained particularly close connections to taverns. In large cities and small villages alike, stagecoaches picked up and deposited passengers at taverns (see figure 1.1). In the 1790s, Philadelphians taking the Federal Line to New York City boarded the stagecoach at the White Swan Inn on Race Street. In the next century, passengers heading south from Philadelphia on the New Line Expedition alighted at taverns in Chester, Wilmington, Elkton, Havre de Grace, or Baltimore.[20]

Into the 1830s and beyond, newspaper advertisements identified stagecoach lines with tavern services. In the late 1830s, the Alligator Line of stage-

Nearest and best route.
Providence and Albany Mail Line of Post-Coaches,

By the way of Hartford, in two days,

LEAVE Providence Tuesdays, Thursdays and Saturdays—lodge at Hartford; leave Hartford Mondays, Wednesdays and Fridays—lodge at Albany.

RETURNING, leave Albany Tuesdays, Thursdays and Saturdays—lodge at Hartford—leave Hartford Mondays, Wednesdays and Fridays, and lodge at Providence.

N. B. This Line runs to meet the Steam Boat at New-Haven, the Hudson, Litchfield and Northern Stages, and the Boston, Bristol, Newport and New-Bedford Stages. Books kept at Blake's Hotel, Horton's Globe Tavern and Wesson' Coffee-house.

> D. CORNELL, *Glocester,*
> D CLARKE, *Ashford,*
> E. POMEROY, *Coventry,*
> L. KING, *Hartford.*

May 7. tf.

FIGURE 1.1 *Providence Gazette,* January 7, 1824. The Providence and Albany Mail Line linked the capital cities of Rhode Island and New York and offered passengers connections to steamboats on the Long Island Sound and to several other stage lines. The stock image of a stagecoach that embellished the advertisement may suggest female passengers in the rear seat. Like many stagecoach operators, especially those over routes that took a day or more, the Providence and Albany line relied on tavern keepers to collect passengers' fares, inscribe their names, provide meals for drivers and passengers, and probably to care for the horses and the stage itself. Courtesy of the American Antiquarian Society.

coaches and steamboats serving Alabama, Georgia, and Florida promoted its regular meal stops. Also operating in the late 1830s, the People's Line between Montgomery, Alabama, and Augusta, Georgia, advertised that passengers on their line would get "sleep and refreshment" in a wayside tavern, while passengers on the competition's coaches jolted through the night. A stage line running from Richmond to Charlottesville, Virginia, received public praise from its passengers for offering "good accommodations on the road" and "no travelling by night."[21]

Passengers' records of stagecoach travel further confirm the continued significance of taverns as waiting rooms and refreshment stops. While returning to Philadelphia from a family visit to Ohio in the mid-1830s, widowed Jane B. Haines noted the tavern stops during her stagecoach journey. About one two-day stint, she wrote, "breakfast at Washington dined at Brownsville stopped at Union town and lodged at *Smithfield* . . . took an early breakfast, dined at Frostburg, lodged at Bevans ville . . . Breakfast on Sideling Hill." During her own Pennsylvania travels around the same time, Ann Haines—Jane's unmarried contemporary and a family connection—repeatedly found herself in taverns waiting for stagecoaches that were scheduled to depart at midnight. Nor was she alone, either in waiting in taverns or in writing about the experience. One October evening in 1836, Andrew Lester alighted from a stagecoach at Mr. Ramsey's Hotel in Fredericksburg, Virginia, and remained there until eight o'clock in the evening, when he boarded another stagecoach to reach the Potomac River, where he waited until three o'clock in the morning for onward transportation.[22]

In addition to passenger services, tavern keepers provided logistical support directly to stagecoach operators. The proprietors of any stage line needed to consider where and how they would furnish and feed their horses, maintain and repair coaches, and feed their drivers. Tavern keepers sometimes stabled extra teams of horses to ensure a consistent rate of speed or as insurance against stagecoach horses' high rates of injury and death. Keepers also kept horses fed and watered. Early in the nineteenth century, tavern keeper Samuel Kirby of Dinwiddie County, Virginia, had a contract with a stagecoach line. His contract obliged him to provide hay, corn, and oats for the stage horses and to arrange for a blacksmith to shoe them as needed. The contract also made Kirby responsible for maintaining and repairing the stagecoach by, for example, replacing the axle and furnishing tar for waterproofing and grease as a lubricant. Finally, the contract required him to feed both the stage drivers and the mail carriers at his own expense. Kirby would, in theory, recoup all these costs by selling meals and drinks to stage passengers, but his surviving papers do not confirm whether he was pleased with his bargain.[23]

Compared to stagecoach lines, steamboat and railroad companies had less need for tavern services. For starters, many passenger boats offered a "*Tavern on board*," providing both refreshments and places to sleep. By the late 1830s, some trains began offering occasional sleeping cars, although dining cars became common only much later in the century. Even so, taverns still mattered to passengers, and keepers knew it. Andrew McLaughlin, the owner of the Patapsco Hotel outside of Baltimore, advertised the "easy access" from his house to the new Baltimore & Ohio Railroad. Five years later, William Howlett promoted his Union Hotel in Richmond with the information that he could convey guests to and from the steamboat and railroad in "Hacks kept for that purpose." Far to the north, D. A. Gage promoted his establishment in Bellows Falls, Vermont, as being "within a few rods" of the depot that served two New England railroad lines. Such advertisements reflected and fueled keepers' competition for the patronage of hungry and tired passengers alighting from boat or train.[24]

Although steamboat and railroad companies did not feel obliged to publicize public accommodations near their wharves and depots, their passenger business presumed the availability of wayside taverns and hotels. The growing volume of passengers, tight scheduling, and frequent transfers made points of departure into potential grit in the machinery for all forms of commercial transportation. The higher the capital investment in vessels, rails, engines, and carriages, the less a carrier could afford any delays or additional expenditures. Handling tickets and corralling passengers at all hours of the day and night, keepers provided a valuable service to passenger carriers. Travelers on the infant Baltimore & Ohio Railroad boarded the cars in Baltimore not at a company depot but at the Three Tuns Tavern on Pratt Street; outside the city, the Patapsco Hotel served as a waiting room through the mid-1850s. During an 1857 tour through the South, wealthy young Prudence Swift and her travel companion, astronomer Maria Mitchell, spent their waiting time between train segments in public accommodations. In Augusta, Georgia, for example, the pair spent one afternoon at a hotel and the evening and night on the Atlanta-bound train. Reaching Atlanta at four o'clock in the morning, the women went straight to the Trout House and "took a room" until they boarded the train for Chattanooga, Tennessee. Railroad corporations would eventually invest in elaborate passenger depots and hotels, but during the key transitional period when railroads were first being adapted to the American context, taverns eased the rapid growth of lucrative passenger traffic.[25]

For a short but formative period, keepers even played a role in servicing some railroads' and steamboats' equipment and workers. In the first years of the Baltimore & Ohio Railroad and the Granite Railway in Massachusetts, horses pulled the cars. Horse-drawn trains stopped much like stagecoaches to rest, feed, or exchange teams of horses. Early locomotives also made regular stops for water and fuel. One such engine carried only enough water to travel fifteen miles before refilling.[26] Steamboats likewise made occasional stops for wood or coal. Whether along rail or waterway, such stops already were or soon became tavern sites, serving drivers, conductors, deck hands, and firemen. Likewise, tavern keepers on the banks of the Erie Canal fed the mules who pulled canal boats and poured whiskey for the boatmen and many passengers. Much like towns faded or thrived as a function of transportation, some keepers found travelers whizzing past their doors or drawn to other routes altogether, and others found new opportunities in serving passengers, carriers, or both.[27]

In both conceptual and practical ways, the links between commercial transportation and taverns helped potential passengers accommodate themselves to inconvenient schedules and sometimes downright alarming travel conditions. While some Americans could complete trips on modern transportation alone, many more people continued to live at a distance from hubs served by multiple water, rail, or stagecoach lines. Along with noncommercial transportation, including walking, taverns served to connect transportation lines and hubs not only to each other but also to communities that would otherwise have had no connections to the emergent national transportation grid. Travelers such as Maria Mitchell and Prudence Swift were thus beneficiaries of a technological revolution that built on an existing network. Only the combination of static and moving, old and new components made it reasonable for passengers to arrive in a town or city in the middle of the night and find nearby accommodations. Yet the experience of traveling rested on more than the transportation network and the ability to pay one's way, for neither guaranteed access to wayside taverns nor determined the terms of a traveler's reception once inside.[28]

White Men's Mobility

White men traveled for many reasons: to resettle in a new place, scout out land, settle debts, buy or sell goods, visit friends and family, seek work, and attend court. Smaller numbers also traveled to and from capital cities and towns as elected or appointed officials. Whatever their reasons for being on the move, when white men came to wayside taverns, they expected to talk, much as they did in their home taverns. Their conversations nurtured both opportunities and challenges. Opportunities often took the form of information that might guide their next steps, literal or figurative. Travel writers and private citizens acknowledged "the occasional amusement and information to be derived" from talking "with the landlord's family, and casual travellers." When James Gibbons and his father-in-law "contemplated removal" in 1804 from their eastern Pennsylvania home to Ohio, every other traveler the pair encountered on the way there and back represented a potential font of information. Decades later, migrants on the same route remained eager to quiz other "movers" on the road. Even foreign tourists could be useful, as British visitor Captain James E. Alexander learned from the "interrogatories" of an elderly settler and an "improving" lawyer he met in Kentucky.[29]

The self-interested prospect of gathering valuable information in wayside taverns encouraged the potentially democratizing assumption that nearly anyone could possess useful intelligence. In taverns as in stagecoaches, however, one man's reasonable query was another's impertinence. Europeans sometimes ascribed quizzing to Americans' bumptious republicanism, while white Southerners identified it as an offensive Yankee habit. Yet how was a man supposed to take the temperature of the company in which he found himself without speaking? How could he dodge invasive or tiresome questions without causing himself more trouble? Every man from congressmen to drovers had to consider when, how, and with whom he spoke, even as he gauged whether the strangers around him were honest or criminal, well-informed or ignorant, peaceable or prone to violence.[30]

As strangers talked, they attempted to suss each other out in a context where the visible and audible signs of identity were often ambiguous. Americans in the early republic were accustomed to taking cues from strangers' dress, manners, and speech, but wayside taverns assembled unusually heterogeneous mixtures of people. At the turn of the century, indentured servitude and other forms of legal subordination remained widespread enough that inhabiting a white man's body was not in itself an automatic passport to tavern services. Regular advertisements for runaway servants and slaves suggested that both people who were shabbily dressed and those who were better clad could be illicitly on the move.[31] Once servitude became rare among adult white men, the conditions of travel still complicated visible status markers. One early guide implied that wealthy travelers might as well leave their "expensive attire" at home because after a day on muddy or dusty roads, a gentleman could only hope "to appear clean and neat." The advent of steam travel, with its smoky, spark-belching engines, confirmed the value of clothes that could stand up to "rude usage." In taverns, crowded conditions only made social identifications even more difficult. The signs of wealth, occupation, and social capital that usually distinguished laborers, drovers, and peddlers from jurists, legislators, and other people of "consequence" blurred wherever exhausted men vied for a share of a tavern floor.[32]

Although many white men acted as if they personally had no concerns for either their ego or their safety in such circumstances, some men made their concerns explicit. A common source of tension in wayside taverns concerned the risk that a stranger would prove to be a thief or a confidence trickster. Newspapers, travel literature, and personal anecdotes abounded with tales of travelers falling prey to men of plausible mien but hidden motives. As a young man traveling alone in 1804, James P. Parke feared for his safety among strangers. As far as he could judge, the men sharing his room in a New Jersey tavern "looked like gentlemen," yet their conversation gave Parke reason to suspect the pistol-carrying strangers were well-camouflaged "Reprobates" intent on "plunder." The next night, he fretted that a "drunken man" might set their shared room ablaze with his ill-placed candle. Only after his close friend Reuben Haines joined him the following night did Parke record that he "slumbered and slept."[33]

How white men coped with the risk and opportunity of wayside encounters varied, but experienced travelers had a distinct advantage. When John Wight Bill stopped at a familiar tavern in Philadelphia, early in his extended 1835 trek, the sense of being in a place and with people "we have seen before" enabled him to enjoy "quite a jolification." In newer surroundings, Bill was more cautious, but by the time he reached Georgia, he had developed a facility with code-switching. Arriving at a Georgia tavern with a wagonload of commercial property, he "supped" with a newly elected congressman, Jacksonian Democrat Hopkins Holsey and "his Lady," who came in their private carriage. Later the same evening, Bill socialized with a group of drovers, who arrived on foot, driving herds of livestock to market or slaughter.[34] Other men also recognized that travel created opportunities to alter their self-presentation. Retired soldier and commission merchant Robert Patterson indulged in this flexibility during a mid-1830s trip from Philadelphia to the Iowa Territory and back. Patterson undertook the early legs of this trip with his daughter and sister-in-law. In their company, he noted his pleasure in refined taverns and peaceable tavern companies. On his own one day, Patterson relished the prospect of "seeing a real knock down, drag out, bit[e] and gouge Kentucky fight." Later the same day, Patterson rejoined his kinswomen at the stage tavern, apparently unruffled by his transition from homosocial rowdiness to chivalrous respectability.[35]

Conversational dexterity mattered not only because wayside taverns assembled motley crowds but also because men's conversation often turned to politics, a source of bitter and sometimes violent debate in the early republic. Venturing through the American interior after the turn of the century, Fortescue Cuming concluded that "politicks, throughout the whole of this country, seems to be the most irritable subject which can be discussed." As Roberts Vaux, another young friend of James P. Parke, suggested, a white man on the road might find himself "up to his arm pits in politics" even before exchanging introductions. And if violence did break out in a tavern, whether for political or other reasons, a man had to decide on the spot whether his personal safety and reputation depended on joining in or staying on the margins.[36]

John Wight Bill had weighed such risks even before leaving his Connecticut home in late 1835. Long-standing tensions between North and South had lately grown far more heated in the aftermath of Nat Turner's rebellion, an insurrection scare in Mississippi, and repeated acts of violence against Black and white activists who called for slavery's immediate abolition. The circulation of information through the transportation network fueled much of this tension. Recognizing the suspicion that might greet him as a Yankee bookseller, Bill inscribed an acknowledgment of slavery's constitutional status into his journal. He also vowed to "keep aloof from any and all intermedling with the local concerns and institutions of the South." Yet he could no more avoid conversation with fellow travelers than he could help noticing public slave auctions or the summary justice meted out to Black southerners. To his aid came his journal. What he could not safely say aloud, he confided to its pages. Poor southern whites were "not the one half as good citizens as are the *slaves*," he wrote one day. Another day, he described South Carolina's pro-slavery nullifiers as "trumpet-tongued," "designing," and "disordered." Eventually, he concluded that the North had far more "bold chivalrous daring enterprizing men" than the South. For him as for many other comfortably literate men, wayside writing helped him hold his own tongue around men who might leap to injurious or even dangerous conclusions about him.[37]

Over the following decades, competing understandings of politics, manners, and masculinity continued to produce fraught moments in wayside taverns. Brash young urbanites could easily offend older men in New England's village taverns, as New York City's Abram Hewitt and his friend Edward Cooper learned during a tour to celebrate Hewitt's twenty-first birthday. After a leisurely week of sightseeing, sea bathing, bowling, fishing, and dancing, the pair wound up in a tavern near Dover, New Hampshire. Although their other stops had gone smoothly, Hewitt thought that the "villainous looking" keeper of this tavern seemed "as likely to knock us down as to pick his teeth," while another local combined "the characteristics of the bull dog & cut[throat]." Eager "to pick a quarrel," the second man seized Hewitt's and Cooper's hefty walking sticks and "commenced a sweeping invective against . . . aristocrats." Although Hewitt joked later that his shapeless gray coat and durable fustian pantaloons did not give him "any appearance of possessing a dollar," at the time he launched into "a general eulogy on [laborers] & democrats in particular," hoping to appease "this ferocious gentleman." In confiding this episode to his journal—writing in another tavern the next day—Hewitt played up the humor and cast himself as the quick-witted hero.[38]

While Abram Hewitt updated his journal in the bedroom he shared with Edward Cooper, much tavern reading and writing took place in public spaces. In taverns, literacy had long been associated with sociable activities, such as reading newspapers and discussing the news they contained. For related reasons, perusing a travel guide, map, or gazetteer often served as a prelude to conversation, an excuse to ask where a stranger was bound and what he had seen. Yet a book suggested the possibility of sustained reading. In his *Pocket Companion*, George Temple counseled his readers to bring a book or two as a means to avoid "recourse to politics." Even with a newspaper, a man's position in the room—sitting by himself or at a table with others—signaled whether he intended to read quietly or read and talk (see figure 1.2).[39]

Even more than public reading, writing in a tavern's public rooms represented an alternative to conversation, one available chiefly to men of more-than-minimal literacy. By the early nineteenth century, most white men could read at least at a basic level, particularly in the North, but far fewer were comfortable with writing voluminous personal letters or journals. As such, public writing in a tavern had a performative quality. A young South Carolinian on his way home from Pennsylvania expressed as much, explaining to his mother that he wrote to her "regardless of wine & tumult." Francis Lee's writerly devotion presumably pleased his mother, but it also excused him from conversation. Lee did not rely on writing alone to mark his status. He and his father, Colonel John Boykin, traveled in "elegant" style with their own carriage, three horses, servants, and "a young man." Even so, writing helped him choose when and how he interacted with other tavern-goers.[40]

Although many mettle-testing opportunities involved other white men, some travelers also took advantage of women's presence. Married men often passed judgment on tavern landladies and their housekeeping, as if to remind themselves that they possessed better-managed and furnished homes. Bach-

FIGURE 1.2 John Lewis Krimmel (American, 1786–1821), *Village Tavern*, 1813–1814, oil on canvas, 16⅞ × 22½ inches, Toledo Museum of Art (Toledo, Ohio), purchased with funds from the Florence Scott Libbey Bequest in Memory of Her Father, Maurice A. Scott, 1954.13. Photo Credit: Richard Goodbody, New York. John Krimmel's scene suggests the power of tavern reading to produce both sociability and separation. The gray-haired man in glasses at the table reads aloud to his fellows. The younger man, seated by himself with his back to company, reads alone until something, perhaps the arrival of the woman and child, prompts him to turn toward his fellow patrons. Krimmel's painting also illustrates the mixture of people and activities in a small tavern whose floor plan did not allow significant spatial separation. Anyone entering this tavern from the road outside could immediately see nearly everyone in the room. Yet this tavern includes multiple amenities, such as paintings, newspapers, and chairs with well-turned legs. The bar cage pictured in the center served to secure the valuable liquors and glassware.

elors paid less attention to their material surroundings as a rule, but they were quick to notice if they encountered a woman they considered pretty. Married or single, some travelers must have taken advantage of the opportunities for commercial sex, known to flourish along important transportation routes, but both prostitution and rape usually passed without mention in travel writing. In diaries and letters that might later be read by kinswomen, men such as Joseph Brevard and Robert Hunter did little more than mention the attractive women they encountered, including a "very pretty young woman" and a "sweet, pretty young girl, too handsome by far for her station." Such phrases neither prove nor rule out sexual commerce, but J. B. Dunlop veered closer in observing that the "Beautiful Barmaid" at a rural New York tavern was "an invaluable acquisition to the Landlord."[41]

In their letters and journals, some male travelers took pains to frame their interactions with women as flirtation. Although this understanding does not exclude the possibility of assault, harassment, or prostitution, it illuminates the work of masculine self-fashioning. Traveling through North Carolina in the 1820s as a newspaper agent, Hiram Haines (no known relation to the Philadelphia Haines family) noticed many women in the letters he wrote to his fiancée Mary Ann Currie Philpotts. Haines used his encounters with women to tease Mary Ann, perhaps seeking to test her attachment. In one such letter, Haines described seeing the "L-E-G-S" of the Carolina "lasses" with their "pettic—ts tucked up." On the road again later the same year, the now-married Hiram wrote from widowed Mrs. Williams's tavern about his "liking for widows." After a "cocktail," he felt "pretty comfortable" and "looked around to see if I could find a subject for amusement." Spotting an elegant lady's hat, he entertained himself by writing an anonymous poem to the hat's owner, hoping to disconcert her and, through the retelling, tease his wife as well. South Carolina's Colonel John Boykin also found ample opportunities to flirt, as his son and travel companion Francis P. Lee suggested in the epistolary journal addressed to Mrs. Boykin. One evening, Lee related how "the tingling lips of your husband . . . smacked the ruddy girls with pouting lips" as they bade farewell. A week later, at Mr. Wigglesworth's tavern south of Fredericksburg, Virginia, Boykin "spent the after dinner in paying his respects to Mrs. Wigglesworth," the keeper's wife, and "succeeded pretty well in engaging her affections." Farther south, the colonel used his "usual gallantry" to secure "the best room in the house for Mrs. Edgar," a fellow traveler. In this case, Lee suggested that Boykin had shown more courtesy than Mrs. Edgar's own husband, who was also present. Lee appears to have taken Boykin's attentions to other women not as an insult to Mrs. Boykin but as a kind of masculine one-upmanship that burnished the colonel's manly reputation. From his tone, he expected female tavern keepers, other travelers, and even Mrs. Boykin to reach the same tolerant conclusion.[42]

As white men passed through wayside taverns on trips for business and pleasure, they faced both opportunities and risks. While spending an afternoon in a tavern, a man might drink and talk with men from wildly different backgrounds. In these encounters, sometimes a traveler gained an economic advantage or forged a valuable acquaintance; sometimes he lost face; sometimes he inflicted or endured violence. Only some men had the luxury of avoiding conversation by dint of reading or writing. Traveling with respectable gentlewomen represented another resource, a means of avoiding conversational entanglements with strangers and asserting their own status as gentlemen.

White Womanhood on the Move

Middle-class and elite white women had fewer reasons for travel than their husbands, fathers, and brothers, but as the transportation revolution made travel faster and cheaper, they reaped some of the same benefits as white men. Although migration often attenuated familial ties, especially for people of limited means and those who moved into the far west, improved roads, canals, steamboats, and trains made discretionary trips, once feasible only for the wealthiest Americans, more accessible to women from middling households as well. Some privileged women engaged in new practices of tourism, venturing to take the waters, admire booming towns or wild mountains, bathe in the sea, and socialize with other travelers. For all these women, tavern stops became a matter of course. Although the vision of fast transportation to destination resorts suggested that middle-class and wealthy women travelers need associate only with people of their class, a typical multiday trip entailed numerous wayside tavern stops and many encounters with strangers quite unlike themselves.[43]

On newfangled steamboats and trains, the professed goal of protecting white women from danger and insult became a reason to create first-class and ladies' cabins and cars and a pretext for excluding Black men and women from them, whatever their manners and means.[44] In wayside taverns, white women on the move were also overtly favored by contrast to Black women, but they still had to operate within narrow norms to avoid being seen as "public women," or potential prostitutes. White women themselves policed this sexual double standard, as the opinionated travel writer Anne Newport Royall noted. She memorialized a tavern landlady who refused entry to "a poor, but decent-looking woman with a child in her arms, standing in the door." Even Royall's offer to pay double the other woman's charges failed to soften "the brute." Royall fought a largely losing battle with this anecdote. Many of her contemporaries agreed that a poor mother with no visible means of support, no obvious husband, and no one to vouch for her was probably guilty of immorality and thus unworthy of respect or protection from the virtuous. Unlike this unfortunate mother, the white women whose travel writings survive generally traveled with the visible trappings of respectability. A lady—to use the parlance of the period—did not arrive on foot and alone. Her clothing, luggage, bearing, speech, and company all appeared to prove her social position and personal virtue. Yet even a woman who never questioned her standing at home might work hard to reconcile wayside tavern encounters with her sense of self.[45]

Middle- and upper-class white women negotiated a path through wayside taverns using a combination of willful blindness, moral judgment, gendered thinking, and writing. In part because they were themselves judged, middle-class and elite women set themselves up in judgment of the conditions and people they encountered. Like their male peers, they wrote letters and diaries to shape, not just record, their wayside experiences. In 1808, Hannah Marshall Haines, her husband, and her son were arrested in Connecticut for violating an ordinance against Sunday travel. A well-to-do and well-regarded Quaker from Philadelphia, Hannah was flabbergasted to find herself and her family "rudely seized" and "detained" under guard in a tavern like common criminals, "lest we should slip away, and not stand trial." In writing to two kinswomen, Haines expressed distress at being "intirely in the power" of the inimical constable. Equally disconcerting, the next day, the Haines family stood trial before "the Inhabitants of the village," who turned out for the spectacle. When the Haineses resumed their homeward journey the next day, Hannah used letter writing to recast the experience. Although she could not easily forget the public humiliation, she reworked the event as one in a long series of "trying scenes" that Connecticut's "very bigoted Presbyterians" had inflicted on her fellow Quakers.[46]

Ladylike travelers also separated themselves from objectionable settings and people by passing judgment in less dramatic circumstances. When Hannah Marshall Haines's daughter-in-law Jane complained about one of the "dirty miserable" wayside taverns she visited, she did not imagine that the family members who read her letter would consider her tainted by association but rather the opposite. Her extended family knew from experience that travel might mean visiting taverns and interacting with people they would never countenance at home. Still, in emphasizing her disgust at the standard of housekeeping, Haines rejected any possibility of identification or kinship with the women of the tavern. Along similar lines, Sarah Howland used her journal of a family pleasure trip in 1818 not primarily to detail the sights she took in, such as "the foam of the falls of Niagara rising high in the air," but to describe and assess their daily stages. On this trip, she deemed roughly half of the wayside taverns "good," "very good," or even "very excellent." The remainder she dismissed as somewhere between "tolerable" and "wretched." At every point on this spectrum, her judgments asserted her right both to occupy and to express opinions about wayside taverns. At the same time, her remarks invoked the social position from which her standards derived, which any relative or friend likely to read Howland's journal would recognize.[47]

Also significant in women's travel writing were the omissions. Sarah Howland wrote as if she and her family were the only guests in every wayside tavern they visited, highly unlikely in the summer season along the popular route they traveled. This strategy protected Howland's self-image by disassociating her from behavior and people of which she disapproved. Her silence also exempted her husband from any responsibility for bringing his wife and their young daughter to places where, perhaps, whiskey tipplers thronged at the bar or slept on the floor. Even in writing destined for close friends and family members, most well-to-do white women remained similarly discreet, acting as if they could not even recognize licentious behavior in others or as if the other people they encountered in tavern spaces simply did not exist. These tactical silences disconnected familial and feminized leisure travel from masculine vice, despite their simultaneity in wayside taverns and their preservation in letters from men such as Hiram Haines and Francis Lee.[48]

Whereas white women travelers felt free to complain about tavern accommodations and service, they rarely recorded feeling vulnerable around other travelers. S. Schulling's record of a trip through Pennsylvania in 1824 stands out for its atypical reference to sexualized fear. During one stop, Schulling and her female friends fanned each other's alarm at being around strange men. In this tavern, the women "had to pass thro the main lodging room which contained a dozen beds," all of them "filled with men." At the sight, fear took "full possession of our mind's," and the women insisted that their male companion "should occupy the next apartment to us" as a safeguard against intrusion. Still anxious, Schulling and her friends rearranged the bedroom furniture to block what they fancied to be a concealed door. Schulling's implicitly sexual fears suggest the difficult position in which self-identified respectable white women often found themselves. While reliant on masculine protection, Schulling and her peers felt all but unable to share a roof with strange men. Nor could they imagine taking charge of their encounters with other travelers beyond the expedient of sequestering themselves in a bedroom. At the same time, the women's demand for protection presumed that safety in a tavern was possible and that they could commandeer tavern resources to get it. Women on the road sometimes face unwanted sexual advances or outright attack. Yet as white women traveling in a group with the resources to pay for separate accommodations, Schulling and her friends overestimated their danger. Perhaps they did not know, or chose to ignore, that they were comparatively safe *because* of the far greater exposure to sexualized insult and violence that less privileged white women and women of color faced among strangers. Rounding out the anecdote in her diary, Schulling found one more way to make her discomfort bespeak her status. She claimed that "David our driver a good natured son of Africa felt less objection to the place than did we."[49]

Older and especially widowed women felt freer to express displeasure at masculine conduct as they moved through wayside taverns. During a trip from Pennsylvania to Ohio with her children in the mid-1830s, the widowed Elizabeth Lundy Willson recorded several observations about other people on the road. Willson paid attention to fellow travelers because her oldest son was migrating to Ohio and she hoped to learn something about his prospects. Yet she deplored the "rough unguarded language of those young men" she met at tavern and ferry stops. At one Ohio tavern, she was "much annoyed by the oaths of some young men who had made too free with the glass," adding that "the landlord was not clear of the same fault." At another tavern, Willson wrote again about an "intoxicated" customer. This time, however, the keeper acted as a man "of feeling" and helped ensure that the drinker "knew his place," perhaps by keeping him at a distance from Willson's party. Willson used her diary to manage her reactions to those around her: naming the rowdy masculine tavern-going behaviors that troubled her, invoking alternative norms for manly behavior, and memorializing the men who seemed to agree with her.[50]

Anne Newport Royall went many steps beyond Elizabeth Willson in insisting on her right to tavern spaces and opinions. After her husband died and his relatives contested his will, Royall supported herself by writing and selling travel narratives, making several tours to solicit subscriptions and amass material for additional volumes. Her wayside tavern encounters suggested the extent and limits of white women's claim to tavern spaces. Instead of ignoring trouble, Royall almost courted it, stuffing her books with juicy anecdotes to generate publicity and win subscribers. Although men skirted the subject of prostitution, Royall observed that "all taverns" had an "infamous girl about . . . as sly as the owners keep it." When keepers or patrons threatened her because of her published opinions, she fired back, calling them ungentlemanly, sometimes to their faces, and sometimes in print. Even after she was convicted as a common scold, she continued to travel and publish. Yet after a few years of increasingly difficult encounters, she largely stepped back from the immediate confrontations associated with travel and addressed the public through her newspaper, *Paul Pry*.[51]

As they moved through wayside taverns, both women who critiqued rowdy male behavior and those who pretended not to notice it staked a claim to tavern spaces. As the notion of white women's special affinity for virtue spread through American culture and into the temperance movement, middle-class women grew increasingly explicit in their attacks on the common tavern behaviors of drinking, socializing, game playing, and more. Temperance women drew many white men along with them, creating an alternative vision of who and what taverns were for. During the same period, the daily dynamics of travel created opportunities for keepers to profit from respectable white women travelers and their cultural and spatial aspirations.[52]

Black Mobility

In wayside taverns, Black Americans tested connections between the freedom to move and the right to occupy public space, key aspects of vernacular citizenship.[53] Any free Black person who wished to travel in the United States struggled against white Americans' assumption that self-willed Black mobility might be criminal, as Elizabeth Stordeur Pryor and others argue. Free Black travelers also faced novel barriers related to the transportation revolution. As stagecoaches, steamboats, trains, and urban trolleys spread, their proprietors responded to white customers' pressure, developing practices to exclude or segregate free Black travelers. At the same time, those who trafficked in enslaved people took advantage of new forms of transportation. White men's and women's strategies for occupying space in wayside taverns likewise constrained free Black Americans' opportunities to travel and use taverns for their own purposes. In taverns, Black women struggled to get any of the consideration that white men accorded to white women they considered ladies. Black men who sought to use taverns for their economic and political self-improvement faced white resistance and often violence. Most wayside taverns remained so unwelcoming to Black travelers that the prospect of reducing their reliance on taverns represented one reason that their access to railroads and steamboats mattered so much.[54]

Yet some Black men on the move in the early republic were able to use wayside taverns much like white men, harnessing geographic mobility to their personal goals. In the 1810s and 1820s, the magician and ventriloquist Richard Potter made a living by touring not only in New England but also in the Mid-Atlantic and the South, as far as Mississippi. As a traveler, he lodged in taverns. As a performer, he used large tavern rooms, among other venues, as his stage. Potter's racially ambiguous appearance helped him navigate tavern spaces designed to accommodate large, mostly white crowds. Some people thought he was from India or perhaps the Caribbean, while others concluded he was white with a dark complexion, and still others perceived him as Black.[55]

The young Solomon Northup made his living from the transportation revolution. In his youth, he worked on the Champlain Canal in northeastern New York. From this work, he earned enough money to buy horses and the equipment to become an independent contractor, transporting lumber from Lake Champlain to Troy, New York. Later, he and his wife supplemented their farming income through occasional work in taverns and hotels around Saratoga Springs, where they made money from leisure travelers and tourists: Solomon as a violinist and Anne as a cook whose skills earned "high wages" at Sherill's Coffee House. Northup's long experience of the connections between geographic mobility and economic opportunity surely informed his agreement to travel to Washington, D.C., to perform there during New York's slow season. In the event, this trip put him within the reach of professional slave dealers, who transported him by water to New Orleans as a purported slave.[56]

Black travel sometimes combined political and economic motives. A formerly enslaved man known as Aaron traveled through New England, the Mid-Atlantic, and the Midwest in the 1830s or early 1840s, supporting himself as a speaker and seeking contributions toward the publication of his antislavery autobiography. In the text he eventually produced, Aaron related multiple tavern encounters with white men who treated him not as a legitimate traveler but as a Black man out of place. A Rhode Island keeper stole more than twenty dollars from him, which Aaron did not even try to recover. In Windsor, Connecticut, Aaron offered a keeper twenty-five cents to sleep in a "comfortable straw bed." The keeper declined even to let him sleep on "a pallet in the bar-room," claiming that "his customers did not like it when he took in a colored man." In another Connecticut tavern, "eight or nine young men" converged on him, manhandled him in a mock-phrenological exam, and demanded to know "where I was from;—some said that I was from South Carolina." Aaron feared this interrogation meant the men expected to profit from seizing and selling him. He also believed that this tavern's keeper only allowed him to spend the night because he was planning to "sell my sinful body."[57] Aaron and Solomon Northup were hardly alone in encountering taverns as sites of betrayal linked to the larger phenomena of kidnapping and the slave trade. In addition to the well-known fact that slave traders often worked out of taverns, Black men and boys promised work in a tavern were sometimes seized and sold into slavery instead.[58]

Being insulted, refused service, and worse were predictable hazards of traveling while Black in the early republic, but Black abolitionists like Aaron ensured that its significance remained mutable. In this, they surpassed white travelers who used their pens to reframe bad experiences. In an early issue of his *Weekly Advocate*, a newspaper aimed at New York City's Black community, Philip A. Bell published a letter received from John C. Bowers, in which the latter described his ill-treatment in Lancaster, Pennsylvania, after attending an abolitionist convention elsewhere in the state. At the North American Hotel, the barman "molested" Bowers, and the hotel keeper insisted that "it hurt his house, for . . . any colored man to sit at his table." Bolstered by the support of "about fifty" other abolitionists during the "altercation," however, Bowers kept his seat, rising from the breakfast table only when he was "quite refreshed." Although the episode probably had the ring of painful familiarity to many of the *Advocate*'s readers, Bowers insisted that this racist incident had been a unique occurrence during his two-hundred-mile round trip. Publishing this story thus highlighted the possibility and value of Black travel. For his part, Bowers continued to work as an antislavery activist and a subscription agent for the *Advocate*, one of twelve working across six states.[59]

Publishing acts of resistance to discrimination in taverns, like those in trains or streetcars, encouraged other Black Americans to assert their right to mobility in the face of white opposition. These publications also raised awareness that Black travelers constituted a market for public accommodations by blacklisting keepers who refused their business and promoting hospitable keepers. When J. H. Townsend informed Frederick Douglass that Mr. Hall of the Phoenix Hotel in Binghamton, New York, had "ordered me out of his bar-room," Douglass publicized Townsend's passionate critique of the "Satanic" tavern keeper. Douglass also printed Townsend's strategic suggestion that other Black travelers "put this creature in the way of his duty by patronizing other hotels." On other occasions, Douglass used his platform to celebrate establishments, such as Cincinnati's Dumas House, that welcomed Black travelers.[60]

Free Black men who visited taverns while traveling faced special hostility because they were using taverns in pursuit of their own political, economic, and social goals, as white men did. In their turn, free Black women travelers who staked a claim to respectability through their clothes, deportment, and speech challenged middling and wealthy white women's supposedly exclusive claim to the privileges of virtuous ladyhood. As such, in wayside taverns, destination resorts, and urban hotels, Black women often encountered white keepers and fellow patrons who refused to accept them at all or insisted on a marked separation from white women. In his 1848 antislavery testimonial, Wilson Armistead included numerous examples of the unequal treatment that Black travelers faced in the United States regardless of their national origin or class. In one case, an American tavern landlady refused entry to a light-skinned "gentlewoman" from Haiti, telling her to go instead to "the Nigger huts" nearby. The manager of Boston's Marlboro' House informed Mary E. Webb that she could stay at the hotel but could not eat with white guests at "the public table," nor could she attend the on-site weekly worship service. Adding financial injury to the insult, the keeper expected her to pay extra for dining privately in her room. According to the newspaper, Webb decamped for the more hospitable Winthrop Hotel.[61]

Free Black women who traveled as white people's servants had a different but no more equitable experience of wayside taverns. As servants, Black women could count on being received by keepers who might have rejected them outright as self-willed travelers, a pattern they also experienced on stagecoaches, steamboats, and trains. Yet Black women in service could count on sleeping in inferior accommodations and eating separately from white servants. Harriet Jacobs recalled being treated differently than white nannies on a steamboat from New York City to Albany, in land-based accommodations along the way, and again at a Saratoga Springs hotel. At the Pavilion Hotel outside New York City, "a great resort of the fashionable world," Jacobs found that "some of the ladies had colored waiting-maids and coachmen, but I was the only nurse tinged with the blood of Africa." A hotel employee told her to stand as she fed her young charge in the dining room, while all the other nursemaids remained seated. Instead of eating with the other nurses, she alone was ordered to dine in the kitchen with the hotel's servants. Drawing this distinction between white and Black servants extended a degree of racial privilege to white working women who had little claim to ladyhood and its protections. Yet when Jacobs's employer instructed that both Jacobs and his daughter be served in their room, the hotel's white waitstaff complained that "they were not hired to wait on negroes."[62]

For enslaved people, white exploitation of their labor, relationships, and bodies left even less room to make wayside taverns serve their own pursuits of mobility and self-determination. Instead, improved transportation both increased whites' eagerness to relocate hundreds of thousands of enslaved people to new southern territories and made it faster, easier, and more profitable to do so. At the tavern junctures of their involuntary journeys through the domestic slave trade, Black people faced conditions that made most white travelers' complaints look fatuous by comparison. Whereas some white women used an exaggerated sexual threat to improve their accommodations, enslaved women regularly endured rape. For related reasons, enslaved men also faced extreme danger in and around southern taverns: being valuable as property proved scant protection in spaces where white men drank, socialized, and competed.[63]

Forcible relocation from the upper and eastern South to the labor-hungry plantations of Alabama, Mississippi, and beyond brought many thousands of enslaved men, women, and children to wayside taverns during terrorizing expeditions by road, water, or rail. Whether in the grip of a new owner or as part of a coffle bound for auction, enslaved people often approached taverns dazed by weary miles, whips, and the loss of people and places they cared for, probably forever. At these taverns, keepers provided enslaved people with food and drink to sustain the next day's trek, sometimes serving it in troughs usually used for hogs or other livestock. When night fell, enslaved people were likely to sleep not in bedrooms but in barns, on muddy floors, or in barred cellars.[64]

Those few transported slaves who did see the inside of tavern bedrooms, usually women, were rarely brought there for their own comfort. Instead, after a long day's march, an enslaved woman had to prepare herself for the likelihood that one or more of the traders would take her aside and rape her. Traders at Remley's tavern in Lewisburg, Virginia, for example, openly took turns raping enslaved women in the bedroom they rented for that purpose. Women had reason to fear not only for themselves but for anyone else they cared for in the coffle: a daughter or sister who might also face rape; a son, husband, or friend who might be maimed or killed for trying to prevent an assault; a baby reduced to profit or loss in a trader's ledger. Lewis Clarke told of a slave trader who took a crying infant from its mother's arms and handed it to a tavern keeper "to pay one of his tavern bills." Etched in Josephine Brown's familial memory was the slave trader who gave an enslaved infant to a tavern landlady because the baby's crying "affects my nerves." The smiling landlady thanked the trader for his "kindness and generosity." A few days later, the child's mother leaped from the deck of a steamboat and drowned in the Mississippi River.[65]

Enslaved men in the domestic slave trade suffered gendered torment as well. In taverns as in every other house of bondage, Black men's inability to defend themselves, each other, or the women and children near them represented an assault on their masculinity. Enslaved men also faced terroristic violence simply for being in or around a tavern. Whether in the custody of a dealer or accompanying their owner, enslaved men knew that strange white men with time on their hands and alcohol in their bloodstream often meant trouble. Theodore Dwight Weld's influential *American Slavery as It Is*, published in 1839, included multiple episodes that highlighted the volatile cruelty of tavern crowds. In one example, an enslaved man was staked to the ground and gang-whipped by men who happened to be in this particular Mississippi tavern and shared a thirst for violence. Similarly, when Josiah Henson bumped into a drunken white man while trying to extract his owner from a tavern fight, the man took such offense that he later "waylaid" Henson, beating him so severely that his fractured arm and shoulders never fully healed. Charles Ball also encountered aggressive white masculinity while traveling with a new owner. On the way back to the plantation, the enslaver stopped at a tavern for toddy and "toasts in honour of liberty and independence." Left alone outside while the white men caroused, Ball eventually sat down on a bench near the door, only to have a "gentleman, in military clothes," take offense and threaten to "cut my head off."[66]

As insulting, dangerous tavern encounters made their way into abolitionist print, they reinforced the point that most white Americans saw Black access to taverns, like Black mobility itself, as a threat to the early republic's racial hierarchy. Taverns' place in upholding slavery and racism became all the more visible through advertisements and reports concerning the sale, flight, and capture of enslaved people. Yet in small numbers and often in covert ways, taverns also played a role in enslaved people's bids for freedom.[67] When slave owners visited the North, their enslaved servants often "cherished a secret desire for liberty" and sought information about escape routes during their travels. Charles Ball told a fellow slave from the Northern Neck of Virginia, whom he happened to meet in a Georgia tavern, what information he could about "the best means of reaching the State of Pennsylvania." People escaping from slavery sometimes exploited the commercial transportation network and its tavern junctions. Most famously, William and Ellen

Craft escaped from slavery with Ellen disguised as a white gentleman and William passing as her slave. The Crafts stayed overnight in hotels in Savannah and Charleston before taking ship for Philadelphia.[68]

Necessity and a determination to do and be more than white supremacists wanted drove many Black Americans to test both old and emerging limits on their mobility. As free and enslaved people used taverns in their bids for freedom, economic opportunity, and political self-determination, their actions fashioned a "rival geography" in opposition to taverns' use as places of "containment." While the print record made clear to any contemporary reader that escaping slavery or traveling with ease were not normative Black experiences, they happened often enough to make public accommodations, like the transportation network as a whole, a domain in which Black Americans could imagine self-willed as well as coerced mobility in the early republic.[69]

FROM THE 1780S THROUGH THE 1850S, public and private investment in internal improvements brought stunning changes in how long it took to cross long distances, yet travelers' diaries and letters retained an emphasis on daily tavern stops. In ways both practical and conceptual, taverns linked old road-based forms of travel with new steam-powered transportation. Travelers' uses of wayside taverns helped bring into being a reasonably coherent, increasingly national transportation network. Those who planned, funded, and built this imperfect system of taverns, roads, canals, and rails largely imagined its use in terms of white men's economic and geographic mobility. Wayside tavern encounters reflected this vision. Although white men sometimes felt alienated from or even threatened by other white men in the temporary communities of wayside taverns, they also used these moments to articulate for themselves and others their presumed competence to travel on their own account and conduct their own affairs. Through travel and transportation, moreover, white men helped knit the nation together through ties of commerce and culture, while also extending its reach into areas where American sovereignty did not yet hold sway.

The growing ease of early nineteenth-century travel created many new opportunities for white middle-class women to imagine, initiate, plan, and evaluate travel, even though most of them still preferred to travel with and rely on white men. As far as wayside taverns were concerned, the result was a significant uptick in the presence of middling and wealthy women who expected to be treated as respectable ladies, not public women. Greater numbers did not automatically make wayside taverns into spaces that women traversed with ease, however. The codes of respectable feminine behavior prompted female travelers to claim access to wayside taverns with constrained confidence. On the one hand, they believed in their right to extract protective consideration from their menfolk, who sometimes complied in ways that infringed on other men's access to tavern spaces. On the other hand, female travelers did not unravel the double standard that allowed gentlemen the freedom to engage in ribaldry and drunkenness with other men on the move.

Black Americans also moved through wayside taverns in ways that illustrated the early republic's oppressive and liberatory potentials. Together, slavery and racism meant that Black Americans had ample reason to associate taverns with insults, violence, and coercion. Yet free and even enslaved Black Americans wrested a small but important modicum of opportunity from wayside taverns. The reality of Black movement through a transportation network designed to support white men's mobility meant that, like trains and streetcars, wayside taverns became "theaters" in which Black men and women claimed rights: the right to move, receive tavern services, and be treated as self-willed men and respectable women.[70]

CHAPTER TWO

Fitted Up in a Superior Style

Tavern Improvements

In 1819, Isaac Frazier advertised in at least two South Carolina newspapers that he had "opened a HOUSE OF ENTERTAINMENT" in Columbia, the state capital. Frazier informed "his friends and the public" that he was keeping tavern in a "large and well known house" that had "lately undergone a thorough repair." Promising "assiduous and unremitted attention" to render his guests "comfortable," Frazier also offered "appropriate rooms elegantly furnished for the reception of families, entirely remote from the bustle" of a busy tavern.[1] Keepers of leading taverns in locally important towns throughout the settled parts of the country made similar promises to accommodate the public in updated, commodious, and well-managed taverns. Through both their language and their material investments, these keepers signaled their alignment with increasingly widespread ideals of refinement and comfort. At the same time, village and town keepers continued to accommodate men who wanted other things from their taverns, including affordable lodgings and the sometimes riotous sociability that accompanied heavy drinking. Through both small gestures and major investments of time and money, improvement-minded keepers promoted spatial differentiations that helped them accommodate divergent tavern publics.[2]

Changes in taverns' layout and embellishment had little to do with licensing laws passed after the revolution, which largely carried over colonial statutes that required keepers to accommodate travelers and regulated their alcohol sales.[3] Instead, this trend began much earlier in the small slice of urban taverns that had supported elites' public performances of gentility since at least the mid-eighteenth century. Catering to the colonial elite, a handful of urban tavern keepers had provided elegant and well-appointed rooms for elaborate public dinners and balls. At such events, gentlemen and ladies demonstrated their gentility through elegant, expensive clothing, refined conversation, polished manners, and graceful movements that supposedly raised them above the common order of humanity, whose conduct and way of life identified them as rude and even uncivilized. In the infant republic, prominent men in important towns and cities continued to use leading taverns as stages for a kind of republican aristocracy. The need to differentiate themselves from an aspiring middle tier that sought genteel surroundings while also pursuing thrift and respectability helped encourage urban elitists to abandon their former tavern haunts, such as Philadelphia's City Tavern. In the nineteenth century, the ratchet of consumer fashions pushed the owners of would-be first-class hotels into an unending cycle of investment and innovation in the name of improvement. Evolving standards of bodily comfort informed systems for ventilating, heating, lighting, and cleaning, each of which posed technical and labor challenges. The wants and demands that reshaped private homes and the leading urban public accommodations spread slowly yet steadily beyond the eastern seaboard, where the evidence of refinement and comfort was as unevenly distributed as it was in the coastal cities. In both small and sizable taverns, the dynamics of improvement brought physical changes, financial costs, and cultural tensions.[4]

Repairing, expanding, furnishing, and staffing taverns for the sake of gentility and comfort put great demands on tavern keepers, particularly those in small towns and along country roads. For starters, perceived differences between the city and the countryside became entrenched as "elements of an intellectual geography," which might not recognize evidence of refinement in communities far from coastal cities. In addition, late eighteenth-century gentility required not only elegant consumer goods and manners but also a distinct separation between labor and leisure. Long after the turn of the century, however, many tavern-keeping families still lived, worked, and entertained their customers in taverns with a one- or two-room floor plan. To convert such a tavern into one with a separate or detached kitchen, dedicated bedrooms, and distinct rooms for socializing was costly and time-consuming. Many keepers, like private householders, first embarked on the refining process through their choices about the uses of existing space and the purchase of a small number of luxury goods. As a next step, ambitious keepers added onto and reorganized their existing spaces. This trend led to increasingly large, complex taverns, complete with multiple private bedrooms, even as many tavern guests continued to share rooms or even beds. To furnish these spaces, keepers invested in objects associated with refinement and comfort, such as wall coverings, pictures, carpets, tea sets, lamps, mirrors, and washbasins.[5]

Because of taverns' gradual improvements and their heterogeneous patrons, the prosperous cosmopolitans whose opinions saturate the archives often found few signs of either refinement or comfort in small town, village, or rural taverns.[6] When urbane travelers found fault with their surroundings, they often mobilized national, regional, ethnic, and cosmopolitan prejudices.

Some travelers did so not merely to complain but to create cultural distinctions where spatial separation seemed insufficient or totally lacking. Other travelers chose instead to appreciate gestures toward refinement and comfort even in the one-room and log cabin taverns that remained common in new settlements and along lightly traveled roads. For their part, town and village keepers and their patrons did not always agree with cosmopolitan outsiders that shared-use spaces and homespun were backward or degrading.[7]

Keepers of larger taverns increasingly relied on the interior organization of space to differentiate people and activities. The outside and most of the ground floor of many such taverns were overwhelmingly masculine and usually white terrain, while new interior spaces often catered to middle- and upper-class visitors, including women. Improving keepers tried to enhance the public house's resemblance to a genteel private home, yet most taverns offered an uncertain welcome to female patrons. Tastefully furnished private bedrooms and parlors and occasional refined gatherings in more public rooms created zones appropriate to gentlewomen. Yet these zones could feel like small islands in turbulent rivers of whiskey, as hard-drinking men flaunted their refusal to practice a moderation that might please the ladies. In addition, some of the impetus for self-segregation came not from ladies but from men who occasionally found the rowdy forms of masculinity tiresome, repulsive, or threatening. Spatial differentiation provided an imperfect separation among competing norms, most notably between white men's quasi-democratic drinking culture and the middle-class respectability that shaped parlor culture and made an imperfect transition to taverns. In both the more public and the more private rooms, white men and white women sought to enhance their separateness from and imagined superiority to others. And in this evolving, contested environment, people of color occasionally managed to make their own uses of improving taverns.[8]

Log Cabin Refinement

From the road, many of the small taverns that dotted the American landscape were not readily distinguishable from other houses and farmsteads, unless perhaps a sign out front proclaimed their function.[9] Sometimes constructed from rough-hewn logs, small taverns might have a one- or two-room footprint, a packed-earth floor, and a sleeping and storage loft upstairs. In such settings, there could be little separation between sleeping, eating, drinking, socializing, and cooking, either for tavern guests or for members of the household. Lewis Krimmel's "Barroom Dancing" (ca. 1820) suggests the jumble of people

FIGURE 2.1 John Lewis Krimmel, [Barroom Dancing], ca. 1820, watercolor. Krimmel's
genre painting documents the juxtaposition of uses and users found in small rural taverns.
White men and women dance to music provided by a Black fiddler, while other white
men drink and observe. Blankets on a shelf near the door hint that travelers slept in chairs
or on the floor near the fireplace. The tavern also features improving touches, such as
finished walls and floor, paintings, wall map, candle sconce, birdcage, ornamented fire
irons, punch bowl, and a variety of glassware. While a cosmopolitan traveler accustomed
to grand city ballrooms might have scorned rural people's enjoyment of a tavern dance,
Krimmel crafted a middle ground between caricature and romanticism. He also captured
the awareness of watching and being watched: one of the seated women appears to look
out of the painting at the viewer, while the man leaning against the fireplace seems to be
staring at the dancing woman. Courtesy of the Library of Congress.

and activities in a small rural tavern (see figure 2.1). Although Krimmel's paint-
erly vision usually inclined toward sympathetic realism rather than caricature,
it was probably difficult for any wealthy contemporaries to associate either his
scene or the average small tavern with the graceful self-restraint and beautiful
surroundings that gentility demanded. Yet as genteel consumer goods and
ideas circulated farther and farther beyond the Atlantic seaboard, log cabin refinement became something more than a contradiction in terms.[10]

In small taverns where drinking, eating, sleeping, and cooking took place in one apparently undifferentiated space, well-to-do travelers reported feeling distress or even disgust. Writing in the late 1790s, Isaac Weld deplored the small taverns that consisted of little more than a single room, which was "common to every person in the house, and which is generally the one set for breakfast, dinner, and supper." In such a tavern, "all the strangers that happen to be in the house sit down to these meals promiscuously," and in most cases, "the family of the house also forms a part of the company." To offset their own sense of being ill-used and out of place, Weld and other Europeans who thought along similar lines passed judgment on the living conditions, manners, and morals of thousands or even millions of other people based on the conditions they witnessed in taverns. Implicating the new republic and its citizens, Weld condemned American taverns as overcrowded, filthy, and dilapidated. Reaching similar conclusions about the correspondence between uncomfortable taverns and the Americans who patronized them, Weld's contemporary Henry Bradshaw Fearon opined that Americans had little "knowledge of that English word, *comfort*."[11]

Immigrant and native-born Americans who also resented or feared the material and social conditions in the nation's small taverns found other ways to distance themselves from their surroundings. Some northern travelers wrote about southern architecture, foodways, and social norms as if the South and its inhabitants were backward, primitive, or alien. From his brief experience of a few meagerly furnished taverns late in the Revolutionary War—hardly an opportune time to showcase any tavern's qualities—Pennsylvania's Enos Reeves concluded that southern taverns were "not worthy to be called a Tavern in any other country." Traveling through the Deep South on business, John Wight Bill of Connecticut concluded that Georgians were "too indolent" to "improve" the soil.[12] Over time, outsiders' criticism increasingly centered slavery as the source of southern problems, and such remarks helped travelers deflect what they considered keepers' insulting, offhand treatment. In the 1850s, for example, Frederick Law Olmsted refracted what he saw as insolence through the lens of slavery, arguing that keepers disdained work while the enslaved responded only to "bullying or bribing." Evoking decades of complaint along similar lines, Olmsted's language helped him foster detachment from uncomfortable experiences and feelings. Critical northerners were not entirely wrong in noticing differences between North and South, of course, but their critiques of rough, crowded taverns placed themselves at the top of an aesthetic and moral hierarchy when they were feeling ill at ease.[13]

Ethnic stereotypes provided another means of creating separation within cramped taverns. In Pennsylvania, Anglo-American visitors to German settlements passed judgment on so-called Dutch manners, architecture, and food. When English aristocrat William Strickland described the Germans as "a race not thought to be very refined in their manners," he may only have expressed the views he brought with him. Yet his claim that German Americans remained "the merest drones in the creation never having . . . made any improvements of any kind" suggests that he had also absorbed some specifically American prejudice about this immigrant group as well. English-born Quaker Pim Nevins concluded that the Germans "pay more attention to having large Barns than good Dwellings," and he surely intended no compliment when he claimed that they cared more for their cattle than for people. A prosperous Philadelphia paper manufacturer, Joshua Gilpin betrayed his own presumptions when he observed that a particular tavern was kept by "a Dutch man but we found the house a very clean one."[14]

Another geographic construct that created social distance within heterogeneous taverns involved the imagined declension in civilization from coastal cities to the countryside. As urban elites had done for generations before, prosperous cosmopolitans such as Philadelphia's William Parker Foulke used their country cousins' lack of refinement as a means of orienting themselves in unfamiliar places. Through a sequence of chatty letters to a favored aunt during travels through central Pennsylvania in the late 1840s, Foulke mapped his distance from home by judging his tavern hosts on their dwellings, furnishings, manners, dress, and foodways. An urban gentleman had to relax his "accustomed standard" in out-of-the-way villages and their small taverns, the young lawyer and reformer explained to Eleanor Foulke. In such places, a traveler could not expect to find "*salmon coloured pork*" but must eat rustic ham. Foulke suggested that a sensible urban gentleman who relished "terrapins & champaign" at home would understand that his hosts at a rural stage tavern "struggled for sausages." The same sort of man would recognize that the whiff of a "badly ventilated dissection room" was "merely the savoury emissions of an unmitigated *sourkrout.*" By likening rural foodstuffs to anatomical specimens, he evoked disgust while aligning himself with modern, scientific Philadelphia and his probably German hosts with "primitive customs." In keeping with his commitment to penal reform and colonization, Foulke asserted his faith in improvement, noting that the standards of people with "cultivated taste" would eventually prevail "in the communities of latest foundation."[15]

While carefully archived letters allowed Foulke and other well-off tavern-goers to have the last word on tavern conditions, keepers' perspectives and choices sometimes emerge from the same sources. When John Clifford complained in his travel diary about receiving "used" sheets in 1804, he also left clues about his hosts' side of the story. By the time Clifford had noticed the sheets, he had already insulted the keeper's household by insisting on having a fire laid for him in a separate room, instead of agreeing to share a room and a fire with his hosts. The extra work and expense of the fire, along with the implied dislike of their company, had probably irritated the landlady well before Clifford complained about the sheets. Rejecting his criticism, she informed him that her sheets were "clean enough" and he "might sleep on the floor" if he preferred.[16]

As Clifford's reactions suggest, by the turn of the century, some cosmopolitan travelers believed that to be satisfactory, a tavern must offer privacy by night, separation from the tavern household, clean, airy rooms, and well-constructed furnishings. At this time, most people did not enjoy such refinements and comforts in their own homes, and few taverns anywhere in the republic met all these standards. Yet even in small wayside taverns, some keepers took steps toward refinement, comfort, and the spatial differentiations they implied. A few years after Clifford's travels, Joshua Gilpin recognized Mrs. Dickie's efforts in what he considered a "miserable place," a small village roughly fifty miles east of Pittsburgh. At her tavern, a single downstairs room served as "kitchen, bar room, sitting room for all the guests of whatever description & family lodging room." The keeper's family bed sat "in one corner" of the room. Additional beds "occasionaly made up for lodgers" vied for space with tables, chairs, and other furniture. Upstairs, Gilpin found three beds "ranged head to foot along the wall"; the middle bed alone had a "rude curtain," made from a black muslin gown. Serving as the "general store room," the loft also contained bins and barrels of oats, whiskey, vinegar, and other goods. The "open" staircase allowed "uninterrupted" conversation with everyone downstairs. Even so, Gilpin concluded that "Mrs. Dickie did her best." First, she furnished "clean sheets." She also assigned the loft and its beds to the Gilpins and a prominent local judge who had arrived at the same time, separating them from the tavern household and the other patrons. Once supper was ready, Mrs. Dickie served the judge and the Gilpin family first. When they finished, they "retired" upstairs. Only then did the Gilpins' servants and the other travelers eat what remained of supper. Finally, "our servants & a concourse of waggoners & others" slept downstairs with the Dickie household.[17]

Through their choices, village keepers such as Mrs. Dickie made limited but important distinctions among guests where architecture was not sufficient to the task. In 1810, Virginia's Martha Lewis Cocke observed that in order to entertain "all classes of people at once," a keeper must "of course have separate tables, as genteel travellers would not like to eat with waggoners and they would not like to wait nor either would it be reasonable to expect it."[18] While staying at a small tavern near Fayetteville, Tennessee, some years later, Anne Royall noted that this "neat" house offered little in the way of functional separation, since the main room served as dining area, kitchen, and bedchamber. Yet she did not complain because she had a good bed "with curtains" in which she could lie "snug out of sight." Even when a pair of late arrivals sat down to supper "at a table hard by" her bed, she still felt "quite delighted with a place of concealment." Contributing to her satisfaction, this tavern accommodated overnight travelers in a "separate building" from the one where locals gathered to drink and socialize.[19]

Such gestures did not appease all travelers, but they suggest the evolving tavern vernacular of refinement and comfort. Further clues come from keepers' advertisements. Impressive but vague adjectives such as "superior" coexisted with references to repairs. In 1810, for example, John Beard announced that he had just bought and "repaired" a large tavern in Centreville, Delaware, which he had "fitted up in a superior style." The managers of the Planters Hotel in Camden, South Carolina, asserted that "their establishment has undergone complete repairs" and would be "convenient and comfortable for travellers."[20] Keepers also made much of their expansions. In 1817, William H. Slaughter promoted his tavern in Salisbury, North Carolina, as "improved and enlarged." Advertisements of taverns for sale or lease often mentioned the dimensions of both buildings and rooms to help prospective keepers envision the kind of business they might be able to run: large rooms implied not only greater capacity but also greater opportunities to separate uses and users. In 1799, an advertisement for the Spotsylvania Court House tavern in tidewater Virginia paid careful attention to its sizable rooms: "2 rooms, 28 by 18 each, and one 28 by 12 feet on the first floor." Also noteworthy was a "new two story house" that formed part of the stand, containing "very commodious dining and lodging rooms."[21]

References to commodious or spacious rooms, reinforced by detailed measurements and functional descriptions, represented concrete promises that particular taverns had left behind the hugger-mugger conditions that some travelers so loathed. Larger and more elaborate interiors did not, however, resolve the competing values and demands that patrons brought to and made on taverns. To understand spatial changes and their implications for social differentiation and tension among tavern clients, we approach improving taverns as arriving patrons did: from the outside.

Facades, Porches, Barrooms, and Beyond

If the sight of a one- or two-room log cabin primed a traveler to expect dark, smoky, crowded conditions, roughly constructed furniture, and homespun blankets, the same traveler had reason to hope for different arrangements in a "neat, two-story" tavern made of brick, stone, or wood frame, according to regional preference. In Pennsylvania and Ohio, a "handsome, roomy, well finished stone house" with a sign out front made a welcome sight to travelers hoping for more than a glass of whiskey and a share of the floor. Two-story brick taverns similarly suggested the possibility of airy and spacious rooms in the Chesapeake region. Further south and in much of the west, wood-frame buildings with extensive wings or multiple stories, in addition to outbuildings, promised amenities that smaller structures necessarily lacked. Whatever the building materials, glazed windows, well-built chimneys, and a full second story suggested a roomy and well-lit interior and the possibility of domestic comforts. The exterior of many town and village taverns, however, left an impression of masculine busyness and manual labor (see figure 2.2).[22]

As town and village taverns grew in overall size, so did the yards and stables for patrons' horses and other livestock. This tendency was especially evident in Virginia, where owning and riding one's own horse represented an important gentlemanly attainment. By 1816, the Spotsylvania Court House tavern could stable one hundred horses. A few years later, the courthouse tavern in Orange County had room for nearly two hundred mounts, having doubled its capacity in twenty years.[23] Highly bred riding horses were far from the only animals visible in and around rural and town taverns, however. When Isaac Frazier of Columbia, South Carolina, advertised his tavern, he mentioned not only his "elegantly furnished" rooms but also the "vacant lots" where drovers could secure dozens or even hundreds of pigs, horses, or cattle. Although many country women were familiar with livestock and some could both ride and drive, men were usually charged with tending to any livestock that tavern guests brought with them. Keepers often advertised the services of their "faithful," "good," and "attentive" hostlers, many of whom were Black men or boys, especially in the southern states. At a busy wayside establishment, the bustle of patrons combined with the labors of the hostlers, porters, and stable boys coping with horses, wagons, carriages, luggage, freight, and droves of livestock gave an overall impression of purposive masculine effort.[24]

Arriving patrons could see other kinds of work taking place on the porches that almost invariably adorned the front and sometimes the sides of good-sized taverns. Roofed or unroofed, and also known as a portico, balcony,

FIGURE 2.2 The Bull's Head Tavern in the Bowery (1801–1886). A subset of urban taverns, such as the Bull's Head in New York City, specialized in receiving drovers, who brought herds of livestock from rural areas to cities for slaughter and consumption. A paddock separates the tavern from another building, perhaps a barn that housed animals awaiting sale. Although the presence of numerous cattle surely added to the noise, smell, and dirt, and while this tavern lacks elegant exterior details, the artist figured the main building as a tidy, well-built two-and-a-half-story structure with large, glazed windows. Courtesy of the Miriam and Ira D. Wallach Division of Art, Prints and Photographs: Print Collection, New York Public Library.

veranda, patio, or piazza, this feature was one that taverns shared with fancy urban and resort hotels but was meant for quite different people and purposes. In hotels serving wealthy tourists, vast shaded verandas served as social spaces for women and men together and sometimes offered scenic vistas as well. At the Cape Ann Pavilion in Gloucester, Massachusetts, guests ventured out to the "wide, beautiful covered veranda" to enjoy the view: a "narrow strip of beach, then a low stone wall, some rocks, and then the Atlantic." Outside New York City, the Marine Pavilion hotel provided similar amenities for its prosperous visitors (see figure 2.3).[25]

At a typical tavern, porches likewise served as places to sit, talk, and observe, but they rarely afforded a scenic natural vista nor were they designed for genteel heterosocial leisure. Instead, tavern porches operated as a vantage point for men to lounge and to observe goings-on outdoors. From a tavern

FIGURE 2.3 Horatio Black and Alonzo Reed, Marine Pavilion, Rockaway, Long Island, ca. 1833. The Marine Pavilion combined the virtues of ocean views with proximity to New York City. This illustration indicates the hotel's vast size, which implied a sizable number of bedrooms and the possibility of separate rooms for dining, dancing, reading, and socializing. Like the Cape Ann Pavilion near Boston, the Marine Pavilion featured a veranda spanning the front of the hotel, where guests could mingle and enjoy the view. Like many other images of resort hotels, this one includes an extensive foreground, used for heterosocial leisure rather than homosocial business. No herds of livestock graze on the grass, nor did the artist depict servants who worked for the hotel or its guests. Courtesy of the American Antiquarian Society.

porch, men also exchanged the news of the day and dickered over the merits of horses tied up out front. Standing on the porch, an auctioneer could point to livestock in the road, force enslaved people to display themselves for sale, or hold up smaller articles before a crowd milling around in the road or the yard. Almost any business that men transacted in taverns could take place on the porch. An early 1850s lithograph of "The Tavern" suggests how the typical tavern porch was a relatively informal masculine space, as white men leaned and sat in relaxed postures while reading newspapers and talking (see figure 2.4). Entering a tavern often meant running the gauntlet of men lounging or working out front.[26]

Once indoors, visitors might have the choice of entering a barroom, the first room-based spatial improvement that many keepers adopted. Long a feature of multiroomed taverns in coastal cities and towns, a barroom typically

FIGURE 2.4 Augustus Kollner, [The Tavern], ca. 1852. Published by the American Sunday
School Union, this image probably served as an illustration in a book for children's moral
instruction. Less extreme than many temperance images, which suggested that a single
drink could lead to a habit of debauchery and ultimately to the grave, this image appears
to recommend that young men or boys walk past rather than stop in at a tavern. The scene
suggests how men occupied a typical tavern porch, sitting in casual postures while talking
or reading, in contrast to the more formal stances and heterosocial groups at resort hotels.
Also present on this porch is a Black man. Alone among the figures in sitting on the floor,
he remains apart from the white men, not sharing the space they simultaneously occupy.
Courtesy of the Library Company of Philadelphia.

retained the bar cage, or a wooden framework around the place where the liquor was stored and poured.[27] A distinct barroom became one of the first
signs that a tavern keeper anticipated patrons who preferred more separation
of people and activities than could exist in a one-room structure. In a tavern
with a barroom, any ladies might still have to pass by or even through the barroom, but they did not need to linger. As Benjamin Shackelford noted about
his Culpeper Court House tavern, "the front room may be occupied as a public bar room without interfering with the other rooms" on the ground floor.
Although people could and did drink throughout taverns, the barroom made
the fewest demands for respectability and self-restraint. In fact, some men

found that tavern barrooms tested their tolerance for obvious drunkenness, coarse language, and overt competition.[28]

Yet tavern barrooms also supported distinct drinking subcultures, often tied to class. Public officials who set the prices for tavern goods and services authorized the sale of alcohols at a wide range of price points, indicating that men from all walks of life should be able to afford access to the barroom. Baltimore's 1789 price list, for example, allowed keepers to sell three distinct tiers of Madeira wine, an imported luxury, as well as "Best" and "Second Quality" claret, also imported. Ounce for ounce, the best Madeira cost more than three times as much as whiskey, the cheapest alcohol, and since Madeira was sold by the quart and whiskey by the gill, a four-ounce measure, the wine was still further out of reach for most patrons.[29] Even during the Revolutionary War, leading city keepers advertised that they stocked the "best wines" and "best liquors." Similar claims diffused into the countryside in the early nineteenth century. In 1830, for example, Benjamin W. Cook of Lenox announced to people in western Massachusetts that he served imported wines "of the finest flavour," but whiskey remained the most common and usually the cheapest tavern drink.[30]

A second type of public room found in some improving taverns, the news room, likewise had the potential to create distinctions among taverns' male patrons. As J. B. Dunlop observed in the early nineteenth century, a tavern was often "crowded with people waiting to hear the News."[31] News came not only from travelers such as Dunlop but from newspapers, whose numbers grew steadily after the Postal Act of 1792 ensured newspapers' economical delivery. In small taverns such as those featured in Lewis Krimmel's paintings, people waiting for the news did so in the same place where others drank, ate, and even slept. Creating a specific room for reading newspapers and other printed material suggested a new take on the act of public reading. As early as 1808, Mr. Gautier's tavern in northern Virginia included an "excellent newsroom, where the most respectable papers on the continent are taken." The same year, Hannah Haines understood the news room at a New York resort hotel as a place for "the Gentlemen to Lounge and read the News pappers." By 1830, a well-stocked reading room in a first-rate urban hotel featured "the papers from all parts of the continent and with maps conveniences for writing &c." By midcentury, however, print remained more available than news rooms in the smaller wayside taverns. In 1848, in a central Pennsylvania village served by at least one turnpike, William Parker Foulke found "a newspaper, & a geographical account of Canada, & an article on Mr. Clay's resolutions" but no news room. A reading or news room suggested that reading "the most respectable papers" was a serious and potentially solitary activity. A person with letters to write or a journal to update might also sit in the news room, the better to avoid interruptions. By contrast, a barroom seemed, in Francis Lee's words, "hardly possible" for writing.[32]

The proliferation of designated spaces for observing newcomers, drinking, and consuming the news did more than increase taverns' overall size and capacity. The zone defined by barrooms, porches, and news rooms accommodated multiple forms of white masculinity. With options for both the rowdy and the restrained, the leisured and the enterprising, these spaces allowed different sorts of men to occupy taverns while also allowing some men the opportunity to shift at will between more sociable and more reserved modes of interaction. At the same time, the valences of reading, writing, and drinking could express distinctions of wealth and culture in ways that the inclination of a moment did not erase. Overall, white men continued to dominate the spaces that most visitors encountered first, even as increasing numbers of middle-class white women passed through them on their way to more congenial spaces.

Dining Rooms and Long Rooms

Keepers who sought to provide genteel hospitality needed to do more than enclose the bar or provide a news room. Two additional types of rooms found only in the finest urban taverns in the mid-eighteenth century spread far and wide in the nineteenth: dining rooms and the large, flexible rooms known variously as long rooms, assembly rooms, or ballrooms. Both types of rooms functioned at multiple levels. The presence of a dining room helped keepers serve timely meals to people in a hurry to get back on the road or to their stores and offices. Dining rooms also afforded space for voluntary association gatherings and public dinners. Long rooms hosted informal and formal social gatherings during the daytime and evening, including performances, exhibitions, and balls. Some of the activities held in these rooms welcomed women as well as men, which created additional opportunities to both expand and filter tavern patronage. In these ways, dining and long rooms did more than increase a tavern's capacity: they catered especially to middling and wealthy white people whose notions of propriety and comfort called for separation between the spaces dominated by men, such as porches and barrooms, and those that men shared with women. At the same time, tavern workers—male and female, white and Black—also circulated through these spaces. Their presence undergirded the comparatively favorable terms on which respectable white women moved through certain parts of the tavern interior.[33]

Keepers had multiple reasons to invest in and advertise capacious dining rooms that were architecturally distinct from the barroom. A dedicated dining room signaled that a keeper expected to feed a regular flow of travelers, locals, or both. Provided a tavern had the kitchens, tableware, and staff to match, a dining room created the possibility for speedy or leisurely mealtimes, according to demand. At stage taverns, stage drivers expected rapid service for themselves and their passengers. An enslaved man who labored at a Virginia hotel recalled that when he heard the stage driver blow the horn from "'bout two miles 'way," he was supposed to "hustle round" to meet the stage. According to some reports, the driver also sounded "as many distinct blasts as there are passengers" to let the keeper know how many places to lay at table. A dining room also helped town keepers feed crowds of local diners in a rush. As Basil Hall observed at one New York tavern, the officers and privates of a militia company "snatched up their dinner in such a hurry" that Hall found the dining room abandoned "in less than fifteen minutes."[34] Similarly, in Augusta, Georgia, which a traveler described as a "mere merchants station," the Eagle Tavern served as a kind of commissary for the town's businessmen. "When the door of the dining room is opened," he observed, "they rush in seizing the nearest seat . . . & before I could decently get half through my dinner," many of the locals had raced back to work.[35]

Beyond the logistics of capacity and turnover, advertising "commodious dining" allowed picky customers to imagine they would not be eating in the kitchen or in a sleeping area. It also suggested that genteel visitors would not eat cheek by jowl with other patrons. In many jurisdictions, this spatial refinement appeared long after the expectation, encoded in tavern price lists, that people would dine and drink according to their means and occasions. New Jersey rate-setting officials, for example, allowed for both "common" and "good" dinners and suppers. In Hunterdon County, an "extraordinary" dinner cost 50 percent more than a regular dinner, and keepers could also offer "extraordinary" breakfast and suppers, with comparable price differentials over the standard fare. To entice customers to purchase the higher priced offerings, ambitious keepers boasted that they served "the best viands the country can afford" or "the best the market affords."[36]

Making an even greater investment in space, labor, and gentility, some large-scale keepers created a separate dining room for female patrons. This amenity welcomed not women in general but ladies, whom most Americans of this era identified with whiteness, genteel behavior, financial comfort, and the social capital of being the acknowledged wife, widow, daughter, or kins-woman of a reputable white man. Ladies' dining rooms, sometimes called ordinaries, gratified respectable white women's self-image and encouraged their patronage. In addition, they tended to keep such women out of other spaces where they might find fault with other guests or the tavern household. For similar reasons, these rooms marked distinctions among men: they relied on male waiters' labor, while remaining open to ladies' male guests and travel companions. The existence of a ladies' ordinary enabled gentlemen to shun the more eclectic company in the main dining room, while framing this masculine sifting as consideration for ladies.[37]

As men's presence at the ladies' ordinary implied, men were much more likely than women to experience the privilege of homosocial tavern dining. Keepers of leading city taverns advertised their dining space and services to men's societies and clubs before the turn of the century. In the 1790s, Charles-ton's "Gentlemen" could dine at the Shakespeare tavern whenever they liked, but they could also repair there as members of "Societies or select Parties" to dine and conduct business in "PRIVATE ROOMS." In 1815, John MacLeod emphasized that his Sign of the Phoenix tavern in the nation's capital offered "private rooms" to "Societies, clubs or parties . . . at a short notice." Prear-ranged dinners of this sort tended to fall on the extraordinary side of the tav-ern price list, and patrons also lingered far longer than for the average tavern meal. For both reasons, when keepers advertised their ability to host societies and parties, they cultivated their more prosperous patrons. In 1810, for exam-ple, the July Fourth dinner at Thomas's tavern in Wilmington, Delaware, cost one dollar, enough to buy at least two meals plus drinks on any ordinary day in most taverns in the country. While societies tailored annual dues to their memberships, subscriptions to special events like anniversary dinners could be costly in both money and time, marking the men who came to taverns for such events—and particularly those who attended events of multiple societies—as men of considerable resource. Such dinners were almost always exclusive to men, nor did keepers identify groups of women as potential cus-tomers for private rooms and prearranged dinners. Even in small towns with few societies and thus few society dinners, partisan and patriotic holidays provided annual occasions for public tavern dinners. At these events, men were the primary guests and women attended for a portion of the proceed-ings, if at all.[38]

The large multipurpose rooms used for meetings, balls, performances, and dining proved most useful to middling and well-off patrons and, within that group, more useful to men than women. These large rooms had their origin in the urban colonial gentry's demands for elegant rooms suitable for balls and performances. By the end of the eighteenth century, such amenities were spreading to leading taverns in small towns a day's ride or more from any metropolis. Fifty miles north of Boston in Exeter, New Hampshire, Widow Folsom's tavern had a second-story long room running the depth of the house by the end of the eighteenth century. This room could be divided into two, using a convenient channel in the ceiling to hold a partition. When the space was so arranged, men could gather in one part of the room for a political meeting or a dinner, while other patrons used the remainder of the room. When opened to its fullest extent, the room could serve as a ballroom or performance space. In the mid-1810s, the Culpeper Court House tavern in Virginia had a similar arrangement. By "opening a folding partition," the keeper could join two rooms into "a large dining room." In the busy shipping town of Port Royal, Virginia, Philip Lightfoot's tavern featured "three large well finished rooms" on the ground floor, the largest of which could serve at need "as either a drawing room or ball room."[39]

Contemporaries agreed that the best ballrooms were not just capacious but also "decorated with much taste, elegance and splendor." The *Nashville Whig* used these words about the ballroom at Mr. Lewis's tavern in that city when describing a ball commemorating the Battle of New Orleans. Matching the setting were the "numerous and fascinating" ladies, while the gentlemen included "the first citizens of the country" and "the HERO himself," Andrew Jackson. On the walls hung oil portraits of Jackson and fellow Tennessee generals William Carroll and John Coffee. Across the country, tavern ballrooms hosted similar patriotic celebrations at which local elites displayed their finest attire and manners while hitching themselves to emblems of national glory.[40]

Like balls held in other spaces, some tavern balls operated on a public basis, open to nearly anyone who could pay the entry fee. Others, like some concerts, were organized on a subscription basis. Self-consciously determined to preserve a genteel exclusivity, organizers of these events made tickets available only to peers and friends, at a high price, or both. Local elites did not enjoy exclusive rights to taverns' long rooms, however, as these rooms also hosted entertainments and performances marketed to a wider audience. Families with children could attend an exhibit of political and historical wax figures at Sullee's long room in Charleston, one of the city's leading taverns; adults' tickets cost fifty cents, and children's half as much. In the 1820s, a sequence of taverns throughout New England hosted a "GRAND Caravan of Living Animals" at which children's tickets were again half price. In the early

1840s, the modest prices for a menagerie and a "superlative band of Music" attracted "factory girls" to a tavern in Dover, New Hampshire.[41]

Large, multiuse rooms offered possibilities for tavern entertainments that were at once heterosocial and respectable. White men who were or hoped to be considered gentlemen could buy tickets to events that implied refinement. Some of the same events also appealed to middle- and upper-class white women. Yet although these rooms operated as a kind of tavern set-aside for respectable and genteel folk, the sights and sounds of rowdy fellows enjoying a merry evening in the barroom or on the porch could easily impinge on people attending a society gathering or a ball. Some adventuresome gentlemen doubtless accepted the implicit challenge to move back and forth between the two milieus and their modes of behavior. Other attendees hungered for ways to drive the rowdy men out or sought out different venues altogether.[42]

Domesticating the Tavern: Bedrooms

Just as dramatic as the changes in taverns' spaces for drinking, eating, and socializing were those in public houses' sleeping accommodations. At the end of the eighteenth century, travelers often slept wherever they could, including in chairs, on the floor, in lofts, and in beds shared with strangers. Although these arrangements persisted in many taverns through the mid-nineteenth century, keepers made a serious commitment to refining sleeping accommodations: increasing privacy for overnight guests, creating dedicated guest bedrooms, and investing in manufactured textiles and other consumer goods associated with beauty and comfort. Keepers' pursuit of well-furnished bedrooms had cultural and economic implications. Intended to make taverns more homelike for patrons accustomed to private bedrooms in their own homes, these changes anticipated a steady stream of overnight guests, particularly middling and elite women and families participating in leisure travel. This partial domestication both won approval and aroused conflicts about who had first claim to these accommodations.[43]

The class of patrons who had always slept in a bedroom in their own homes, which they shared only with close kin, friends, or perhaps servants, were often uneasy or disgusted at the prospect of sleeping in public and around strangers. What travelers saw as unseemly sleeping arrangements sometimes reflected extrinsic exigencies rather than a tavern's architecture or its keeper's aspirations. In the fall of 1793, thousands of people fled Philadelphia to escape a devastating yellow fever epidemic. Among them was Thomas Jefferson, then secretary of state, who complained in two letters of sleeping in "a bed in a corner of the public room" of a tavern outside Philadelphia, "the other alternative being to sleep on the floor in my cloak before the fire." Because of the circumstances, Jefferson's remark may reveal little about everyday accommodations at this tavern, but it does illuminate his reaction to the keeper's manners. Jefferson grumbled that the keeper offered him the bed "as a great favor."[44]

Crowded sleeping arrangements and unapologetic keepers remained routine both in busy taverns and in those that saw few travelers. Whenever courts or legislatures were in session, nearby taverns often attracted more visitors than they could accommodate in any sort of comfort. In the fall of 1786, Robert Woodruff noted that Trenton and its taverns were "very full" during the sitting of the New Jersey Council and Assembly. In 1810, Hannah Haines found the taverns in Hudson, New York, "crowded with Company" because "it was the time of the Court setting." Similar problems recurred in newly settled western towns. In Cahawba, the temporary capital of Alabama in the early 1820s, the state's senators were "obliged to sleep three upon one mattress laid upon the floor." At midcentury, in what he called an "unadulterated" log tavern in a small Pennsylvania village, William Parker Foulke had a bed to himself but shared the bedroom with the keeper's sons.[45]

As taverns welcomed more travelers, keepers might invest in one or more bedrooms dedicated to guests. This improvement created spatial separation between guests and the tavern household but did not preclude crowding. While visiting Newport, Rhode Island, in the mid-1780s, Robert Hunter likened a room with six beds to a hospital ward. Nearly half a century later, Captain J. E. Alexander reached for the same metaphor, complaining that the otherwise "respectable establishment" he patronized in Memphis, Tennessee, offered "a room like the ward of an hospital with a dozen beds in it, all doubly occupied save one, from which a voice asked me 'to bundle.'" The captain "declined the invitation."[46]

Despite such reports, the spreading preference for privacy by night had begun to reshape town and even village taverns by the turn of the century. An early form of privacy entailed spatial separation from locals in and around the barroom, which might mean a dedicated guest bedroom, a separate building for overnight guests, or both. By 1799, James Frazer's tavern at Virginia's Spotsylvania Court House featured "sundry lodging rooms" and one "convenient private room" located in a new building, itself "more privately situated" behind the main building and away from the road. In 1816, another Virginia tavern had seven "handsome lodging rooms" on its second floor, "divided into 3 separate apartments by 3 separate staircases." The staircases helped insulate overnight guests from each other and from other patrons using public rooms.[47] Such trends also affected big urban hotels. Leading city hotels such as David Barnum's City Hotel in Baltimore boasted of their "private entrances and passages" which made them "as desirable for ladies as any private house." At Howard's Hotel in New York City in the late 1840s, "City Gentlemen engaged in business" used the main entrance. Travelers, "generally Gentlemen with their Ladies and families," used "a more private entrance" around the corner.[48]

Although travelers continued to encounter shared bedrooms and even beds well into the nineteenth century, taverns that welcomed a steady flow of tourists and other prosperous travelers usually offered at least one bedroom for private use. This amenity became common enough that in the late 1820s, England's Captain Basil Hall could observe "that during all our journey, there never was the smallest difficulty about our having at least one bedroom exclusively for our use." Even in the most crowded inns, he continued, "this amount of accommodation was in every case afforded as a matter of course." In addition to choosing his taverns well, Hall had the money to spend on private accommodations. For most guests, privacy remained out of reach. In the Pennsylvania tavern where S. Schulling's travel party had two bedrooms to themselves, "the main lodging room . . . contained a dozen beds . . . filled with men."[49]

To the best of their ability, keepers equipped their private bedrooms to meet evolving middle-class domestic standards. Doing so meant investing significant labor in cleaning floors and bed linens. It also required spending money on selected manufactured goods. Shortly after the turn of the century, Joshua Gilpin found "neat rooms with carpets, glasses &ca & excellent beds" thirty miles west of Philadelphia. In the mid-1820s, Carl Bernhard, Duke of Saxe-Weimar Eisenach, found "wide and comfortable" beds with "fine and perfectly clean" linens, along with "the necessary washstands, &c" at the largest of "three fine taverns" in Utica, New York, a town of roughly three thousand people.[50] By the early 1840s, the Globe Hotel of Springfield, Illinois—the state capital and home to some four thousand people—featured thirty bedrooms. An inventory described a host of furnishings associated with genteel living and clean comfort, including two dozen candlesticks, at least nine mirrors, twenty-five tablecloths, thirty-seven feather beds, fourteen washstands, and multiple stoves. The Globe also featured "Superior" carpeting in the bedrooms but had only rag carpets elsewhere. Some patrons slept on feathers, but others at the Globe made do with straw.[51]

Travelers' satisfaction with their accommodations often involved a comparative element. Some people took pleasure in recognizing that at the very least, they fared better than someone else. Traveling with a sheriff and jury to address a land dispute, Reuben Haines of Philadelphia described to his wife, Jane, how they had slept at a wayside village tavern: "some in the hay loft some on benches and some on the floor, and six of us fortunate enough to get to three comfortable beds that had been provided for us." Haines did not question why he was among the favored six, nor did he mention whether those on the floor paid less than those in beds. Authorized tavern rates did not typically distinguish a shared bedroom from a private one, while surviving sources rarely clarify how much more than the posted rates travelers might pay for privacy and comfort. People who boarded at a tavern could, however, be charged differently—often more—than travelers. At one urban establishment, "transient" patrons paid $1.50 per day, while "for those otherways," such as boarders, "the charges are reasonable, according to what rooms are occupied, and what is ordered." Whatever Reuben Haines paid at his Pennsylvania tavern, his silence on this point suggests that he took for granted that he and his peers needed, appreciated, and deserved better accommodations than their hosts and anyone from the rural laboring classes.[52]

One point of agreement between keepers and those patrons whose opinions predominate in the archive concerned the observation that private bedrooms made taverns suitable for families. Basil Hall believed that traveling with his family had ensured him private bedrooms "as a matter of course." "Travellers with families" need fear no "inconvenience on this score" in the United States, he asserted. Not all families were equal, however. For Hall and like-minded Americans, the traveling families who deserved privacy not only were white and in possession of sufficient funds but also included women. Without pleasure but also without surprise, an anonymous traveler in the mid-1830s described being denied a private bedroom one night because "the single rooms are kept for ladies."[53]

Newspaper advertising made the limits of family especially clear. Side by side with sale notices that confirmed the routine breakup of enslaved families for profit and with fugitive ads that documented enslaved people's strenuous efforts to visit family members, southern tavern keepers spun familial fantasies for potential patrons. A Boston-area advertisement for the Bell Tavern in Washington, D.C., asserted that "families coming to the city, can be accommodated in the best style, as private as in their own house." Isaac Frazier offered families accommodations "entirely remote from the bustle of the tavern." John G. Ballard provided "private rooms" for "Travelling Families" at his Eagle Tavern in Camden, South Carolina. Keepers of resort taverns were especially likely to reference the needs of families since visiting these destinations was so often a family affair. At South Carolina's Rice Creek Springs, the managers built "Camp Houses convenient for the accommodation of families." At the Sweet Springs in Virginia, families could get "cabins of two, three, or four rooms," while solo travelers were consigned to "log-houses, roomy or crouded according to the increase of the company." North and south, the wealthy families who enjoyed these resorts usually came with free or enslaved servants, who knew that privacy for "Travelling Families" often meant more work, greater vulnerability, and familial separation for themselves.[54]

Racialized notions of family were not the only grounds for improving tavern amenities. Threading through keepers' advertisements over the decades were multiple references to genteel people in general and gentlemen in particular. At the Globe Tavern in Camden, South Carolina, C. E. Williamson promised that "his house is well furnished with elegant bedding and furniture, of every kind necessary for the reception of genteel persons." Other keepers from the southern states to New England solicited the patronage of "genteel boarders."[55] Advertising to "gentlemen planters" as well as "families from the country," Mrs. Calder of Charleston made much of the fourteen "newly white-washed and painted" rooms at her Planter's Hotel, with their "*new Furniture, Bedding, Carpeting,*" and the "observance of cleanliness through every department."[56] Over the next decades, tavern and hotel keepers alike continued to market their "new and spacious" options to "single gentlemen," not just ladies or families. In 1840, C. G. Saunders promoted his establishment in Springfield, Illinois, with a poem whose opening lines suggested the importance of home comforts to men traveling on business: "Ye strangers who for enterprise may roam, / We here invite you to a friendly home." The remaining lines detailed the keeper's "anxious care," the "choice substantial fare," and the "beds and bedding of the best" but made no appeal to families or ladies. At the extreme, some keepers spurned female travelers altogether. In an 1856 brochure, J. D. Brown promoted his Arcade Hotel in Philadelphia as an economical yet comfortable option that would satisfy "the fullest wants of all the guests," but only if they were "gentlemen," for "*Ladies* are not accommodated at the ARCADE HOTEL."[57]

For most keepers, their taverns were their family's livelihood and their home. As such, keepers had their own and their families' comfort and reputation to consider. Advertisements of taverns for sale or lease hint at how keepers might esteem their own privacy. When James Frazer's executors noted that his tavern included a "privately situated" secondary building, with a "convenient private room for a family," did they hope that a prospective keeper would envision his own family in that room? Two decades later,

Villeboro, a "large and convenient tavern" on the "great post road from Fredericksburg to Richmond," was offered for sale with the note that the stand had "a house in the back yard for the accommodation of a proprietor's family." Whereas some travelers mocked keepers for any presumption of gentility, others accepted that a keeper could be a "gentleman" in his own house. Improving keepers invested in privacy and refined goods for their own immediate use, not only for their guests' pleasure.[58]

Contesting the Tavern Parlor

In the first half of the nineteenth century, parlors became an important element of domestic sociability for middle-class Americans and an additional source of conflict for both tavern keepers and their guests. Such conflict was both predictable and anathema to emerging norms for parlor culture. In the mid-eighteenth century, only members of the colonial gentry had parlors. Lavishly decorated rooms for formal sociability, gentry parlors attested to their owners' status. By the mid-nineteenth century, parlors had spread into middling homes but were now more associated with feminized domesticity and familial leisure, including reading, writing, conversing, and singing or playing music. In both incarnations, parlors made an awkward transition to early republican taverns.[59]

Tavern parlors came in three varieties. Sizable taverns whose keepers could count on a regular supply of wealthy patrons began to offer private parlors or sitting rooms, usually in limited numbers, and only of interest to those willing and able to pay the extra charges associated with their use. In 1820, Mrs. John Reed reported that guests at David Barnum's City Hotel in Baltimore could be "handsomely accomodated with a chamber[,] private parlor and bath." A decade later, English writer Frances Trollope and her traveling party also received two parlors at a tavern in much smaller Hagerstown, Maryland, "without asking at all." Farther west, private parlors spread slowly. In Cincinnati, with seven times Hagerstown's population, a keeper "literally" scolded Trollope for requesting such a room, perhaps an assertion of democratic western manners in the face of eastern and British expectations. Where private parlors existed, they found favor with travelers who endorsed both the price and the social statement they made. As Carl Bernhard observed, a "separate sitting-room" with "a separate charge" appealed to the prosperous traveler, "especially when he travels with ladies."[60]

As rooms that amplified cultural and economic stratification, taverns' private parlors were on occasion put to subversive use. Parlors played a small but important role in Reverend Jermain Loguen's escape from slavery, or so he suggested in his third-person autobiographical narrative. Along with another man, the young Loguen had set out for Ohio from a plantation south of Nashville. Mounted on horseback and with ready money in hand, the pair twice posed as free people of color when they stopped at taverns south of the Ohio River, the local border between slave and free states. In both cases, Loguen and his friend demurred at entering the barrooms, each "literally filled with white men, in all stages of intoxication." Having good reason to fear such company, the pair requested private accommodations. "We are free colored men," Loguen recalled telling the keeper, "and want to be by ourselves, and have supper, and go to bed." Both keepers agreed that the men could retreat to another room, which Loguen identified as "a private parlor." While the "bellowing of the crazy and drunken men" kept the pair awake, no one accosted them, and in the morning, they paid their bill and "prepared to journey again." Frederick Douglass had his own tale about being shown to a private parlor in a New York City hotel to meet some white English friends, although in this case, the keeper insisted that the interracial gathering take place in seclusion. These and similar episodes indicate that the growth of privacy in public houses occasionally served Black travelers. Loguen's and Douglass's accounts also suggest that white men did not invariably see Black men's distaste for barroom sociability as an intolerable affront to their own masculinity.[61]

An alternative to private parlors, the ladies' parlor further reinforced respectability's toehold in early republican taverns but in ways that rarely offered any benefit to Black women. Most white keepers and guests questioned or outright rejected any Black woman's claim to ladyhood, so unless such a woman successfully passed for white, she was unlikely to enjoy the comfort and shelter of a ladies' parlor. In addition, since access to ladies' parlors was not usually a matter of paying a fee but of invitation, such spaces heightened the significance of dress, carriage, behavior, speech, and complexion. A white planter's daughter such as Margaret Steele took for granted her right to "a very well furnished private parlour for the ladies entirely seperated from the rest of the house and boarders." Some female guests might have felt overawed, uncertain whether they, their outfits, and their manners belonged. Still other women circulated through parlors as tavern servants or ladies' maids, facing constant judgmental scrutiny from the patrons.[62]

Compounding these fraught dynamics, the ladies' parlor remained open to men who could claim kinship or acquaintance with any of the women who were using it. Like Frederick Law Olmsted, some men sought out the ladies' parlor because they preferred it to standing on a porch in the "freezing cold" or lingering in the "stinking" barroom with men who were "smoking and chewing and talking obscenely." From another perspective, ladies' consignment to the parlor, like the ballroom, had the benefit of preserving most of the tavern for men who did not want to curb their behavior in deference to ladies. Yet despite this dual masculine interest in ladies' parlors, these rooms became typical only in the finer town taverns, resorts, and urban hotels, which tended to attract a more homogenous patronage than most public accommodations.[63]

Both more common and more contested than private or ladies' parlors were parlors for the shared use of all tavern guests and sometimes the keeper's family. Whether such rooms even deserved the name of parlor depended on who was doing the judging. Grounds for doubt included a room's uses and cleanliness. In 1808, in a tavern near Princeton, New Jersey, for example, Caspar and Reuben Haines slept on "cott Beds" carried into the parlor. Fortescue Cuming questioned whether "a small dirty room with a bed in it" deserved the name "breakfast parlour." Yet some British travelers had more positive impressions of mixed-use quasi-parlors. In the 1820s, Captain Basil Hall dined "in a cheerful sunny parlour" in a Connecticut tavern. Elsewhere, Hall encountered "a smiling sort of kitchen-parlour."[64]

In large, complex taverns, dedicated parlors proliferated alongside barrooms, dining rooms, and ballrooms. In Boston, the better sort of tavern might have "a parlour and two sitting rooms, where strangers who have nothing to do pass the day." In Utica, New York, in the 1820s, a particularly "fine" tavern featured "several sitting, reading, and writing parlours." Whereas costly private parlors remained rare in western taverns, public parlors were not. By the mid-1840s, the former Globe Tavern of Springfield, Illinois, boasted "four front parlors." The state capital was still a modestly sized town with no direct connection to railroad lines, so the tavern's most frequent patrons were local residents and visiting legislators, lawyers, and other men of business. The parlors also served these men's wives, including Mary Todd Lincoln early in her marriage to Abraham Lincoln.[65]

One possible motive for identifying a room as not quite a parlor was to defuse issues of access and behavior. If it were not a true parlor, it mattered less who was present and what one did there. In practice, guests and members of tavern households often jostled for precedence as they sought to establish norms governing access to and behavior in tavern parlors. As parlors spread far beyond colonial gentry mansions to middle-class homes, and as mobility and tavern inclusion became evident components of vernacular citizenship in the imagined nation, more people staked a claim to tavern parlors.

One Black traveler articulated his conditional entitlement in the language of middle-class respectability, which he defined in terms of work, dress, and cleanliness. When working as a "hostler or cook, or any thing of that sort," he wrote, "I did not think that my place was the parlor." If, however, he was "clean and well dressed, in occupations not offensive, then I think I am as good as anybody, and deserve as good treatment."[66] Condemning a different conditional logic, Frederick Douglass observed that in England, he shared parlors with white travelers and "no one is offended," but in the United States, even the most respectable Black Americans were "caricatured, scorned, scoffed, mocked, and maltreated with impunity by any one" so long as he had "a white skin." With these words, Douglass highlighted American racism while pointing out that people like him regularly tested their access to public parlors, asserting their claim on citizenship and the rights it supposedly conferred.[67]

Black Americans were not the only ones to find their parlor presence a matter of debate. Competing understandings of parlor etiquette produced numerous conflicts among white people. Anne Royall condemned a "Dr. Somebody," who "bolted into the parlor" where she and another woman were sitting, "and without saying a word, stalked through into another room." "If he had had a spark of politeness," she continued, "he would at least have taken off his hat" to the ladies rather than ignoring their presence. When Royall complained and requested another parlor, the barkeeper told her there were none, and in any case, "the other man has a right to get to his room." Learning that the other woman in the parlor at the same time did not share her feelings only intensified Royall's indignation at this lack of gendered deference.[68] Royall's brisk pen also captured parlors' potential use as a backdrop for conflict among men. During a visit to Charlottesville, Virginia, Royall stayed in a tavern where a group of "genteel" locals welcomed her. At the same tavern, she also encountered "ruffians"—supposedly students at the University of Virginia—who repeatedly tried to storm into the room where Royall was sitting with her "friends." When the keeper brought Royall "by a private stair-case" to a more sheltered parlor, the "rude fellows" broke open the door "and rushed in," forcing the gentlemen to cover Royall's retreat to her bedroom "at the risk of their own lives." As Royall fashioned it, the scene spoke to the tension not only between rowdy students and respectable gentlemen but also between moralizing hypocrites and truly virtuous men, a common refrain in her writing.[69]

A woman did not have to be as notorious as Anne Royall for a man to undermine her right to the parlor. Consider the voluble William Parker

Foulke's description of his evening in a village tavern in 1848, where the keeper "took special pains to make me comfortable—lighted a fire in his parlour, & supplied me with all his available means of enjoyment." Sometime later, the landlady asked "whether I had any object[ion] to a couple of ladies sitting in the parlour!" Foulke remarked that "the room was hers," as if his hosts had not given him exclusive possession of the parlor since his arrival. When the new travelers entered, Foulke set his book aside and engaged in a "brisk confab" with "the 'ladies.'" As he related the episode, after half an hour, he returned to his book, a signal the women apparently understood as a tacit request that they should leave the room, which they did. Foulke framed the episode as a comic interlude, assuming that his aunt would agree that he had been sufficiently polite to women who did not quite meet his standard of ladyhood.[70]

Even more than in news rooms, parlor reading and writing set people apart, yet the quiet literate did not have it all their own way. Anne Royall believed that when she and another traveler entered a tavern parlor and "sat down to write," the men who were already there drinking and "disputing on politics" ought to "take the hint" and either leave or modify their conduct, "but no! here they sit." The spread of tavern parlors made some elite and middle-class women and men more at home in taverns, yet different interpretations of respectability and good behavior created opportunities for conflict among strangers. Architectural complexity helped tavern keepers serve multiple publics but could not eliminate tensions among taverns' varied users.[71]

Keeping House in Public

Across the spectrum of public accommodations, guests' compliments and complaints implicated far more than the material arrangements. "Civil, obliging," and "attentive" keepers sometimes made up for deficiencies of space or furnishings, while perceived inattention or rudeness made it difficult to enjoy even the most refined accommodations.[72] As taverns grew larger and more complex, even the most "assiduous" keeper required more labor. While degrees of refinement could be found in small taverns that ran on family labor, as the variety and number of rooms increased, so too did the tavern workforce. By midcentury, a large hotel easily employed dozens or even hundreds of people in a variety of job descriptions. Across the spectrum from village taverns to vast urban hotels, keepers, servants, and guests tested each other's understanding of both the work and the manners required to accommodate the public.[73]

Most tavern keepers who operated on a small scale relied on family members for the essential work of the household, as did self-working farmers, artisans, and retailers. As Thomas Fairfax noted in 1799, New England's tavern keepers kept "as few servants as possible," relying on "the daughters of the family" to "make the beds, set out the the table &c. &c." In the "western country," Fortescue Cuming observed that the keeper's wife and daughters managed "the business of the house, and the accommodation of their guests," often in multipurpose rooms that they shared with whatever patrons happened to be present.[74] Guests walked through, ate in, and slept in rooms that doubled as kitchens and family living space for the tavern household. In the process, patrons of small family-run taverns became witnesses to the work and manners of family members and servants. One common practice in this setting was for paying guests to eat with their host's family. Basil Hall noted one "pretty young woman, apparently the daughter of the master of the house," behaving "exactly as if she had been one of the party" at the table. From his vantage point, her manner was not "in the least degree forward or impudent," but guests often had quite a different reaction.[75]

While middle-class and wealthy Americans and European travelers sometimes found family-style taverns uncomfortable, some took the liberty of indulging their curiosity about strangers' domestic arrangements. When John Melish heard a spinning wheel, "the first I had heard in America," he followed his ears upstairs to a room where he found "a black girl carding cotton, and a daughter of the landlord spinning." Returning downstairs, he further satisfied his curiosity by pressing the landlady for information about domestic manufactures. Melish seems not to have questioned his entitlement to look or inquire as he pleased in a public house, nor did he appear to wonder how any of the women he met felt about his curiosity.[76]

At the scale of a small village tavern, adding a servant or two did little to alter the interpersonal tenor of guest, keeper, and servant relations, except that household problems became public ones. Like many householders, Virginia's Martin Browne saw Minty Johnson, a woman who worked for him, as something less than a free agent. Regarding her as a member of his household, not just his workforce, he expected to wield quasi-paternal authority over her. When she left unexpectedly, he grumbled that she "left our House in a dirty manner," a phrase that implied moral as well as material failings on her part. Any private householder might have said the same in the equivalent position, but in small, family-run village taverns, there was even less opportunity to hide household concerns from public notice.[77]

Keepers who invested in expanding and refining their premises needed people to meet guests at the door; care for their horses; carry their bags; tend bar; prepare, serve, and clean up after meals; wash sheets, towels, floors, and dishes; tend fires; and draw endless buckets of water. Because much of this work involved feminized labor, tavern improvements tended to increase the number of women on the premises. In large taverns, male and, especially, female servants often worked in areas beyond guests' sight, yet the fruits of their labor demonstrated their presence and importance. Keepers of large taverns assured potential guests that they had "good," "faithful," or "competent" maids, cooks, waiters, and hostlers, but outsiders seized opportunities to judge whether the sheets, dishes, and floors were clean, the food well cooked, and the stables well tended. Complaining about inferior servants was practically a badge of honor among people wealthy enough to hire or enslave them.[78]

The challenges of supervising servants and pleasing guests left many improving keepers struggling to assert their refinement or even their authority within the tavern household. If the tavern stand was not big enough to let the keeper's family live in their own building, then the guests could dispute the tavern family's claims to both gentility and physical space. This problem most often arose with travelers who rarely knew or cared for the tavern family's status in the local community. At an Alabama tavern, Anne Royall found "the landlady seated in an elegant parlour, on an easy sofa, dressed like a princess, all in white . . . with all the *hauteur* of an Empress." Royall thought "she had better be in the kitchen." Royall even claimed a preference for bachelor keepers because in their taverns, "I am always mistress of the servants." Then again, she complained when other patrons acted like masters in the keeper's house. In one such case, she noted that it was "the *consequentials* of the neighborhood" who treated the "'sanctum sanctorum' of the landlady" as their own.[79] Royall was hardly the only traveler who expected to boss around the servants. Andrew Lester abandoned an otherwise promising Virginia tavern because the "boys" he encountered did not leap into action when he told them to tend to his horses. Whether youths or grown men, the enslaved workers "did not dare" obey Lester without specific instructions from the keeper. Apparently, they had learned to fear him more than any transient guest. Yet keepers who expected guests to treat them as the masters of their own households risked being written up as insolent or neglectful.[80]

Keepers' advertisements probably contributed to some guests' readiness to treat them as social inferiors. In newspapers, broadsides, and circulars, people in the business of commercial hospitality promised their personal "assiduity and attention to business." The discourse of hospitable service could be found throughout the early republic. In 1793, a keeper in Martinsburg, Virginia, told potential patrons that his "attention" to them would be "minute and pointed." Some forty years later, Hector H. Crane announced that he would "spare no pains to gratify and accommodate" the patrons of his Eagle Tavern in Rochester, New York. Female keepers likewise promised, in Ann Gatewood's words, that "no exertion will be wanting to make every thing perfectly agreeable."[81]

As many private householders did with their servants' or slaves' labor, keepers' promises appropriated the credit for the work required to run a tavern, but this gesture toward their own household authority could not always protect them from others' condescension. Even at midcentury, the keeper of a considerable hotel, such as Jacob Kline of Wheeling, Virginia, could be patronized in print. In April 1841, the editor of the *Wheeling Times and Advertiser* praised Kline's hotel, noting that he had been "well fed," and wrote favorably about Kline's "very thorough repair and renovation." Indeed, he took "much pleasure in recommending" the Virginia Hotel "to the traveling community." Yet while he accorded Kline an "Esq" after his name, he also diminished Kline by dubbing him "as a worthy Boniface as ever tapped a cask." Used in comic fiction, character sketches, and travelers' writings, the moniker Boniface usually indicated that a tavern keeper was jolly and competent, but not someone who demanded significant respect.[82]

For his own part, Jacob Kline represented himself in print not as a hands-on tavern keeper who bustled about pouring drinks and listening to yarns but as the proprietor of a sizable establishment, as indeed he was. Kline's "Servants' Book" indicates that from 1841 to 1849, he employed the services of over 130 people at his Virginia Hotel in Wheeling. He also hired a hotel superintendent to do the day-to-day managerial work. A. W. Fleming, Kline assured his readers, had many years of experience "in some of the first hotels in the east," as well as five years in a rival Wheeling establishment.[83]

Whereas Virginia Hotel's keeper and superintendent were both white men, people of color made up a significant proportion of the staff, one-third or perhaps much more. Among the workers whose occupations Jacob Kline identified, a large majority of the waiters were Black, as were perhaps half of the porters and chambermaids, while the staff also included some German, Irish, and French immigrants.[84] Whatever their race, most of the men with identified occupations worked in highly visible roles, either indoors as porters, waiters, or general servants or outdoors as hack drivers or hostlers. Waiters often wore white jackets, and the other workers in regular contact with guests probably wore distinctive clothing as well.[85] While most women and girls worked in the kitchens and laundry rooms, where they had little or no chance of encountering hotel guests, perhaps as many as one-third of the female staff worked as parlor or chamber maids. They probably wore matching aprons, if not uniform dresses. All of them likely had first- or secondhand knowledge of the ways that guests' privacy could mean jeopardy for serving women: closed doors simplified harassment, assault, and accusations of stealing or ruining guests' property.[86]

Black workers also made opportunities in improved taverns and hotels. In the Niagara region of New York, Black men and women worked in many of the prominent hotels, and some managed or even owned public accommodations. Working in hotels and taverns, they likely had opportunities to provide information and practical assistance to people escaping from slavery who wanted to cross the border into Canada.[87] Black workers could also be found in hotels farther south, where their conditions and remuneration varied. At least one formerly enslaved man recalled that free Black barbers and waiters dressed and spoke like the white gentlemen and that "white folks speak 'spectable to 'em." Barbers had gained access to taverns and hotels because of changing standards for both tavern amenities and personal grooming. Many white men who would never sit down to eat with a Black man were perfectly comfortable with both proximity and touch in the context of service, provided the barber refused to shave Black clients on the same premises. Within this constraint, free barbers who did business on their own account had far more independence in their work lives than enslaved staff, as well as control over their own money. In rare cases, Black barbers became prosperous enough to have their own shops. Most famous of all was William Johnson of Natchez, who eventually became a substantial landowner and even mingled with rich planters at Natchez's famous racecourse.[88]

Not everyone agreed on the virtue of having "'spectable" interactions with white people, however. At the 1848 Colored National Convention in Cleveland, for example, the delegates resolved that Black barbers who refused "to treat colored men on equality with the whites" were "base serviles, worthy only of the condemnation, censure, and defamation of all lovers of liberty, equality, and right." This bold language entailed far more than access to hairdressing services. The conveners insisted that when anyone, white or Black, accepted Black people in service positions but rejected them as patrons, whether in a tavern or anywhere else, they endorsed race as a valid boundary of belonging in the new nation.[89]

A similar point could be made about white women's presence in tavern parlors and their absence from the barroom, but with a strong caveat. Most middling and wealthy white women came to see their gendered separateness as a privilege rather than a liability. Many had limited control over their families' socioeconomic standing—a function of economic volatility and gendered property law—but they could police the boundaries of ladyhood. The tavern improvements that made some female patrons feel more at home in public houses made other women feel less so, whether because the idealized middle-class home had no bearing on their daily realities, or because making a living through domestic labor constrained their family lives. At the same time, tavern improvements that made it easier for respectable white women to visit taverns complicated white men's own sense of belonging, making some feel less welcome and others more so, thanks to competing ideals of manly virtue.[90]

WHILE REPORTS OF UNCOMFORTABLE and even disgusting conditions left many travelers expecting the worst of American taverns, the slow process of refinement that remade middle-class homes in the late eighteenth and early nineteenth century also reshaped many taverns. As contemporaries saw it, taverns improved when they were repaired and expanded, when their interiors became more complex through subdivision by uses and users, and when they were furnished and decorated with well-made and fashionable consumer goods, not just serviceable homemade wares. Refinements in spatial organization and furnishings induced other changes in how people used taverns. In large improving taverns, white men lost some of their freedom to roam wherever they pleased, while some white women gained a new ability to feel at home—literally and figuratively—because of the subdivisions that feminized some key spaces. Yet despite the many changes in public accommodations, rural, village, and town taverns remained uneven, much like American motels and hotels to this day. This unevenness explains much about early republican travelers' frequent expressions of dissatisfaction. Private bedrooms with clean linens and decorative touches made at least some travelers want the same in all taverns, yet partial improvements, such as freshly washed homespun sheets, might be all that a particular keeper's trade or inclination would support.

In conjunction with their material investments, the language that keepers used for their trade suggests a certain proto-professionalization in commercial hospitality. Although professional hospitality schools and associations would not develop until the late nineteenth and early twentieth centuries, the early republic witnessed an evolving sense of what it meant to manage a good public house. By the mid-nineteenth century, commercial hospitality had begun to bifurcate both in and beyond the nation's coastal cities. Experienced practitioners were hired to manage hotels, which increasingly lived up to the ideal that they should be altogether bigger and better than most taverns. Whether as hirelings or lessors, the keepers of improved taverns and good hotels often specialized in their trade, remaining in the business and building valuable reputations over decades. The keepers of smaller, less improved taverns tended to own or lease their premises. In small towns and villages, they often combined the trade with other endeavors, taking up or abandoning tavern-keeping as other opportunities ebbed and flowed. Although keepers often managed a farm, store, or another enterprise that meshed well with the tavern business, some practiced trades with little obvious overlap. In the 1790s, for example, New England doctor Samuel Adams added tavern-keeping to his medical practice in hopes of improving his family finances.[91]

Given the difficulties of the work, the consistent claims of assiduity across the spectrum of public accommodations suggest that something important was at stake. The emergent middle class of the mid-eighteenth century through the mid-nineteenth century pursued aspects of gentility through industriousness: too much leisure could be both unseemly and counterproductive. From this perspective, the hard work of tavern-keeping, whether in small or large taverns, might be seen not as servile or degrading but as compatible with the goal of making a respectable living. Equally, the emphasis on effortful attention countered the notion that keepers had only to slop whiskey into glasses and tankards to make a tidy profit, an idea that aligned with temperance criticism.[92]

At the same time, town and village keepers had to remain pragmatic about the realities of their trade. As Joshua Gilpin understood, village and town keepers juggled competing demands, such as providing "accommodation for genteel Travellers" while also maintaining "a vast establishment in stables & needs for Waggoners." Not only did these patrons make different spatial demands, but they also were increasingly likely to observe contrasting habits of behavior and consumption, including drinking. As the next two chapters explore, while temperance advocates often represented tavern-going as choosing idleness and vice over industriousness and respectable pastimes, many Americans recognized that the practice could support a far more fluid set of sociable and economic opportunities.[93]

Part II

Enterprise

CHAPTER THREE

A Statement of Your Account
The Circulation of Goods and Credit

In 1797, Virginia tavern keeper Martin Browne sent Luke Burns "a statement of your account" detailing Burns's repeated and sizable purchases of alcohol. In the spring of 1794, for instance, Burns racked up £2.19.14 in alcohol debt, most of it for half-pints of distilled spirits. He bought alcohol at least thirty-eight times that season and seventeen times in March alone. At the end of his brief note, Browne modified the valediction used in many business letters from the period: "am as usual (when Captn Grogg does not rule your better Judgment)—your friend &c." Browne's language hints that Burns was, at least occasionally, the kind of drinker who made so many small taverns and bar-rooms unappealing to respectable women travelers and considerable numbers of men as well.[1]

At first or even second glance, tavern accounts suggest that village and town tavern-going promoted inebriation and little else. In some ledgers and day-books, the tallies of drams, gills, half-pints, pints, quarts, and gallons of alcohol run for pages, with little or no interruption by entries for lodgings, meals, stabling, horse feed, or anything else, and often with scant reference to any form of payment.[2] Drawing on a selection of taverns in varied settings, table 3.1 illustrates the predominance of alcohol in tavern keepers' sales. Yet the relationship between village and small-town drinkers and their taverns was often far more complicated than the count of liquor sales alone might suggest. A skilled itinerant cooper, Luke Burns lodged at Martin Browne's while working in the neighborhood and paid off part of his tavern debt through his craft. Browne in turn furnished Burns with a place to live, an introduction to his other customers, and essential goods such as shoes. Shaped not only by drunken conduct but also by prolonged acquaintance, debt, and the circulation of goods and skills, the relationship between Burns and Browne illustrates some of the complex dynamics common in village and small-town tavern-going in the early republic.[3]

The prominence of travelers among a tavern's customers and the significance of their custom owed much to location. Depending on their proximity to routes for trade or migration, centers of population, political capitals, and to competition with other keepers, among other factors, some taverns

TABLE 3.1 Alcohol sales, as percentage of sales covered by tavern licenses

	Alcohol	Lodgings, meals, and horse care
	as percent of tavern sales	
Browne Tavern, near Winchester, VA, 1803–1804	95.4	4.6
Elkton Tavern, Elkton, MD, 1806–1814	69.9	30.1
Marriner's Tavern, Lewes, DE, 1812–1813	91.5	8.5
Warsaw Tavern, Warsaw, NY, 1830–1831	96.2	3.8
Ellis's Tavern, Decatur, MS, 1837–1839	40.8	53.9
Adair's Tavern, Greenville, GA, 1843–1844	98.8	1.2

Sources: Calculated from Browne Papers, Vol. 6; Elkton Ledger; Marriner Daybook; Warsaw Daybook; Craft and Tingle, *Old Account Book Entries, 1837–1841, Decatur, Newton County, Mississippi*; Adair Papers, Account Book 1843–1844.

welcomed enough travelers to justify making significant improvements. In many village and town taverns, travelers were far too rare to warrant much outlay on keepers' parts yet still represented a valuable diversion and news source. For both local and traveling patrons, their alcohol purchases had a variety of meanings. Some tavern drinking customs, such as clubbing and treating, could encourage lingering and drunkenness while operating as modes of inclusion and exclusion. Further complicating the picture, an indeterminate proportion of the alcohol purchased in village and town taverns was not swallowed on the spot but bought for household or workplace use.

Whatever the contours of their traveling and alcohol trades, keepers often did business in goods and services far beyond the narrow range required by a tavern keeper's license.[4] Unlike the hospitality specialists who managed the largest, capital-intensive hotels, many tavern keepers operated an ancillary business such as a farm, store, or both. Some keepers maintained well-stocked, physically distinct stores and kept separate accounts, but in many small taverns, the store and the tavern were all but indistinguishable, their accounts commingled. As villages grew sufficiently populous and integrated into local transportation networks to support both taverns and stores, keepers were more likely to specialize, sometimes becoming more drink-centered than ever and sometimes reorienting toward other forms of consumption.[5]

Village and small-town keepers did much, if not most, of their business with repeat customers who lived no more than a day's travel away or rarely more than twenty miles. To such patrons, keepers usually offered credit, building up transactional webs that connected them to their neighbors over time. In part because of this credit, tavern transactions remained vested in personal reputations and mutual knowledge. Keepers traded in many items that formed part of the global circulations of goods, including imported wines and spirits and international plantation commodities such as sugar and coffee. They also handled multiple forms of payment, including minted coins, bank notes, personal notes of hand, manufactured goods, farm products, and labor, all of which they recirculated as sales, payments, loans, and wages. Indeed, keepers' sales often reflected the farm products and domestic manufactures that they accepted in payment of tavern bills. From the late eighteenth century to well into the nineteenth century, keepers and patrons of village and town taverns participated in forms of exchange and production that were tied both to local reputations and demands and to regional, national, and international market flows of goods, credit, and information.[6]

These local and extralocal circulations informed tavern sociability. What men ordered to drink and whether they bought for themselves, for their households, or for their fellow drinkers both expressed and informed individuals' relative standing within the tavern. In similar ways, who purchased nontavern goods and whether they did so in person or by proxy implicated hierarchies of gender and race. White women and people of color were rare yet significant customers in small and not-so-small taverns. Patrons' tavern sociability and purchasing behaviors helped fashion the social and economic matrix that individuals, households, and whole neighborhoods inhabited. And as they transacted, they took part in the protracted struggle to define the significance and boundaries of economic activity in the early republic.[7]

"A House for the Entertainment of Travellers"

In the early nineteenth century, legal authorities and other observers often insisted that taverns should exist only if they entertained travelers, but many taverns—licensed or not—arose in places where travelers were rare. Being located along a vibrant transportation route improved the chances that a tavern would do a reasonable business in overnight accommodations, meals, or stabling and fodder for horses. Keeping tavern in a local market town or county seat further enhanced the likelihood of a significant traveling trade, provided that the tavern was also located on the main business street, near the courthouse, or along the main through-road. Even when outsiders were rare, however, they could have an important impact, whether because of the size of their bills, the interest they stirred among locals, or wider historical contingencies. Conversely, taverns mattered to people on the move: they helped make both local and long-distance travel possible. Tavern accounts from varied neighborhoods, selected to highlight both continuity and change over time and space, illuminate how physical and social geography shaped the prevalence of travel and the context of local patronage. And once we have a better understanding of differences across taverns, we can also appreciate the differences and commonalities in consumer behavior within them.

At the close of the eighteenth century, William Brown kept tavern and operated a ferry in the town of Bath, colonial North Carolina's first port of entry. His accounts suggest the importance of navigable waterways for cheap, swift, and easy transportation and the ways that taverns helped people use them. Bath lay on Bath Creek, which fed into the Pamlico River, which in turn reached the Atlantic Ocean via the Ocracoke Inlet. Bath was a sufficiently important shipping destination for shipmasters to advertise their departures for that port in New York and Philadelphia newspapers. By land, the town lay along a locally important northbound road to Virginia. Although Bath had lost some of its commercial and political importance by the end of the century, residents in the surrounding county were accustomed to visiting the town for both business and pleasure.[8] Brown himself had a direct interest in water transportation: he kept a ferry that traversed the creek and collected fees from the masters of the brigs, schooners, and sloops that entered the port to load and unload their cargoes. Brown also played an occasional role in shipbuilding and repair, furnishing labor for such jobs as "cawking the ship." Over 40 percent of Brown's customers in the 1780s took meals at the tavern from time to time, and the area's wealthy residents were especially likely to gather at Brown's for dinner. By contrast, Brown provided few patrons with overnight lodgings, suggesting that most visitors lived near enough to visit for the day or continued their journey by land or water. Like most of his fellow keepers, Brown poured prodigious amounts of alcohol, but his tavern's business rested on and supported the local and extralocal circulation of goods and people.[9]

Two hundred and fifty miles to the west, brothers John and Alexander Lowrance kept a tavern and store from the 1750s through the mid-1790s in a rural community in North Carolina's Rowan County. By the late eighteenth century, two major roads converged in the eastern part of the county, bringing a steady stream of migrants and enough settlers to populate a network of small villages and towns, each with a handful of artisans who served the surrounding farmers as well as passing travelers. Salisbury, the county seat and largest town, lay west of the two roads, and the Lowrances' tavern still farther west. As a result, few travelers came to the Lowrances' tavern, and from 1780 through 1795, alcohol accounted for almost all of the transactions that pertained to a tavern license—namely, alcohol, lodgings, meals, horse feed, and stabling. Local farmers, artisans, and some travelers visited for drink and conversation, but few stayed for meals, let alone spent the night. By contrast, the keepers of a popular tavern in Salisbury proper did a respectable business in meals and lodgings as well as alcohol. Small differences in location made significant differences in tavern keepers' trade.[10]

Nearly two decades later and back on the coast, water-based shipping shaped the traffic at Sarah Marriner's tavern in the mid-1810s in Lewes, Delaware, yet her customers little resembled the wealthy and sociable crew at William Brown's tavern on Bath Creek. Sheltered by Cape Henlopen at the mouth of the Delaware Bay, through which shipping from Wilmington and Philadelphia reached the Atlantic Ocean, both Marriner's tavern and the town bore witness to the importance of water. Marriner's customers included numerous pilots who guided ocean-going vessels through difficult coastal waters. Because of its more northerly latitude, Lewes's maritime connections were more seasonal than in Bath. Maritime traffic in Delaware Bay declined in the winter, when ice sometimes "stops the navigation" on the Delaware River and Bay. Marriner's business ebbed and flowed somewhat with this seasonal pattern, averaging nearly seven customers a day from July through October, but fewer than five from November through February. Yet unlike William Brown's accounts, Marriner's daybook includes no charges for ferry passage or ships' fees, and she did very little business in meals or accommodations.[11] A decade earlier, the artist Charles Willson Peale observed that the removal of the county court from Lewes "has been a considerable loss" to the town, and most vessels moored at the harbor only when they were "weather bound." While "a considerable number of Visitants" came to "take the benefits of the salt air and bathing," Peale concluded that many villagers made a rather "precarious" living since the loss of the court meant less reason to come to town. In the latter half of 1812, Marriner herself did almost no trade except in alcohol, which accounted for over 93 percent of her transactions. The tavern's location explained the popularity of grog, a sailor's drink and the overwhelming choice of Marriner's patrons.[12]

The tavern's proximity to major shipping lanes took on new significance for Marriner and her neighbors when the coast became a local front in the ongoing British-American War of 1812. In February 1813, a British naval squadron began blockading Delaware Bay, part of Britain's campaign against American shipping and naval maneuvers. Stifling traffic in and out of the bay, the blockade also afflicted people on the coast: British forces suppressed the coastal trade and raided local farms for livestock and other foodstuffs. For Sarah Marriner, this alarming period had its compensations. For starters, as the American forces responded to the British threat, she hosted many more people, including militia officers, many of whom bought food and lodgings for themselves and their horses. Pilots also appeared with greater frequency, in part because of the warmer weather but perhaps also because their skills had a new application: tracking and evading the British squadron. Marriner's drinking trade increased as people thirsty for news visited in far greater numbers than in the preceding six months. Daily attendance at Marriner's peaked in April, when Commodore John P. Beresford of the Royal Navy threatened to bomb Lewes unless the citizens furnished his squadron with foodstuffs and fresh water. Through April and May, the tavern's monthly visits more than doubled the average attendance in the second half of 1812, thanks in no small part to the militia forces who mustered in the town's defense.[13]

By the time that war reshaped traffic at Marriner's, well-situated taverns along major roads stood a good chance of doing a sizable trade in meals and accommodations. One of the most commercialized transportation routes of the late eighteenth and early nineteenth centuries ran roughly north-south from New York to Philadelphia, Baltimore, and Washington, D.C. Stagecoach taverns in the intermediate towns along the way saw significant traffic in both stage passengers and private travelers.[14] In sharp contrast to Marriner's daybook, the surviving ledger of a stagecoach tavern in Elkton, Maryland, documents the steady business in meals and accommodations for both people and horses that resulted. Being a stage stop guaranteed this tavern the custom of travelers along a busy route. Although keepers who were not co-proprietors of stage lines had no guarantee that stagecoaches would continue to stop at their taverns, this keeper, possibly Joshua Richardson, was likely secure in the short term because stagecoach proprietor Daniel Richardson had named him as the executor of his will. When Daniel died, his executor retained authority over the stagecoach business as he settled the estate.[15]

As a location, Elkton had major advantages for a transportation-minded tavern keeper. Not only did it lie on the Philadelphia-to-Baltimore route, but it also sat along a waterway that fed into the busy Chesapeake Bay. The town was thus an appealing destination for farmers in the surrounding areas who wanted to get their crops to market. The tavern stood ready to refresh thirsty wagon drivers and stagecoach passengers, while absorbing local farmers' surplus horses and grain to support the stagecoach line. Neighbors from the town and nearby countryside joined the stage at the tavern, consigned freight, and hired gigs and livery horses from the keeper. Locals also visited because of politics: the keeper noted that several of his customers incurred charges for meals, drinks, and lodgings because they were attending courts or elections. Overall, customers for travel-related services made up an important slice of this keeper's business: 20 percent of his account holders came for meals or lodgings, and roughly one-third for any combination of meals, lodgings, provender, or stabling.[16]

Improvements to land- and water-based transportation accelerated after the War of 1812, with new turnpike roads, canals, and steam-powered water travel. Yet transportation improvements worked uneven transformations, as two anonymous tavern keepers' daybooks from northern and western New York illustrate. An 1822 daybook from Antwerp Township in northern New York suggests the primarily local scope of a village tavern reasonably close to major transportation routes but with nothing to attract a steady stream of travelers. Antwerp and the surrounding Jefferson County had significant potential for rapid development in the early 1820s. Reasonably close to both the St. Lawrence River and Lake Ontario, the area included fertile soil and natural resources for quarrying and mining, while rivers provided water power for grist and timber mills. Navigation on the St. Lawrence was challenging, but the river linked Lake Ontario to the Atlantic Ocean, and area farmers found a market for their crops in Montreal.[17]

Antwerp itself lay on the post road that stretched north from Utica in the center of the state to Ogdensburgh on the bank of the St. Lawrence River. In 1822, a stagecoach carrying mail came through town twice a week on the post road, but it brought few passengers to Antwerp. The tavern's daybook shows almost no business in overnight accommodations and only slightly more in horse care and meals. Only three out of seventy-one customers spent the night in the late summer and early fall of 1822, and the stage driver himself accounted for almost half of the meals sold in that period. Such numbers represented scant encouragement to invest in bedrooms or parlors. However, the stagecoach's regular stops benefited the tavern in other ways. On days the stagecoach came through, the tavern saw more customers: a median of almost five customers on stage days versus three on other days. In addition to drawing people in for drink and news, this tavern also extended its influence out into the neighborhood whenever the keeper hired out his ox team and a wagon to people who needed to haul goods to or from one of the nearby mills.[18]

A second New York village tavern had a similarly attenuated relationship to the rapid pace of transportation-related change visible in the Philadelphia-Baltimore corridor. In fertile but hilly Wyoming County, east of Lake Erie, the county seat of Warsaw remained relatively poor for many years after its founding in 1803. Eventually, local residents benefited from nearby Oatka Creek, which afforded water power for local mills, and even more from the Erie Canal, which eased the transportation of heavy goods. Yet five years after the great canal's opening, one Warsaw tavern still did little business in meals, lodgings, or horse care, in no small part because the canal, over thirty miles north of Warsaw, absorbed most passenger and freight traffic. In a two-month period at the end of 1830, when short days and the chance of snow made over-night shelter a serious matter, the keeper furnished lodgings to only four of seventy-four customers and did even less business in costly meals and horse care. The following June, a better season for traveling but a busy time for farmers, the keeper made over two hundred distinct daybook entries but furnished only five meals, and no guest slept at his house. In such circumstances, keepers were likely to make minor improvements rather than to invest in major building and renovation projects.[19]

By the early 1840s, the overall increase in commerce and travel meant that even in towns with only road-based transportation options, some tavern keepers saw enough travelers to warrant significant structural improvements. One instructive example comes from the Eagle Tavern in Watkinsville, Georgia. Incorporated in 1815, Watkinsville was the seat of Clarke County and lay on a well-traveled road between Milledgeville, the state capital, and Athens, the site of the state's university. In its earliest incarnation, the original structure might possibly have been used as a blockhouse, one of many small fortifications that white Americans built for protection as they encroached on Indigenous lands, in this case, the territory of the Muscogee Creeks.[20] By the early 1820s, the building had become the Eagle Tavern—one of the most popular tavern names in the period because of its patriotic national symbolism—and is believed to have featured two rooms on each of two floors. A decade later, a stagecoach traveled between Athens and Milledgeville three times a week, stopping in Watkinsville along the way. As a result, townsfolk and farmers could now visit the Eagle and mingle with through-passengers on the stage. Both these passengers and private travelers kept the Eagle's staff busy with their demands for meals, lodging, and horse feed. Almost three-quarters of the Eagle's customers came for meals or lodgings, and more than half came with their own horses, who needed stabling, feeding, or both. That sort of demand from both private and commercial travelers spurred major structural changes once Richard Richardson bought the tavern in 1836. Richardson expanded and refined the four-room Eagle, wrapping an extensive two-story addition around the exterior (see figure 3.1). This addition increased the number of

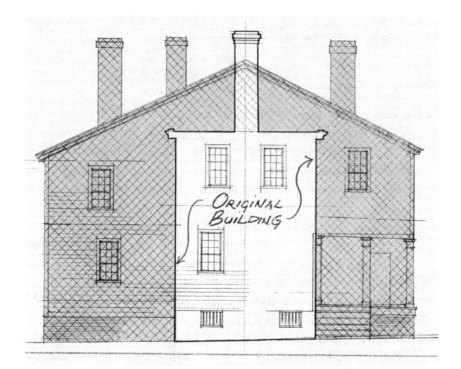

ORIGINAL
BUILDING

FIGURE 3.1 Elevation of the Eagle Tavern, Watkinsville, Georgia. This drawing illustrates the Eagle Tavern's expansion in the 1830s. The tavern may have begun as a simple two-story tavern with a two-room floor plan. When stagecoach traffic seemed to justify a significant expansion, then-owner Richard Richardson chose not to erect an entirely new building. Instead, he built an addition that wrapped around the existing structure. The expanded tavern offered many more bedrooms and more opportunities to separate uses and users. Drawing by Christa Kelly after Thomas G. Little architectural drawings, ms4249, Hargrett Rare Book and Manuscript Library, University of Georgia Libraries.

bedrooms severalfold and added both a large ground-floor dining room and a substantial porch fronting the road.[21]

Demand for travel-related services increased markedly and unevenly in the first third of the nineteenth century, producing both strong contrasts between taverns that operated around the same time and significant similarities over the decades. Where demand was steady or growing, ambitious keepers with access to credit had reason to make speculative investments, producing larger and more refined accommodations. Where demand remained slack, taverns might not see an overnight visitor from one month to the next, even if the keeper had whatever beds, bedding, stabling, foodstuffs, and provender the law required. The relative scarcity of travelers meant that village and town keepers could call most of their patrons neighbors, in the loose sense of the neighborhood defined by a day's travel by road.

Tavern Drinking Cultures

Tavern drinking encouraged white men to mingle with neighbors and occasionally strangers, whether in a separate barroom or simply near the bar cage in a mixed-use room. Ledgers filled with references to drink—whiskey, rum, cider, ale, brandy, and more—and sometimes to tobacco and cigars provide strong hints about the smells, sights, and behaviors likely to be encountered in such spaces. Yet tavern drinking was more complicated than one might guess from the often-scandalized reports of outside observers. With the masculine prerogative of lingering in tavern barrooms came the necessities of choice: what to drink, how much to drink, and with whom. As keepers poured and patrons drank, they engaged in both quasi-democratic mixing and hierarchical sifting with other members of the tavern company.[22]

In their daybooks and ledgers, keepers took pains to identify their patrons by name because they so rarely received payment at the point of sale. At times, they also recorded details that indicated their knowledge of each patron's social standing and connections. Most white men received first and last names, which tacitly communicated their right to a father and a lineage. Some patrons were explicitly identified as the father or son of another patron, but keepers surely left out much of what they knew, including the familial relationships that bound people whether they shared last names or not. Even without the deep local research required to establish kinship, however, the repetition of surnames in many account books suggests multiple possible connections among patrons. Another type of information comes from the occasional patrons who received professional, occupational, or military titles such as doctor, esquire, pilot, captain, or major. Such descriptors increased precision in the case of common family names and hinted at the ways that rank and occupation might inflect keepers' interactions with their patrons.

Where strangers were concerned, by contrast, keepers might be forced to rely on a description rather than a name. On November 16, 1821, six patrons visited a central Virginia tavern known as the Traveller's Rest. Two were unnamed, identified not as first and second stranger, but as "Pedlar" and "Mr. Gentleman." Both men came with horses, paid for supper, and bought grain and hay, so what made one a peddler and the other a gentleman? If the two men did not use these words to describe themselves, perhaps their conversation, clothing, and baggage communicated one's hardworking itinerancy and the other's affluence. Their transactions also fleshed out the tale. "Pedlar" had but one horse and made do with the whiskey and water that usually accompanied a tavern meal. "Mr. Gentleman" arrived with two horses, ordered brandy, and spent nearly twice as much money. Neither money nor drink made a gentleman, but what men drank mattered.[23]

The sociable drinking practice known as clubbing further illuminates the links between drinking and social status. On its face, clubbing meant only that a group of people had agreed to share the costs of their drinking, but the practice often drew lines of genteel inclusion and exclusion. Clubbing seems to have been most common in refined urban venues, and men who clubbed almost always drank at the upper end of the tavern price list. At the Old Coffee House in late eighteenth-century New York City, patrons had made clubbing an informal rule: everyone who drank wine clubbed expenses, whether they drank one glass with dinner or opened multiple bottles over the course of "three or four hours." A newcomer to this arrangement objected because it encouraged men to drink and linger more than they wanted, forced them to subsidize other men's drinking, or both. But he probably recognized the underlying social logic. For starters, the Coffee House denizens clubbed in wine, not the much less expensive rum or whiskey. In clubbing, they signaled their taste for wine, their desire to associate with men of similar tastes, their indifference to the cost, and perhaps their dedication to long bouts of imbibing. In the process, they imposed a particular understanding of gentlemanly behavior on strangers visiting the Coffee House.[24]

Reasonably common in leading urban taverns, clubbing did not diffuse widely into village and small-town taverns. Wherever it appeared, however, it often retained a modicum of the ostentation seen in refined urban settings. When town and village tavern-goers clubbed, they did not drink the cheapest alcohols around, usually rum, whiskey, or hard cider. Instead, like their urban brothers, they clubbed in costly brandy, punch, toddy, or similar preparations that easily cost twice as much as the cheapest tipple because they involved top-shelf liquors, additional ingredients, or special drinkware like a punch bowl. At William Brown's tavern and ferry in Bath, North Carolina, more than one-third of the patrons participated in clubbing, and they almost always drank toddy or brandy, usually while sharing a meal that further increased their costs. Brown's most frequent clubbers included some of the most prominent men in Beaufort County, including the county's largest enslaver, Thomas Respess Sr., the leading officer of the county's Continental Army regiment, Colonel James Bonner, and other Respess and Bonner men. Since Brown himself held the rank of major in the same regiment and had represented the county in the state legislature, his tavern represented an obvious place for distinguished men to engage in highly visible yet exclusive forms of sociable drinking.[25]

Even though clubbing remained infrequent in town and village taverns in the decades after the revolution, keepers found customers for drinks at the expensive end of the menu. At Sarah Marriner's tavern, grog, an inexpensive rum-and-water mixture, accounted for 84 percent of the drinks she sold. The small number of men whom she identified as officers or gentlemen accounted for a sizable proportion of the pricier drinks—more than a quarter of the brandy and nearly three-tenths of the toddy—and only 4 percent of her grog orders. Men already known to their neighbors by their profession, property, or military rank and uniforms did not need to buy costly drinks to communicate their status. That they did so anyway and in wartime suggests that they felt free to flaunt their tastes and affluence or, alternatively, obliged to spend in proportion to their status.[26]

Whether they chose freely or under obligation, gentlemen had ample scope to distinguish themselves through drink. At the busy stage tavern in Elkton, Maryland, most people drank neat spirits or cheap fermented cider. One-quarter of the patrons, however, also ordered more expensive drinks, including fortified wines, toddy, punch, or sangaree, a chilled sweetened spirituous drink. Even if the keeper served these rarefied options with the minimum of theater, other patrons could easily identify the difference between them and their own glasses of whiskey or cider.[27] In the far less cosmopolitan milieu of Warsaw in western New York, men who shared a tavern barroom still made distinctly different choices. At this tavern, inexpensive whiskey—three cents per glass—accounted for more than 70 percent of the drink orders. One-third of the tavern's patrons drank nothing else. But the keeper also sold significantly more expensive options to a minority of the drinkers. Other men did not automatically defer to a man who ordered a double sling, wine, or cocktails, but in a small tavern or barroom, it was easy to notice distinctions among drinkers.[28]

Treating and toasting, two common patterns in tavern drinking, had similar potential to draw lines of inclusion and exclusion. Whether reciprocated or not, treating meant paying for others' entertainment, usually of the alcoholic variety. Contemporaries maintained that treating and toasting produced a dangerous sort of leveling: in both "places of low intoxication" and in "respectable" or even "splendid" venues, these sociable practices seduced men into drinking to excess.[29] Village and town tavern accounts suggest that whether men bought rounds for each other or simply bought enough to return others' toasts, sociable drinking could easily lead to drunkenness. Martin Browne's customers regularly bought whiskey by the half-pint or pint, amounts large enough for sharing with or toasting fellow patrons. Rarely did Browne's patrons order a single gill, or four ounces, and they were somewhat more likely to do so on days when the tavern saw the fewest customers. This pattern does not prove either toasting or treating, for nothing prevented the pint and half-pint men from drinking it all or taking it away with them. However, finding others at the bar apparently encouraged Browne's neighbors to order more than they otherwise did.[30] Several decades later, when temperance was spreading into the Deep South, William Adair in west central Georgia sold alcohol in volumes that suggested treating, toasting, or both. Adair recorded most of his sales by price without reference to volume; his liquor sales usually cost multiples of $.06¼, the amount he charged for four ounces of ordinary distilled spirits. Assuming his patrons were not buying more expensive alcohols, more than a third of Adair's generic "drink" sales cost enough to supply patrons with between sixteen and thirty-six ounces of whiskey. In other words, Adair's patrons often ordered liquor in volumes large enough to treat a sizable number of men or indulge in a protracted exchange of toasts, always assuming they did not simply take their liquor away with them.[31]

The meanings of treating and the related practice of toasting extended beyond the potential for heavy drinking. In wayside taverns, some men sought to make strangers drunk just so they could cheat or rob them. Yet toasting and treating among men who knew each other were often reciprocal practices, expressive not only of goodwill but also of a kind of equality. Men often drank together when they concluded a successful transaction, and reciprocation nullified the sense of obligation that otherwise resulted from accepting a favor. In other situations, inviting men to drink had a coercive edge since declining a toast was likely to be read as churlish, cheap, or weak. The practice not only resulted in more drinking and greater expense but also reinforced a particular version of competitive masculinity, sometimes to literally toxic degrees.[32]

Toasts and treats also created boundaries. Sometimes these boundaries were obvious: when only part of the company indulged, for example, or when reciprocal toasting excluded the tavern staff. Political treating drew distinct lines of inclusion and exclusion. On the October day in 1842 when Georgians elected their new congressmen, the "Democrat Ticket" incurred five and a half dollars in alcohol charges at William Adair's tavern, enough to buy twenty quarts of whiskey. Fourteen customers ordered an additional seven dollars' worth of alcohol on the same day, providing opportunities for even greater inebriation. Partisan treating allowed Adair's customers to drink copiously, in public, in the fellowship of Democratic voters. Simultaneously, they set themselves apart not only from Whig voters but also everyone who lacked the franchise, on the premises and off. As it happened, Georgia Democrats had reason to celebrate, as the electoral returns showed them gaining five seats in this election.[33]

Whether partisan treating demeaned voters was a matter of perspective and perhaps a function of victory. Partisan operators were often accused of buying votes with drink, an interpretation that cast doubt on the average voter's independence and fitness for the franchise. One anonymous diarist who visited Augusta, Georgia, in the late 1810s lamented that "the man who will *treat the mob* . . . commands their votes." In the absence of well-organized political parties, wealthy men might treat their neighbors to alcohol at rallies and polls in part on the premise that such largesse to the community bespoke their fitness for office.[34]

On occasion, treating expressed a clientage relationship, thanks for a favor, or a reward for a job. When Martin Browne's lodger Luke Burns treated a "strange Cooper" to whiskey, their shared occupation may have explained Burns's generosity, but it put the stranger under an obligation and elevated Burns, however temporarily. At other times, Burns treated "Old Sam" to a drink, and another patron purchased several drinks "for Old Joe." Listed without last names, both men were almost certainly Black, probably enslaved, and possibly members of Browne's household. The treats might have been a form of payment for services rendered, but as recorded in Browne's ledger, they also underlined the purchaser's status. If Luke Burns owned no land, he like many other white men in Virginia could not vote. His ability to treat others, however, conveyed the informal but potent prerogatives of a self-employed, skilled white man.[35]

Perhaps ironically, another kind of information visible both in ledgers and to other patrons involved the varied forms of temperance practiced in the early nineteenth century. Punch bowls, bottles of wine or brandy, and glasses of spirits did not look like quarts of lower-alcohol cider or ale. At the Elkton stage tavern in the 1810s, one-quarter of the patrons ordered no spirits but did consume cider and wine.[36] Into the 1830s and 1840s, a significant slice of tavern-goers continued to drink while eschewing spirits. Some tavern keepers seized on this trend, like S. B. Miller of Sandyville, Ohio, who promoted his "temperance tavern" as serving only wine and beer.[37] In Warsaw, New York, a majority of the tavern-goers in the early 1830s drank at least some whiskey, but more than one in ten patrons drank only cider. Since the two were equally cheap at three cents per serving, the cider drinkers probably made a deliberate choice in favor of the lower-alcohol beverage.[38]

In the early 1840s, as temperance propaganda increased the stigma against public drinking, men who were willing to drink at all in taverns remained likely to drink spirits. Most drinkers at William Adair's Georgia tavern remained committed to whiskey. Nearly 43 percent of Adair's patrons ordered only whiskey, while less than 2 percent shunned distilled spirits. Adair's most regular patron, Henry Floyd, ordered sizable amounts of whiskey and "drink," yet he seemed to prefer lower-alcohol drinks. Floyd was single-handedly responsible for 45 percent of the tavern's ale sales in the early 1840s and nearly a quarter of the beer. By 1845, Floyd appears to have rethought his public drinking, making occasional visits to Adair's tavern for foodstuffs and gunpowder without buying any alcohol. A minority of Adair's patrons, perhaps one quarter of those who visited in the sampled period, visited far less often than Floyd and never purchased alcohol in any form. Instead, they came for household goods such as sugar, salt, and nails.[39]

Tavern-going provided opportunities, encouragement, and even pressure for white men to drink to excess. Yet notwithstanding these inducements, patrons continued to vary in what they drank, how much, and how often. In addition to reflecting men's different tastes, tolerances, and means, tavern drinking also involved positioning oneself both alongside and in contrast to other white men. Drinking (or not) was far from the only means of doing so.

"A Tavern and a Store"

Visiting a local tavern to provision a household could make as weighty a statement of manhood as the ability either to treat the company or hold one's liquor. More durable and more valuable by weight than grain, whiskey could be consumed on the spot, used at home or in a workplace, and exchanged in trade. Other tavern goods shared this treble character. Men on the move bought quarts of oats and sheaves of corn for their horses to eat. When bought by the bushel, the same provender fed animals in the buyer's household or was exchanged for yet other goods. On the often-spotty credit side of tavern ledgers, alcohol, provender, and foodstuffs mingled with labor, bank notes, and notes of hand (personal promissory notes) in payment for tavern goods and services. Through repeated and overlapping exchanges over months and years, tavern commerce bound patrons to keepers and each other even as cash payments became predominant in tavern ledgers.[40]

In village and town taverns at the turn of the nineteenth century, sales of manufactured goods and both raw and processed foodstuffs accounted for an important share of keepers' trade and patrons' reasons for tavern-going. Usually operated under the same roof and documented in the same ledgers, tavern and store overlapped for both keeper and patrons. Fully 70 percent of William Brown's customers in Bath, North Carolina, bought goods beyond the standard fare of drinks, accommodations, meals, and provender. Brown's additional sales included bulk quantities of durable provisions, such as bacon, and other supplies that had many applications, including long sea voyages, such as tar and pine trees.[41]

Tavern keepers could keep "a store of very well-assorted goods" or focus on liquor, but whatever they sold, they had to accept payment in forms that their customers could supply. At the turn of the century, the credit side of these ledgers reflected the mixture of productive activities in which local householders engaged. In western North Carolina, the Lowrance brothers took payment in liquor, cash, grain, deer skins, salt, iron, indigo, old pewter, and wooden boards. Some debtors paid by trimming trees or working in the fields at harvest time. On the coast, William Brown took alcohol in payment. In the mid-1780s, Captain John Gladen settled his account with twenty-eight gallons of rum, perhaps acquired directly from a distiller in New England or the West Indies. Brown doubtless welcomed a commodity that he could resell either in bulk or by the small measure. Keepers accepted many other forms of payment that could be used in their own households or sold to patrons. Samuel Garrett paid some of his debt to Brown with corn, sugar, hats, and women's gloves. A local doctor paid in corn and women's shoes. Several patrons settled in part or in full through unspecified sundries. Skilled workers paid with their handicrafts, including shoes, textiles, and barrels.[42]

Most patrons paid their tavern debts piecemeal and often long after they received goods or services from the keeper. Keepers expected through-travelers such as "Mr. Gentleman" and "Pedlar" to pay in full. Yet they extended generous credit to local patrons, sometimes carrying debtors on their books for weeks, months, or even years, often without charging interest, a practice known as book debt. One of William Brown's credit entries reflected a payment of ten shillings, less than 2 percent of the patron's total debt. Another of Brown's debtors, the largest enslaver in the county, took six years to settle his account.[43] Tavern keepers' accounts give the impression that they were not chiefly concerned with calculating profits. In addition to offering credit, keepers rarely settled their accounts at the end of the year, nor were they known for keeping systematic records about their business expenses. Of greater interest than profit were the webs of mutual obligation that formed as patrons transacted on credit with multiple people in their community. Tavern keepers took care to record the ways in which their patrons' mutual financial obligations intersected with their own accounts. In the mid-1780s, for example, William Brown noted that Samuel Garrett had paid part of his debt by an order on Richard Blackledge. Blackledge himself appeared in Brown's ledger as a debtor in part for cash advanced to yet other members of the Bath community. Such skeins of mutual obligation wound throughout turn-of-the-century tavern accounts, creating both strength and risk.[44]

Operating in Virginia's fertile and rapidly growing Shenandoah Valley, Martin Browne resembled both the Lowrance brothers and William Brown in that his considerable liquor business depended on and facilitated an extensive trade in domestic and commercial manufactures and agricultural produce. In 1803–1804, less than 5 percent of the transactions in Browne's tavern daybook involved lodgings, meals, or food and shelter for horses, while nearly 90 percent included alcohol. Many of his alcohol sales involved comparatively small measures for the period—namely, half-pints of whiskey—and customers who carried their whiskey away in a "pocket Bottle" likely made at least a start on it while still at the tavern.[45]

The modest proportion of Martin Browne's sales beyond the limits of his tavern license attracted a wide swathe of his customers. More than 40 percent of his patrons bought bulk foodstuffs such as vinegar, molasses, sugar, potatoes, and fish at least once in the period covered by one ledger. Nearly two-thirds bought sundries. Almost a fifth of his patrons owed him for textiles or clothes, such as the red waistcoat and footed stockings charged to one William Dalloway, goods that likely reflected the labor of Martin's wife Molly, a weaver, or another woman in the household. Although the lack of information about Browne's expenses prevents any calculation of his profits, these unlicensed transactions amounted to nearly 30 percent of his gross sales.[46]

On the credit side of the ledger, Martin Browne's customers paid in labor, goods, and money. Consider Browne's accounts with his household and tavern servant, Betsy Duty. Duty received her wages in money, shoes, snuff, stockings, and "two Linsey petty coats," each item assigned a monetary value in his ledger. Betsy also settled her brother Thomas's account with Browne. Browne himself assumed his customers' debts to third parties, while tavern debtors instructed their own debtors to pay Browne. In one such case, Edward Talbot instructed a Mr. Hardy to pay to Browne "the balance which you owe me."[47] Among more than one hundred customers represented in Martin Browne's 1790s ledgers, the vast majority bought on credit. Browne recorded interest charges in only seven cases. Perhaps for that reason, only one-quarter of his debtors had paid in full by the time Browne stopped making entries. Flexible credit combined with the ability to pay in various forms over multiple years made it possible for some people both to spend more time in taverns and to pursue a higher standard of living than they could otherwise have achieved.[48]

Yet although book debt helped keep patrons visiting, goods flowing, and households consuming, it did not always work to keepers' advantage. Extending credit and juggling many forms of payment eventually wore thin for Martin Browne. By 1805, he was attempting to clear his own debts and move to Kentucky. The tipping point for Browne may have involved his flour speculations, and yet his records suggest the tavern was also a drain. Erratic record-keeping ought not to have been a factor because Browne trained as a clerk in England before emigrating. Even so, in February 1796, he wrote that Thomas Burns's account "may have been ballanc'd." Thanks to sporadic payments and the commingling of tavern and other accounts, Browne could only "imagine" that Thomas Burns had paid his balance in an account that had stood open since 1789. One possible factor in Browne's accounting trouble was his widely shared habit of combining debts for tavern drinks with those for household quantities of alcohol and many other transactions. A 1792 law had decreed that Virginia keepers who extended more than five dollars of credit for tavern drinks to people who lived less than twenty miles away could not sue their neighbors for payment. Browne's accounts left him no easy way to identify which debts he could pursue through the courts. He may have rested his slim hopes on continuing to extend credit while pleading for payment from his debtors and for patience from his own creditors. Long after Browne's day, systematic double-entry bookkeeping remained the exception rather than the rule among tavern keepers, and archival materials suggest that keepers did not make a priority of documenting what they spent to provision or improve their taverns.[49]

Despite these accounting shortcomings, the lack of interest charges, and the many forms of payment, the transactions that wove through Browne's and other turn-of-the-century tavern ledgers had clearly defined monetary value. Well before the 1800s, keepers recorded the value of goods and services in shillings and pence, later switching to dollars and cents. At the same time, these exchanges remained deeply enmeshed in social relations because the unsecured credit that keepers offered their local customers hinged on reputation and the information contained in everything from gossip to dress and manners. Keepers had to keep their ears to the ground for information about individuals' solvency while gleaning what broader economic clues they could from newspapers, strangers, and general tavern talk.[50]

One of the topics about which keepers had to stay informed was the use and value of paper money. Where paper money was readily available, tavern-goers were more likely to pay in cash at the time of purchase for at least part of what they bought. In the 1800s and 1810s, Elkton's Joshua Richardson bought and sold a variety of farm goods, including oats, buckwheat, pigs, flour, and beef. Thanks to his location, he received a higher proportion of cash payments than someone like Martin Browne. Elkton had been saturated in commercial relations for decades and was home to at least one bank branch. Since many banks printed notes but were not equally sound in their financial or political capital, consumers did not always accept a bank note at face value. Depending on a bank's local reputation, its notes might trade at par or at a significant discount. The steady flow of leisure, political, and commercial travelers bound for Washington, Baltimore, Philadelphia, New York, and points beyond increased the likelihood that Richardson and his neighbors had the "monetary knowledge" to handle many different notes with ease. Richardson's ledger confirms this suspicion: only rarely did he annotate a discounted note in his ledger and without any indication of why or which bank had issued the note. For other discounted transactions, he may have written the agreed value on the notes themselves. As Joshua Greenberg argues, Americans found many ways, written and otherwise, to make bank notes communicate their variable value.[51]

In long-settled yet still-rural areas in the 1820s and 1830s, village and town keepers' business continued to reflect both their immediate economic context and broader developments in trade and transportation. In New York, the initial similarities between the taverns in Antwerp and Warsaw fade in considering the store side of the business. The keeper of the Antwerp tavern dealt in locally produced farm goods, such as potatoes, beef, and pork, but sold few manufactured goods besides alcohol. The Warsaw keeper sold a narrower but more discretionary selection of foodstuffs, including cheese, crackers, and sugar. Neither keeper had reason to stock a larger range of goods but for different reasons. In the mid-1820s, Antwerp was the poorer town, and its households did without many luxuries, although the more prosperous among the local farmers may have shopped in towns along the St. Lawrence River and Lake Ontario. By that time, Warsaw already had roughly twice the per-capita taxable property of Antwerp, considerably more horses per capita, and the money to provide more schooling for its children. It also supported at least three other taverns and multiple stores that did "considerable business," probably in goods that came overland from Buffalo or the Erie Canal. Locals used the tavern far more as a sociable resort than as a source of essential goods and credit. The contrast between the two towns had initially sharpened when the opening of the Erie Canal in 1825 dimmed Antwerp settlers' prospects, by comparison with those in easier reach of that instantly successful transportation artery. After 1840, the gap grew wider still because the opening of the Genesee Valley Canal gave Warsaw's residents safe and dependable water access to the Erie Canal.[52]

Farther south, the overlap between tavern-going and provisioning a household remained robust. In the mid-1840s, the accounts of the Eagle Tavern in Watkinsville, Georgia, document much trade in supplies useful for farming households, including manure, a literal by-product of the tavern's stagecoach traffic. The Eagle also furnished its neighbors with labor: the accounts included charges for plowing a garden, using the Eagle's horses and mules, and hiring human workers, probably enslaved people. Payments came in cash, sometimes by note of hand, and occasionally through labor or a third party's payment.[53] Around the same time in Greenville, Georgia, another county seat, keeper William Adair sold copious amounts of liquor and handled a wide array of local and nonlocal manufactured and agricultural products: many pounds of nails, tobacco, sugar, and coffee left his premises, along with shoes, wooden plank, lead, gunpowder, copperas (used in dyeing), and barrels. Adair also made small cash advances. On the rare occasions he noted credits in his daybook, they were usually in cash and worth less than a dollar.[54]

In newer western states and territories, the complementary relationship between tavern- and storekeeping continued to depend on proximity to major transportation routes and on the establishment of populations big enough to support stand-alone stores. Even quite small county seats could become commercial hubs on a modest scale, where tavern keepers vied with other retailers to supply local residents.[55] By the late 1830s, recently founded Decatur, Mississippi, had at least one store that supplied an extensive range of textiles and other goods used in making clothes, along with spices, books, small tools, soap, paper, and general "merchandise." Such a well-supplied store is noteworthy considering the county's small population: about 2,500 people in 1840, 20 percent of whom were enslaved and thus far less free to consume than other inhabitants. Yet Decatur sat a manageable thirty-some miles away from the village of Enterprise on the Chickasawhay River, which eventually fed into the Pascagoula River and into Mobile Bay. By contrast with the store, James Ellis's tavern in Decatur did a much more limited trade, usually in

TABLE 3.2 Percentage of customers purchasing tavern and other goods and services

	Meals or lodgings	Horse care	Alcohol	Other goods or services
Browne's Tavern, near Winchester, VA, 1803–1804	7.4	8.6	83.3	22.2
Richardson's Tavern, Elkton, MD, 1806–1814	20.0	20.8	45.8	71.7
Marriner's Tavern, Lewes, DE, 1812–1813	27.3	16.1	86.5	15.2
Warsaw Tavern, Warsaw, NY, 1830–1831	6.8	2.7	87.8	41.9
Ellis's Tavern, Decatur, MS, 1837–1839	73.3	30.0	50.6	36.7
Adair's Tavern, Greenville, GA, 1843–1844	1.4	0	73.8	57.6

Sources: Calculated from Browne Papers, Vol. 6; Elkton Ledger; Marriner Daybook; Warsaw Daybook; Craft and Tingle, *Old Account Book Entries, 1837–1841, Decatur, Newton County, Mississippi*; Adair Papers, Account Book, 1843–1844.

bulk foodstuffs such as meat, sugar, and coffee. Ellis often sold those items in large volumes, such as the eighty-three pounds of beef he provided to Silas C. Walker. As the head of a seven-person household that included an enslaved woman and a girl, Walker may have hoped to feed his household from this purchase or to consume some and resell the rest. As for Ellis, sales of this type accounted for over 40 percent of his gross sales.[56]

Well into the second third of the nineteenth century, tavern keepers continued to serve drinks and furnish their neighbors with household provisions. As tables 2 and 3 suggest, two patterns held true across a variety of settings. On the one hand, keepers sold alcohol more often than any other good or service, licensed or not. On the other hand, alcohol was not important to every patron, and it was not necessarily more significant in financial terms than keepers' other goods and services. In the absence of full information about what keepers spent to provision their taverns and stores, a definitive answer is impossible, but ledgers and daybooks suggest that keepers had good reason to stock a variety of goods: they sometimes grossed as much for their store goods as for alcohol, or even more. By contrast, even though providing meals, lodgings, and horse care was a requirement of the tavern keeper's license, it was less obvious that doing an extensive trade of that sort was essential to the keeper's prospects.[57]

TABLE 3.3 Frequency and gross value of tavern goods and services and other sales

	Alcohol		Meals, lodgings, and horse care		Nonlicensed goods and services	
	Frequency	Gross value	Frequency	Gross value	Frequency	Gross value
Browne Tavern, near Winchester, VA, 1803–1804	88.9	65.9	3.6	3.9	7.4	29.2
Richardson's Tavern, Elkton, MD, 1806–1814	27.3	1.7	11.8	1.7	51.4	93.6
Warsaw Tavern, Warsaw, NY, 1830–1831	82.1	43.3	3.3	0.7	14.6	64.6
Ellis's Tavern, Decatur, MS, 1837–1839	31.7	16.7	41.8	38.9	26.5	44.4
Adair's Tavern, Greenville, GA, 1843–1844	77.2	68.3	0.7	1.7	20.3	30.0

Sources: Calculated from Browne Papers, Vol. 6; Elkton Ledger; Warsaw Daybook; Craft and Tingle, *Old Account Book Entries, 1837–1841, Decatur, Newton County, MS*; Adair Papers, Account Book, 1843–1844.

Note: This table excludes Marriner's tavern because her account book did not record prices.

Whether they specialized in alcohol, sold diverse or limited store goods, or served many travelers, keepers persisted in conducting many of their transactions not for cash but on credit. Some keepers also speculated in other ventures as well, such as flour, slaves, internal improvements, manufactures, or banking. All these practices entailed considerable risk, and keepers' diverse sales and payments did not insulate them from panics and crashes. The depression that followed the panic of 1837, for instance, affected tavern keepers even if they had not invested in tavern improvements or other speculations. By the late 1830s, cash predominated on the credit side of the ledger of one anonymous Virginia keeper, but as banks failed, even the notes of still-functioning banks lost much of their value. Of sixty payments sampled from this ledger, thirty-eight were made in cash but rarely in full of patrons' debts.[58] In the South Carolina upcountry around the same time, partial payments by cash or note were also far more common than other forms, perhaps because some agricultural commodities had held their value even less well than some bank notes. Some patrons managed to pay up to 10 percent of their accumulated debt by the summer of 1838, but this keeper also noted multiple cases where customers made payments only after a justice of the peace got involved.[59]

When hard times began to improve, payment in full at the point of purchase remained but one of several options. In the mid-1840s, Georgia keeper William Adair accepted numerous payments in cash, but he still recorded payment in other forms, including corn, potatoes, pork, and poultry. And when he attempted to balance accounts with fourteen account holders in and after 1845, he noted eight were paid in full: two by note of hand, four by cash, and two by settlement. In the latter two cases, Adair may have accepted payment in multiple forms and perhaps forgave some of the debt to close these accounts. Yet neither the prevalence nor the vulnerability of bank notes had prompted this small-town keeper to give up on book debt. Instead, he and his patrons remained financially entangled over time.[60]

Throughout the period, hostile observers deplored the generous credit that keepers offered, while lawmakers curtailed keepers' right to sue their debtors. Offering drink on credit made it easy for people to drink too much and accumulate excess debt, but tavern keepers' sales also connected them and their neighbors to local, regional, and international trade circuits. With a stock of goods that traveled anywhere from a few to a few thousand miles, tavern keepers helped village and rural households consume items that had either been inaccessible or confined to the wealthiest families a generation ago. By carrying debt on their books for weeks, months, and even years without charging interest and by accepting payment in many forms, town and village keepers also helped their neighbors sell their labor and market their agricultural produce. The risks of all this mutual and market entanglement were real and more complex than those inherent in transacting in an alcohol-soaked environment. At the same time, many thoughtful contemporaries associated making, selling, and consuming goods and services, even in taverns, with individual and collective prosperity and with the day-to-day work of nation-building.[61]

The Privilege to Consume

While poor accounting practices and a volatile business cycle left many people unable to calculate or even imagine their financial risk with any accuracy, keepers and patrons continued to rely on what they read in others' appearance, conduct, and purchases. In terse yet revealing ways, account books illuminate how tavern transactions reflected and shaped notions of worth.

Tavern ledgers identified account holders, the people who were financially responsible for all the drinks, bacon, nails, and paper that keepers furnished. For legal reasons, married women and enslaved people were unlikely account holders, yet commerce often trumped the strict letter of the law. White women and Black men did not occupy space in taverns or ledgers on the same terms as white men, but their presence further complicated the notion that white manhood alone unlocked all the opportunities of tavern-going. Buying a peck of salt, fifty pounds of sugar, or a side of beef reified white men's position as household heads, a visible testament to their right and responsibility to make choices for themselves and for others. These dynamics took on additional dimensions in the presence of other white men who could view and judge. White women and people of color were not merely an audience for such dynamics, nor did their appearance in tavern ledgers serve only to highlight their relative social, economic, and legal subordination. As workers, they moved openly throughout taverns, which sometimes brought them into focus in tavern accounts. Occasionally, they appeared as economic agents and even as householders.[62]

Sarah Marriner's daybook both illuminates the paucity of Black account holders and suggests the various positions they may have occupied in her tavern and the wider community. She named three Black men, each only once, in nearly a year of entries, although nearly 15 percent of the local population were free people of color. "Solomon Gibs, Negro" was a known quantity in the neighborhood, having lived in the area as the head of a household since at least 1800. "Moses Harris, Negro" may also have been familiar to Marriner and some of her regular customers: the 1810 census identifies a possible residence in Murderkill Hundred, some thirty miles from Lewes. Both Gibs and Harris drank at least once at Marriner's in the year covered by the daybook, and it would not be surprising if Gibs, at least, appeared in and around the tavern more often than the daybook indicated. Marriner held the third man, Jack Nicny, responsible for breaking a tumbler but felt no need to record how the accident had happened. Since he consumed nothing, perhaps he worked in her household and she charged the glass against his wages.[63]

Marriner's daybook lists no women among over three hundred account holders, but this absence meant less than it appears. Women traveling with men did not as a rule get named in ledgers, but a hint to their presence sometimes survives. In May 1813, for instance, some "Ladi[e]s" came to Marriner's with a "Gentelman." Besides these unnamed strangers, Betty was the only woman in the daybook, and Marriner knew her well enough not to identify her further. Betty visited multiple times in the summer and fall of 1812. Each time, the daybook associated her with grog and cider charged to Jeams (or James) Holland. Did Betty consume the drinks herself, or did she deliver them to Holland? Was she his daughter, wife, servant, apprentice, or slave? We do not know, in part because Marriner or her proxy almost certainly *did* know and had no need to write it down. Marriner's daybook was equally silent about any women who labored in the tavern. Even Marriner herself is a nebulous presence. Yet Betty and the anonymous ladies cannot have been the only women ever to cross Marriner's threshold. Her female neighbors could easily have stopped by to pass the time of day—even if they did not come to drink—pick up news about the threatened invasion, or, in peaceful times, attend a social gathering without ever appearing in Marriner's ledger.[64]

The routine exchanges of goods, services, and labor sometimes incorporated white women or people of color with no evident fuss, but the political valence of such moments varied. The presence of white women or Black men in taverns could affirm racial, gender, and legal hierarchies. Often, both their transactions and how keepers documented them marked a subordination rooted in domestic dependence, wage labor, or slavery. Stretching over more than a decade, Martin Browne's accounts include multiple references to Black people. "Negro Wench Pegg" appears in passing in an explanation of how young Andy Simpson came to buy a "pocket Bottle of whiskey." According to Browne's entry, Andy claimed he had acquired the bottle on his mother's orders while transporting Pegg from one place to another.[65] Some cases involving Black men and whiskey suggest a unilateral favor, something like a gratuity within the context of slavery. Thus, Browne recorded purchases of alcohol "for Coe's Isaac," the possessive suggesting that Isaac was enslaved and by whom. He also noted that Matthew Wright acquired a quart of whiskey "pr order of Miss Eliza Wright for Old Joe." Several unnamed Black men came and went to fetch whiskey at the behest of white account holders. Roughly 20 percent of the county's population was enslaved, so the occasional appearance of enslaved men at Browne's cannot have surprised the keeper or his other patrons. Many of these appearances created small opportunities to articulate local hierarchies as Browne knew them. He noted the mature female authority behind some of Matthew Wright's and Andy Simpson's purchases. He inscribed the hierarchies of race, gender, and bondage in his references to Andy Simpson's whiskey bottle: he did not have to refer to the enslaved Pegg at all, nor did he have to call her a "Negro Wench," but he did both.[66]

Martin Browne also documented Black men as account holders at a time when free people of color made up less than 1 percent of Frederick County's population.[67] Based on his lack of last name and his classical first name, "Black Hercules" was probably born into slavery: some planters gave enslaved children similar neoclassical names, usually in mockery. Hercules may still have been enslaved when he bought two shillings' worth of rum from Browne, which he paid for with nine days of work and cash. Perhaps he had the limited freedom of hiring himself out, or perhaps he was now free yet pinned to his slave name in Browne's accounts. "Black Cato" showed up in Browne's book as the recipient of cash which Browne advanced on behalf of "Black Robbin." Robbin appears to have been a skilled harness maker: part of his debt stemmed from the cost of a pair of chains that Browne had returned and an overcharge for a pair of new harness traces. Between mid-1789 and early 1792, Robbin made additional appearances in the ledger when he visited Browne's for liquor and sundries. On one of those visits, he might have met up with "Black Manuel," who visited Browne's multiple times in 1789 for rum, molasses, and cider, accumulating debts amounting to almost two pounds in the process. Manuel paid part of his debt in work and cash but the majority in agricultural produce, including wheat, rye, and potatoes. As far as the ledger reveals, Browne took for granted Manuel's right to dispose of this property. Like Browne's white customers, Manuel received goods on credit and made payments in a staggered sequence that kept patron and keeper connected by debt. Although visiting white-dominated taverns posed real dangers, for Manuel, Robbin, Hercules, Cato, and some of the other people of color mentioned in account books, tavern-going formed part of their strategies for meeting their economic needs. Perhaps they also seized the opportunity to socialize with kin or friends working in the kitchen, stable, or fields. In other words, tavern-going sometimes functioned for them much like it did for white men but with greater inherent risk and usually without the third leg in the stool of white men's vernacular citizenship: the prerogative of participating in formal politics.[68]

White women also appeared in Martin Browne's books although their written presence understated their involvement. The constant presence of wife Molly and daughter Juliana—their work in the tavern, at the loom, or in the kitchen gardens—is implied in notes appended to others' accounts. Juliana was "present" when Martin settled with Betsy Duty, who worked in the tavern for several months. Molly may have done the weaving that furnished Betsy with the petticoats she took in partial payment of her wages. Two additional women, Mrs. Sears and Miss Wright, were also peripherally involved in the Brownes' textile production. Molly Browne appeared again in connection with Mrs. Simpson, a rare female account holder. Mrs. Simpson secured bacon and labor from Browne and paid Molly in beef and two heifers. Mrs. Simpson also made thirty-five purchases of alcohol between April and December 1803.[69]

While female account holders were rare in village and town taverns, within that small group, Mrs. Simpson was not unusual in buying whiskey in quantities suitable for taking home. Simpson usually purchased whiskey by the quart. Those quarts could have furnished several members of her household with an acknowledged whiskey ration, fueled a not-so-secret addiction, or been used to acquire yet other goods. Whiskey was also medicinal: Browne annotated one sale of three pints as taking place "at night, the old Lady at their House having Tooth drawn." Whatever Mrs. Simpson consumed within her own household, she did not buy whiskey to linger at the bar and drink. Indeed, Mrs. Simpson rarely appeared at the tavern "Herself." Instead, she dispatched a third person: usually Calvin, sometimes Charlotte or Lotty—possibly enslaved people in the Simpson household—and sometimes "her son Andy." Mrs. Simpson's physical absence and fiscal presence spoke volumes. In this period and for decades to come, most contemporaries regarded public drinking as a masculine prerogative and especially a white man's, even though some urban taverns had their share of female drinkers. For someone like Mrs. Simpson, however, not drinking at the bar was hardly a social liability: quite the opposite. Instead, by drinking at home—if she drank at all—and transacting through subordinates, she provisioned her household while both manifesting and protecting her reputation as a reputable female householder.[70]

A generation and more later, middling and wealthy white women who visited their local taverns did so either for special social occasions, in which case they rarely entered the ledger, or because of the tavern's retail side. What white women bought in taverns reflected their gender and domestic responsibilities. In the early 1820s in Louisa County, Virginia, for instance, women dispatched kinsmen and slaves to the Traveller's Rest to buy goods for both personal and household use, including alcohol by the gallon and both sugar and eight-penny nails by the pound. Unusually, Katharine P. White visited in person. A middle-aged woman, householder, and substantial enslaver, she had considerable social and financial capital. When she went to the Traveller's Rest for calico, she did so not because she had no one to send but because she wanted to see and handle it for herself; as Ellen Hartigan-O'Connor argues, white women had long been comfortable with this form of skilled consumption.[71] Nearly a quarter century later, William Adair had several female account holders. They appeared in his books multiple times over a period of years, buying many of the same goods that men bought, including whiskey, cheese, molasses, lead, plank, and nails. Also like their male peers, women received credit and paid in varied ways. Rebecka Moffitt, for one, bought three and a half pounds of nails, perhaps using them to maintain fences or improve buildings, and paid cash in full over two years later.[72]

Buying patterns differed where white women had access to at least one well-stocked retail store. In Warsaw, New York, where the presence of several stores limited what the tavern keeper tried to sell, Barbara Utter, the head of an eight-person household, was the sole woman to appear in the tavern accounts at the end of 1830. Utter bought only whiskey, usually by the half gallon, and she sent a kinsman to transact for her.[73] In Decatur, Mississippi, James Ellis's tavern stocked a wider range of goods but had almost no female customers. By contrast, several women made comparatively frequent purchases at the Decatur store, buying a dozen types of textiles, dyes, needles, thread, ribbons, medicines, soaps, paper, books, metal goods, and dishes. The one woman in the tavern daybook, Mrs. Lena Moore, made a single purchase, but that one transaction, a quart of whiskey and fifty-seven pounds of beef, bespoke her responsibility for household provisioning.[74]

Whether by proxy or in person, by choice or by necessity, a small number of white women and people of color entered taverns' economic orbit. Even as taverns became more complex in their internal organization, women's transactions remained knowable to the white male majority gathered at and around the bar. In the smallest taverns, a person who wanted a bushel of corn or a pound of nails entered through the same door as everyone else. Even if the store goods were kept in a distinct place, such as the loft of Mrs. Dickie's western Pennsylvania tavern, a customer had to speak to the keeper or their agent, who was usually to be found at the bar.[75] In a slightly larger tavern, such as the 1820s iteration of the Eagle Tavern in Watkinsville, Georgia, the keeper had the space to set up his store in one room and the bar in the other (see figure 3.2). At the Eagle, the store and the bar each had their own door to the street. Yet these doors were mere feet apart, and the rooms shared an interior door. Whenever this door stood open, people in one space could both see and hear people in the other. In such spaces, female and Black patrons became known as consumers, whether in person or through proxies who were familiar to the keeper or carried written instructions.[76]

By the 1830s, wealthy female account holders likely had first- or second-hand knowledge of improving taverns whose keepers solicited ladies' and families' patronage. In this context, they likely read their own absence from the barroom as a privileged choice, which set them above most white men, at least in moral terms. By the mid-1840s, the combination of road and tavern

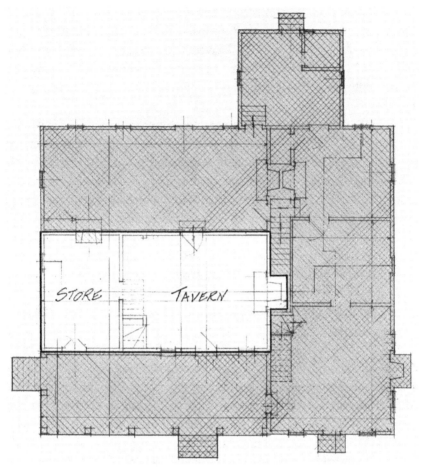

FIGURE 3.2 Floor plan of the Eagle Tavern, Watkinsville, Georgia. This drawing suggests the internal organization of the ground floor of the Eagle Tavern before and after its expansion in the 1830s. In the 1820s, when the tavern had a two-room footprint, the keeper operated the tavern and the store in separate rooms connected by an interior door. Patrons who wished to reach the tavern's upper rooms did so via the staircase in the barroom. Drawing by Christa Kelly after Thomas G. Little architectural drawings, ms4249, Hargrett Rare Book and Manuscript Library, University of Georgia Libraries.

improvements could well have made it congenial for white women to shop in tavern stores such as Adair's. His accounts suggest that his female customers may not have relied on proxies when they shopped for store goods, as their mothers' and especially their grandmothers' generation had done.[77] Propertied white women's tavern consumption marked them as people with resources and household responsibilities who were both like and unlike the masculine majority. In contrast, free Black patrons could not so easily interpret their exclusion from barrooms as a choice, even if they genuinely preferred the quiet of a private parlor or the informal friendliness of a Black-staffed tavern kitchen. As far as enslaved Black tavern users were concerned, their presence could be both illegal and under the aegis of their enslaver: a testament to taverns' ability to both cut across and reinforce the hierarchies beyond their doors.[78]

Rare yet revealing, white women's and Black men's transactions for alcohol and other household staples complicated the meanings of tavern commerce for white men. The usual absence of respectable, propertied white women from town and village taverns, especially those whose keepers had not made major architectural improvements, freed—or compelled—white men to focus on establishing their place in an often-contested masculine pecking order. At the same time, the fact that white women and people of color occasionally visited taverns in person or by proxy for themselves and their households signaled that they contributed to the same economic networks on which white men relied. For white men, the presence of these other tavern patrons increased the stakes of tavern-going as an index of and a prop to their own mobility and transactional authority.

TAVERNS' CRITICS OFTEN SUGGESTED that tavern-going was a waste of money, time, human potential, and even life. The gallons of whiskey and other drinks that crossed tavern bars and store counters confirm that the early republic had good reason to worry about drunkenness and its consequences. Yet to focus on alcohol and drinking culture alone, as temperance critics often did, is to overlook many other aspects of tavern-going in early nineteenth-century towns and villages. As they extended credit and negotiated cash, notes, labor, and a wide range of goods, keepers ensured that their taverns remained more than dram shops even when they were not in great demand as travelers' refuges. In such taverns, white men—and small numbers of female and Black patrons—could provision their households and build up networks of obligations, information, and interests. White men in particular benefited from being able to satisfy multiple needs in one place. Equally important was the chance to be seen in public as a person with the opportunity and authority to move about while managing their goods, credit, time, and labor.

For town and village tavern keepers, casual storekeeping articulated well with the licensed trade in alcohol and accommodations. If keepers sold groceries and dry goods, they could both increase their sales to drinkers and do business with people who rarely or never drank in taverns. By accepting diverse forms of payment, keepers further facilitated their own retail sidelines and related occupations such as farming. While the credit they extended underwrote public and private drinking, keepers also created markets for local products and labor, supplied their neighbors with necessities and some luxuries, and eased an often-tight money supply.

Through transactions large and small and through networks of exchange and labor that sometimes lasted for years, tavern-keeping and tavern-going helped shape the circulation of people, goods, information, and money. While some of the patterns in tavern accounts looked broadly similar across nearly a century of dramatic change in the nation's population, territory, and economic engines, taverns did not represent a hidebound corner of the early republican economy. Instead, tavern transactions connected individuals to each other and neighborhoods to national and even global trade networks, forging connections that were both imagined and as tangible as quires of paper and bottles of physic. The keepers involved in these networks, especially those who invested in improvements, stretched the meanings of tavern-going and the practice of vernacular citizenship in the nation's small cities, towns, and villages.[79]

CHAPTER FOUR

Convenient to Business

Entrepreneurial Networking and Innovation

In 1834, Hector H. Crane advertised his Eagle Tavern in Rochester, New York, as an "airy and commodious" accommodation that was also "central and convenient to business." Favorably situated on the main street through town, across the way from the courthouse and a bank, the Eagle was "convenient to business" in more than its location. Men in multiple lines of business boarded there, including attorneys, physicians, merchants, judges, clerks, surveyors, bank tellers, machinists, and a professor of music. Since many of these men listed no separate place of employment in the city directory, anyone who hoped to do business with them would likely have sought them out at the Eagle. People came to taverns like the Eagle when their affairs required them to travel, negotiate sales, promote products and services, and meet with clients, customers, or investors. Smaller and less favorably situated taverns across the country also served people who were pursuing endeavors ranging from land speculation and corporate investments to commercial entertainment and confidence tricks.[1]

The early republic witnessed a veritable explosion in the ways people made their livings, even though agriculture absorbed most of the nation's labor power through 1860. North and south, agricultural production itself underwent rapid changes linked to aggressive territorial expansion and shifts in the ways landowners used land, labor, and machines.[2] Over the same period, the number of different occupations listed in any good-sized city's directory grew severalfold. The variety of goods and services available even in modestly sized towns also grew, as did the numbers of specialized retailers and providers.[3] In all corners of this expansive, creative but also volatile and often brutal economy, financial success rested on many factors, including individual initiative, access to credit, the willingness to use force to tap the nation's abundant resources, and the law in all its complexity.[4]

People engaged in enterprises as different as manufacturing and commercial entertainment also needed places to conduct business and ways to communicate with potential customers for their goods or services. They needed a means to act at a distance and often relied on informal associates to do so. Not least, they looked for cultural and social contexts in which their ventures might be welcomed, or at least not rejected out of hand because they were strangers or because of pejorative assumptions about their trade. Infrastructural development would eventually make it easier to satisfy some of these needs. Improved transportation reduced the impact of geographic sprawl, while steam-powered printing presses increased the volume and reach of commercial intelligence. The invention of the telegraph, which first connected Baltimore to Washington, D.C., in 1844, further enhanced the speed and reach of communications.[5] By the late nineteenth century, a growing number of corporations found that they gained control and saved money if they handled transactions such as acquiring raw materials and gathering information internally, not via the marketplace. In some sectors, enormous vertically integrated corporations resulted, such as railroad companies that owned their own network of hotels. In the first half of the century, however, most firms remained small and many of their basic transactions occurred not in-house but through market-based transactions with individuals or other firms. In this context, taverns and their keepers helped people in many lines of work address material, informational, and social needs, both in conjunction and in tension with the world of print.[6]

In the early republic, individuals, family businesses, partnerships, and corporations all had occasion to use the kinds of supportive services that taverns offered.[7] Endeavors in manufacturing, agriculture, the professions, entertainment, financial services, and education each needed space, networks, and information. Taverns and keepers were also useful across the legal and moral spectrum of capitalist possibilities. People with exacting obligations to the law, such as executors and other people acting in a fiduciary capacity, used taverns for business purposes. So did people who stretched or broke the boundaries of the law, including speculators and counterfeiters. Wherever they fell on the legitimacy spectrum, people who were trying to market innovative goods and services valued taverns not only because these spaces attracted potential consumers and clients but also because people came to town and village taverns in part to learn the news from lately arrived strangers and mails. Leveraging the network and reputation of a locally respected keeper mattered at a time when authorities from the county courthouse to Washington, D.C., drew shifting and contradictory boundaries between proper and improper forms of economic activity.[8] Tavern settings helped blur distinctions between conservative and speculative investments, between respectable and disreputable conduct, and even between those who could move freely and take risks in pursuit of a livelihood and those who could not. Not all taverns were well situated to provide strangers with accommodations and locals with places to meet and work, however, nor were all keepers influential enough to loan much credibility to would-be business users. The presence of many different users, as at Crane's Eagle Tavern in Rochester, thus hinged on and testified to a tavern's material improvements, its location, and its reputation.[9]

People who used taverns for business often depended on keepers to act in formal and informal ways as their agents. Keepers dispensed information, handled money, took names, and made connections. Self-interest suggested several reasons for keepers to involve themselves in other people's business. First, these business users paid for their use of taverns, sometimes in rent and sometimes in drink, food, or other charges. Their presence also helped frame taverns in the public imagination as sites of economic opportunity and innovation. Even as temperance advocates insisted that tavern drinking led to alcoholic excess, corroded drinkers' character, and undermined their financial prospects, many Americans harnessed taverns to economic innovation and growth.[10]

The people examined here suggest the breadth of taverns' business users. They include executors, sheriffs, land speculators, sellers of patented machines, corporate directors, stockholders, performers, teachers, and counterfeiters. Separately and together, their ventures illuminate the use of taverns as physical spaces and nodes within commercial and informational networks, which made taverns an important component of the nation's entrepreneurial growth in the early republic. At the same time, taverns' use by people in many different types of business enhanced their value for the people who used them most easily—namely, those white men who had a propensity for risk-taking and discretion over their own mobility, property, and time.

Legitimating the Transactional Landscape

Taverns' role in the early republic's commercial landscape stretched far beyond keepers' interactions with their own customers. Private travelers by road used taverns as landmarks guiding them from place to place. Many entrepreneurs also relied on familiar taverns to put themselves and their ventures on the map. Using taverns as landmarks for their own businesses, entrepreneurs oriented themselves both spatially and in relationship to other businesses and their commercial networks. For related reasons, taverns made sense as venues. As public spaces in both the official and everyday sense of the term, taverns made appropriate sites for auctions and any sales that had to take place in the public eye for the sake of fair competition. As landmarks and venues, taverns both drew people in and disseminated information outward.

At a time when city and town maps rarely plotted businesses and city directories often included no or imprecise addresses, retailers and tradesmen used taverns to direct people to their own businesses. Richmond publisher T. Nicholson told readers of the *Virginia Almanack* that he could be found "two doors above the Eagle-Tavern," which distinguished him from another Richmond publisher, "next door below the Columbia Tavern."[11] Storekeepers advertising their wares likewise told their readers to find them "next door to," "opposite," or "west of" particular taverns in midsize towns across the country. A "Ladies Habit Maker" in Gallatin, Tennessee, informed the public that he could be found "one door above Mr. Robert Mitchel's tavern." Even business advertisements that included a street address sometimes kept the tavern referent. When a New Hampshire grocer promoted his Concord store in the late 1840s, he included both his street address and the description, "two doors north of Phenix Hotel." Such persistent uses of taverns as landmarks involved a more-than-spatial orientation: they encoded certain taverns as both appropriate for and "central to business," as Rochester's Hector Crane claimed about his Eagle Tavern.[12]

A closely related indication of taverns' practical and symbolic value came from their use as venues for transactions over which the law had special oversight. Like its English precursors, American property law insisted that certain sales be conducted with scrupulous attention to transparency and probity. Every time a property owner died, the process of settling the estate involved multiple legal checks on the individuals who, acting as executors or administrators, shepherded that estate through the elaborate probate process. Throughout, executors and administrators had to document their care in resolving the competing claims of creditors, debtors, and heirs fairly and in the prescribed order. Similar guardrails constrained the acts of legal guardians, trustees, and sheriffs, who often sold others' property as part of a legal process to settle unpaid debts. Whenever a person acting in one of these fiduciary capacities sought to sell property, the law imposed special obligations intended to secure a fair price at a competitive sale. Estate sales and auctions following a foreclosure usually required a well-advertised public event, held in a location likely to attract multiple bidders.[13]

Reputable taverns on major streets or at significant crossroads hosted both public notices and public sales. Legal texts often required posting notices about upcoming public sales in "the usual and most public places" in the neighborhood. More than a mere landmark, the sort of tavern suitable for posting notices tended to stock newspapers and attract the kind of customers who might both spread the word and bid themselves. In addition, such taverns offered spaces suitable for public sales, such as the front steps, porch, or yard. While taverns' outdoor and public character satisfied the auctioneer's need to attract a big audience, sizable taverns also had interior rooms where the parties to a transaction might negotiate the terms of a purchase or finalize paperwork.[14] As sites embedded in local networks of sociability and obligation, taverns did not guarantee competitive bidding or fair dealing, however. A creditor might find that his debtor's property sold for far less than expected. If the debtor had many connections in the neighborhood, they might act together to constrain the bidding so that a family member could buy the property at a low price. This dynamic was especially likely when the creditor did not also have significant local standing. Fair or fraudulent, such outcomes made clear that although taverns were legitimate public venues, they were not neutral ground.[15]

Locally prominent town and village taverns hosted auctions for ordinary commercial purposes as well as estate and foreclosure sales well into the nineteenth century, even as large cities and commercially important towns turned to quasi-professional auctioneers and dedicated auction houses. Boston and New York each had at least one auction room before the revolution, and Charleston had an auction house no later than 1783. By 1815, the much smaller town of Fredericksburg, Virginia, supported at least one professional auctioneer. The emergence of urban auction houses stemmed less from an aversion to taverns than from the increasing importance of wholesale auctions as a means for retailers to supply their stores.[16] In smaller towns and villages, by contrast, taverns remained commonplace as auction venues. Such activities found favor with the law even as temperance thinking increased its hold on public and private behavior. Nowhere was this pattern stronger than in New England. In 1830, for example, when a probate court judge in western Massachusetts ordered the public vendue of real estate belonging to a man who had been adjudged a "lunatick," the sale occurred at a tavern, and public notices appeared in the *Berkshire Journal*, a local newspaper friendly to temperance.[17] In regions where towns were fewer and farther between, such as the South, real estate auctions were more likely to be held on the property itself. Even so, taverns remained in occasional use as auction sites and as venues for negotiations and depositions in ongoing lawsuits.[18]

The widespread reliance on taverns for business that at once required an audience and remained subject to legal scrutiny meant that white women, too, resorted to taverns for estate sales. When acting as executors or administrators of their husbands' or other relatives' estates, women had the same obligations as any man in the equivalent role. Neither law nor custom prevented white women from working through, with, and even in taverns to fulfill them. Anna Maria Hollyday of Easton, Maryland, chose Mrs. Troth's tavern as the site for auctioning land that she may have inherited from her husband's estate. In her public notice, she named two men as her agents, with the stipulation that she would "annex A GENERAL WARRANTY to every deed," perhaps signaling that the men would conduct the auction, while she attended to the paperwork.[19] Like professional slave dealers, executors also used taverns for slave auctions. A tavern was especially appropriate in the case of a "young man" sold by a Virginia widow's agent because the unnamed man had been working in a local tavern for several years. Advertised as possessing the skills and reputation of an "excellent dining room servant," perhaps he eventually found the means to turn his tavern intelligence to his own interest. Perhaps he even had an opportunity to share some information with fifteen other men, women, and children belonging to another estate, whom the agent auctioned off at the same tavern that day. From the agent's perspective, stacking the sales at this location likely fanned interest and facilitated attendance among local farmers, slave dealers, and their agents.[20]

Whether Black women also made use of tavern venues in a fiduciary capacity is less clear. Although some free Black families acquired enough property to go through the probate process, they did not necessarily see taverns as good venues for their estate sales. The possibility was greatest in a city such as Charleston, where free Black families accumulated significant property and a few kept notable public accommodations. Yet cautious Black executors and administrators might have considered a tavern or hotel an unwise and even provocative venue. White men who were prone to rowdy behavior might too easily be inspired to disruptive or violent conduct if confronted with evidence of Black prosperity in a tavern setting.[21]

Speculating in Land

Another type of auction often associated with taverns in the early republic concerned the sale not of private property but of public lands. In the decades following the revolution, Americans hastened to privatize millions of acres of land over which the United States claimed sovereignty through a combination of economic coercion, military force, and diplomatic negotiation in both good and bad faith. Whereas waves of land speculators and settlers meant misery for many hundreds of thousands of Indigenous and enslaved people, many white Americans pinned their hopes for financial security on western land. In some states, landownership carried additional weight, being the threshold for full political citizenship.[22] More intoxicating still, land could not only be lived on, improved, partitioned, and bequeathed to one's heirs but also speculated in and mortgaged. In boom times, land speculation could be the means to a quick fortune. Speculators and would-be settlers first devoured massive tracts within the contested borders of the thirteen states. After the Louisiana Purchase, Americans took for granted that most of the new territories would ultimately end up in private hands. When public land went on the block, taverns provided accommodations to would-be speculators and settlers, hosted sales, and facilitated efforts to manipulate prices.[23]

The roles that taverns played in supporting land speculation depended on location. In the east, land speculators interested in faraway tracts often gathered in prominent urban taverns to promote joint land ventures. In 1786, notices in the *Continental Journal* invited veterans and "other good citizens who wish to become adventurers" in the Ohio Country to a meeting at Boston's Bunch of Grapes tavern. This meeting led to the founding of the Ohio Company of Associates, which paid one million dollars for one and a half million acres of land in the Ohio portion of the Northwest Territory. The Bunch of Grapes was an appropriate venue for such a meeting thanks to its long reputation and its multiple uses. For years after its founding, the Ohio Company's Boston-area shareholders continued to meet there and in other local taverns. As places where people visited on business, strangers met by happenstance, and alcohol sometimes encouraged risk-taking, such taverns offered many opportunities to recruit investors for real estate combinations.[24] As surveyor Joseph Ellicott pointed out, savvy land companies also built taverns, mills, and similar improvements on their vast holdings. These essential institutions attracted settlers, whose investments would further increase the value of yet-unsold land.[25]

Well into the nineteenth century, potential land speculators and settlers had recourse to taverns even as they availed themselves of new printed materials to aid their research and land purchases. Men in search of land could consult a growing wealth of geographic, economic, and demographic information in newspapers, maps, gazetteers, and booster literature, often available to them in taverns. They could buy shares in land lotteries, such as one drawn at Richmond's Eagle Hotel for lands near the Dismal Swamp Canal in Virginia. While at the Eagle, a hotel much frequented by Richmond's sociable risk-takers and businessmen, would-be purchasers could also "confide their land business" to a land agent such as Henry O. Middleton, who proposed to visit "the Western Counties throughout Virginia, Kentucky, and Ohio" and offered "every benefit" of his firsthand knowledge to potential investors.[26]

Men who planned to settle on the land they bought often preferred to gather their own firsthand intelligence. As they explored, they stopped in taverns for refreshment and information. Because wives, sisters, mothers, and daughters rarely joined their menfolk on such ventures, their absence freed men to pass their time in whatever tavern spaces they preferred and to talk as much as they liked to any men they found about land, geography, farming prospects, infrastructure, prices, and the virtues of various neighborhoods. Sometimes the mere fact of meeting others on the same quest solidified men's enthusiasm for a particular location. While exploring the area around Huntsville, Alabama, in 1818, Virginia's John Campbell happened to meet "a number of young Virginians with who I am intimately acquainted" in a tavern. The men's "cordial" encounter helped convince Campbell to "not think of Tennessee." A year later, Campbell had settled in Huntsville and had been named secretary to Alabama's constitutional convention, an opportunity even more unavailable to his female relatives than the original exploratory trip.[27]

Not all such speculative encounters were as happenstantial as Campbell claimed about his own. Wherever great public land sales were imminent—as they were in Huntsville during Campbell's visit—taverns in the vicinity teemed with men keen to find good land at low prices. In the 1830s, enormous tracts went up for sale from Georgia to Mississippi, for example, following protracted state and federal campaigns to dispossess the Creek, Cherokee, Chickasaw, and Choctaw Nations. In 1833, many white men flooded into the village of Cocchuma, Mississippi, for one such sale, at which 250,000 acres were offered up. A significant proportion of the buyers ended up joining forces with or buying land from the Cocchuma Land Company. Founded for the purpose shortly before the official sales began, the company operated out of Mr. Pratt's tavern. Like others of its ilk, the company hoped to engross a substantial percentage of the public land for sale. To do so cheaply, it strove to enlist as many buyers as possible to reduce competition and thus prices. Once the public sales concluded, it and similar companies turned around and auctioned off much of their new holdings in a competitive environment, reaping great profit in the process.[28]

The questionable activities of federal land officials at this and other public sales in the 1830s triggered congressional investigations. The Cocchuma Land Company had allegedly purchased three-quarters of the public lands offered at Cocchuma, and Congress wanted to know whether the officials who conducted the public sales had conspired with the company to depress competition and cheat the federal treasury. How and where the Cocchuma company had organized thus became a pertinent question. Witnesses testified that the company had originally formed "in the south room of the upper story of the tavern of Mr. Pratt." What began in the relative privacy of an upper room could not have succeeded, however, unless "its existence was generally known of." After all, the company's prospects depended on absorbing as many buyers as possible before the sales began. To this end, the company relied on the tavern's public character to spread the word. Multiple witnesses testified that a leader of the combination "called the attention of the people, before the tavern door." The same taverns that helped speculators stifle competitive bidding in one instance served to excite it in another. According to tavern keeper Robert W. Carr, a "company of speculators" who had bought public lands at Columbus, Mississippi, auctioned them off at his tavern just a few days later.[29]

From Congress's point of view, the rub was not the involvement of tavern spaces and keepers but whether the federal land agents had knowingly acted against the public interest. From this perspective, the fact that the federal land officers "appeared to be boarding" at Pratt's tavern tended to undermine the claim that they had been unaware of the land company's machinations. From the vantage point of the other men in and around the tavern, however, it was not so obvious that these on-the-spot land companies were engaged in illegal dealings. They may have reasoned that since the land officers must have witnessed the company's planning and allowed the sale to go ahead, the process was licit, or licit enough. Moreover, since groups of men attending an auction easily whipped each other up into a land-buying frenzy, acting together might have seemed like a necessary and even virtuous precaution to men of small capital. The would-be buyers also heard from company agents such as R. J. Walker that their desire for good land at low prices was perfectly just and reasonable. Walker told them that "it had always been the wish of the President, for the people to get the lands at $1.25 per acre." With such assurances, the men who gathered at Pratt's tavern in Cocchuma and Carr's tavern in Columbus in the 1830s had as much reason to think themselves good citizens as those who had assembled at the Bunch of Grapes in Boston to speculate in the Ohio territory nearly half a century before. Whatever the sins of federal officialdom, white men who were eager to speculate in western lands understood that taverns could be places to gather information, raise capital, and sometimes, collaborate in pursuit of their personal dreams for improvement.[30]

Incorporating Capital

Much like land speculators, corporations chartered to start banks, build roads, and erect factories found taverns useful places in which to recruit and consult investors. Americans were of mixed minds about incorporation early in the century; one might even say that corporations looked as legitimate and as questionable as many real estate speculative combinations. At first, Americans knew corporations as legal entities authorized by state legislatures to accomplish a specific public good, such as building a bridge. Incorporation might include a monopoly privilege, such as the exclusive right to operate a toll road in a particular area. Some corporations also received public monies because of the value they promised to bring to the community. Although such privileges made many contemporaries uneasy about the blending of public authority and private profit, incorporation became increasingly popular and, eventually, easy to achieve. Initially, incorporation required a special act of the state legislature, but New York paved the way toward the widespread adoption of general incorporation statutes, which made the process a matter of routine administration. New York also stretched the notion of public good, extending eligibility for general incorporation first to colleges and medical societies and then to turnpike and textile companies after the turn of the century.[31]

However created, the corporation had important advantages as a form of business organization. Like joint stock companies, corporations could raise capital by selling shares but had the added advantage of limiting the investors' personal liability for corporate losses. For many corporations, especially those that were relatively small in capital, investors, organizational complexity, and geographic reach, tavern spaces and networks represented an important resource. Gathering in taverns helped directors and investors with important operational tasks, including raising capital, gathering and disseminating information, managing costs, and making internal decisions.[32]

To mobilize capital, a new corporation needed not only the imprimatur of the state but also a means to get the word out to potential investors who would buy shares. Many corporations relied on a hybrid strategy that combined print media, correspondence, word of mouth, and physical space. Newspaper advertisements told the public where they could go to inspect the articles of incorporation and subscribe their names in corporate books, often the most prominent taverns in the neighborhoods where the directors expected to find capital. Early manufacturing corporations often raised the bulk of their capital in one place and invested it somewhere else with the required water power or other natural resources. At the turn of the century, the New Hampshire Iron Factory Company operated in the village of Franconia, but most of its investors lived 150 miles away, in the Boston area. Accordingly, the company advertised its operations in Boston newspapers and conducted its meetings in Boston taverns.[33] Many costly internal improvement projects also depended on urban capital. A project to improve the navigation of the Mohawk River in New York, for one, led to the forming of the Mohawk Navigation Company, which relied on investors in New York City, some two hundred miles away. The company's favorite venue, Cornelius Bradford's New York Coffee House, was a familiar haunt for New York merchants and bankers. Somewhat later, the early railroad corporations likewise drew much of their capital from city folk. As Jon Majewski argues, most of the investors in central Pennsylvania's railroads lived in Philadelphia and New York City, beyond the railroads' service area. These investors anticipated direct benefits from owning stocks, namely, dividend payments and their stocks' potential appreciation.[34]

Once a corporation launched its operations, the regular cycle of business meetings also brought corporate officers and investors to taverns. Although some decisions could be made via correspondence or by agents and much information circulated in print, face-to-face meetings and their associated public visibility remained important when corporations needed to elect new directors, solicit shareholders' approval, or raise additional capital. Most small corporations could not afford to invest their scant capital in headquarters spacious enough to host large meetings. Since many investors had to travel to attend, taverns made practical, reliable, and comparatively inexpensive venues for corporate meetings. At the same time, holding meetings in taverns multiplied the opportunities to see and be seen, which represented a passive means to mobilize financial and social capital. Meetings of the "friends" of Alexandria's Farmers' Bank took place at local taverns. Richardson's stage tavern in Elkton, Maryland, hosted bank elections and held checks until account holders could pick them up. Locating this business at the stage tavern served the convenience of stockholders and directors coming from out of town, while the conjunction of bank branch, tavern, store, and through-travelers bolstered the circulation and acceptance of the bank's notes.[35]

The benefits that corporate investors hoped to get from their shares did not end with dividends or stock appreciation. Instead, many investors hoped as much or sometimes even more for indirect benefits. Depending on the sector, these benefits might take the form of increased land values, cheaper transportation to and from distant markets, and more demand for local goods and services. For small turnpike projects that connected rural towns to a waterway, or a series of road segments that debouched into a distant commercial metropolis, investors usually came from the immediate area served by the planned improvement. Small-town residents met in taverns to garner support and capital for projects that would improve local roads or waterways. The Hudson Branch Turnpike Company, for one, built a ten-mile stretch of road on the east bank of the Hudson River roughly one hundred miles north of New York City. The company's stockholders met at a tavern in the town of Hudson on the river. Both the scale of the project and the location of these meetings suggest that most investors lived nearby: most were probably local landowners who wanted to get their farm products to New York City's markets and perhaps reap the benefits of rising land values as travel costs declined. They might not have expected dividends from the corporation, but they had multiple reasons to want the road.[36]

A similar logic informed the Third Turnpike Road Company in New Hampshire, which built, maintained, and collected tolls on fifty miles of road that ran from Bellows Falls, Vermont, through southwestern New Hampshire toward the Massachusetts state line. This turnpike existed to connect the Bellows Falls area to roads leading to Boston. Such a road might in theory have garnered investment from Boston-area merchants who wanted to tap the agricultural products of southeastern Vermont and southwestern New Hampshire. In fact, both the capital and the corporation's directors were local. Once the road was complete, locals made good use of it, sending many wagons to Boston. The road also made it possible to run a stagecoach from Keene, New Hampshire, to Boston, cutting passenger costs by 25 percent. The turnpike company's directors convened regular shareholders' meetings in the small towns along their road. On their way to these meetings, investors traveled the road they paid for and saw firsthand how well it served the neighborhood and whether it was in need of maintenance.[37]

Corporate meetings of the Third Turnpike Road Company took place in the roadside taverns of Keene, New Ipswich, Jaffrey, and Marlborough. At these taverns, investors could expect to meet their friends and neighbors. In addition to their corporate business, they could conduct private transactions on the side, either with the keeper or with other patrons, a minor but not unimportant efficiency. Tavern settings also created opportunities for shareholders to influence their neighbors during sociable interludes before or after corporate meetings. In good times, tavern meetings facilitated a positive local feedback loop that encouraged continued investment in ways that could address what economists call the free rider problem. A potential hurdle in raising capital for small infrastructure projects was the fact that investors were unlikely to see large dividends and major appreciation of their holdings, while at the same time, people who had invested nothing in building a bridge, road, or waterway could still reap the rewards of cheaper transportation and

rising land values. Tavern networks provided a partial solution to this problem because it was difficult to ignore one's neighbors when face-to-face in
the tavern. Intersecting layers of financial and social obligation intensified the
moral leverage on potential investors. The conversational one-upmanship
that often went along with men's sociable drinking further increased the
pressure.[38]

When small corporations encountered financial difficulties, they continued to lean on the networks of obligation and interest that flowed through
taverns and communities, but tavern suasion had its limits. The proprietors
of New Hampshire's First Cotton and Woolen Factory held regular meetings
in Jaffrey taverns. At these meetings, investors chose their officers, voted on
assessments (shareholders' future financial obligations to the concern), and
transacted "any other business." When the corporation ran short of money,
its agents published multiple notices in the local newspaper and convened
additional tavern meetings. Readily visible in print and in person, the corporation's activities helped ratchet up the pressure on delinquent shareholders.
Peer pressure could not work magic, however, and the textile company was
forced to auction off the stock of people who remained in arrears. When
those shares went up for auction at still more tavern meetings, the corporation's short-term financial prospects again rested on tapping residents. In
the case of the Third Turnpike, its local success contributed to its undoing. The
road brought significant benefits to the towns along its route, prompting
other nearby towns to invest in new roads that ran past their own front doors,
drawing traffic from the Third Turnpike. Thanks to this competition, the Third
Turnpike had become obsolete as a toll road by the early 1820s, and the
state legislature allowed the corporation to dissolve, turning control of the road
over to town authorities.[39]

As the Third Turnpike's misadventure suggested, the course of local roads
mattered: a few miles made a material difference in whether a landowner or an
entire town supported or opposed a given road. Newspapers printed countless
notices about meetings held to determine the course of a road, each segment
being contested among landowners and surveyors. Tavern keepers had particularly strong incentives to take notice of local improvement projects. Keepers along the route of a new turnpike road benefited somewhat from hosting
company meetings on their premises. If the road thrived, they benefited far
more from the overall increase in traffic, as farmers, wagoners, and perhaps
stagecoaches stopped in to refresh themselves, their teams, and their passengers. And if they owned land in the area, they welcomed the prospect that it
would rise in value. At the same time, the benefits of road building were often

impermanent and unevenly distributed, which sometimes prompted keepers and other locals to speculate in multiple local road ventures.

Such incentives and concerns help explain patterns in keeper involvement in infrastructure corporations elsewhere. In the area around the nation's capital, for one, rural tavern keepers joined with other local landowners to improve short stretches of road that would enhance access to Washington, Alexandria, and Baltimore for both people and goods. In 1816, keeper William Wiley hosted meetings of a newly incorporated turnpike company. His interest in the road and its route is reflected in the fact that the company operated as the Falls Bridge and Wiley's Tavern Turnpike Company. A few years later, Wiley campaigned for public support for another local turnpike project that would further connect his tavern to still other improved roads in the vicinity. As Jonathan Wells has argued, for white southerners, investing in local internal improvements did not always indicate a commitment to "economic modernization" across the board, let alone a "broader program" of social, legal, and political change. In Wiley's case, he had multiple interests in these turnpike corporations, independent of his political commitments. Any meeting held at his tavern promised a spike in his sales, if only for an afternoon. Improvements in the local road promised to bring additional travelers to his tavern, both locals and through-travelers who wanted to reach Alexandria, Washington, or Baltimore. The overall growth of the area's population promised to increase commercial traffic and land values. Not least important, his public role in supporting area turnpikes helped make his name as a local leader.[40]

For reasons of convenience, cost cutting, and the complex social dynamics of investment, turnpike corporations, factories, and even a few railroads continued using taverns as occasional meeting venues through the 1840s. Buried within the financial reports that several public works corporations made to the Virginia legislature, for example, appear payments to tavern keepers. Turnpike companies' expenses for the early 1830s either included "tavern bills" or hinted at them in references to unspecified "expenses of the board at their several meetings," which may have included transportation, lodging, and room costs. Newspapers likewise bore occasional witness to railroad stockholders' tavern meetings, such as one convened at Hardy's tavern in Amherst, Massachusetts, for the stockholders of the Souhegan Rail Company in the late 1840s.[41]

While the overlap between tavern-going and corporate projects often encouraged local participation, it did not hold equal promise for all investors. Propertied white women made up a small but significant proportion of investors in a variety of corporations.[42] Although the evidence is mixed, it

seems probable that many women invested more for dividends and appreciation than for the prospect of indirect benefits. An exceptional case, Rosalie
Stiers Calvert of Maryland took charge of her own and family members' investments in bonds and bank stocks. She voted her shares, acted as her
father's proxy, and kept a close eye on dividends and alternative investments
such as real estate. Calvert also understood the value of local roads and the
importance of their exact route. She hoped, for example, that a proposed
turnpike would take the route she preferred, "giving us an excellent road to
Washington and Baltimore." She invested in a plot of land that included
McCoy's busy stagecoach tavern, which "frequently" stabled between forty and
eighty horses, thanks to the several stagecoach companies "which converge
on this route." She later bought a second tract nearby, in part to prevent anyone from building another tavern on the new turnpike road to Baltimore,
which would "greatly decrease" the value of McCoy's tavern. Some years later,
McCoy's hosted meetings of the Washington and Baltimore Turnpike Company. Despite Calvert's active involvement in all these affairs, it is not clear
that she attended company meetings, including the one held at Gadsby's
Hotel in Baltimore at which the shareholders elected her husband president
of the company. Calvert devoted a considerable amount of time to her and
her father's business interests, but domestic duties and gendered sensibilities
alike made conducting business through writing more congenial than tavern-
going, even for such an important and savvy stockholder.[43]

In contrast, male investors had considerably greater freedom to attend tavern meetings. Many of them visited taverns anyway, and they could stack
their various business and sociable needs into a single afternoon if time were
pressing. In addition, some men who wanted to invest were not as comfortable with a pen as Calvert was, and they may well have preferred getting and
exchanging information orally. Being seen as a stakeholder, investor, and de-
liberator in the company of their peers also mattered to white men's sense of
self and their position in the local pecking order. But even men who never
expected women to attend corporate meetings understood that women
might visit taverns on business of their own. In fact, the nexus of tavern-going
and economic innovation sometimes generated explicit appeals for women's
attention and approval.

Selling Technology

Taverns' ability to attract an audience, combined with keepers' opportunities
to gauge and vouch for outsiders, made them useful to innovators who

sought to sell patented technology. While the early republic's economic growth owed as much to land and labor factors as to machine technology—or more—new machines increased productivity in many firms and households.[44] The textile industries of both Great Britain and the United States relied on complex machines, and textile innovators sought patents and licensing to prevent their competitors from getting rich on their inventions. By contrast, independent machine makers usually wanted to sell as many of their machines as possible. Comparatively simple patented machines had a dramatic impact in enabling householders to intensify their farming or domestic manufactures. The starkest example from the period is the cotton gin, which unleashed massive investments in land and slavery in the southern interior. Enough southern farmers had been desperately seeking their next profitable crop that the gin required little salesmanship to be widely adopted in the 1790s. Machines that addressed less obvious problems often required greater effort in marketing and demonstration.[45]

In urban markets, placing an advertisement in a newspaper might result in sales without patent holders or their agents having to leave home. To make sales elsewhere, patent holders needed to travel, find a place to demonstrate their machines, and stir up interest. Newspaper advertisements suggest that like corporations, patent holders relied on a combination of printed promises and face-to-face salesmanship. Although patent holders sometimes worked to put their devices into stores, they also made their domestic and agricultural inventions available for inspection and purchase in taverns. William Tunstall marketed patented threshing machines to local wheat farmers at Richmond's Swan Tavern at the turn of the century. The busy Swan attracted the custom of both Richmonders and planters from the surrounding countryside, who visited the state capital on private or public business. The Swan's keeper did not need Tunstall's machine to attract customers, but Tunstall needed the Swan's patrons.[46]

For keepers of less busy taverns, hosting novelties could inspire regular customers to make additional visits and strengthen keepers' networks of exchange and obligation. Both dynamics were in evidence in a letter Thomas Jefferson received in 1817 from Thomas Wells, who kept a tavern in the area near Monticello. Wells and Jefferson moved in different social circles but had multiple points of connection. Beyond the basic patron-keeper relationship, Jefferson had bought land from Wells years before, and the two men shared an interest in supporting local educational institutions. As a surviving letter indicates, Jefferson also asked Wells to conduct business on his behalf from time to time. While writing Jefferson about his efforts to complete a particular commission, Wells seized the opportunity to mention a "Stranger" who was staying at his tavern. This stranger held a "patton" for a machine that, in Wells's opinion, "shaves a Side of leather with greate virility." Encouraging Jefferson to pay him a visit, Wells added that the man would "at any hour to day be Ready" to demonstrate his machine's use. Wells may have written similar notes to other planters in the neighborhood, cultivating his own network while promoting the stranger's device.[47]

Whereas agricultural machines were generally intended for use by free men or enslaved people, some of the patented machines displayed in taverns were marketed for free women's and children's use. John Brown's "FARMER'S SPINNER," suitable for "family purposes," could be seen at Major Porter's tavern in Hartford, Connecticut. The advertisers informed local farmers that investing in the spinner would enable them to "furnish work and amusement for [their] daughters with great profit." Since the machine was "principally designed" for women, the advertisers invited them to Porter's tavern to "examine for themselves." Although the advertisers were incorrect in assuming that farmers' daughters had much idle time, they were more astute in recognizing that farmers might indeed bring their kinswomen to a tavern, especially in pursuit of new ways to turn women's domestic labor into cash.[48]

While the advertisers of Brown's spinning machine imagined harnessing underworked women, advertisers for other domestic machines promised to release women from domestic drudgery. "The hard labor of *Washing*, as it devolves upon the *femenine sex*" had inspired "our inventive countrymen," declared Daniel Mills, Connecticut tavern keeper and agent for selling Coxe's washing machine. Mills noted that the machine had been "put to trial in the family of Mr. Dudley," a tavern keeper, where it was "unanimously declared . . . the best machine for this purpose." Mills observed that he too had used the machine "for a considerable time" in his own tavern. His marketing capitalized on more than demonstrating the machine's successful operation in a busy tavern setting. In addition, he positioned himself as a forward-thinking keeper who took good care of both his tavern's linens and his *"femenine"* dependents. In practice, such machines tended to redistribute rather than ease women's domestic labor.[49]

Some distributors of domestic technology relied on especially prominent tavern and hotel keepers' endorsements. In the mid-1830s, advertisements for James Ralph's Patent Improved Clothes Mangle—suitable for "getting up silks, linens, woolens and cottons of every description"—leveraged the endorsements of several well-known Baltimore keepers for whom laundering clothes as well as bed linens had become an important business consideration.

George Beltzhoover of the Fountain Inn praised the mangle as "the best we have ever seen," and George Peacock of the American Hotel agreed it was "one of the best." David Barnum, who had bought three of Ralph's mangles, "perfectly" agreed with these assessments. Barnum's word mattered perhaps most of all because he was known well beyond Baltimore as a manager of high-end public accommodations. He had been hired away from Boston to assume the management of Baltimore's Indian Queen and later ran the City Hotel, famous for its comforts.[50]

Most tavern keepers had nothing like Barnum's reputation, yet even keepers with merely local eminence could influence public opinion by offering space to novel inventions and spreading the word through their existing networks. In practice, this meant that tavern-goers who lingered in taverns, and keepers who encouraged them to "stand gossiping," helped diffuse innovative ideas and machines into their neighborhood and its households.[51] Keepers could not determine the overall commercial success of a machine any more than they could keep a turnpike corporation solvent. However, by displaying models and tapping their network of patrons, they could ease the path. Keepers had direct and indirect incentives to be helpful. When acting as agents, they hoped to make money from selling machines. When they acted only as keepers, they received some financial consideration for the use of their space and stood to attract extra traffic and thus additional sales of drink, horse feed, and other tavern basics. At the same time, they linked their taverns with visions of improved productivity and greater household earnings. Depending on the machine's target users, keepers could also present themselves to the public as contributing to women's and children's welfare. If nothing else, that posture made a refreshing contrast to doleful tales of how tavern-going wasted men's vigor and ruined their families. Promoting machinery thus reinforced the association between taverns and valuable novelty.[52]

Performing Respectability

Another strand of entrepreneurial inventiveness that wove through both taverns and print involved culture and entertainment. At the turn of the nineteenth century, the emergent commercial entertainment sector included much that stretched the borders of respectability, such as bawdy songs and off-color stories. Yet popular performances and exhibitions often contained content understood to be both entertaining and informative or even uplifting, including historical anecdotes, illuminations, wax figures, meteors, animal specimens, and electrical demonstrations. Some cultural entrepreneurs combined performance with instruction in genteel accomplishments, including French, music, dancing, or swordsmanship. For that slice of the nation's entertainers and instructors who positioned themselves on the respectable or refined end of the spectrum, well-regarded and improved taverns had much to offer: temporary lodgings while on tour, spaces in which to perform and teach, and ways to market their offerings.[53]

The most established actors and musicians in the early republic worked in the nation's leading cities, where they increasingly had opportunities to perform in dedicated theaters and performance halls. Before the revolution, numerous colonial leaders, especially in New England, discouraged theatrical performances as a dissipated extravagance, but some cities boasted dedicated playhouses. After the war, Philadelphia, Boston, and New York built new theaters, and other cities eventually followed suit. That large and small cities invested in permanent buildings for musical and dramatic performances did not mean that most performers could stop touring, however. Instead, itinerancy remained a fact of life for most, although musicians and dancers were sometimes able to settle down by making teaching their primary occupation.[54]

For touring entertainers, taverns provided temporary accommodations and places to perform. A "Grand Caravan" of wild animals toured extensively across New England and New York in the 1820s and 1830s, visiting both large cities and small towns. In the latter, they most often displayed their curiosities on the grounds of a local tavern. For twenty-five cents—half off for children—patrons could see animals that at times included an elephant, a lion, a camel, a baboon, llamas, and a monkey who rode a pony. Many of the taverns where the caravan exhibited hosted other traveling entrepreneurs as well. In early October 1821, for instance, the caravan was on display at Major Porter's stage tavern in Hartford, Connecticut, the same tavern that had displayed the Farmer's Spinner a few years before.[55] Successful performers such as Richard Potter also toured extensively. Potter staged performances of ventriloquism, magic, songs, dances, and tumbling in Canada, New England, the Mid-Atlantic, and eventually the South in the 1810s and 1820s (see figure 4.1). He performed in a variety of venues, including small-town taverns, coffee houses, and hotels such as the Golden Ball Hotel in Haverhill, Massachusetts. Around the time of Potter's visit, the Golden Ball hosted a variety of entrepreneurial, entertaining, and civic activities, providing premises for an itinerant dentist, a circus featuring equestrian tricks, militia assemblies, turnpike company meetings, and political gatherings.[56]

By Particular Desire,

And POSITIVELY the LAST NIGHT.

MR. POTTER,
The Ventriloquist,

RETURNS his most grateful acknowledgments to the Citizens of Haverhill, and its vicinity for their very liberal patronage on his former Evenings, and has it in his power to inform them, that he will, by particular request, perform many wonderful and very interesting exploits, at the Golden Ball Hotel of Mr. L. D. White, on Monday Evening next, April 12, when he anticipates a return of that highly distinguished encouragement hitherto extended to him.

Among many new experiments he will introduce his celebrated

NE PLUS ULTRA.

TICKETS.—25 CENTS,

Without distinction of age, to be had at the Golden Ball Bar. Performance to commence at 7 o'clock. For particulars see bills.

FIGURE 4.1 *Haverhill Gazette & Patriot*, April 10, 1824. Richard Potter's advertisement for a performance at the Golden Ball Hotel in Haverhill, Massachusetts, combined several elements that performers and other itinerants used to cultivate public interest, including short engagements, support from local notables, references to novelty, and eye-catching typesetting. Other issues of the *Haverhill Gazette* documented the Golden Ball's value to other itinerant entrepreneurs as well as its use for local political and business meetings. Within a few months of Potter's performance at the Golden Ball, keeper Leonard White was dead, and his widow Ann assumed management. Courtesy of the American Antiquarian Society.

Performers and teachers made much use of improving taverns' sizable public rooms for both their capacity and their implied respectability. In 1802, the renowned American-born performer and dancing master John Durang offered a "GRAND SPECTACLE" in a "commodious and large Room" at Mrs. Wood's Sign of President Washington in Reading, Pennsylvania.[57] A decade later in Albany, New York, dancing teacher Mrs. Martely was able to teach and offer demonstration balls in the ballroom at Gregory's Eagle Tavern. An attraction such as the Grand Caravan, by contrast, probably displayed its "natural curiosities" in a tavern yard or pasture, perhaps resorting to a barn in inclement weather. But even in this case, keepers sometimes offered more than the bare minimum of space. At Barker's Hotel in Portland, Maine, for example, the caravan's venue was "neatly fitted up for the accommodation of visitors, with an awning, where ladies and children" could gaze at the animals "without the least apprehension of danger."[58]

Having found a workable and affordable space, performers and instructors needed to secure a paying audience or clientele. Word of mouth augmented print advertising in newspapers and broadsides. Both those who performed in taverns and those who used other spaces relied on tavern keepers to sell tickets to concerts, performances, exhibits, and balls. In addition to handling tickets and collecting fees, keepers probably promoted upcoming events to their regular customers in casual conversation and perhaps through broadsides pasted up in the tavern and around town. Would-be teachers submitted advertisements to local newspapers, which urged students to find them in the tavern where they lodged or taught and to speak with the keeper if they happened not to be available.[59]

Operating out of an improving tavern helped itinerant performers navigate numerous prejudicial stereotypes. In the popular imagination, itinerancy was associated with humble origins, spendthrift behaviors, and sometimes outright criminal practices, including theft and fraud. Successfully pretending to be someone else struck some Americans as a kind of trickery, while the lure of public adulation might dissolve self-restraint and reason. Finally, actresses had to face down the widespread assumption that they were kept women or prostitutes. Racism compounded these problems for the small cohort of Black performers. Working with the keeper of an improving tavern could not erase any of these social stigmas, but such keepers commanded a degree of respect in proportion to their transactional footprint and their taverns' elegance. Their support helped outsiders gain entrée to a neighborhood and its notables.[60]

Performers in the early republic capitalized on and reinforced taverns' positive associations with new people, new ideas, and new things. When advertisements insisted that a spectacle would be staged for a limited number of performances, they alerted readers to the risk of missing out. John Durang warned the citizens of Reading, Pennsylvania, that he would perform *"for a few Nights only."* Describing oneself as "lately arrived" from a more cosmopolitan place put a second positive spin on itinerancy. Durang himself noted that he had come from Philadelphia, a means of asserting his own cultural capital.[61] At the turn of the century, many immigrant artists sought to capitalize on their European backgrounds. Mr. Duperon highlighted his experience as the "late Fencing Master of the French Academy." English dancing master Mr. Phillips promised to teach the steps being danced "at all courts, and polite assemblies of Europe." Monsieur Lalliet advertised that his daughter Emma, "lately arrived from Paris," would teach that city's "most fashionable" dances to the people of Albany, New York. These advertisements not only reflected the fact that Americans still took many cultural cues from Europe, but they also highlighted village and town taverns' role in drawing Atlantic gentility into the American interior.[62]

While fanning their cosmopolitan credentials, teaching performers had to be careful not to offend their potential students or hosts by implying that they were rustic and ungenteel. Accordingly, John Durang used the flattering language of patronage to thank "those gentlemen, who have, in a friendly and generous manner, assisted in procuring the privilege" of using Mrs. Wood's long room. Nearly thirty years later, J. Morgan maintained that his dancing school in Middletown, Connecticut, hosted at two local taverns, was the fruit of "several polite invitations from Gentlemen" in the town. This claim, in turn, bolstered the expectation that other local gentlemen and ladies would indeed pay Morgan to teach them "the principles of politeness, and the art of dancing" in a tavern.[63]

Leveraging novelty, respectability, ties to a wider cosmopolitan world, and local connections mattered to all itinerant cultural entrepreneurs, but they were especially important to the small cadre of Black performers in the early United States. Most Black performers were hired to accompany white performers or to furnish music for dancing, rather than making their own engagements as headliners. Yet white people would also pay to see magicians, tumblers, and acrobats even if they were Black or made themselves racially ambiguous, like Richard Potter. Potter worked hard to calibrate his performance to white Americans' tastes. Suggesting that he was foreign-born made his physical appearance hard to read and prevented him from being pigeon-holed in white American terms as "mulatto" or "negro." Like other itinerants, he fanned interest by stressing his short engagements, such as one in Albany, New York, "*FOR TWO NIGHTS ONLY*." He repeatedly referred to his audience as "Ladies and Gentlemen" and mentioned the "highly distinguished encouragement" he had received. He described his feats as "*Philosophical Performances*" and noted that the ballrooms and other halls where he performed were "in ample order . . . handsomely illuminated, with good music," suggesting tasteful spectacles in improved venues. Perhaps most important, Potter framed himself as an Atlantic performer, using a largely British repertoire of songs and dances, which he identified with Sadler's Wells, a London venue famous for its entertaining but still respectable productions. In contrast with his Scottish teacher John Rannie, Potter did not perform gruesome tricks like fake decapitations, nor did he use ventriloquism to frighten or humiliate audience members.[64]

Richard Potter continued performing into the 1820s, and white performers esteemed him enough to steal his repertoire. Yet mainstream white audiences grew less willing to support performances that highlighted Black skill, preferring racist caricatures instead. Potter himself encountered a mixture of support and opposition when he returned to New England to tour. First, he faced a possibly racially motivated prosecution for an illegal performance in Rhode Island. A hostile public notice described him as a "mulatto juggler" who practiced "deceptive arts." Shortly after, a New Hampshire paper reprinted this notice and added that his performances were of an "*immoral* and *irreligious* tendency." Another critic complained that the "first people in town" set a bad example by wasting their money on the "fashionable" diversion. Although another local asserted the "good moral tendency" of Potter's showmanship, the controversy mired Potter in costly legal trouble for years.[65]

Thirty years later, respectable Black performers were few but could recruit an audience among people friendly to antislavery. Mary E. Webb made a name for herself as an orator and actor who appealed to abolitionist audiences. Her repertoire included work that novelist Harriet Beecher Stowe adapted for the stage.[66] Elizabeth Greenfield performed a vocal concert repertoire to packed houses but only of white audiences, as "no colored person can be admitted." Nationwide, many more white Americans consumed minstrel shows that caricatured Black speech and bodies. By midcentury, however, few refined or popular entertainers had much need of urban taverns as performance venues because the growing taste for all sorts of commercial culture had fostered many competing performance and entertainment spaces, including playhouses, pleasure gardens, circuses, concert halls, museums, and sporting venues.[67]

In small towns, by contrast, tavern keepers faced less competition from rival entertainment venues and benefited in tangible and intangible ways from hosting itinerant performers and instructors. Early in the century, John Durang had framed his performance in Reading as a means to assist his host, reminding "an encouraging public" that attending his performance would help keeper Mrs. Wood in her "peculiar predicament," perhaps connected with her recent widowhood. Any keeper with importunate creditors certainly needed as many patrons as possible. Well into the century, events designed for ladies and gentlemen were likely to attract the sort of patrons who paid more for an evening's entertainment than a whiskey-and-cracker patron might spend in a month. Aspiring keepers could also perceive indirect benefits: hosting respectable performers and instructors linked their taverns with the latest genteel fashions and helped them perform their own respectability.[68] In such ways, small-town taverns supported the diffusion of cultural and commercial innovations beyond the nation's elite and its eastern urban seaboard.

Counterfeiting Legitimacy

Both the taste for decent novelties and the presumed respectability of certain tavern venues were subject to manipulation, as an 1816 cautionary tale suggested. As the story went, a man came to Richmond on a stagecoach from the north, calling himself Vanhorn and claiming to be the advance agent of a famous French balloonist. After selling several hundred dollars' worth of tickets to watch the balloonist's ascent, Vanhorn left town on another stagecoach, "bilk[ed] the tavernkeeper, the printer and the public—and *vanish[ed]*." This possibly fictional confidence trickster had many real-life counterparts who used taverns both to help them move about and to find potential marks.[69]

Among the criminals drawn to taverns on business in the early republic were counterfeiters, who took full advantage of paper money's labile status in the early republic. In the absence of a national paper currency, banks printed their own bank notes. Although each bank's notes were in theory exchangeable for gold or silver coin, some banks printed so many notes, backed by so little specie, that their notes were hardly more trustworthy than counterfeits, while a financial panic could undermine even a well-regarded bank's paper money. In addition, men with privileged information and access to banking had incentives to protect the bank and its account holders rather than the general public. To take but one minor example, in 1810, John Steele, former Federalist congressman and comptroller of the U.S. Treasury and current agent of the Bank of Cape Fear, received a letter warning him about counterfeit bills on the bank. His correspondent instructed Steele to "keep from the Public" the news that the fake bills were circulating unless he personally detected one.[70]

In this context, where definitions of licit enterprise so often reflected the definer's self-interest, the conclusion that counterfeiters operated out of taverns because such places attracted people of shaky morals was more political than explanatory. The overlap between crime and tavern-going owed little to taverns' propensity to attract rule breakers and quite a bit more to the services that taverns offered all their business users. Like auctioneers, inventors, stockholders, speculators, and instructors—and like the confidence trickster Vanhorn—counterfeiters relied on taverns because of their need for mobility.[71] Counterfeiters rarely produced and distributed their fake notes in the same place. Some created their goods in the relative seclusion of small villages or rural areas. At least one canny practitioner justified his secretive habits with the excuse that he was developing a machine he hoped to patent. The famous Cogniac Street gang produced their counterfeit bills on New York's Canadian border, while Ira Johnson of Ohio worked in Covington rather than much larger Cincinnati or Cleveland. Wherever they fabricated their fake notes, counterfeiters usually insinuated them into circulation elsewhere. Like licit entrepreneurs, the most successful criminal gangs depended on networks of trusted agents who handled bills, property, and information and who often moved through taverns in the course of their illicit work. Cogniac Street relied on an "extensive network" of traveling and resident agents to pump counterfeit notes into the nation's financial circulatory system. Taverns where strangers routinely transacted, socialized, and drank represented opportune places to pass counterfeit money. In New York City, tavern keeper John Connor and his wife Hannah accepted and passed on the Cogniac gang's notes to a network of tavern keepers and counterfeit dealers, some of them kin. With a much smaller network to draw on, Ira Johnson planned to push notes into circulation in riverside taverns as he and his family floated down the Ohio River on a flatboat. In the event, the Johnsons used their boat to evade the police.[72]

As the number of counterfeit bills grew nationwide, mainstream newspapers warned about counterfeiting activities, and specialized counterfeit detectors became a new print genre. As a result, wayside keepers and their patrons had ample opportunity to learn about the risk of encountering counterfeiters and their notes (see figure 4.2). A typical notice in the *Baltimore Patriot* warned that wagoners had reported that two travelers were passing counterfeits "to tavern keepers along the road" west of the city. Advertisements warning

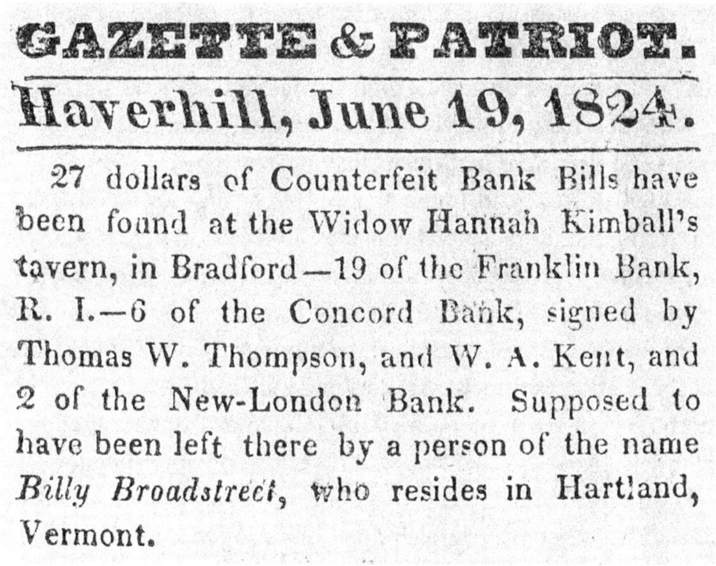

GAZETTE & PATRIOT.
Haverhill, June 19, 1824.

27 dollars of Counterfeit Bank Bills have been found at the Widow Hannah Kimball's tavern, in Bradford—19 of the Franklin Bank, R. I.—6 of the Concord Bank, signed by Thomas W. Thompson, and W. A. Kent, and 2 of the New-London Bank. Supposed to have been left there by a person of the name *Billy Broadstreet*, who resides in Hartland, Vermont.

FIGURE 4.2 *Haverhill Gazette & Patriot,* June 19, 1824. Like many of their contemporaries, Hannah Kimball and her customers in northeast Massachusetts dealt with bank notes and people from multiple states. Hartland, Vermont, lies more than eighty-five miles to the northwest, near the Vermont–New Hampshire border. New London, Connecticut, home of the most distant of the several banks mentioned, sits near the junction of the Thames River with the Long Island Sound, over one hundred miles to the south-southwest. The public links between Kimball's tavern and counterfeit notes did not ruin the tavern's reputation. Two months later, for example, locals held a political gathering there. Courtesy of the American Antiquarian Society.

about a "club of counterfeiters" and their fraudulent bills on a Maryland bank appeared in newspapers across several states in 1816, heightening readers' awareness that counterfeiters, like other people, relied on taverns as temporary lodgings and as a base of operations. The details in this notice included the claims that one man in this gang had traveled through Virginia exhibiting a racing horse, presumably stopping in taverns as well as consorting with "noted gamblers and Swindler[s]."[73]

Further grounds for general alarm came from the suggestion that counterfeiters could pass for gentlemen. As Stephen Mihm observes, most "shovers" of counterfeit money were working class, but some "counterfeited class and cash." The fake impresario Vanhorn displayed a "demeanor smooth and genteel." Counterfeiter David Lewis was described in many newspapers as being "genteel in his appearance, easy in his gait, polite in his manners, serious in his conversation." One of his associates, known as James Crawford, was supposedly young, slim, about five foot and eleven inches tall, with "sandy whiskers and light hair," and a supposedly telltale fondness for "brandy grog and smoking cygars." Such descriptions surely heightened men's mutual scrutiny in tavern barrooms and elsewhere, particularly for young men on the move.[74]

How often men on the road found themselves facing hostile attention from other tavern-goers because of their appearance or manners, we will never know, but Allen Trimble's autobiography shows how the need to negotiate bank notes could increase the dangers of traveling on business. As a young man—probably nineteen years old—the future legislator and governor invested in a speculative venture in 1803: driving hundreds of hogs from his Kentucky home to eastern Virginia for sale. Homeward bound after successfully selling his drove, Trimble stopped in a tavern one morning for "my breakfast and horse feed" and offered a five-dollar note on a northern bank in payment. The keeper rejected Trimble's notes, insisting that he would only accept "Virginia paper." "Much provoked," Trimble was obliged to take off his vest to reach his money belt, which contained a "good supply" of bank notes. With his suspicions of counterfeiting heightened by this stash, the keeper promptly rejected a ten-dollar note on a Virginia bank. As he recalled the events much later, the frustrated Trimble next went to a nearby store, where the clerk deemed the notes genuine and made change for him. Meanwhile, the dispute attracted "a crowd of rough looking men and boys who had collected to see the boy who had offered to pass counterfeit money, of which he had a great quantity, (for that was the news spread through the town)." Later the same day, two men sped past Trimble on the road. "Their appearance and manner" made Trimble suspect that they intended to waylay him for the contents of "my belt of bank notes." Only by riding hard well into the night did he escape the would-be robbers and reach another tavern, whose keeper agreed that "I had made a fortunate escape."[75]

Several decades later, counterfeiting was, if anything, a far more serious problem, yet this reality did not mean that all strangers greeted each other in wayside taverns with reflexive hostility. In one of his letters to his aunt, the ever-opinionated William Parker Foulke described a young man he met at a village tavern while deciding on the next leg of his trip. His temporary companion was tall, with "quite a civilized face, but a strong Yankee twang." Based on what Foulke learned about the other man's "extensive & rapid tour," he concluded that this stranger "must be a seller of patent rights—or of watches jewelry & the like; or a trafficker in counterfeit money." To Foulke, "it did not much matter *which* of these functions he was performing," implying that all these itinerant means of making a living were suspect, although only one was illegal. Foulke himself was leading a reasonably peripatetic existence at the time, yet he seemed never to worry that anyone would question his probity. In the event, Foulke put his life and property in this stranger's hands by accepting a ride in his sled. As he explained the matter to his aunt, he preferred not to let the snow delay him, but perhaps he also wanted to avoid looking overcautious and thus unmanly. For both men, like many of their peers, movement was a business necessity. Striking up conversations with strangers represented one means to forge—in either sense of the word—connections that greased the circulation of people, goods, services, and information.[76]

DESPITE AND SOMETIMES BECAUSE OF their association with enterprises of dubious moral and legal status, taverns and keepers helped individuals and firms cope with the practical difficulties of migration, itinerancy, and mobilizing audiences, buyers, and capital. Tavern keepers' material assistance in the form of lodgings and space is the easiest to document but may not have been the most important. As keepers gathered and distributed local news, bought country produce, sold manufactured goods, extended credit, furnished space, acted as agents, and helped travelers reach their destinations, they accumulated information and contacts that other people could tap to publicize and normalize their own activities, from auctioning property to staging performances. These roles helped entrepreneurs cultivate a market while managing costs and risks.

Throughout this process, tavern keepers, business users, and their customers bridged the worlds of orality and print. Most of the evidence in this chapter comes from low-circulation newspapers published in locally important towns, but the printed advertisements that helped pay for the paper did not stay inert on the page. Through conversation, keepers and clients amplified advertisements printed in newspapers and broadsides that sat on tavern tables or were pasted on the wall. Local tavern talk did not merely chew the cud of old feuds and family gossip but infused new information and paved the way for entrepreneurs and innovators. Whether purposeful or incidental, the oral transmission of information in the early republic remained critical in a vast country where many day-to-day economic transactions took place locally and face-to-face or not at all. Even as the transportation and communications revolutions began to remake the nation, many Americans continued to experience the interdependence of print and writing with oral, face-to-face persuasive and commercial communication. Those transactions and that talk were neither unimportant nor disconnected from larger economic trends.

Instead, they represented a kind of capillary action that pulled goods, people, ideas, credit, and information back and forth between neighborhood networks and much broader, long-distance circulatory flows that often depended on written communication between individuals and firms who might never meet in person.[77]

While tavern services, spaces, networks, and talk represented a valuable resource for many ambitious Americans, access to that resource was no more evenly distributed in the early republic than were property and the right to control it. Speculators, corporate directors, inventors, teachers, and others did not do business in taverns *because* those spaces were often unwelcoming, off-putting, or dangerous to white women and people of color. Indeed, some of them relied on improving taverns and their modest but real outreach to respectable white women. Yet doing business in taverns helped teach generations of American citizens to associate their new nation's entrepreneurial spirit with what they simultaneously came to believe were white men's prerogatives—or responsibilities—of risk-taking, networking, and mobility.

Part III

Representation

CHAPTER FIVE

Tavern Legalities
Orderly Freedoms and Republican Accommodations

In 1787, an essay about "Federal Sentiments" warned that any man inclined to "loitering a day at the tavern" squandered his ability to "be a good citizen of any free country." Despite such concerns, the new nation's federal, state, and local lawmakers often relied on taverns and keepers to serve their own and the nation's purposes. One of the earliest and best-known examples involved George Washington, who opted to stay in taverns when he toured the country in a campaign to strengthen the people's attachment to the new federal government. Knowing that he would incur much physical and social discomfort, he nonetheless selected public houses to avoid either burdening private citizens, as English royals had long done, or appearing to favor political allies. Washington's presidential tours threw into sharp relief the importance and difficulty of the travel, trade, and communications needed to bind the young nation together. Over the ensuing decades, many men in state and local government struggled on paper and in practice to make taverns serve their republic's needs. Although much of their work stemmed from fears of drunkenness and disorder, the nation's lawmakers also strove to harness taverns to the orderly freedoms of a mobile, entrepreneurial, republican citizenry.[1]

In the early republic as in the colonial period, the chief mechanism for regulating taverns took the form of laws requiring tavern keepers to take out licenses, a process that usually involved local officials such as justices of the peace or town selectmen. The substance of tavern licensing remained broadly consistent with colonial precedents until the advent of temperance legislation. Licensing laws held keepers responsible for both serving and surveilling the public. Keepers were expected to facilitate mobility for some people while curtailing it for others. Lawmakers imposed numerous restrictions on what keepers sold to their local and traveling customers, while leaving them considerable leeway to combine tavern-keeping with other enterprises. Similarly, lawmakers sought to control or eliminate some of the ways that patrons tried to use taverns for their private benefit, while tacitly allowing many others. Beyond the realm of licensing, state and local lawmakers harnessed taverns to the work of republican rule by making them temporary sites of government in practical as well as symbolic ways. All these choices reflected and impinged on major developments in the early nineteenth century, including territorial growth and settler colonialism, infrastructural developments, the spread of free wage labor, and slavery's unraveling in the northern states.[2]

From the 1830s onward, temperance convictions prompted a growing number of jurists and legislators to rework the legalities of alcohol in American society. Even as the marketplace offered one solution in the form of temperance taverns, whose keepers met sober citizens' demands for travel accommodations and gathering places, some lawmakers sought to remake taverns altogether. Their efforts added the force of law to long-standing private attempts to make taverns appealing to respectable, self-restrained men and women. From a strict temperance perspective, even if keepers and patrons had obeyed every letter of standard licensing laws, those laws remained unequal to the task of eliminating heavy public drinking. But if tavern-goers refused to adopt temperate habits, they might be compelled to do so by exiling alcohol from taverns and retail stores.[3]

Even as lawmakers debated a range of prohibitory options, however, they continued to treat taverns as important resources for republican citizens. In the 1850s, state courts heard many suits that pivoted on the relationship between tavern keepers and their guests. In ruling after ruling, judges determined that the public interest required protection for travelers and their property. Like much licensing law, this legal argument was not new in itself but took on additional contours at midcentury. Against the backdrop of tightening restrictions on Black mobility, motivated in large part by sectional conflict over slavery and the territories, jurists tied white men's freedom to travel, especially on business, to the nation's economic and political vitality.[4] At the same time, legal endorsements of white men's ability to move, exchange, and conduct politics in taverns appeared both to undergird and to flow from white men's status as the republic's most favored citizens.[5]

Mobility

From a licensing perspective, the reason for taverns' legal existence involved supporting legitimate travelers. American protections stemmed from English law, which construed travelers as deserving special consideration. As strangers, the thinking went, travelers relied on tavern keepers for essential shelter and food. This reliance spawned multiple licensing requirements. Tavern keepers could not decide on the whim of the moment that they did not want to receive travelers; they were "bound from their situation in life, to perform the work tendered to them," as New York legislator and jurist James Kent phrased it. A keeper who refused to entertain travelers "without a very sufficient cause" faced substantial financial penalties, potentially amounting to hundreds of dollars and the loss of their license.[6] Tavern regulations gained in significance as the new nation's vast claimed size but comparatively small band of settled territory called forth sustained efforts to promote the union, protect its borders, and encourage the domestic circulation of commerce, people, and information. Both the federal and state governments invested in these ends while attempting to stave off the kinds of mobility that people in power saw as threats to property rights, public order, and productivity.[7]

The evolution of the federal postal service demonstrates the federal government's appreciation of domestic mobility's value to the early nation. In the colonial period, the royal postal system had been a revenue-generating system confined to the major ports of the Atlantic coast. Although it provided what Richard John calls "a remarkably high level of service by the standards of the day," the British administration had not designed the system to get up-to-date information into the hands of the general reading public. With independence, the infant republic struggled to maintain even this level of service and could not keep pace with the population's growth and migration. Through the Postal Act of 1792, however, Congress authorized an enormous expansion of the mail service that involved a system of post roads, village post offices, and regular deliveries. In the same act, Congress provided for newspapers to travel at a subsidized rate, underwritten by people who mailed letters, which in turn created the conditions for a multifold expansion in the nation's printed news, greatly expanding its reach beyond the ranks of urban coastal merchants and public officials. In the long run, the post office, the mails it carried, and the sprawling network of post roads would help unite the nation.[8] At key moments, however, this public communications network contributed to political divisions. In the 1810s and the late 1820s, evangelicals tried to impose Sunday closing on post offices and the taverns that often housed them, interrupting the flow of information and people for religious ends. In and after the 1830s, southern planters sought to suppress the circulation of abolitionist print, hoping to protect themselves from federal intervention and domestic insurrection against slavery. In the 1850s, pro- and antislavery publications continued to circulate through the mail, contributing to growing doubts that the Constitution and strong interregional economic ties could bridge the tectonic gap of sectionalism.[9]

Efforts to constrain the movement of people and ideas recurred in no small part because the post office helped remake the nation's transportation infrastructure. Stagecoach companies and postriders received federal contracts to carry the mails, which subsidized the costs of passenger road travel. On many routes, government contracts represented such a large share of a stagecoach's potential earnings that whoever lost out in the competitive bidding process often chose not to operate a stagecoach at all. Like any other road transportation of the day, mail stages made regular tavern stops to refresh both horses and drivers. Some of these taverns doubled as post offices and their keepers as postmasters, a common pattern in the nation's small post towns and villages. The links between local taverns, newspapers, and stagecoaches that shaped daily tavern-going patterns thus rested in no small part on the federal government. By 1830, the postal network carried sixteen million newspapers, nearly fourteen million letters, and untold numbers of passengers and packages annually. Once built, the nation's post roads also served all manner of private conveyances.[10]

Because of the rapid but uneven development of the nation's transportation network, lawmakers began adopting geographic variations in tavern licensing requirements early in the nineteenth century. The most important examples involved horses. When so many road travelers moved by horsepower, the ability to care for horses represented an essential aspect of a tavern keeper's support for travelers. Caring for horses meant building and maintaining stables or pastures, keeping provender on hand, and providing the labor to muck out, feed, and otherwise tend to the horses. Yet even the relatively high charges that keepers could levy for these services did not make horse keeping an appealing prospect in places where most patrons arrived on foot or as passengers in commercial stagecoaches, trolleys, steamboats, or trains. As early as 1803, New York State exempted licensees in New York City from the requirement that tavern keepers accommodate horses.[11] Other states also began allowing tavern keepers in far less imposing cities and towns to shuck off the obligation of stabling guests' horses. Already in the late 1820s, county courts in the territory of Michigan could "release" a tavern keeper from the provisions related to "hay, stabling, pasturage, provender and grain." Back east, Maine's legislators permitted officials of "populous towns" to waive the requirement of pasturage for horses in the 1830s. By the 1840s, it was commonplace for licensing laws to craft lesser horse-care requirements for urban keepers or to give municipal authorities discretion over local requirements. Such legislative concessions reflected both the growth of commercial transportation and the pressure that dense populations put on urban land use. Legislators may also have reasoned that keepers might show greater respect for locally tailored requirements.[12]

To preserve the travel-centered logic of tavern licensing—and limit the number of drinking establishments—most states did not follow New York's experiment in allowing city keepers to dispense with lodgings for people as well as horses. Instead, they upheld requirements that tavern keepers must "actually keep the necessary spare bedding, stabling, hay and provender" to accommodate travelers.[13] In South Carolina, keepers had to have "clean and wholesome meat and drink, and lodging for travellers" at all times, or risk losing the £100 they staked as part of the licensing process. In Michigan, any person could sue a keeper for five dollars—many times the cost of a night's lodging—if he or she did not meet the required standards, including "good and sufficient" bedding.[14] In addition, many states and territories required keepers to abide by fixed rates, to post their rates publicly, or both. To prevent price gouging and reduce the risk that travelers would be unable to afford shelter at night, rate-setting bodies tended to assign comparatively low prices to overnight lodgings, while a cheap drink or two could be parlayed into a few hours of shelter.[15]

As the persistence of tavern rate-setting suggests, legislators intended to keep lodgings affordable, which meant that licensing laws had little direct effect on the trend in tavern improvements. Tavern keepers faced reasonably modest minimum standards for travelers' accommodations. In the 1810s, New Jersey required proof only that the applicant had "two spare feather Beds more then is necessary for his Famelyes use." Rarely did the neighbors who endorsed a license petition certify that an applicant had more than the legal minimum, such as "two good feather beds" or "in every way has good accomodation for men and horse." Somewhat later in the Michigan Territory, territorial legislators expected every would-be licensee to have "at least two spare beds for guests, with good and sufficient sheeting and covering." Legislators did not, however, require that each traveler have a set of bed linens, let alone a separate bed. In fact, the Michigan statute insisted that keepers maintain space and food for four guest horses, a strong suggestion that lawmakers accepted that four strangers might share two beds.[16] In more urban settings, minimum standards were sometimes higher. In 1823, the corporation of Washington, D.C., passed an ordinance requiring taverns to have "at least three good bedchambers" dedicated to guests, "with two good feather beds and bedsteads, and suitable bedding" in each. Although this ordinance did not prohibit strangers from sharing a room or even a bed, it increased the pressure on keepers at the lower end of the spectrum to adapt to middling and wealthy Americans' understanding of decency and comfort.[17]

Even without requiring significant improvements, however, lawmakers gave indirect support to keepers who sought to make distinctions among their guests on socioeconomic grounds. In addition to allowing keepers to offer basic and better meals, priced accordingly, some jurisdictions gave keepers the right to demand advance payment in "ready money" from travelers, a power that keepers were free to apply selectively. Anti-vagrancy laws, which sometimes made dirty clothing an "arrestable offense," further justified keepers' skeptical evaluations of strangers. A keeper was unlikely to face legal consequences for turning an impoverished-looking stranger away, even if such a traveler stood most in need of tavern services.[18]

Legislators' concern for the needs of those they deemed legitimate travelers shaped their thinking about tavern conduct. Everywhere, tavern regulations required keepers to prevent drunkenness and usually idling, gambling, and "lewd" behavior, yet lawmakers often exempted travelers from some of the requirements intended to promote public morality. In the early 1780s, Connecticut law proscribed spending more than an hour drinking in a tavern, yet exempted travelers and "Persons upon Business, or any extraordinary Occasions." Connecticut did not take the further step of excusing travelers from its ban on Sunday tavern-going, as Hannah Haines and her family learned to their cost. South Carolina, in contrast, stipulated that tavern keepers could not "suffer any person" to "abide . . . drinking or idly spending their time on the Lord's day"—"excepting strangers and lodgers." Such provisions suggested that travelers and "Persons upon Business" were people whose well-being while on the move served the public interest.[19]

Travelers' favored status also implied the imperative of controlling unauthorized mobility. In direct and indirect ways, licensing laws required tavern keepers to uphold other citizens' rights over slaves, servants, and other subordinated people. The early republic's tavern licensing laws retained colonial restrictions on selling alcohol to enslaved people, indentured servants, apprentices, minors, sailors, or soldiers without the "leave and consent" of a lawful superior. Restricting keepers' freedom to sell alcohol bolstered the right of individual masters, enslavers, parents, and other authorities to command obedience and labor from people bound to them in relationships of "authorized power." These restrictions also had implications for mobility. Keepers had an implied obligation to question and potentially refuse not just alcohol but also shelter and food to anyone who might be running away from obligations to a legal superior.[20]

The significance of keepers' responsibility to surveil both drinking and mobility changed in tandem with shifts in the landscape of legalized subordination. Whereas various conditions of unfreedom had been a normal and often lengthy stage in the life cycle of most colonial men and women—and a literal lifetime for those bound in slavery—legal freedom became the default condition for adult white men in the early republic. With important exceptions, including indentured immigrants, soldiers, and sailors, most young white men came to experience relatively short periods of legal subordination because the availability of western lands and urban wage labor attenuated paternal authority over them. Even apprentices were not always bound by legal articles but were often free to seek new employment if they chose.[21] White men thus had reason to expect that keepers would acknowledge their freedom to drink on their own recognizance, even if they looked young or worked for someone else. That freedom came to look a lot like a right that inhered in white men's bodies, although buying and selling alcohol were, in fact, privileges that legislatures could curtail, as the frustrated drinkers of the 1840s and 1850s learned. Notwithstanding these limits, white men's authorized tavern drinking and mobility undergirded the emergent conviction that white men's freedoms were their natural entitlement in a just republic, not revocable privileges.[22]

The situation for Black Americans could not have been more different. The overwhelming majority of the nation's Black population remained in permanent, hereditary slavery as the institution spread to new states and territories. Whites' fear of unauthorized mobility among the enslaved motivated not only the regular mustering of southern militias to suppress potential insurrection but also the first federal fugitive slave law of 1793.[23] As northern lawmakers slowly unmade slavery, they ensured that Black men and women continued to face legal roadblocks in their pursuits of mobility and livelihoods. New York decreed that any slaves in the state born before July 4, 1799, would become indentured servants for life. Children born to people partially emancipated by this law would themselves be bound to servitude until well into adulthood: twenty-eight years old for men, and twenty-five for women. At the same time, the state's tavern keepers faced legal consequences if they served alcohol to anyone they had "reason to suspect" was a slave, apprentice, or servant. As more white men experienced fuller measures of freedom, perceptions of Blackness became the most obvious grounds for doubting someone else's right to visit taverns. In Pennsylvania, which also took a gradual approach to emancipation, legislators incorporated racial language into their tavern licensing laws. There, the ban on keepers selling alcohol to enslaved people became a ban on selling to "negro servants." From one perspective, this language implied that Black Pennsylvanians who were not servants could drink like other members of the commonwealth, yet white people easily believed that challenging Black tavern-going had the color of law. Across much of the rest of the nation, tavern laws were mute about free Black patronage, but other laws combined with popular prejudice to make entire states, not just taverns, hostile to Black mobility, among other forms of self-determination.[24]

The penalties for drink-selling infractions provide further evidence of how legislators envisioned improper drinking and mobility. In Mississippi, where enslaved people were numerous and slavery bound almost all Black residents, state legislators imposed fines up to one hundred dollars on keepers who served alcohol to an enslaved person without authorization. Keepers who served apprentices, servants, or minors—who were likely to be white, given Mississippi's demographics—faced fines of only fifty dollars. In Wisconsin, Black people were vanishingly rare, but the Anishinaabek remained numerous. There, legislators levied fines of up to $150 on tavern keepers who served alcohol to any Indigenous person. A keeper who sold liquor to a white minor could only be sued for twenty dollars.[25]

Under tavern licensing and alcohol retailing laws, as in the federal constitution itself, issues of sovereignty and race marked most Indigenous people as outsiders within the republic. Under an 1822 law, no one in Mississippi could sell alcohol to Indigenous people without written permission from the superintendent of Indian affairs. In 1832, Congress banned alcohol sales and production in "Indian country," yet allowed alcohol in the region for the U.S. military's use.[26] While acting as governor of Michigan Territory a few years before, Lewis Cass had claimed that taverns and liquor played antithetical roles in white and Indigenous societies. Addressing Potawatomis and Miamis at a meeting to discuss land cessions and removal, he maintained that "it is necessary" for white people to "have roads and taverns and ferries," and equally necessary for the Potawatomi and Miami people to "fly from this mad water," meaning whiskey.[27]

Yet even in this hostile ideological and legal context, mobility could authorize exceptions. In 1840, Ohio updated its law, allowing keepers to sell "traveling Indians . . . any quantity of liquor, not exceeding one gill" apiece. This paternalistic limit did not apply to other travelers; it both set Indigenous people apart and imagined them as having legitimate reasons to be on the move. In the context of ongoing removals in the Midwest, several possibilities may have been on the Ohio legislators' minds. Bands who remained in Ohio might travel for treaty-making, and midwestern legislators faced considerable incentive to smooth that process. Tavern keepers themselves were eager to sell liquor to Indigenous people. People in bands that had switched from Indigenous to Euro-American farming techniques also visited market towns to buy and sell, and they likely saw taverns as places to meet some of their needs, much as their white neighbors did.[28]

A final group's freedom to move under tavern licensing laws deserves comment. Although race and servitude constrained many women's access to taverns, tavern regulations neither targeted women for exclusion nor required keepers to police female drinking. Selling liquor to a married woman without her husband's consent did not violate the terms of a tavern license, even though selling to a slave or servant without explicit permission did. The law of coverture, not tavern licensing per se, governed married women's freedom to buy in and move through taverns, and husbands had no special right of action against tavern keepers. Widows and single women who were legally accountable for themselves and not excluded on the grounds of race went unmentioned in tavern laws as customers. This silence was not inherently permissive; it likely reflects lawmakers' faith in other laws' power to restrain women's conduct, regardless of race. Perhaps they also reckoned on the force of custom to do what the law did not. Yet the absence of explicitly gendered regulation—with the important exception of prostitution, discussed below—can also be read against the backdrop of white women's travel. As more white women used commercial transportation and public accommodations, they staked new claims to mobility. In the process, the notion that ladies deserved and needed protection justified racial segregation in public accommodations and transportation, complicated mobility for all women who were not considered ladies, and impinged on white men's tavern freedoms.[29]

The importance of mobility in legislative imaginations entailed much more than concern for public order at the local level. Discouraging some forms of mobility while supporting others served the wider goal of securing the vast nation. Provided that Indigenous, enslaved, free Black, and impoverished white people were appropriately removed, exploited, or constrained, men in power could see how westward-bound settlers might solidify American territorial claims and grow valuable crops that could feed hungry urban populations both at home and abroad. Western households would in turn create new markets. From another perspective, mobility would also undergird American manufactures, which needed both raw materials and labor. Much of the latter came from teeming port cities and older farming districts whose young people migrated into cities and new factory towns for work. Trade in regional crops and manufactured goods linked disparate regions together, west to east and south to north. Even itinerant sellers, long objects of suspicion to men in authority, could be reimagined as weaving rural households into networks of trade and consumption that might bind the nation together.[30]

Enterprise

Much like mobility, numerous forms of economic activity in the early republic were heavily regulated. William Novak suggests that these regulations construed tavern keepers as "virtual public officials." Keepers practiced their trade not as a "private economic activity" but as a "public responsibility." These observations capture critical features of the legal imaginary and the thicket of laws through which keepers and patrons moved. At the same time, through positive statements of law and regulatory silences, legislators construed taverns and keepers as props to other people's private enterprises in ways that extended well beyond keepers' support for mobility.[31]

Tavern licensing laws included many sections restricting keepers and patrons by establishing punishments, usually financial, for keepers who allowed patrons to behave in ways that regulators wished to restrain or suppress. In addition to defining legitimate patrons and requiring services for travelers, legislators regulated certain forms of play that many men enjoyed, including blood sports and gambling. Cockfighting and a variety of card, dice, and other games were widely banned from taverns even if they were unregulated in more private places. In a typical maneuver, the Virginia legislature banned from taverns any items used in games on which spectators staked wagers, including dice, cards, and billiard tables. In 1798, the state went further, calling for the outright destruction of billiard tables. By 1819, Virginians had loosened up to the point of allowing backgammon, chess, or draughts (checkers) in taverns or any other public place, but betting on these games remained illegal.[32] Northern states passed similar laws authorizing local governments to penalize keepers who provided gaming implements or merely tolerated proscribed forms of play. Keepers caught allowing or encouraging gaming faced a variety of financial penalties, including fines, the loss of their security bonds, and the loss of the license itself. Licensing laws did not, however, require tavern keepers to surveil or interrupt financial risk-taking that could be construed as work or business related. Keepers had no obligation or authority to oversee any of the financial speculations that took place in and around taverns, no matter how much of a gamble men took in the process.[33]

A similar ambiguity emerges in considering how legislators regulated keepers' alcohol sales. Keepers faced a sliding scale of penalties according to the racial and legal status of those they served. As concerns about both public and private drunkenness mounted, potentially ruinous fines also awaited keepers who allowed otherwise legal patrons to drink to excess.[34] Yet in the decades before legislative temperance, licensed tavern keepers remained free to sell everything from the lower-alcohol ales and ciders to the potent fortified wines and distilled spirits, usually with no cap on the volume sold to a given patron at any one time. Requirements that keepers prevent patrons from becoming "scandalous" or "idle and disorderly" involved subjective limits. Kentucky adopted the whimsical provision that keepers could not allow "any person to tipple or drink more than is necessary." Virginia instructed keepers to stop people from drinking "more than is necessary, on the Lord's Day." South Carolina ordered its keepers not to allow anyone to "remain drinking and tippling" but put no time frame on remaining.[35] Given the number of business-related activities that people conducted in taverns—including reading newspapers that arrived under the aegis of the U.S. mail—it took barely any finessing of the law to allow some locals to remain in taverns for hours on end. In contrast, legislators got more precise with sailors and rivermen, both because authority figures considered these workers prone to rowdy behavior and because their labor was essential to commerce. South Carolina barred its keepers from entertaining "any seaman or mariner" for more than "one hour in twenty-four." Many states also sought to limit tavern-going by capping the amount of credit that keepers could extend. However, such provisions did little to prevent patrons from getting significant credit from keepers for alcohol and other goods; they simply made large debts unrecoverable at law, shifting the risk from patrons to keepers.[36]

In states and territories that instituted tavern price caps, moreover, local officials often created perverse incentives by making alcohol cheaper than meals and whiskey as cheap as or cheaper than the lowest-alcohol beverage. In the mid-1810s, a Kentucky tavern-goer could buy eight ounces of whiskey and shelter for the night for less than the cost of a meal. In addition, keepers remained free to dispense whiskey in quart and gallon jugs to patrons who went on to use them in their households and workplaces or as items of trade. Although concerns about public drunkenness motivated multiple licensing restrictions, in the first decades of the nineteenth century, most legislators tacitly acknowledged alcohol as a prop to sociability, a palliative in cases of pain or extreme exertion, and a valuable commodity. As a result, people whose credit the keeper trusted or who could furnish ready money could walk off with as much liquor as they could carry.[37]

As with alcohol, legislators both relied on and limited the ways that keepers could leverage their taverns' ability to attract a crowd. In addition to authorizing public auctions in taverns, the early republic's lawmakers initially did little to prohibit tavern keepers from combining their trade with any other legal business, even though the prospect of visiting both a tavern and a store, for example, created additional incentives to linger. As concerns about drinking mounted, however, some states began to impose novel restrictions. In 1839, Ohio's legislators stipulated that tavern keepers could sell by small measure (less than a quart) only in "the common bar of the tavern," not in any contiguous store or room. New Jersey passed a stricter law in 1846, mandating that no one could keep a tavern and a store "in one house," although the law allowed both businesses to operate "under the same roof" if they were "entirely distinct." (Had the Eagle Tavern in Watkinsville, Georgia, been subjected to the same law, keeper Richardson would have had to close off the interior door between his store and the barroom and turn over the management of the store to another person.) Neither of these laws banned large-volume alcohol sales, however. Nor did they prevent customers from buying alcohol at the bar and then retiring to another room. Whereas reducing public drinking represented one end of such laws, an equally important goal involved the retail environment: such laws sought to protect those consumers who wanted to shop without confronting whiskey-sodden sociability.[38]

Tavern keepers faced more restrictions on whom they could host for business purposes, whether through their own licensing requirements or through codes regulating other occupations. Although lawmakers did not single tavern keepers out in their anti-prostitution laws, they presumed not only that tavern-goers were prone to disorderly conduct but also that keepers might seek to capitalize on the financial possibilities of prostituting women to their patrons. In practice, some keepers faced repeated charges of running a "lewd house or place for the practice of fornication" or "a common, ill-governed, and disorderly house." Yet many states that penalized "open lewdness, or any notorious act of public indecency" made no attempt to police all exchanges of sex for material gain.[39] Although none of these laws stemmed from wholly new concerns, they seemed more urgent as rapidly growing cities created degrees of anonymity that appeared to promote sexual license. Keeping prostitution out of orderly public houses—or well concealed within them—helped preserve the fiction that respectable women should be sheltered from the realities of carnal commerce, while imposing little real constraint on those men who enjoyed the freedoms of the sexual double standard.[40]

At one level, the legal expectation that taverns should be public, orderly, and decent places provided indirect support to those performers and impresarios who sought to operate on the respectable end of the entertainment spectrum. Yet public performers remained objects of distinctive legal regulation. Although revolutionary-era bans on theatrical performances eased in the early nineteenth century, numerous states banned some exhibitions while authorizing others, or gave towns the power to grant or withhold licenses to perform on a case-by-case basis. Keepers themselves sometimes faced penalties if they allowed unlicensed performances in their taverns. In practice, such laws could be used to police who benefited from the use of taverns for commercial entertainment.[41]

In the mid-1820s, performer Richard Potter stood trial for two unlicensed tavern performances in Smithfield, Rhode Island. As Potter's modern biographer John Hodgson notes, Potter may not have known about the state's law and its unusually high penalties, passed while he was touring southward. The keeper of the tavern where Potter performed had reason to know, however, since the same law exposed him to fines of fifty dollars per offense. The prospect of personal gain likely motivated the initial complaint against Potter. The informer stood to collect half of the crippling four-hundred-dollar fine assessed against the erring performer, two hundred for each performance. The local official who pursued Potter at law was the informer's first cousin. In contrast, tavern keeper David Farnum faced no charges for his role in the two unlicensed performances. That Potter became mired in costly legal trouble while Farnum did not probably reflected the former's double outsider status as a person of color and an itinerant performer. By contrast, Farnum had standing in the neighborhood. As the keeper of a sizable tavern and a member of a prominent local family, Farnum had connections that were at least as useful as the informer's. In addition, a stiff fine levied against him would have reverberated through the neighborhood on webs of debt.[42]

David Farnum's escape from legal and financial harm reflected another important dimension of tavern licensing laws. Lawmakers counted on keepers' neighbors to guarantee their fitness for a license, yet the thick social and economic links between keepers and patrons functioned as a potential constraint on the enforcement of licensing laws. State and territorial legislators charged tavern keepers themselves with policing their patrons, yet placed few categorical limits on who could hold this consequential position. Licensing laws did not presumptively bar women from becoming licensed keepers, for example, although some states began imposing racial restrictions in the early nineteenth century. Rhode Island, for one, barred its town councils from licensing "any colored or black person" in 1822.[43] More often, state legislators identified finances and reputation as the means both to filter candidates for licenses and to bind keepers to good behavior. A typical licensing statute required would-be keepers to pay a license fee, stake a considerable sum of money on their own good behavior, and get friends or relatives to stand surety for them. In some jurisdictions, keepers submitted documents signed by up to twelve of their neighbors, attesting that they were "fit and proper" for the trade, of "good moral character," or "of sober life and conversation." Lawmakers hoped such fiscal and moral requirements would ensure that keepers had the standing and character needed to enforce the law against their own patrons and neighbors. In practice, these requirements rooted taverns in firsthand local relationships shaped by proximity, friendship, kinship, and economic advantage. At the same time, the authority to punish infractions devolved on municipal, town, and county officials, judges, and jurors. As Laura Edwards argues, the law in practice, like keepers' character witnesses, often remained a local affair, shaped by local networks and perspectives.[44]

The enmeshment of town and village taverns in long-standing economic and social relationships thus became part of the legal context in which taverns operated. Licensing petitions from one New Jersey county suggest the role of kinship as well as transactional networks in tavern licensing. In this period, nine different family names appeared repeatedly among the sixty-odd signatures on licensing petitions from Deerfield township. Some individuals signed more than one petition, and multiple men with the same family name signed individual petitions. Twelve families contributed a witness in more than one town, and nearly one-third of the signatures across nine petitions came from men who attested to multiple applicants' fitness. These overlapping signatures testified to the network of interpersonal ties that continued to shape both legality and commerce in many parts of the country. These ties did not mean that keepers could evade the law with impunity. They did, however, increase the chances that both keepers and local officials would interpret the law differently for their own friends and connections, for less well-connected locals, and for evidently poor or otherwise suspect outsiders.[45]

Lawmakers' silences and actions together authorized taverns' and keepers' catalytic role in networks of exchange and innovation. Licensing laws that sought to police slaves, servants, sailors, drinkers, counterfeiters, gamblers, sex workers, itinerants, and performers left ample space to use taverns for a wide range of commercial, social, and other purposes. Keepers generally remained free to offer space for business meetings, social and civic events, and the myriad enterprises of inventors, teachers, corporate investors, and speculators. Unintentional or partially considered loopholes in the licensing regime even created possibilities for white women and people of color to use taverns in their own pursuits of mobility and economic gain. Those loopholes complicated tavern dynamics without compromising lawmakers' more conscious intention of making taverns serve the needs of propertied, rights-bearing citizens.

Representation

Just as lawmakers understood that well-conducted taverns could support the new nation's needs for orderly mobility and enterprise, they also recognized that taverns' physical spaces, commercial character, and local familiarity could sustain the work of republican self-governance. One of the early republic's repeated challenges involved giving the citizens access to government. Access had multiple dimensions in the early republic: it included the privilege of casting votes, holding public office, and tapping government's administrative functions. But access involved more than privilege. To be meaningful, it had to include the practical ability to exercise those privileges. Voters needed not just the right to vote but an opportunity, which required a time, a place, and a means of public notification. Ordinary property-related tasks such as registering deeds and probating estates required both legal personhood and the ability to appear in person before the appropriate official, such as a justice of the peace or county court clerk. Individuals had to appear in court if they were involved in private legal actions or public prosecutions. Created by legislative action, the early republic's new states, territories, counties, and towns had an abstract existence independent of local circumstances, but government needed to be physically incarnate to function fully, which meant both public officials and built environments. Across many jurisdictions, lawmakers relied on taverns and their keepers as they sought to facilitate access to government services and the exercise of political privileges and responsibilities.[46]

For many citizens, geography represented a major barrier to their interactions with government. People who had moved to acquire land or establish a new town often ended up inconveniently far from the nearest courthouse. In many lately settled districts, the burden of distance from the nearest court often coincided with legislative underrepresentation, leaving residents of these areas at a distinct disadvantage both individually and collectively. In the late eighteenth and early nineteenth centuries, backcountry inequities fueled waves of discontent that resulted sometimes in electoral revolts and sometimes in popular protests. Given this history, planting government institutions in new geopolitical communities remained an important consideration deep into the nineteenth century.[47]

In nascent political communities that could not yet afford public buildings, taverns had much to commend them as temporary sites for government. Not only were they one of the first institutions built in a new village, but also keepers built them at their own expense. In the nation's newer states and territories, some county courts sat in taverns for several years before moving into a purpose-built courthouse. In the early years of Terre Haute, Indiana, the circuit court sat at Henry Redford's Eagle and Lion Tavern, originally a two-story log house and one of the town's first buildings. Terre Haute moved swiftly to build government buildings, and Redford's tavern may have housed the court for four years or less. Yet as a stage tavern, the Eagle remained "a place of great resort," while Redford himself remained connected to town affairs and received the contract to build the town jail.[48] Even after the first public building appeared in a county or town, local officials' reliance on taverns sometimes persisted because the multiple jurisdictions and branches of government all needed space. The town of Cincinnati illustrates the point. Within a decade of its founding in 1790, Ohio's Hamilton County built its county courthouse in Cincinnati, but that building did not also house the municipal government. The town's select council owned a building that was inadequate for meetings, so the councilmen met in taverns for roughly thirteen years, before finally committing the funds to make the town house usable. During renovations, the council returned to its reliance on tavern venues.[49]

In the early republic, the movement from tavern to courthouse or town house evoked a much older process of spatial specialization in American public architecture. In colonial Massachusetts, early courts met in a variety of places other than courthouses, including taverns, private dwellings, and meeting houses usually used for sacred functions. In Virginia, too, colonial taverns hosted judges and juries. Over the course of the eighteenth century, however, many communities began building courthouses as one part of a larger process of making the law more formal, dignified, and hierarchical. In places where this process had begun to unfold locally well before the revolution, post-revolutionary courts were unlikely to sit in taverns, although lawyers and judges still lodged there, and sometimes juries were sequestered there as well.[50]

Yet while links between taverns, foundings, and governance surged westward with the waves of acquisitive settlers, they also lingered in the eastern states. The original thirteen states created their own new counties, townships, and towns in the early nineteenth century. In these infant jurisdictions, eastern lawmakers looked again to taverns in ways that older settlements in the same states had outgrown. Legislative acts creating new towns or townships sometimes designated a particular tavern as the venue for inaugural town meetings. The act by which New York established the town of Seward in Schoharie County, for one, called for the initial town meeting to be held at the place "lately occupied by John C. Wooden, as a tavern." Ironically, the movement from village taverns to dedicated courthouses and other government buildings helped to reinforce taverns' growing spatial complexity over time. Both architectural trends enabled new ways of marking political power, social capital, and wealth.[51]

In related ways, the use of taverns for elections expressed both democratic and exclusionary aspects of republican government. Over time, property and taxpaying qualifications for voting declined for white men. In turn, election days became highly visible statements of ordinary white men's power to decide who wrote and enforced the laws. Election judges or other officials selected the polling places in each voting district, usually choosing prominent and convenient locations for the purpose. Some officials preferred stores, mills, and other commercial venues, and others opted for schools, churches, and other places less associated with either commerce or drinking. In Philadelphia, voters cast their ballots at the state house. Yet in many places, election officials' choices suggested that they found taverns peculiarly appropriate venues. Early in the nineteenth century, voters in Alexandria, Virginia, and Cincinnati, Ohio, went to the council chamber or courthouse if they lived in its district but to taverns in one or more of the remaining districts or wards in each city.[52] In rural areas, election judges and supervisors also endorsed taverns as polling places. Near Philadelphia, Pennsylvania's Chester County appointed taverns as polling places in twelve of thirteen electoral districts. The thirteenth district contained the county courthouse (see figure 5.1).[53]

Not all taverns made equally eligible polling places, however. The chosen taverns tended to be local landmarks and regular gathering places for business and pleasure, not marginal, out-of-the-way spots. Certain election notices from northwestern Virginia, for example, directed voters to "the house of Adam Moudy" in Smithfield. Like many other taverns, Moudy's needed no further identification to its neighbors. Moudy kept tavern for at least a decade, and repeated public notices identified his tavern as a venue for public auctions, foreclosures, estate proceedings, and other tasks prescribed by property law. Moudy's tavern also provided a platform for transactions that showcased and extended the wealth and power of some of the area's largest enslavers. At the end of the year, local planters offered up large groups of "Negroes for Hire" at the tavern. For the white men in the audience, this spectacle had several potential meanings: it allowed men of lesser means to become partially vested in slavery; it highlighted the bonds of racism that seemed to

FIGURE 5.1   George Caleb Bingham, *The County Election*, 1852; oil on canvas; Saint Louis Art Museum, Gift of Bank of America 44:2001. Bingham's painting suggests the spectrum of possible behaviors and attitudes on an American election day. Some voters, dressed variously as merchants, lawyers, farmers, or laborers, discuss the issues of the day. One man, the worse for drink, is being propped up in line to vote. Several men actively solicit votes from the men waiting in line. The scene also suggests the potential links between tavern-going and voting. The polling place, possibly a courthouse, sits in the foreground. Behind it appears the Union Hotel, a substantial two-story structure. From the hotel's windows, dim figures survey the crowd waiting to vote. On the Union Hotel's other side lies a small single-story grocery, a type of business often associated with illegal liquor sales. In the absence of a courthouse, a tavern such as the Union Hotel made a suitable polling place in many jurisdictions.

unite white men; and it summoned up the differentials of wealth and power that divided them. All of Virginia's voters, and most of its tavern patrons, were white men. Not all its white men possessed the suffrage, however, because the state tied voting to property ownership until 1851. In all these ways, the use of taverns as polling places articulated the relationship between voters, government, and private property.[54]

Lawmakers never stopped worrying about taverns' potential to encourage disorderly, illegal, or subversive behavior. Perhaps in part for that very reason, in the early nineteenth century, they expanded taverns' use as venues for elections, courts, and other government functions, marrying tavern-going to white men's political rights. In short, lawmakers harnessed taverns to the orderly functioning of government and thus to the interests of its most powerful stakeholders. At least two states made this point by protecting certain tavern assemblies from interference. In 1809, Ohio passed a law to safeguard gatherings at "any tavern, court or election or any other meeting of the citizens, for the purpose of transacting or doing any business appertaining to, or enjoined on them." Anyone who provoked "any contention or disturbance" at such a meeting faced temporary imprisonment and a fine. In 1827, Michigan passed a nearly identical law to safeguard its public meetings. These laws enhanced local authorities' power to protect citizens' assemblies from both dissent and disorderly conduct.[55] In all these ways, lawmakers sought to make taverns accommodate the republic. As a result, an important kernel of legal truth lay behind the commonplace notion that the building of a tavern made a couple of houses into a village. As George Flower recalled about the settlement of Albion, Illinois—part of an English emigration project led by Morris Birkbeck—once settlers built a tavern and blacksmith shop, Albion was "no longer a myth, but a reality, a fixed fact."[56]

The Orderly Freedoms of Temperate Citizens

In the second third of the nineteenth century, the legal context for keeping and visiting taverns changed. The available evidence suggests a marked decline in per-capita alcohol consumption during and after the 1830s, combined with the emergence of taverns run "on the temperance plan," chiefly in New England. Those changes did not satisfy the temperance movement's stalwarts, however, because significant numbers of urban workers, recent immigrants, and rural laborers showed no inclination to temper their intake. As a result, temperance-minded officials at all levels of state and local government began to act against drinking in new ways. Even as they explored novel constraints on public drinking and sought to make public houses accommodate their own sensibilities, however, lawmakers continued to wrestle with taverns' importance to a mobile, entrepreneurial, republican citizenry. That vision of taverns' potential endured even as temperance activism swept into the nation's legislatures and courts.[57]

According to their legal and moral views, jurists articulated varied understandings of taverns as necessary refuges for travelers and potentially disorderly resorts for locals. In 1840, two cases from South Carolina—a state far removed in both geography and politics from the prohibitory enthusiasms associated with New York's "burned-over district"—provide instructive examples of how temperance convictions shaped judicial thinking. These cases provided opportunities for the state's judges to try to disentangle drinking from taverns while reckoning with the demand for public accommodations, an acute need for road travelers in rural districts like their own. In the Palmetto state, in fact, the state's commissioners of roads had authority over tavern licenses, and license fees funded road maintenance.[58]

The first of these cases, *South Carolina v. John Chamblyss*, originated in a tavern keeper's conviction for selling alcohol. Over the next century, judges referred to this case in legal treatises and in rulings in other states. Keeper Chamblyss had been convicted in Darlington district's circuit court not for selling to slaves, or to drunks, or on Sundays, but simply for selling alcohol as a stand-alone purchase, as tavern keepers in and beyond South Carolina did as a matter of course. When Chamblyss appealed his conviction, the state's court of appeals ruled that the circuit court judge had given fatally flawed instructions to the Darlington jury.[59] That judge, who also served on the appellate bench, had attempted to separate what taverns had so long combined: public commercial drinking and travelers' accommodations. Judge John Belton O'Neall had informed the jury that South Carolina authorized a tavern keeper "to furnish guests with drink, as a part of their entertainment," but not to "sell spirits, as a separate business, even to his lodgers and guests."[60] This interpretation of the state's licensing law aligned with O'Neall's personal convictions. He had "learned to abhor the liquor traffic" from working in his father's store as a youth. As an adult, he abandoned first liquor and then all alcohol. His career as a lawyer, circuit court judge, and state representative required him to travel extensively within the state, and perhaps encountering drunken, rowdy tavern-goers during his circuits helped strengthen his temperance convictions. O'Neall's instructions to the jury suggest that his antipathy to alcohol extended beyond personal dislike. He advanced a legal interpretation that would have significantly reduced tavern alcohol sales in the state, and he later attributed much of the state's crime to alcohol consumption. Shortly after this case, he became president of the state's temperance society.[61]

Writing to overturn Chamblyss's conviction, the appellate court's Judge Josiah Evans took aim at O'Neall's interpretation of tavern law, while acknowledging temperance's influence. According to Evans, the "popular sense" of taverns as furnishing both drinks and lodgings was "clearly shewn by Webster's definition," which he quoted at length. Under South Carolina law, he continued, a tavern provided accommodations, meals, and alcohol, and the requisite tavern license covered both the hospitality and the drink. Therefore, as a licensed tavern keeper, Chamblyss committed no crime when he sold alcohol by the small measure. In tracing the precedents, Evans referenced not only Webster's dictionary but also the English lexicographer Samuel Johnson, William Shakespeare, English and colonial laws, Joseph Brevard's digest of state law, and contemporary legal thought across "most of the States of the Union." In concluding, Evans asserted that he went into such depth not because the law was unclear, but because of the "deep and exciting interest" at stake. Arguing that it was "my duty to expound, not to make, the law," he also insisted that preserving the traditional legal definition of taverns would not "interfere with that great reformation in the habits of our people, which has already taken place."[62]

In dissenting from the majority's decision in this case, Judge O'Neall had the support of fellow temperance judge Richard Gantt, but neither man wrote an opinion. However, in another 1840 case that turned "on the same point," O'Neall wrote a lengthy decision, which the influential politician and lawyer Langdon Cheves described as "his Honour's dissenting opinion" in Chamblyss's case. The facts in *Commissioners of Roads v. James H. Dennis* involved not the sale of alcohol but the license fee: specifically, whether the commissioners had been "entitled to demand" fifty dollars from tavern keeper James H. Dennis as the cost of his liquor license. Dennis maintained that since he kept a tavern but did not retail liquor, he required no license. Whether Dennis furnished alcohol with meals did not appear in the ruling, but he apparently did not sell alcohol on its own, by either the small or the large measure. In finding for Dennis, O'Neall reiterated that despite his "great respect" for his appellate colleagues, "I regard the tavern license and the license to retail [alcohol], as two distinct things." A tavern, he argued, existed for the "relief, and lodging of wayfaring people, travelling from place to place" and not for the liquor trade. O'Neall offered hope that keepers like Dennis who did not sell alcohol could avoid the high fee assessed for a liquor retailer's license, but he also insisted that tavern keepers must take out a license binding them to the conventional obligations of policing their patrons and protecting traveling guests.[63]

If Cheves was correct in describing O'Neall's ruling in *Dennis* as revealing the logic of his thinking about the original Chamblyss case, then O'Neall stopped short of claiming that existing law barred alcohol from taverns altogether. In his instructions to John Chamblyss's jury, O'Neall had observed that a tavern keeper could furnish alcohol as part of a meal and even adjust his charges to cover the cost. This line of argument created a loophole for a sub-set of tavern drinkers. By this logic, people who could afford a tavern meal could also enjoy liquor or wine with their meals without being considered "'*lewd and idle.*'" By contrast, people who wanted to waste "'*their money and time in* [a] *lewd and drunken manner*'" had no right to drink in taverns.[64]

Judge Richard Gantt's brief concurrence in *Dennis* likewise pivoted around the imagined tension between respectable travelers and local rowdies. By serving liquor freely, he suggested, keepers attracted people who annoyed travelers with their "riot and disorder." As a remedy, he invited the legislature "to do away the impolitic and mischievous amalgamation" of public accom-modations and liquor retailing altogether. Although he may have been imag-ining sober travelers affronted by local drunks, by the 1840s, the term also easily summoned up the idea of interracial sex. Given the tavern context and southern setting, moreover, Gantt's phrasing invited speculation about inter-racial prostitution involving white travelers and enslaved women. Whatever the sources of Gantt's queasiness, he took for granted that with new restric-tions on alcohol sales, "travellers may rest in quiet and peace" in wayside tav-erns. Gantt's vision left little room for travelers who enjoyed talking to strangers or sought out boisterous forms of sociability.[65]

Temperance-minded judges had legislative colleagues working to achieve similar ends in their own sphere. At least fifteen states adopted some form of local option law. Indiana and Vermont, among others, experimented with versions that allowed voters to decide at the town or township level whether annual liquor licenses would be issued locally. Massachusetts gave county commissioners the authority to refuse all applications for liquor licenses.[66] By the mid-1840s, multiple states were regulating temperance taverns as well as acting against liquor sales. New Jersey required that temperance tavern keepers undergo the same licensing process as other keepers, including a char-acter witness from twelve local freeholders. Vermont accomplished a similar purpose with an 1846 statute that distinguished tavern keepers from inn keep-ers. Both had to provide "suitable provisions, lodgings and accommodations," but if local authorities allowed alcohol sales at all, only tavern keepers could sell liquor and wine by the small measure (here, less than one pint), while inn keepers could sell only cider or small beer.[67]

States that took the path to prohibition presumed that taverns would con-tinue to exist because citizens needed places to stay and gather. Most prohibi-tory laws of this period followed the precedent set in Maine. Various iterations of that state's law banned the sale of any liquid that could cause intoxication, with exceptions for use in medicine and manufacturing. To oversee these authorized sales, the state instituted a new licensing procedure to designate town liquor agents. While tavern keepers could remain in business on a dry basis, they were barred from serving as liquor agents because legislators believed that the taste for liquor—and liquor profits—created powerful temptations to break the new law.[68] Delaware made the mere presence of alcohol in a tavern into "presumptive and *prima facie* evidence" of the criminal intent to sell. New York likewise made it illegal to sell, give away, or store alcohol in taverns or any other places of "public amusement." As in Maine, New York's new liquor agents could have no financial interest in a tavern or any competing "place of public entertainment." They also had to be eligible to vote, which excluded most Black men and all women, and they could drink no alcohol, which meant that they had to embody temperate masculinity.[69]

Across lines of sex, race, and class, temperance advocates insisted that everyone would be better off without the alcohol trade. Public drunkenness would no longer affront respectable people's sensibilities. Intoxicated men would no longer pollute their homes and injure their dependent wives and children. Working-class households would achieve a comfortable standard of living when wages no longer went for drink. Some propagandists even maintained that keepers themselves would thrive. One keeper who had "'opposed the law with all my might'" allegedly discovered that he made "'much more money'" trading in foodstuffs and "'other necessaries.'" His claim might even have been true. As James Dennis and other temperance tavern keepers demonstrated, although prohibition hurt many keepers, some managed to accommodate travelers, deal in varied goods and services, and provide a hub for public and private activity without alcohol.[70]

The overt contestation of tavern spaces did not stop when the wishes of the temperate became law, however. While some keepers who violated new liquor laws did so covertly, others did so in open defiance of the temperance regime. In the late 1830s, Massachusetts tavern keeper Thomas Wesson was tried for violating a Massachusetts law that prohibited retail sales of distilled spirits in volumes less than fifteen gallons. Wesson admitted breaking the law and insisted he would do so again. A few years later, Wesson joined twelve other retailers and innholders in calling for a local convention in Concord to discuss "the course taken by the County Commissioners." Later still, Wesson received a jail sentence for a liquor-related offense.[71] Across the nation, temperance laws faced challenges not only in taverns but also in court, from gubernatorial vetoes, and from popular votes. Opposition encompassed personal preferences, antipathy to temperance pieties, economic self-interest, and alarm about governmental overreach. Multiple states and territories had voided, repealed, vetoed, watered down, or otherwise altered their prohibitory laws before 1861, but the struggle for respectable public accommodations would continue.[72]

"The Great Traveling Public" at Midcentury

During the 1840s and 1850s, many of the same courts that ruled on the constitutionality of prohibition also explored the nature and purpose of taverns in lawsuits that had nothing to do with alcohol. Many of these cases involved suits for damages because of property losses that travelers suffered while staying in a tavern. Legal attention to travelers' financial risk was hardly new, but the growing volume of travel and its importance for business heightened the concern. The same cases also gave judges and lawyers opportunities both to affirm the links between mobility, enterprise, and legal personhood and to reflect on what mobility meant to the republic and its citizens. Their arguments sometimes found an audience beyond legal professionals, making their way into publications intended for businessmen and other travelers.[73]

Jurisprudence on both sides of the Atlantic had long established that in addition to their general obligation to accommodate travelers, keepers had a particular responsibility to protect travelers' personal property. If travelers suffered theft or property damage in a tavern, they could sue the keeper to recover the value of their lost property, and keepers had limited legal grounds for self-exculpation.[74] Although most such liability cases were decided on the facts, legal questions still emerged. Keepers often tried to argue that guests' choices had abrogated their own liability, a claim that judges usually dismissed. In *Taylor v. Monnot*, a case that came before New York's superior court in 1854, the keeper insisted that his guest was to blame for his own $350 loss because he had placed the money in his baggage rather than keeping the important sum on his person. Although the court agreed with the keeper's statement of the facts, the judges still found in the guest's favor, reasoning that a traveler had a right to decide for himself how much money his travels required and where to keep it. Previous legal commentators had confined keepers' liability to travel necessities: personal baggage, a carriage or wagon, horse, and associated equipment, and only those monies needed for travel. In this case, the judges concluded that keepers had no right to dictate their guests' luggage or habits. Indeed, keepers must anticipate that travelers differed "according to the character of the journey, the sum necessary to be carried, and the personal habits of the traveller," which meant their belongings would vary, too. This line of thinking raised the stakes on keepers' ability to read their patrons' appearance and possessions. It also suggested that lockable private bedrooms represented at once a genteel refinement and an attempt to reduce the risk of thefts for which keepers were financially responsible. Equally, keepers' claims of employing only good and reliable servants reflected both housekeeping standards and the fact that keepers were liable if their servants stole from guests.[75]

In the mid-1850s, Vermont's supreme court aligned with New York in reckoning with the reality that people traveling on business might carry very large sums of money. In an 1854 case involving the loss of $4,000 in gold, the fruit of "business connected with the Stark Bank," Vermont's chief justice, Isaac Redfield, concluded that keeper George Robinson was liable to Isaac McDaniels for the loss. McDaniels had left this sum at Robinson's tavern, advising Robinson to hide the money in the bed in McDaniels's room while he, McDaniels, visited in the neighborhood. (Keepers in Vermont could not sell alcohol at this point but remained bound by the weighty obligations of commercial hospitality.) In what would become a widely cited and republished ruling, Redfield concluded that the key issue was not whether the money represented personal baggage or fell into the category of "other goods" for which the keeper had no heightened responsibility. Instead, the case turned on whether McDaniels had been Robinson's legal guest at the time of the loss. Two years later, when the matter returned to the supreme court, the judges ruled that McDaniels was no longer a tavern guest when the theft occurred and saw no fresh cause to question the propriety of his traveling with so much money in the first place.[76]

A further wrinkle in determining keepers' liability emerged in *Neal v. Wilcox*, a North Carolina case that pivoted on the uses that a legal guest made of tavern space. This 1856 case suggested that the usual liability did not apply when guests used taverns for certain commercial purposes. Using the example of a traveler who hired a tavern room to display and sell his stock of "clocks and watches," Justice Richard Pearson of the North Carolina supreme court ruled that property brought to be sold at an inn or tavern was not covered by the precedents establishing "the special liability of inn-keepers." For Pearson, a guest's choice to use a tavern as a commercial venue—"for the purpose of showing and selling" goods—reshaped the relative obligation of guest and keeper. Keepers' liability served "to encourage travelling and intercourse among the citizens," Pearson concluded, but "does not reach so far as to take in consideration of trade and commerce." Since the risk of loss fell on the guest in such cases, this ruling suggested that keepers were free to allow and even encourage guests to use tavern and hotel rooms for retail and other business purposes.[77]

Both the North Carolina and Vermont cases pivoted around the legal construction of a tavern guest. As judges explored the borders of guesthood, they articulated what was becoming a widely shared consensus on the economic and political importance of travel and mobility more broadly. From the liability perspective, guest status reflected geography as much as the use of space. Chief Justice Redfield's much-referenced ruling affirmed the long legal understanding that only some tavern patrons were also guests in the eyes of the law. Keepers' special liability extended to patrons with "the transitory character of a guest." People who did not live in the neighborhood became tavern guests whether they visited for "mere temporary refreshment," such as a drink or a meal, stayed overnight, or remained for days on end. Local residents, by contrast, did not enjoy guest status whether they drank, ate, hired a room, or slept in the tavern. As in many aspects of licensing, legal authorities did not usually specify the minimum distance between residence and tavern required to make a patron a guest. Redfield simply noted that a guest "comes from a distance." Whatever the distance, if a patron was indeed a guest, keepers remained liable for thefts committed by their servants and dependents and even for burglaries by outsiders, unless the keeper had evidence that a burglar had used "superior force." Redfield conceded that keepers might find this legal construction oppressive, but he insisted that the "severe" standard of keepers' liability was "indispensable to the quiet and comfort of travelers."[78] The same year, Redfield further supported one version of comfortable travel by finding that Vermont's law prohibiting alcohol sales in taverns and other retail establishments was constitutional, as newspaper editors far from Vermont noticed.[79]

The principle that tavern keepers could be held liable for travelers' commercial as well as personal property filtered out into the business world. *Livingston's Monthly Law Magazine* publicized notable court decisions about keepers' liability, including Vermont's *McDaniels v. Robinson* and New York's *Taylor v. Monnot*. Alexander Davis's *Traveler's Legal Guide and Business Men's Directory* similarly affirmed the protections for business travelers, summarizing the mixture of case and statute law that protected guests' goods, including those being transported for sale, such as "a sleigh-load of wheat." *Hunt's Merchants' Magazine and Commercial Review* publicized a decision in the chancery court of Louisville, Kentucky, that brought tavern keepers' liability into a ruling concerning a steamboat operator. The magazine included Chancellor Henry Pirtle's reasoning: preserving the safety of the "great traveling public" was now a more urgent priority than it had ever been in old Europe because "we have a necessity of intercourse, a traveling beyond anything seen in any other age, or in any other country."[80]

Arguments about travel's importance to the nation occasionally supported contrary arguments about keepers' liability. Acting as attorney for the keepers of an Alabama hotel, Charles P. Robinson hoped to consign the doctrine of travelers' vulnerability to the past. In "earlier and ruder times," he argued, a "sense of insecurity accompanied every act of traveling." Keepers' liability for their guests' property had helped mitigate that fear. But "in this age and country," Robinson continued, travel had been transformed: "a common language, common ideas, common laws, the habit of traveling, equal knowledge, and an active intelligence, have disarmed traveling of most of its terrors, both real and imaginary, and clothed the traveler with a citizenship wherever his journey leads him." The keepers lost their case, but Robinson's fantasy of confident travelers clothed in citizenship resonated powerfully at midcentury.[81]

In the 1850s, white Americans had reason to associate mobility with economic opportunity, personal freedom, and citizenship. As Alexander Davis's *Traveler's Legal Guide* noted, keepers had "to receive all guests who come." Yet lawmakers had also added new layers to keepers' long-standing surveillance obligations. For starters, public health concerns prompted multiple efforts to keep track of strangers and required the operators of urban hotels and boarding houses to monitor their residents. As Davis explained, keepers had to receive all guests "unless they are drunk, or disorderly, or afflicted with contagious disease." This framework preserved the ancient suspicion that outsiders might bring trouble into otherwise orderly communities, while suggesting that some keepers and some patrons were victims of disorder, not its source. This reframing reflected the spread of local and state prohibition and the related investment in self-restrained, respectable travelers and newcomers finding suitable accommodations. It did not take much imagination to interpret disorderliness as meaning simply that a keeper or other patrons disapproved of another's conduct or appearance.[82]

Taverns' monitory functions heightened still more with the passage of state and federal laws restricting Black mobility in new ways. Most notoriously, the 1850 Fugitive Slave Act, a component of the Compromise of 1850, gave Americans fresh reasons to link mobility with opportunity or terror, according to their vantage point. Significantly amplifying enslavers' power outside their own states, the law obliged all citizens to assist federal marshals, who were in turn empowered and required to help enslavers in pursuit of alleged fugitives. Once seized, moreover, a Black person faced a process that, among its other biases, was worth ten dollars to the commissioners appointed to hear such cases if they found that the individual before them was enslaved but only five dollars if free.[83]

Together, this law and the long history of state tavern regulations crystallized keepers' responsibility for racialized surveillance. Black newspapers reported multiple instances of keepers confining Black people based on the suspicion that they might have escaped from bondage. Yet as Vermont's Chief Justice Redfield emphasized, it was "absurd" to imagine that a keeper could detain guests. Even if guests tried to slip away without paying, keepers could not forcibly stop them, for "no such right to detain the person of the guest can be for a moment tolerated in a free country."[84] However, the new fugitive slave law enhanced keepers' implied obligation to question and perhaps detain any people of color they did not personally know to be free. In practice, keepers could raise the alarm about possible fugitives, refuse to accord Black travelers guest status, or take Black travelers at their word and provide hospitality. Samuel Williams, the Black keeper of Philadelphia's Bolivar House tavern, used his distinctive information-gathering opportunities to resist the law. A member of the "Special Secret Committee" of the Underground Railroad, he helped to foil the recapture of at least one group of self-emancipated slaves from Maryland. His warning helped set off a bloody confrontation at Christiana, Pennsylvania. William and Eliza Parker, members of the local Black community, sheltered the group and defended them when Maryland enslaver Edward Gorsuch, his kinsmen, and supporters arrived, killing Gorsuch in the process.[85]

At midcentury, American judges and legislators created new means to police both how people moved about and how they used taverns. Similarly, legal efforts to constrain or harness Black mobility greatly increased the stakes of defining the public's access to and uses of public accommodations as well as common carriers such as trains and steamboats. Yet attempts to remove alcohol, control Black movement, and protect white travelers' interests represented as much a continuity as a change in legal thinking about the roles that taverns could play in an expansive, mobile, and increasingly commercial republic. Amid the startling new powers embedded in prohibitory laws and the heightened racial policing of mobility and citizenship, judges still envisioned white citizens as appropriately on the move in a nation knit together through travel and private enterprise.[86]

THE ARC OF TAVERN LEGALITIES in the early republic cannot be described as the simple replacement of colonial tavern licensing statutes by new anti-licensing and prohibitory laws. Instead, licensing laws, temperance legislation, case law, and legal administration worked together, illuminating powerful men's understanding of taverns as both a hazard and a resource in the young republic. Territorial growth and infrastructural development heightened taverns' legally acknowledged importance as accommodations for a mobile, entrepreneurial, republican people. Lawmakers imposed significant restrictions on tavern keepers and patrons while also leaving substantial freedom for both public officials and private citizens to use taverns in myriad ways. Private economic ambitions created many calls for tavern services, which sometimes fueled new demands for lawmakers to make taverns safe for respectable citizens. Yet taverns' place in this hotly contested arena was shifting. On the one hand, prohibitory legislation gladdened the hearts of those who hoped that all taverns would become—and remain—temperance taverns. On the other hand, in some parts of the country, taverns' value was already declining in ways that often had little to do either with temperance or with fears about disorderly patrons. In the nation's rapidly growing cities and many large towns, the proliferation of both commercial competitors and public buildings steadily reduced the reliance on taverns as both public accommodations and republican venues.

Even at midcentury, however, most Americans still lived in rural areas or in smaller cities, towns, and villages, where local and state officials persisted in appointing taverns as venues for public functions. In New England, taverns remained tied to civic and economic aspects of village life and hosted public sales to settle public and private debts well into the 1850s. Beyond that region, even temperate lawmakers continued to regard taverns as appropriate republican gathering places. In 1840, when Judge Richard Gantt suggested that locals should be kept out of taverns for travelers' sake, and when the South Carolina legislature received multiple temperance memorials and petitions, the legislators also designated at least one tavern as a polling place. By 1842, many thousands of Pennsylvanians had pledged total abstinence from alcohol, but the legislature also sent a portion of the state's village and town voters to taverns on election day.[87] The founding of new political jurisdictions likewise continued to prompt lawmakers to think of taverns. Three years after passing a local-option prohibitory law, the New York legislature specified that the first town meetings of at least four newly created towns should take place at taverns. In these acts, the legislators saw no need to explain whether these were temperance taverns or in dry towns. A few years later, after passing statewide prohibition, Delaware's state legislators passed an election law that designated taverns as polling places in more than half of the state's hundreds (a hundred was similar to a township).[88]

In 1846, New Jersey's legislators affirmed that taverns existed "to accommodate and entertain travellers and strangers, to serve the public occasions" of their respective counties, and "for the convenience of men's meeting together to transact business." To this affirmation of taverns' tripartite value, they added the warning that inns and taverns that promoted drunkenness and other vices should be prevented "as much as possible." Across multiple jurisdictions and levels of government, lawmakers continued to recognize that taverns sat at the potentially fruitful crossroads between public affairs and private business. Fruitful, that is, for those who enjoyed some or preferably all of the prerogatives associated with whiteness, masculinity, full legal personhood, property ownership, and temperate habits.[89]

The intersection of taverns and government functions extended far beyond taverns' important yet intermittent use as jails and polling places or temporary sites of government. By supporting the circulation of goods, people, and ideas, taverns encouraged people to form and recognize economic, social, and cultural ties between settlements across the rapidly expanding nation. Taverns' uses for and by government fostered political continuity as well. For all these reasons, taverns became important venues for the local development of grassroots political activism. Returning now to the country's first years under the Constitution of 1789, we can better appreciate why and how taverns contributed to the powerful tide of local collective political action.

CHAPTER SIX

Collecting the Sentiments of the Sovereign People
Taverns and Collective Politics

In 1797, a Federalist newspaper in Connecticut attacked a Republican tavern keeper in Philadelphia who was standing for election to the Pennsylvania state legislature. Connecticut readers had reason to be interested in a Philadelphia election because what happened in the nation's capital could both predict and shape events throughout the nation. Rising partisan conflict also whetted voters' appetite for scandalous news about the other side. "A public house is a most excellent stand for collecting the sentiments of the *sovereign people*," the *Connecticut Courant's* editor smirked, because the average voter "never speaks his mind right freely except when he's half drunk." A half century later, Ohio's Curran Swaim reached a similarly scathing conclusion about popular participation in the republic's governance. After watching Democratic events at a Virginia tavern before the 1852 presidential election, he sneered that "shabbiness, patriotism, whiskey, and political zeal generally go together." Both complaints disparaged democratic politics and ordinary voters. Both reflected the fear that alcohol aggravated partisan enthusiasms and corrupted the electoral process, which in turn augmented doubts about the value of tavern venues for all sorts of political work.[1] Yet many thousands of Americans persisted in choosing taverns as appropriate places to pursue collective projects with overt or implied political goals. Habits of tavern-going and ideas about those habits contributed to a wholesale expansion in what it meant to be a politically active citizen from the 1790s through the early 1850s. To understand how, we need to look both at and beyond partisan electoral politics.[2]

Taverns had been political spaces throughout the colonial period. They played a significant role in the revolutionary era as places "to organize and focus popular sentiment" and negotiate "political questions of authority and power." Following the ratification of a constitution that centralized much power in the hands of the federal government—although less than some delegates to the Constitutional Convention had wanted—conservative Federalists in George Washington's administration hoped that popular political engagement would remain orderly and limited. In their estimation, the republic required all its citizens to cherish its independence, but voters need only play an episodic role in the nation's governance: casting their ballots on election day and trusting their representatives to rule until the next election gave voters the chance to return them to office or replace them.[3] When Federalist policies began arousing significant resistance, however, grassroots political actions proliferated. Although collective efforts to resist enforcement of particular laws seemed illegitimate to most Americans and both Federalists and Republicans tended to regard the rival party's existence in the same light, partisan organizational meetings in advance of elections became a routine practice within a decade.[4]

Gathering in taverns advanced the goals of both partisan and nonpartisan groups in the early republic. In the critical first decade under the new constitution, the choice of tavern venues for partisan meetings stemmed from taverns' appeal as local gathering places and even more from the legitimacy accorded to citizens' assemblies in such places. Meeting in the same taverns where voters met personal and household needs week in and week out suggested that candidates and parties remained vested in the communities where voters lived, not just in acquiring power for its own sake. Local meetings never guaranteed voters' influence on public officials and policies, but they did shape understandings of participatory citizenship's legitimacy.[5] As individual parties faded and new ones emerged, partisan organizing and policy-making became increasingly centralized over time. Yet even the massive party conventions that attracted thousands of delegates in the 1840s and 1850s preserved the principle that the people should represent and be represented through their local communities. Alongside the work of prominent men in and out of office, grassroots actions helped create and legitimate parties at the local, state, and national levels.[6]

Many of the people who visited taverns to do business, vote, or support a party in the early nineteenth century returned there to participate in organized voluntarism. Partly in reaction to electoral partisanship, voluntary societies proliferated even in the absence of an explicit constitutional right to associate. Some of these societies predated the nation and the revolution and thus were dignified by their longevity. Societies organized around a shared heritage, such as the Scottish Saint Andrew's Society, attracted relatively little concern. Mutual aid societies were also usually uncontroversial, if only because they promised to reduce the number of people who might tax the public coffers. Groups that seemed more overtly interested in influencing the political status quo beyond their own membership, in contrast, aroused skepticism in proportion to their imagined capacity to wield that influence. Threatening to some and desirable to others were societies founded to improve the arts, education, agriculture, and public health. From the standpoint of their supporters, such societies complemented local improvements in transportation or manufacturing. The most controversial associations developed in the turbulence of the Second Great Awakening and promised to transform American society and politics: they promoted such causes as temperance, abolition, and women's rights. Despite the continuing friction over the legality of associating, the habits of collective voluntarism drew strength from many corners of the nation. By the early 1830s, they had become so widespread that French visitor Alexis de Tocqueville took the "immense assemblage of associations" as characteristic of American society, even though neither the drive nor the freedom to associate was universal.[7]

As with partisan meetings, taverns appeared to be peculiarly appropriate venues for much of this work. What John L. Brooke calls "monitoring" societies, such as militias, were well known for frequenting taverns: they leveraged taverns' long-established links with surveillance, vigilantism, and hard-drinking men who were not averse to violence in the name of order. For other associations, especially of the secular improving type, the right taverns bolstered that improving impulse. White men who visited taverns to invest in infrastructure, learn about new technology, or partake in the culture of refinement had good reason to form associations with their neighbors. When people gathered in taverns to build a better society, they yoked taverns to the future they imagined.[8]

Although Americans who associated did not always see themselves as engaged in political work through their voluntarism, they tended to organize their societies along republican lines. Members drafted and ratified constitutions, elected representatives and officers, wrote resolutions, and practiced persuasive and deliberative politics. As particular associations formed connections to like-minded people in different communities, they sometimes organized umbrella societies and held national conventions for which local societies elected delegates and prepared statements. Across the nation, Americans filled the calendar with meetings where they did the work of voluntarism while practicing basic political skills.[9]

Voluntarily organized gatherings *in taverns* represented only a portion of this political activity in the early republic, but they shared an important common subtext. The typical absence of white women, Black women, and usually, Black men from political gatherings convened in taverns, when members of all three groups gathered and organized elsewhere, meant that collective tavern politics embodied the distinctive privileges of manly and especially white men's citizenship. At the same time, tavern politicking represented a means for ordinary white men to express opinions and build coalitions around such topics as the best people and the best means to lead and improve their world. As men in many of these self-created societies learned to act collectively, they concocted vernacular citizenship practices that drew both legitimacy and structure from the evolving, contested norms of tavern-going.[10]

By the 1840s and 1850s, however, taverns engrossed a far smaller share of organized popular politics than they had a generation before. At the same time, the slow process of improving taverns, promoting temperance, and integrating the nation through transportation made some public accommodations newly important to female and Black activists. Because of their radicalism and notoriety, abolitionists provide an especially useful index of public accommodations' political value in both practical and symbolic ways. Black abolitionists were particularly attuned to the importance of access to taverns and hotels in asserting their own freedom to move, pursue opportunity, and act as citizens. As white women and free people of color converted voluntarism into political influence at the local, state, and national levels, contests over public accommodations continued to intersect with efforts to stretch, maintain, or contract the definition of "the *sovereign people.*" Throughout, tavern-going helped shape what Americans thought it took to be and behave like a citizen at midcentury.[11]

"To Exert Their Interest in Support": Campaigning and Associating in the 1790s

In the 1780s and 1790s, taverns provided more than a backdrop to grassroots politics. In rural communities struggling with disputes over land titles, crushing debt, or burdensome taxes, men visited their local taverns to complain about legislative inaction, draft remonstrances, organize with men from other villages, and plan direct action against landlords, courts, or tax collectors. The protests known as Shays's Rebellion in Massachusetts, for example, built on networks rooted in both official town meetings and more informal tavern gatherings.[12] In the same period, taverns also hosted patriotic celebrations of the Constitution's ratification, July Fourth, and similar occasions. Through the careful selection of speakers, music, toasts, and processions, local arrangements committees encouraged participants to embrace the republic and their place within it. By circulating descriptions of such events across the country, moreover, newspapers helped some Americans understand themselves as belonging to a nation, not just to their local communities or states.[13]

Similar dynamics of coalition and consensus building also informed taverns' use for electoral competition. Instead of contenting themselves with showing up on election day to cast their singular votes, many voters either learned or already knew from revolutionary-era activities that they could "exert their interest" by working together. Although tavern politicking took place across the nation, Philadelphia's 1790s experiments with partisan electoral tavern politics deserve special attention for their outsized importance. The city housed the state and the national capitals in the pivotal decade following the Constitution's ratification and was home to some of the nation's most widely circulated and excerpted newspapers, as the *Connecticut Courant's* attempt to discredit the civic-minded Republican tavern keeper Israel Israel suggests. Compounding the significance of grassroots politics in Philadelphia, in 1790 the state replaced its democratic 1776 constitution with a document that created a much more centralized state government and a powerful governor. What room the state and federal constitutions left for the people to influence their government would be worked out in many places, some of them taverns.[14]

Pennsylvania's first gubernatorial election under the new constitutions pitted General Thomas Mifflin against General Arthur St. Clair. Both men had well-established records of public service, but St. Clair ran with the open support of the "political elite," while Mifflin claimed and ultimately won the backing of most ordinary voters. In the words of historian Kenneth Owen, supporters of both candidates clashed "over the legitimacy of their arguments for public support." Newspapers and taverns became important, interconnected theaters in the struggle for voters.[15] At an early stage in the competition, St. Clair supporters privately circulated a letter from "a respectable meeting of the Members of the late Convention and Assembly" to well-placed friends in and beyond Philadelphia, soliciting their "strenuous support" for St. Clair. Apparently intended for circulation only hand to hand via manuscript copies, the letter made its way into the *Pennsylvania Gazette*, where it inspired a barrage of criticisms. Among other complaints, Mifflin's supporters implied that the prominent men who received the St. Clair letter would use their influence to "dictate" to the public. St. Clair's men, in turn, accused Mifflin's allies of mobilizing voters through their own secretive channels: only "*select* friends" of Mifflin's had been invited to attend the supposedly "very numerous and respectable meeting of the Citizens of Philadelphia held at Mr. Epple's tavern." That meeting was, they claimed, "much more dictatorial" than anything St. Clair's friends had devised.[16] Although charges of secret maneuvers were hardly novel, the reworked state constitution raised this election's stakes because the newly created gubernatorial office included veto power over the state legislature.[17]

The elusive boundary between illicit and licit forms of electoral campaigning provides the key to interpreting subsequent notices describing meetings in support of Mifflin, the more democratic of the two candidates. Published accounts of meetings that had taken place specified both venue and processes. One notice stressed that a meeting held at Peter Merkel's tavern represented the sentiments of "the citizens of the township of the Northern Liberties," north of Philadelphia proper. The same notice reported that the attendees had "considered the proceedings of their fellow citizens assembled at Mr. Epple's tavern" and resolved to publish their support for Mifflin "in the several English and German newspapers of the city and county of Philadelphia." Together, these statements implied that ordinary voters had deliberated on the facts and acted with transparency, a combination that the writers believed would be convincing in print.[18]

Newspaper advertisements for upcoming Mifflin meetings likewise crafted political narratives for public consumption. Organizers invited "the Inhabitants of the County of Chester" or "the Freeholders, and other Electors, in the County of Montgomery" to various taverns to "form a Ticket." Advance notice of this sort made meetings accessible to the voting public while reinforcing the connection between the political community and its taverns. Since most people did not subscribe to newspapers, the taverns where they met as voters were often the places where they learned the news. In addition, open-ended invitations encouraged people in each county to imagine themselves as participants and supporters. The combination of the publicity, its phrasing, and the venue implied that these meetings would represent the needs and interests of the geographic community in which each tavern operated. Framed in this way, holding public meetings in places regularly patronized by locals helped identify Mifflin's supporters as legitimate community stakeholders.[19]

These characteristics became even more important when Democratic Republican societies and the Whiskey Rebellion cast grave doubt on the right to engage in collective criticism of the government. In the early to mid-1790s, the policies of the Washington administration and its congressional supporters struck a considerable number of both urban and rural Americans as overreaching the Constitution and betraying the revolution. In coastal cities, numerous societies cropped up to articulate members' collective disagreement with Federalist men and their measures. Whether they met in taverns or other settings, such as Philadelphia's Philosophical Hall, or publicized their activities but not their venues, Democratic Republican societies found themselves on the defensive when farmers in and beyond western Pennsylvania moved past verbal protest to direct action against officials who sought to enforce the federal whiskey tax. Acting as commander in chief, President Washington eventually mustered thousands of troops to suppress the so-called whiskey rebels by force. He also drew a damning connection between the rural protesters in the countryside and "self-created" Democratic Republican societies.[20] While leading society members rejected that link, they also hastened to distance themselves from crowd actions against duly elected government. Instead, they insisted that organized societies were indeed an appropriate means for the people to criticize their government. A Republican himself by this time, Governor Thomas Mifflin insisted that "Freemen" must both "obey existing laws" and "remonstrate against actual wrongs." In such terms, Mifflin and his fellow Republicans sought to legitimate forms of collective politics that extended well beyond the equally self-created ethnic, mutual aid, and elite societies that had experienced what David Waldstreicher calls a period of "revival and emergence" in the 1780s.[21]

As the Democratic Republican societies scrambled for cover, some voluntary societies continued to meet without incurring the president's wrath. Most of these societies did not exist to debate policy or criticize men in office, yet their existence had political implications all the same. Often composed of gentlemen or respectable artisan-class men, ethnic, mutual benefit, and literary societies took their good intentions and their contributions to the public interest for granted.[22] In the 1780s and 1790s, leading taverns in New York and Philadelphia became well known for hosting fraternal and benevolent societies. In Charleston, Harris's tavern hosted groups with diverse purposes: the local Society of the Cincinnati, the Société patriotique française, the Agriculture Society, the Republican Society, and the Friendly Club, among others. Under Mrs. Coates's management, the same tavern hosted the Agriculture Society, the South Carolina Society, and the Saint Tammany Society. In the next decade, at least six voluntary societies met either at William Robinson's, also known as the Planter's Hotel, or the Carolina Coffee House.[23]

Not all locally prominent taverns could boast as steady a cycle of society meetings as in sociable Charleston, however, and not all societies met in taverns. Most religious societies in particular avoided taverns as much as possible. The practice of associating also continued to arouse skepticism in the late eighteenth and early nineteenth centuries. By their nature, voluntary societies compartmentalized the imagined American public into special interests.

Outsiders sometimes fretted that the secretive Freemasons or the elitist, hereditary Society of the Cincinnati might even become a shadow government. Meeting in public houses and publicizing their gatherings tacitly addressed such fears, suggesting that societies had nothing to hide even if their meetings were closed to the public. By frequent gatherings in reputable taverns, associators also helped reinforce the understanding that respectable men gathered in taverns to do together what they could not accomplish alone.[24]

Concerns about associating illuminate related developments in partisan organizing in the mid- and late 1790s. With the Whiskey Rebellion's forceful suppression, the Federalists had the momentary luxury of believing that they had discredited the very idea of an organized opposition. At election time, voters who favored George Washington and his allies did not need to identify as Federalists, for they saw their elected leaders as representing not a faction but the whole people. In the fall of 1794, for example, "a large and respectable meeting of the Freemen" from Philadelphia County met at Widow Lesher's tavern in Germantown, a village outside Philadelphia, "for the purpose of forming a ticket." The assertion of both size and respectability mattered, and so did the venue. Widow Lesher's tavern had a local reputation as a political gathering place, having hosted multiple previous meetings to debate public measures and candidates for office. The voters at this 1794 meeting endorsed one man for Congress and seven others for the state assembly and resolved to publicize their ticket "for the information of the county." The notice avoided any explicit reference to party or faction, but six of the men endorsed are identifiable through other sources as Federalists. The "Freemen" of the county who assembled at this tavern over the next several years endorsed Federalist candidates at least twice as often as Republican men yet avoided partisan labels until the turn of the century, unlike many of their city brethren.[25]

Within Philadelphia and the neighboring communities of Southwark and the Northern Liberties, two types of taverns loaned themselves to pre-electoral meetings in the 1790s. One was the eminent genteel tavern that catered to gentlemen and merchants, such as the City Tavern or the newer Oeller's Hotel, which hosted many associations and patriotic celebrations. Many events at these taverns, such as the subscription balls designed to accommodate the local elite, were not open to everyone likely to attend so-called respectable meetings at election time, let alone the general public. When Federalists entered such venues to engage in collective civic or political work, they suggested both their meetings' importance and their elevation above the often boisterous culture of Philadelphia's streets and ordinary citizens.[26]

For their part, Republicans also needed spacious premises when organizing meetings intended to be citywide, but they tended to seek out spaces that aligned better with their more democratic norms. "Respectable" meetings of "Democratic Republicans" convened at Louis Fouquet's hotel to agree on tickets for state senator, assembly, and several local offices. Located on the relatively less developed western edge of the city between Tenth and Eleventh Streets, the former Richardet's tavern became "l'Hôtel François" under Fouquet's management. Fouquet advertised in French and English: the French component had particular appeal for Democratic Republicans, who identified with republican France and deplored the Federalists' commercial and diplomatic attachments to Great Britain.[27]

In addition to these large, notable taverns, both Federalists and Republicans relied on two more types of taverns. Urban stage taverns such as John Dunwoody's and George Lesher's served both their neighbors and a steady stream of travelers; meeting at such places represented an excellent means of gathering and disseminating information. Another group of taverns likely served more purely local clienteles. Although their keepers appeared in city directories, they did not usually advertise their taverns in newspapers. Across Philadelphia, the Northern Liberties, and Southwark, meetings held in this type of tavern gave the impression not merely of numbers but also of diffused, local, grassroots deliberation.[28]

State senate elections in 1798 inspired numerous electoral meetings in and around Philadelphia. In the fall of 1797, Republican Israel Israel won election to the state senate, largely with support from the Northern Liberties and Southwark, home to many recent immigrants. Federalists insisted that many unqualified people had voted and that voting had occurred outside designated polling places. Eventually, a second election was called for late February, 1798. In advance of this second election, supporters of both Israel and his opponent, Federalist Benjamin Morgan, worked to rally voters across the city and its outskirts.[29] Both parties adopted tavern venues that helped put partisanship in a neighborhood context. Israel meetings took place at taverns across the city and the Northern Liberties but usually in the densely populated neighborhoods within a few blocks of the busy waterfront, such as Lewis Bender's tavern on Second Street in the Northern Liberties. To support Benjamin Morgan, Philadelphia Federalists likewise fanned out to local taverns throughout greater Philadelphia. Federalists also reached across neighborhood boundaries to invoke the larger political community, as when "a number of the citizens of Philadelphia, the District of Southwark, and the Northern Liberties" assembled at Dunwoody's tavern on Market Street.[30]

The fact that Federalists and Republicans both met in taverns did not preclude each side from attacking the other's tavern meetings. Federalists in and beyond Philadelphia railed that "tavern demagogues" won votes only through their alcoholic corruption of weak-minded voters.[31] At the same time, Federalists cast their own tavern gatherings as legitimate citizens' assemblies. Any unseemly conduct at their gatherings was the fault of Republicans on the (literal) street, as when "*a numerous and daring mob*" tried to interrupt a meeting of Benjamin Morgan's supporters at James Cameron's tavern on Shippen Street. When they failed to break into the tavern, they resorted to making a "clamour and confusion out of doors."[32] On other occasions, Republicans defended the sanctity of a tavern gathering against the violence of the Federalist street. When Republicans in Reading, Pennsylvania, gathered at a leading local tavern to celebrate Republican congressman Albert Gallatin, a group of young Federalist men rang bells, sang offensive songs, fired a cannon, and allegedly attempted to storm the tavern. When they failed to gain entry, they contented themselves with making a disturbance "during the whole night" and tried again to lay hands on the congressman when he, his wife, and their child left the next morning. Anticipating this attempt, the Republicans had already smuggled Gallatin out the back of the tavern, putting him on a horse and then escorting his wife and child in their carriage through the crowd to the outskirts of town.[33]

Through both rowdy gatherings and more orderly meetings, turn-of-the-century voters turned their electoral powers into rather more than the constrained participation Federalists had originally imagined. Both Federalists and Republicans adopted pre-election tavern meetings at which ordinary voters had opportunities to deliberate on men and measures and practice crafting persuasive messages for publication. In New York City, for example, even as Federalists' prospects for national election faded, Federalists organized ward-level meetings for voters in each of the city's eight wards, most of them in taverns. Voluntary society meetings at which men also voted, deliberated, crafted strategies, and celebrated further expanded the popular practices of citizenship.[34] It would, however, be easy to overstate both the degree and the breadth of popular engagement in this period. Whether at partisan or nonpartisan meetings, the processes of electing chairs, clerks, and delegates and tasking committees to draft resolutions and notices for publication created potential hierarchies of political distinction. People of means had more time to devote to political work. Some men were personable and persuasive. Some men labored to read, while others wrote fluidly, and still others could tap unusually rich networks of relations and friends. While men born into wealthy families did not monopolize these strengths, social capital and financial standing were not wholly independent variables. At a minimum, the overlap between extensive involvement in partisan meetings or voluntary societies and having a good deal of discretion over one's time and money remained considerable.[35]

Another aspect of democracy against which to measure tavern politics in this period concerned Black men's and white women's inclusion. The American Revolution had opened up new possibilities for both groups. In Rosemarie Zagarri's words, rights talk had "an elastic quality" at the turn of the century. Some white and many Black Americans associated the cause of independence with emancipation from literal slavery, not just the more metaphorical slavery of empire. New paths to freedom included the chaos of war and legal manumission, both individual and statewide. Free Black Americans asserted their claim to civic and political rights, including suffrage. After the revolution, seven states allowed Black men to vote, sometimes with property and other qualifications. Many white women considered themselves mothers of the revolution or daughters of the republic. Small numbers of propertied white women went much further, insisting that the principle of no taxation without representation applied to them. In New Jersey, both women and Black men with sufficient property could vote from 1776 to 1807.[36]

The growing importance of formal tavern meetings for political purposes had mixed implications for Black and female politics. Black voters in urban areas—where most of the free Black population lived—sometimes convened their own partisan tavern meetings and may occasionally have attended racially mixed campaign gatherings. Early in the nineteenth century, Black Federalists in New York City convened as "Electors of Colour" in local taverns. As Sarah L. H. Gronningsater argues, they combined tavern meetings with print. In 1808, for example, the *New-York Herald* published a notice of a meeting of Black voters at Heyer's tavern on Lower Manhattan's Chatham Street. Since Heyer's also hosted Fourth Ward Federalists' meetings, this tavern was friendly ground, or at least more so than any tavern that hosted Republican gatherings. At this meeting, voters condemned President Thomas Jefferson's unpopular trade embargo against Great Britain, which they attributed to "Executive imbecility and Foreign Influence." The assembled voters also pledged to support their chosen ticket "by all just and honourable means" and resolved to reconvene at Heyer's throughout the election period. The following year, Black New Yorkers again met at Heyer's Long Room to discuss and support another round of electoral nominations.[37]

White women's political participation in the same period differed considerably. In contrast to Black voters, white women enjoyed regular public acknowledgment of their importance to the republic. Numerous authors and public speakers framed white women's interest in current affairs as one of the republic's strengths, while ignoring both the struggles and the work of Black women. Nationwide, however, white women had even less access to suffrage than Black men, while their role in formal tavern politics was complementary rather than analogous to white men's. For the wives, daughters, and sisters of prominent public men, familial and political interests often intertwined at salons, dinner parties, and balls, sometimes held in leading taverns. July Fourth and similar festivities included men's toasts to the "Daughters of Columbia" and the "American Fair," more often invoking women as men's inspiration and moral compass than as equal or independent tenders of the revolutionary flame.[38] Even in New Jersey, where propertied women could vote, public references to them at patriotic celebrations generally framed their contributions in terms of their relationships to men and the feminized work of sewing or cookery. When the Sons of Cincinnati celebrated July Fourth at Wales's tavern in Elizabeth in 1791, the *New Jersey Journal* noted with approval that the "fair friends of the Cincinnati" invited the men "to a participation of cake and tea in a bower prepared for the occasion." Nearly a decade later, on the cusp of Thomas Jefferson's election as president, women attended a Republican celebration in northern New Jersey but ate separately from the men and offered no toasts. For their part, the men made one toast acknowledging women, which urged "the fair daughters of America" to marry only "real republicans." If the Republican women had formed any part of the arrangement committees that organized the day's events, the published notice provided no hint of it. The notion that white women might assemble and make their own political toasts provoked more satire than praise.[39]

Newspapers also provided an unclear picture of female tavern keepers' involvement in partisan organizing. Consider Widow Lesher, whose Germantown tavern hosted multiple Federalist events in the 1790s and early 1800s. Unlike her contemporary Israel Israel, she can have entertained no aspirations to high elected office.[40] Print advertisements show that pro-Constitution Federalists and propertied men were using Lesher's as a gathering place in the 1780s, when her husband was still alive. Local newspapers provide no indication that the widowed Mrs. Lesher herself played a role in organizing Federalist events in the 1790s. Then again, meetings and notices created a public link between the woman and the politics in her house at a time when Germantown was becoming evenly contested between Federalists and Republicans. In the 1797 state senate election that pitted Benjamin R. Morgan against Israel Israel, Morgan beat Israel four to one in Germantown. In the special election the following spring, Israel polled only eighteen votes fewer than Morgan in Germantown, and in October of the same year, Israel outpolled a different Federalist by over thirty votes, while losing both elections overall. In other words, the Federalism of Widow Lesher's tavern meant taking a stand— however indirectly—within a changing electorate. Whatever her own political inclinations, notices about her tavern's use as a partisan venue meant that she appeared often in print as a woman at the intersection of business and politics.[41]

In New Jersey, taverns also served as meeting and polling places, yet evidence for women's and Black men's involvement in tavern politicking appears equivocal notwithstanding their enfranchisement. Pre-election meetings for inhabitants and "electors"—the state's term for voters—were in theory open to female and Black voters, but newspapers provided scant evidence that people from these groups were actively involved or even present. In 1806, for instance, "a large number of electors" from Orange met "a respectable committee" of "gentlemen from Newark" at a local tavern to deliberate the county's ticket. After a "free and satisfactory conference," the electors "unanimously resolved" on a slate. Such notices do not rule out female and Black attendance, but they suggest that incorporating these voters into the public narrative of partisan activism was no priority.[42]

The unequal political opportunities in turn-of-the-century taverns were more than a projection of prejudices that existed in the wider world. Locating political celebrations and organizational gatherings in taverns made it clear that although many people used taverns for a variety of overlapping purposes, the work of deliberating and voting set white men apart. Similarly, the steady repetition of male names in notices of political meetings—in contrast, for example, to notices of performances and lessons, which often included women—quietly undercut the heady discussions of women's rights and Black liberty throughout the mainstream press. The same meetings and notices also tended to single out the well-to-do, professionals, and officers in the militia or former Continental Army. Men with militia titles or an esquire to their name were rather more likely than other men to fill special roles, such as moderator, clerk, committee member, convention delegate, or candidate for office. Equally, men with these distinctions were known collectively as gentlemen, as in the case of the Newark committee. Just as the ability to use some tavern spaces for particular purposes did not give everyone equal access to partisan or associational gatherings, attending those gatherings expressed white men's shared political citizenship in the early republic without conferring equal leadership opportunities.[43]

Contraction, Expansion, and Unease
in the "Era of Good Feelings"

In the twenty years after 1800, when the Republicans became the dominant national party, the prospects for Black men's and white women's involvement in collective tavern politics grew cloudier. Black men faced growing obstacles to their exercise of voting rights, and white women's readiness to express partisan convictions in public shrank during and after the War of 1812. It also became clear that taverns rarely welcomed white women's or free Black people's collective political work; more frequently, these groups met in members' homes, churches, libraries, and similar noncommercial venues. Meanwhile, white men continued to find the combination of print with tavern meetings a potent means to address concerns about the efficacy, transparency, and honesty of their own partisan work. In addition, white men participated in a growing variety of formal associations that met in taverns, deepening the connections between their tavern-going and their vernacular citizenship while broadening their avenues to and exercise of political privilege.[44]

During the War of 1812, New York City papers indicated that some Black voters continued to gather, organize, and publicize their work. Under the heading "AFRICAN LIBERTY FOR EVER!" a notice in the *Commercial Advertiser* from the "General Committee of the Electors of Colour" invited Black voters who were "friendly to the cause of Liberty, Peace and Commerce" to Johnson's tavern "on business of extraordinary importance." A few days later, a piece in the *Evening Post* mentioned "a numerous and respectable meeting of the Electors of Colour" at Williams's tavern. This notice acknowledged a regrettable "division in politics among the electors of colour" but upheld the "respectable" character of the meeting and noted that the assembled men had appointed a nonpartisan "committee of grievances" with delegates from the city's lower wards to "promote habits of industry, honesty, and sobriety." In all, the public notice identified the chair, secretary, and five ward delegates by name and provided the time and place of a future meeting, suggesting a fair degree of confidence that they could continue to organize and meet in public.[45]

In their repeated use of congenial taverns, face-to-face deliberations, and newspapers, New York City's Black voters closely resembled their white neighbors. Whatever their political differences, their electoral coordination apparently brought the Federalists to victory in the 1813 state assembly elections. Or so the disappointed Republicans believed. When they regained power the following year, one of the Republicans who had lost in 1813 spearheaded a successful bill imposing new burdens on the city's Black voters. In less than a decade, most of the state's Black voters would be disenfranchised under the state's new constitution, which eliminated all property qualifications for its white men.[46]

New Jersey charted a similar course, in part because both parties recognized that the small number of female and Black voters could turn an election in one party's favor. When the state allowed white men to qualify by either taxpaying or property ownership, it stripped the vote from both women and Black men, no matter how wealthy. Legislators from both parties had periodically proposed doing away with voting rights for propertied women and Black men over the previous two decades, largely for perceived partisan advantage, but those calls had come to nothing. A "hotly contested election" about the location of the new courthouse in Essex County provided a fresh impetus for disfranchisement. In 1807, Essex voters had to decide whether their new courthouse would be built in Newark, home of the existing courthouse, or in a rural location that might have helped the rival town of Elizabeth achieve a much desired ascendency in the county. Supporters of the two locations used both newspapers and tavern meetings to rally support. They insisted on the advantages of an urban location already well-supplied with comfortable taverns and the inconvenience of traveling into the countryside or, conversely, upon the justice of giving another part of the county a chance to reap the indirect economic benefits that the courthouse brought to its neighborhood.[47]

When the election produced more ballots than legal voters, accusations flew: some so-called Republicans were really Federalists; election supervisors had manipulated the polling hours; underage women had voted illegally; some men had voted multiple times. One Newark supporter who wrote as "Manlius" complained in print that "almost every thing that offered in human shape" had voted, while "some ladies approaching the election poll, was roughly handled." Manlius's solicitude for the "ladies" did not imply protecting their access to the polls, for he described women's voting as an "improper practice." His phrase, "every thing . . . in human shape," hinted at the rumor that white men had voted multiple times by donning women's clothes, but the words might also have contested Black voters' equal humanity. The Essex courthouse fight did not by itself prompt the legislature to strip the vote from female and Black voters, but the gendered and racial framing that men such as Manlius offered helped ensure that the measure faced minimal opposition. And predictably, while the new courthouse was under construction, the locally prominent Eagle Tavern in Newark played host to the court.[48]

Even where women and people of color played no obvious part, white men's participation in local organizing continued to fuel charges and counter-charges of corruption. In New Castle County, Delaware, Republicans maintained a steady diet of tavern meetings despite their overwhelming dominance over county Federalists. In 1809, for example, the county turned out hundreds of Federalists and thousands of Republicans. Nevertheless, New Castle Republicans continued to use meetings not only to mobilize but also to monitor each other. From 1809 through at least 1819, Delaware's *American Watchman* published notices inviting New Castle County's Republicans to meetings at the Red Lion Inn, a conveniently located and well-known village tavern near the center of the county, roughly twelve miles southeast of Wilmington, the county seat. In September 1810, for instance, a Red Lion meeting appointed a three-man committee of correspondence and called for a county-wide nominating meeting, also at the Red Lion, to be attended by delegates elected from voters' meetings in each hundred in the county. (A hundred was similar to a township in other states.) In such ways, pre-election tavern meetings self-propagated: each meeting laid the groundwork for future meetings and generated public notices that kept both cause and venue before the public eye.[49]

At the same time, organizers emphasized the important procedural work that meeting attendees would tackle, in distinct contrast to the agenda at festive events. As one public notice declared, the purpose of an upcoming meeting at the Red Lion was "to agree upon the method of nominating the Representatives of the State Legislature, and Levy Court Commissioners." The following year, Republican organizers convened another meeting at the same tavern to determine the process for selecting candidates for the next election. On paper, at least, these meetings were unscripted, and whoever attended would shape the outcomes by determining the procedures.[50] Published notices usually specified the attendance of "Democratic Republican fellow citizens," "republican citizens," or "democratic citizens," terms that affirmed the legitimacy of partisanship and did not preclude nonvoters' participation, as an invitation to electors did. Both venue and context made it likely that only voters attended, however. Under the state's 1792 constitution, only white men could vote, and they had to be at least twenty-two years old, have at least two years' residence in the state, and pay taxes. At twenty-one, white sons of enfranchised fathers could also vote even if they did not yet pay taxes themselves.[51]

The well-honed routines of shaping slates and mobilizing votes through public meetings did not prevent accusations of corruption from within. In

1810, the *American Watchman* printed a series of pseudonymous letters complaining that New Castle County Federalists had contaminated Republican councils. These letters conveyed a secondary argument about power and influence within the Republican party. As "Locke," one writer protested that "known and avowed federalists" from White Clay Creek Hundred had sent delegates to a countywide Republican meeting at the Red Lion earlier that year. Because of this "flagrant outrage," Locke protested, the Federalist-leaning Thomas Phillips had become the Republican candidate. Phillips was a locally prominent man who headed a substantial household of twenty people, including four slaves and two free people of color. He also owned two mills and could afford to build a new three-story stone-and-wood frame house. Perhaps this wealth as much as Phillips's political choices inspired Locke's accusation of closet Federalism.[52]

Writing as "Aristides," another resident took aim at Phillips's rival, George Massey. Aristides accused Massey's supporters of "riding over the whole hundred" for weeks before the meeting, "begging votes (and federal ones too, which can be proved)." Aristides implied that visiting people to plead for their votes was improper and unmanly. He also derided Massey himself, likening him to a schoolboy who had "not as yet sufficiently matured those lessons he has been, and is still receiving from his worthy tutors." Massey does not appear in the 1810 census for New Castle County, suggesting that he had not yet achieved the manly independence of a householder. While the two antagonists attacked the candidates, they also attended to other men's alleged procedural improprieties. Locke castigated the election judges who had rejected a petition from White Clay Creek Republicans asking for the exclusion of Federalist delegates from their hundred. Aristides condemned the petitioners because they had not attended the meeting at the Red Lion. In Aristides's view, their absence from the tavern meeting cast doubt on their claim to represent the authentic Republican voice of the hundred. A third man, "Honestus," insisted that the petitioners included "a number of men and boys disqualified to vote."[53]

As these complaints implied, the opportunity to cultivate potential leaders by attending face-to-face meetings was neither neutral nor evenly distributed. Not every tax-paying man in New Castle County had either the time to spare for repeated meetings or the social capital to be named to a formal role within the meeting, let alone nominated for public office. White Clay Creek Hundred included the small villages of Newark and Christiana, about ten miles from the Red Lion Inn. Perhaps the aggrieved petitioners had been unable to take the time to attend meetings there. Members of the 1810 correspondence committee, however, had previously served as chairs or secretaries for Red Lion meetings, while respected members of the local meeting were elected as delegates to the countywide meeting, also held at the Red Lion. Massey himself had served as secretary and delegate at previous meetings, suggesting that his candidacy built on his skills in cultivating local networks. The same meetings tended to reward not only those gifted with persuasive charisma but also those endowed with the advantages of wealth, education, or unusually rich connections. Up-and-coming young men and newcomers sometimes had reason to feel thwarted by their more established elders.[54]

At the same time, the controversy reveals the importance contemporaries attached to what happened in public meetings. Local meetings were supposed to reflect, not dictate, local preferences, and attending public meetings thus became a testing ground for individual and group integrity. For this reason, the White Clay Creek petitioners' absence from the Red Lion Inn mattered. Holding a well-publicized meeting in a public place conferred a patina of legitimacy that meetings by the wayside or in private homes could not, at least to many anxious Republicans. As Jeffrey Pasley suggests about this period, Republicans believed that "unfair tactics" including "indoctrination and intimidation" were the Federalists' only path to electoral victory. Even though run-ins with counterfeiters and other tricksters might have made men question their own ability to distinguish truth from lies, face-to-face public meetings among people who knew each other in multiple contexts provided a seeming bulwark against manipulation and falsity. Taverns represented especially important venues for this legitimation because the breadth and variety of tavern interactions could be read as mutually reinforcing opportunities to establish other men's probity.[55]

Much of the time, however, tavern meetings elicited not so much individuals' unvarnished opinions as performances of political manliness. For many white American men in the early nineteenth century, the willingness to speak one's mind in person and not just in print, let alone anonymously, suggested an honorable masculine forthrightness. In this context, even an innocent mistake in convening a public meeting could provoke troubling accusations. In 1816, Samuel Snowden, editor of the *Alexandria Gazette*, came under attack because he had published "an anonymous notice" inviting those who "feel an interest in the establishment of a Branch Bank of the United States" to attend a meeting at John M'Laughlin's prominent tavern in Alexandria. A "numerous and respectable assembly of the citizens" showed up on a Tuesday evening in November, possibly including propertied women with an interest in the bank. The assembled people appointed their own chair and secretary, and the chair called twice for the meeting's conveners "to explain the object and cause of the meeting." No one stepped forward. The disgruntled attendees promptly passed several brief resolutions expressing "disapprobation" of whoever had submitted the original notice and implying fault in the newspaper editors who had printed it. Snowden related all of this, along with extensive "remarks" justifying his printing of the anonymous notice and accusing the group at M'Laughlin's of "an undue degree of sensibility."[56]

The misfire at M'Laughlin's confirmed that the outcome of public meetings could depend on who was present. It also suggested that by the mid-1810s, many people knew the basic practices and procedures for public meetings. Many men had learned these skills from partisan politics, but nonpartisan societies provided a similar education in collective self-governance. Some of those who came to M'Laughlin's for the bank meeting had surely attended previous meetings there, perhaps as stockholders of the Washington and Alexandria Turnpike Company or the Potomac Company. Some might have visited the tavern in its capacity as a stage stop or paid their federal direct taxes there in 1816 and then returned as members of the Alexandria Harmonic Society or the Washington Society, musical and benevolent associations, respectively.[57]

Beyond the nation's largest cities and capital towns, the most common overlap between voluntarism and taverns involved militias. Although exclusively composed of men and usually white men, militias sponsored a variety of community celebrations and commemorative events that women and children attended. In the eighteenth century, self-constituted Regulator militias had sometimes acted against the official colonial militias, but in the early republic, militias more often suggested the state's latent power to defend the status quo. In the nineteenth-century South, state and voluntary militias sought to keep enslaved people in subjection. In the territories, militias took aim at Spanish, French, British, and Indigenous power. Some urban militias had both social and partisan leanings and particularly attracted young men. Whatever the societal implications of their armed power, most militias also practiced an internal politics of voting and rulemaking.[58]

From Illinois to South Carolina, militia companies typically elected their own officers, often gathering at taverns to do so. When they mustered in front of taverns and conducted business within, militiamen embodied the right to occupy this important institution as keepers of public order. In practice, militiamen's version of order often included the prerogative of getting rascally drunk in public. As Captain J. E. Alexander recorded in his *Transatlantic Sketches*, a would-be officer might improve his chances by "treating his friends with sling previous to the election."[59] From a temperance perspective, the tavern connection was pernicious. In a pamphlet about "intemperate drinking," Thomas Hertell proposed that it would be better for the militia "*not* [to be] *mustered at all*" than to assemble at or near a tavern. Not merely a swipe against drinking, Hertell's reasoning devalued the concerns and affinities that often motivated men to form or join voluntary militias.[60]

Across the country, whether militia life absorbed much or little masculine energy, some men also participated in other forms of voluntarism that implied different understandings of the public good. In towns and villages much smaller and less cosmopolitan than Alexandria, locally leading taverns hosted gatherings that gave men practice with procedures and opportunities to act in concert as stakeholders in multiple enterprises. In 1819, voters in the recently settled town of Blakeley, on the east bank of Mobile Bay in Alabama, came to the Alabama Hotel to cast their ballots in local elections. Residents also attended meetings there as subscribers to a variety of improving concerns, such as the proposed Blakeley Academy and the Steam Boat Company of Alabama.[61] Far away in southwestern New Hampshire, where militia activity was less prominent, the village of Walpole sat on the east bank of the Connecticut River and was connected overland to Boston via a sequence of turnpike segments. Holland's tavern hosted many activities for Walpole villagers, such as a county convention protesting the recent change in "the place of holding the Courts," supposedly undertaken without consulting local residents. Improving locals also visited Holland's as shareholders in the Walpole Village Bridge Corporation, as members of the county agricultural society, or, somewhat later, as subscribers to or agents of the mutual fire insurance company. Some of the same people came back to Holland's under the aegis of the Walpole Detecting Society, which pursued horse thieves. And perhaps some of them returned to Holland's yet again, this time with their wives and daughters, for balls organized by the Union Social Assembly.[62]

The voluntary associations that advertised their meetings at taverns often had a practical bent. Members of agricultural societies, for example, hoped to improve their own crops and livestock. Detecting societies hoped to deter crime and recover stolen property. Both types of ventures had political implications and aligned with visiting taverns to exchange credit, information, labor, and goods. Other groups with more idealistic or abstract goals also resorted to taverns. Educational, scientific, and even some religious societies met in taverns and hotels, but not just any tavern or hotel. In 1814, for example, the trustees of the District of Columbia's public schools met at M'Keowin's Hotel. Two years later, a group of citizens met at the same place to "frame a constitution" for the Metropolitan Association, later known as the Columbian Institute for the Promotion of Arts and Sciences. M'Keowin's was an important local landmark on Pennsylvania Avenue: roughly equidistant between the Capitol Building and the White House, it hosted dinners and balls honoring prominent public figures, living and dead.[63] To the north in Ballston Spa, New York, William Clark's Village Hotel operated on a much humbler scale, yet Clark still accommodated the local community, hosting auctions, executive meetings of the board of managers of the Saratoga County Bible Society, and gatherings of the local Masons and the county agricultural society.[64]

The combination of associating and tavern-going did not, in short, appeal only to the subset of men who relished public carousing, as militiamen were often said to do. This cluster of preferences and behaviors complicates our understanding of ongoing tensions between unabashed drinkers and those who embraced temperance not just as a personal creed but as a basis for tireless evangelism. Middle-class temperance men and women developed a gendered critique of rowdy, drink-centered tavern-going, seeking to encourage men to invest their time, emotions, and money not in sociable tippling but rather in their homes, families, churches, and sober forms of improvement. This tension both pitted tavern culture against reforming culture and spurred efforts to reshape taverns to suit more temperate users.[65] In densely populated areas, competing understandings of proper manly behavior helped produce a spectrum among taverns according to the means, affiliations, and behavioral preferences of both keepers and patrons. The same tension cropped up within individual taverns, especially in communities that contained many contrasting viewpoints yet not enough people to support segmentation across taverns. Even temperance reformers such as Thomas Hertell conceded that although tavern venues often led people into "irregular habits," "self-created societies" that were "productive of great benefit" might still convene in taverns. After all, taverns "cannot, perhaps, at all times, be well avoided."[66]

Whatever their mission and membership, voluntary associations in the republic's first decades provided a basis for collective identification and practice in the skills of consultation, deliberation, delegation, and persuasion. Through such activities, both partisan and nonpartisan, "ordinary people learned to think and to act as citizens," as Johann Neem has observed. Associators shared that common experience across lines of gender, race, class, and political affinity. They were most likely to recognize and value these commonalities when their causes, memberships, and venues overlapped. In newspapers and other forms of print, partisan and nonpartisan associators alike crafted a narrative of place, identifying individual establishments and whole categories of institutions with certain people and activities. Both the extraordinarily varied work that white men did in taverns and the voluntarism that other slices of the population pursued in schools, churches, libraries, and government buildings helped shape contemporary thinking about who could be citizens and what citizenship meant.[67]

The Local Dynamics of Rekindled Partisan Competition

After a period when electoral turnout bore scant relationship to the strength of state parties, partisan competition revived nationwide beginning in the mid-1820s. Eventually, new parties amplified local, state, and national struggles over the power of individuals, institutions, and government.[68] Over the next several decades, many Americans came to believe that the nation should be a white man's democracy, with little automatic deference to inherited wealth and social capital. During the same years, the inclination to associate exploded, drawing in ever more people to address a widening array of concerns and causes with both old and new political tools.[69] Some of these causes would prove even more divisive than party politics because they attacked institutions that most Americans believed lay beyond legitimate challenge, including slavery and women's subordination to men. Despite their many differences, the parties and nonpartisan associations continued to have much in common, including the extensive reliance on local meetings to mobilize support and legitimate their work. As in the first decades of the century, Black and white women's groups and those with religious purposes continued to prefer meeting outside taverns, usually in schools, churches, and other civic buildings. The men who predominated in tavern gatherings for political or civic ends presumed that white manhood mattered to citizenship yet remained far from unanimous about what that citizenship should entail or require of them.[70]

In electoral contexts, the habit of attending local meetings and placing notices about them in newspapers continued to reinforce the notion that voters were justified in acting collectively before elections because they did so within local geographic communities. A contested mayoral election in Baltimore bears out this point. In 1822, the supporters of incumbent mayor John Montgomery produced a newspaper narrative to rescue their candidate from a brewing scandal. As described in the pages of the *Baltimore Patriot*, "a general committee" met at Klinefelter's tavern to explain the embarrassing last-minute cancellation of a town meeting. This committee, composed of five representatives from each of the city's twelve wards, *"resolved unanimously"* that Baltimore's "decent" citizens deserved a public explanation. Mayor Montgomery had welcomed the opportunity to participate in "full, free, honorable and candid" public discussion, which would, his supporters claimed, help counter the "malicious and unfounded abuse" that "secret caucuses" had pushed into "the public prints . . . with unwearied industry." Yet, the committee concluded, it would not have been "generous or manly" to hold the scheduled town meeting because his rival for mayor, Edward Johnson, was a "retiring enemy" who had "shrunk from public discourse" and refused to attend.[71]

Charges and countercharges of unmanly calumny were only too familiar in early republican politics, but the committee's arguments were procedural as well as personal. Rebutting the accusation that a town meeting would only provoke angry confusion, the general committee performed measured indignation. By publicizing the meeting's logistics and representative composition, the committee indicted the other side's lack of transparency. In addition, even though only two members of the meeting at Klinefelter's were named, the rest were not masked behind pseudonyms but known by face and name to the voters who chose them to represent their respective wards, the city's voting districts. The following year, another notice in the *Patriot* from "The Voters of Old Town" reasserted the importance of ward and neighborhood politics: "it has been always usual to have a meeting at Klinefelter's, Old Town; therefore, in order to gratify the people in this part of the city, a public meeting will be held on Saturday evening." "The Voters of Old Town" surely did not speak for every voter, let alone every inhabitant, but the combination of the familiar local tavern meeting and the printed notices helped frame a group of voters as a legitimate collective voice.[72]

As the meetings at Klinefelter's suggest, not all electoral meetings were overtly partisan. Through the rest of the 1820s, local meetings and the newspapers that published their proceedings engaged citizens with varying degrees of comfort with partisan organizing. A single issue of a northeastern Massachusetts newspaper illustrates a spectrum of local opinions about electoral politicking in advance of the presidential and congressional elections in 1824. One meeting was purely informational: "persons in Bradford who take any interest in the approaching election" could come to Hannah Kimball's tavern to hear the latest election-related news from Boston. This meeting planned no course of action and did not exclude nonvoters. Across the Merrimack River in Haverhill, "the citizens disposed to send Delegates" to an electoral nominating convention at Newburyport were invited to meet at the Golden Ball Hotel. However diverse the citizens at this meeting, the delegates they selected were almost guaranteed to be white men. Both Black and white men could vote in Massachusetts, but Haverhill had few or no Black residents at the time, and the white majority was unlikely to select Black representatives in any case. (By contrast, Haverhill's white residents were happy to watch Richard Potter perform at the same hotel.) A third notice announced a partisan electoral strategy, requesting "Republicans" in the "several towns" of the Essex North Congressional District to send delegates to a meeting at Steven's tavern in Andover, ten miles south of Bradford and Haverhill, where they would "agree upon a suitable person" to run for Congress.[73]

Elsewhere in 1824, "friends" of General Andrew Jackson were beginning to organize into Jackson clubs, adapting familiar organizational strategies and venues to a new kind of popular campaigning. The notice for a Jackson meeting at Baltimore's Washington Hotel encouraged a narrative of generational realignment, with five references to the youth of Jackson's supporters in a brief paragraph. Rather than inviting people to deliberate on possible candidates or elect delegates to a nominating convention, the "Young American" author encouraged every "respectable" and "patriotic" young man to "attend and proclaim his reverence" for Jackson. Yet Baltimore's Jackson supporters also held meetings at locally important taverns in each ward, including Klinefelter's tavern in the fourth ward. While these notices presumed enthusiasm for Jackson and included few details, they still suggested a regard for local political processes. Presidential election meetings in taverns such as Klinefelter's, where voters pursued both personal business and ward-level concerns, built bridges between individual interests, municipal affairs, and national politics.[74]

In the presidential election of 1828, Jackson's supporters continued to rely on taverns even as they demonstrated new levels of coordination. Baltimore again illustrates the combination of top-down and grassroots action. Strategies for voter mobilization now came from the Jackson Central Committee, who invited "the Friends of JACKSON and REFORM" to meetings in the city's twelve wards. At least half of the Jackson ward meetings in August 1828 convened in taverns or hotels, and the Fourth Ward's chosen spot was, yet again, Klinefelter's tavern. Attendees at these meetings nominated eight people per ward to serve on a superintending committee for the city, which met at the Jackson Reading Room.[75] Smaller towns that lacked the attentions of a central committee still showed considerable organization: village taverns hosted meetings of "the friends of reform and Gen. Andrew Jackson's election," which formed correspondence committees or sent delegates to larger gatherings, often held in other taverns in more populous towns. While the Democratic Party's formation depended on the networking efforts of successful state politicians such as Martin Van Buren, Democratic voters had reason to credit their own local work for Jackson's victory: from their villages and wards, they had helped make a federal democracy from the bottom up.[76]

In power, Democrats insisted that they would make state and national policies reflect the wishes and interests of ordinary voters rather than cosmopolitan elites. Although wealthy men, and especially rich enslavers, reaped some of the greatest benefits from their policies, Democrats, like the Republicans before them, had a somewhat more expansive notion of the kind of white men who could lead than did their mainstream opponents.[77] This expansiveness included the possibility for ordinary men not only to receive patronage positions but also to achieve electoral distinction. Hosting political meetings did not guarantee that a tavern keeper would become locally weighty enough to hold public office, but it could create a path. Baltimore's Michael Klinefelter reached municipal public office through long work in democratic-leaning ward politics. Klinefelter had been an active participant and leader in the meetings at his tavern well before the Jacksonian coalition formed. In 1818, at a "very large and respectable" ward meeting in advance of mayoral and assembly elections, voters named him to the committee that would represent the ward at a citywide meeting. Ward residents met at his tavern to rally support for improving key streets in the neighborhood. In 1822, "Many Voters" promised to support him "warmly" for election to the first branch of the city council, to which he was narrowly elected in late 1824. Around the same time, Klinefelter began hosting Jackson meetings for the ward. After several years of visibility in the Jackson interest, among other activities, Klinefelter won election to the upper branch of the city council, a position he held from 1833 through 1839. As a political host and standard bearer, Klinefelter had both benefited from and helped launch the Jackson movement in Baltimore.[78]

Like Michael Klinefelter, most tavern keepers with political careers remained at the level of municipal or county politics, but exceptional political hosts rose to state and even national office. A man of "considerable influence and abilities," General Abner Lacock kept tavern in Beaver, Pennsylvania, near the Ohio border. The Democratic Republican had served as a justice of the peace and a county court judge before his election to both houses of the Pennsylvania legislature. In 1810, he was elected to the U.S. Senate, one of only two known tavern keepers to reach that office. The other was Joseph Kerr of Ohio, who operated a tavern both before and after serving in the

Senate. His previous public offices included stints as justice of the peace, county judge, state representative, and state senator. In all, at least twenty congressmen and senators from the early republic kept, owned, or worked in taverns or hotels at some point in their careers. Of them, more than half were Republicans, Democratic Republicans, Jacksonians, or Democrats. Only three were Federalists or Whigs. Before the Civil War, two tavern keepers' sons, Martin Van Buren and Franklin Pierce, both Democrats, went on to reach the presidency.[79]

Patterns of partisan affiliation among tavern keepers elected to high national office are scarcely reliable as a predictor of the political fortunes and leanings of all keepers, but there were logical links between Democratic policies and tavern-keeping. Tavern keepers' tendency to be interested in very local infrastructural improvements, such as short turnpikes, suggests one connection. For some keepers, their services to westering migrants and land speculators suggest another. The Democrats' embrace of ordinary men also played an important role. Gathering in male-dominated yet economically heterogeneous spaces—as tavern barrooms and most dining rooms still were in the 1830s—aligned with Democrats' anti-elitism and dislike for outsiders' moral interference. In keeping with this stance, Democrats tended to be skeptical of or hostile to many voluntary associations, in part because urban elites led many of the most prominent ones. Democrats worried that such groups might influence the nation and its policies without ever being answerable to the electorate, a critique they also leveled against the Bank of the United States. Associations that sought to make other people change their way of life usually earned Democratic enmity, even more so if they tried to influence elections and policies. Particularly notable in this regard was the Democrats' disdain for the more coercive forms of temperance, which many on the soon-to-be-developed Whig branch of electoral politics would espouse. Yet Democrats had their own reasons to work together and their own take on improvements: the material improvements that men made to their farms as well as their joint efforts to police their neighborhoods, counter the power of entrenched elites and their institutions, limit the scope of the federal government, and enhance white men's access to land through aggressive territorial expansion. Associations that minded their members' business might also pass muster, including many small-scale infrastructure projects.[80]

Opposition to Andrew Jackson and his Democratic followers fostered both the new Whig Party and many of the voluntary associations Democrats disliked, which sought broad social change through moral suasion or grassroots political pressure. Although Whig stalwarts and radical reformers often found themselves at odds or in wholly different political orbits, both groups embraced overlapping understandings of improvement that distinguished them from many of their Democratic peers. Both tended to attract men and women whose views on improvement encompassed a capacious understanding of what government and nonstate institutions could do. Whigs appropriated the idea of improvements to such a degree that the very word came to seem Whiggish. Whig goals included federal investment in infrastructure improvements, public education, the further development of American manufacturing, and access to capital for improvements through orderly banking institutions. Many Whigs also participated in societies promoting moral improvements for others as well as themselves. A still more radical group, as often at odds as in company with Whigs, believed that Christian duty and the defense of liberty embraced the radical causes of prohibition, abolition, and women's rights.[81]

In the early years of this broad diffuse movement, voters who identified with the National Republicans and Whigs accepted that electoral politics entailed local meetings, tavern venues, and print publicity. In and around Baltimore in 1828, John Quincy Adams's supporters convened their own ward- and district-level meetings at taverns. The "General Convention" for Adams men in Baltimore County brought five men from each of the county's districts to Cockney's tavern to nominate their presidential elector. Rural and town taverns also hosted meetings of "friends of the National Administration."[82] Opposition to Andrew Jackson in Congress and among voters spawned additional meetings in the 1830s, many of them aligned with the new Whig Party. In the fall of 1834, a midterm election year, Baltimore Whigs convened many ward-level meetings, urging "every Whig" to "be at his post." In at least half of the city's wards, Whig meetings convened in taverns.[83]

Around the same time, Whiggish voluntary associations also met in town taverns and hotels. Societies dedicated to improving public health were perhaps the most unlikely candidates for tavern venues because so many doctors attested to the toll that alcohol abuse took on individuals and families. Yet in small numbers in the 1830s, medical societies in the northeastern states, and perhaps elsewhere, continued to meet at least occasionally in taverns. The Fellows of the Massachusetts Medical Society assembled for their semiannual meeting at the Russells' Hotel in Pittsfield in 1829. The following year, the annual meeting of the society's Berkshire district took place at Benjamin Cook's Coffee House in Lenox. Both meetings began at one o'clock in the afternoon and the members may have dined together.[84] Perhaps they even enjoyed some of the "Champaigne, Muscat, Claret, Madeira, Port and

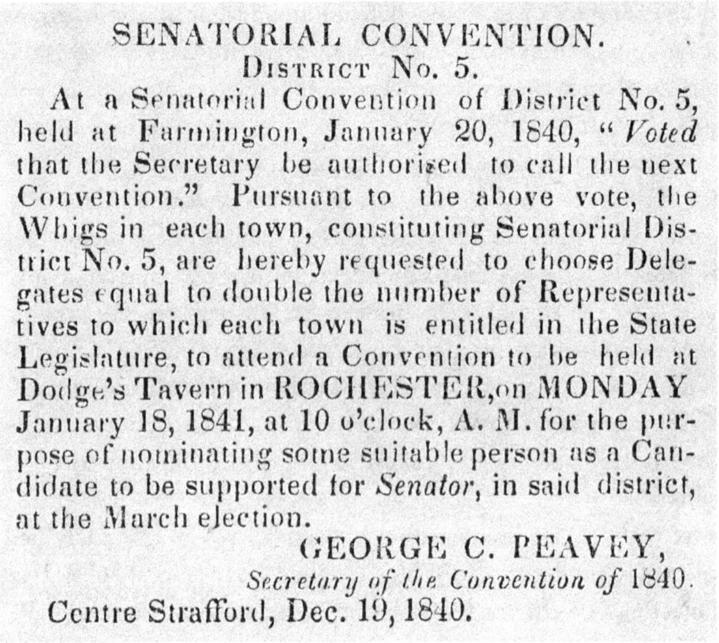

SENATORIAL CONVENTION.

DISTRICT No. 5.

At a Senatorial Convention of District No. 5, held at Farmington, January 20, 1840, "*Voted* that the Secretary be authorized to call the next Convention." Pursuant to the above vote, the Whigs in each town, constituting Senatorial District No. 5, are hereby requested to choose Delegates equal to double the number of Representatives to which each town is entitled in the State Legislature, to attend a Convention to be held at Dodge's Tavern in ROCHESTER, on MONDAY January 18, 1841, at 10 o'clock, A. M. for the purpose of nominating some suitable person as a Candidate to be supported for *Senator*, in said district, at the March election.

GEORGE C. PEAVEY,

Secretary of the Convention of 1840.

Centre Strafford, Dec. 19, 1840.

FIGURE 6.1 *Portsmouth Journal of Literature and Politics*, December 26, 1840. This notice, which appeared with several others under the headline "WHIGS ATTEND!" called on New Hampshire Whigs to convene in local taverns and hotels to select town delegates to attend district conventions. At these conventions, delegates nominated candidates for the state senate. Similar notices calling for town-based representation at partisan and nonpartisan conventions, often held at taverns, appeared in newspapers throughout New England and beyond in the 1830s and 1840s. Courtesy of the American Antiquarian Society.

other wines of the finest flavour," which Cook promoted in his advertising. They certainly made no promise to forswear alcohol in their own meeting notices. Perhaps they, like the Connecticut Medical Society a few years before, opposed "*intemperate*" forms of temperance and defended the strictly "moderate" intake of "wine, cider, and malt liquors" as "subservient to our health and pleasure." Medical societies in New Hampshire and New York also met at least occasionally in improved taverns without asserting that their meetings were temperate or their venues dry.[85]

While the significance of tavern drinking shifted as temperance gained converts, the use of taverns as local gathering places continued. Consider a celebration of and for the Whigs of Amherst, in southern New Hampshire, in December 1840. At the conclusion of the successful log cabin and hard cider campaign, the Amherst Whigs planned to "dispense with the firing of guns" and "the intoxicating cup." Eschewing even wine, their "festival" included mutual congratulations and "an excellent supper" for over one hundred people at Nutt's hotel. Later the same month, multiple Whig nominating conventions across southeastern New Hampshire assembled in local taverns (see figure 6.1).[86] Six years later, the public notice of an 1846 "Temperance Jubilee" at Marlborough, New Hampshire, suggests a similar marriage of political continuity and cultural change. This event celebrated the opening of the Marlborough Hotel, "to be kept as a Temperance Tavern." Held on the Fourth of July, the festivities linked decades of celebrating the nation's birthday in and around taverns to the temperance cause and the commercial imperative of launching a new business. Also in 1846, the New Hampshire town of Dublin marked the conversion of another tavern into a temperance house. With a new name, some newspaper advertising, the removal of liquor, and the support of abstemious men, these establishments operated as taverns in every way but the alcoholic.[87]

In conjunction with temperance and the improving trend in public accommodations, the need to convene and to travel brought some radical reformers into the nation's public houses. County and state meetings in Massachusetts and Pennsylvania, two of the most committed antislavery states, brought activists to hotels on a reasonably regular basis in the late 1830s, as William Lloyd Garrison's *Liberator* made clear.[88] At their meetings, abolitionists shared with far more conservative improvers and partisans a set of organizational strategies that melded republican procedures, face-to-face meetings, and print. In summarizing a Pennsylvania state abolition convention in 1837, for example, the Boston-based *Liberator* mentioned the leadership structure, the naming of people to several committees, and the business conducted by the more than two hundred attendees. Similar processes shaped meetings on a more local scale, such as a county abolitionist meeting held the following year at Wesson's Hotel in Concord, Massachusetts, some fifteen miles outside Boston. At this meeting, the attendees elected a president and secretaries as well as a business committee and two additional committees, one charged with registering the delegates and one with drafting an address to the voters. As with partisan and other causes, antislavery notices also identified many of the men elevated to leadership and committee positions, suggesting the public distinction that men could accrue through activism.[89]

In addition to reporting on past meetings, the *Liberator* printed calls to future action. In late 1838, a notice summoned abolitionists from "every town" in Massachusetts's fourth congressional district back to Wesson's Hotel, also known as the Middlesex Hotel, "for the purpose of considering and deciding on the courses of action to be pursued at the pending election." At this time, abolitionists were divided by multiple questions, including whether to embrace or disavow electoral politics. This notice urged abolitionists to do their "duty" and "give the slave a firm and zealous advocate on the floor of Congress." Amid the controversy within the abolitionist cause, this notice suggested the urgency of representing local opinions as fully as possible: it instructed abolitionists in towns with an abolitionist society to appoint delegates and urged abolitionists in other towns to "resolve themselves into a delegation and come."[90] A similar notice in the same newspaper called for "a large delegation . . . from every part of the state" to attend the quarterly meeting of the Massachusetts antislavery society to be held at White's hotel in Dedham, near Boston. Together, such notices yoked a radical goal to a process that helped individuals act together toward electoral and nonelectoral goals.[91]

Diligent local organizing and networks of friendly newspapers helped parties and societies demonstrate their clout and craft their course through regional or national conventions. In and after the 1830s, improved transportation and public accommodations made it possible for hundreds and even thousands of people to attend partisan and other conventions. Those who could not attend in person could read extensive published coverage and imagine aspects of the experience. Editors described how delegates thronged public accommodations in the large towns and cities that hosted major conventions. William Lloyd Garrison reported that during the 1832 Anti-Masonic State Convention in Worcester, Massachusetts, every hotel in town was "literally jammed with strangers." Some five years later, Harrisburg hotels likewise filled up with "the representatives of the abolitionism of Pennsylvania."[92] In 1848, a newspaper from the Wisconsin Territory informed its readers that the Free Soil Convention in Buffalo had attracted some 75,000 people, a hyperbolic claim that captured slavery's ability to perturb the two major parties.[93]

Party conventions and other large gatherings had economic as well as political implications. After an abolitionist convention in Harrisburg, Pennsylvania, antislavery activist J. G. Whittier shared with the *Liberator* the gossip that a local hotel keeper had forged William Lloyd Garrison's name in his guest register "to attract thither the delegates who were constantly arriving." On another occasion, Frederick Douglass lamented that when people gathered on the First of August to commemorate emancipation in the British Empire, they often spent money at "[h]otels and saloons" whose keepers "appropriated it to pro-slavery purposes." Far better, Douglass thought, for antislavery supporters to patronize a place like Peck's Hotel in Victor, New York, which allowed the women of the Western New York Anti-Slavery Society to hold an antislavery fair, earning over fifty dollars for the cause.[94]

For their part, urban boosters understood the value of attracting conventions, much as a previous generation had recognized the commercial and civic promise of first-rate public accommodations. In 1859, for example, Indianapolis Republicans instructed their delegate to the party to "use his influence" to bring the national convention to their city, observing that its "hotel accommodations . . . were ample." The mainstream press took notice when business-minded improvers crowded city hotels during conventions promoting railroads or other commercial interests. Hosting a major convention marked a city as important while bringing business to the local hospitality, transportation, and entertainment industries. In addition to linking local and national affairs, conventions and the reporting on them reinforced the connections between public accommodations, travel, economic self-interest, and collective action.[95]

As some conventions grew so large that plenary sessions could only take place outdoors, their connection to the local gatherings at which people selected delegates became tenuous, yet it did not rupture. Whatever the organization or issues at stake, massive conventions linked local concerns to national events and local activists to their fellows in distant parts of the country. Organizationally, delegates to regional or national conventions usually were selected through elections in towns, counties, or districts, not by an at-large statewide process. In rural districts, the practical problems involved in convening meetings, generating delegates, and mobilizing voters remained significant even after decades of investment in infrastructure. New England notices sometimes insisted that a meeting needed the participation "of voters living out of the village," not just those who found it most convenient to attend.[96] In 1838, the organizers of a Whig meeting in southeastern New Hampshire urged that "every town be fully represented," and they facilitated this participation by choosing to gather at a tavern in the most central of the four towns named in the notice.[97]

In addition to logistical issues, local tavern meetings also continued to address persistent concerns about authentic representation of local sentiments. National, state, and even county conventions assembled many strangers. But at least in principle, delegates had been vouched for by people who knew them by sight or through local networks. At a local meeting, voters also recognized potential interlopers. The Democratic organizers of New Hampshire hinted at the latter problem in multiple 1850s notices advising that committees would be examining delegates' "credentials" at county and district meetings. The area spanned by the towns represented at one such meeting described a rough circle with an eighteen-mile radius: minuscule from the national standpoint but large enough to make mutual acquaintance uncertain. The committees named to examine credentials relied on yet more local mechanisms by which party men could attest to their delegates' identity and fidelity.[98]

For all these reasons, public accommodations continued to promote and evoke the nexus of mobility, economic opportunity, and representation. Yet by the 1830s and even more by the 1850s, it was no longer clear that a tavern made a preferable venue compared to a town hall, courthouse, meetinghouse, church, schoolroom, or library. For ideological and policy reasons, the Democrats leaned somewhat more on taverns and the Whigs somewhat less in large part because of the latter's greater connections to temperance. Similarly, monitoring societies, such as militias, remained more likely to gather in and around taverns than were religious, temperance, antislavery, and other benevolent or radical groups. This discrepancy reached its greatest extremes for groups that attracted white women and people of color. Whenever Whigs and, especially, radical reformers met in hotels or taverns or used them in traveling to and from national conventions, however, they advanced a powerful argument about what public accommodations should be and for whom. Using such venues represented another step in the long struggle to make taverns, or some parts of some taverns, align with respectability and improvement, notions that were both widespread and far from universal across American society.

"All the Friends of Free Discussion"

However occasional, radical reforming societies' use of public accommodations from the 1830s through the 1850s represented both a continuation of and a threat to long-established norms of tavern politicking. The abolitionist press demonstrated how some public accommodations already aligned with their version of vernacular citizenship, which both constrained white men's tavern behaviors and opened doors for white women and people of color. When William Lloyd Garrison's *Liberator* described how abolitionists visiting Worcester, Massachusetts, converged on the "spacious and beautiful" Temperance House, he meant more than the building's material appeal. In keeping with "their reforming spirit," abolitionists tended to be "te-totallers" and preferred to patronize hotels whose keepers shared at least some of their convictions.[99] For similar reasons, the antislavery press looked favorably on the Revere House in Boston in the late 1830s. The Massachusetts Charitable Mechanics' Association, a mutual aid and educational society, had built the hotel with the intention that "nothing would ever be allowed within the walls which would tend to the subversion of morality or temperance; that no bar should ever be kept in the house; and that in every respect it should maintain the character of a first-rate hotel." The association's president hoped these rules would ensure "many pleasant meetings" for members and like-minded societies. Another Boston venue friendly to white abolitionists was the Marlboro' Hotel, established by the Free Church with the goal of providing accommodations and meeting space for the "friends of free discussion."[100]

Temperance hotels especially appealed to female abolitionists on the move. The best possibility was a temperance hotel run by "active Anti-Slavery friends." Boston's Marlboro' Hotel hosted women's antislavery fundraising fairs and groups that explicitly engaged children and women as moral and political actors, including the Boston Juvenile Anti-Slavery Society and the Boston Female Anti-Slavery Society. Some abolitionist women who convened in congenial hotels organized their proceedings and printed notices like men had done for decades. In 1849, for example, "the Anti-Slavery women of Pawtucket" advertised their upcoming fair at the Pawtucket Hotel in Frederick Douglass's *North Star*. This notice extended an open invitation and identified the ten female conveners by name. While their cause was more radical than most women would endorse, the Pawtucket abolitionists had company both in using print to promote their collective endeavors and in bringing feminine domestic skills before the public eye. Female charitable societies occasionally referenced their own elections and officers in printed notices, and numerous New England women competed at agricultural fairs, sometimes winning premiums and mention by name in local newspapers.[101]

Friendly venues mattered to abolitionists and other radical reformers because they faced significant verbal abuse and sometimes physical violence at their lectures and meetings. Anti-abolitionists hurled verbal insults at abolitionist men and women, dragged speakers from pulpits, and broke windows. At its worst, anti-abolition blossomed into arson, murder, and riot. In Philadelphia in 1838, for instance, anti-abolitionists burned down Pennsylvania Hall, built largely through abolitionist fundraising. Black abolitionists risked insult and attack in hotels and taverns, as on steamboats, streetcars, and trains. Independent of any association with prominent abolitionists, Black neighborhoods faced the risk of riotous attack by white mobs. In this context, Black women who provided food and lodgings for Black conventioneers did critical political work, as Psyche Williams-Forson argues.[102]

In publicizing their difficulties, abolitionists made clear that because some Americans stood ready to use extreme violence in slavery's defense, the institution's tendrils reached far beyond the enslaved themselves. The most radical made the same point about racism. In making these points, abolitionists often indicted crude and aggressive behavior in ways that questioned their antagonists' fitness for political citizenship. As Gamaliel Bailey's antislavery *National Era* reported with approval, the 1847 Maryland State Temperance Convention's resolutions included a call "to induce the political caucuses" to shun "disorderly taverns and filthy groggeries" as venues for both meetings and elections. Such language implied that people who saw no problem in meeting or voting in places that sold alcohol were themselves filthy and disorderly. Garrison himself used dehumanizing language for men who attacked female reformers, calling them "brutal, senseless, polluted, whiskey and wine-bibbing men."[103]

Inverting racist justifications for slavery and Black disfranchisement, such language cast doubt on whether "riotous" drinkers were suitable citizens with the right to political self-representation. According to the abolitionist press, many—although not all—men who impeded abolitionists' work were "ruffians," supposedly rough-mannered, ill-educated, laboring men who would hang out at a "rum tavern." By the 1840s and 1850s, men whose drinking earned temperate scorn were often workers in low-wage and supposedly low-skill occupations, and especially Catholic immigrants from Ireland or Germany. Meanwhile, states enfranchised recent immigrants if they were white men but denied voting rights to all women or stripped them from free Black men, as Pennsylvania did in its 1838 constitution. These changes seemed hypocritical and misguided to people who believed that English fluency, Protestantism, and temperance were as important as white manhood to the fullest measure of citizenship, or even more so. Controversies over voting rights thus overlapped with competing claims on the nation's public houses.[104]

Black activists' personal stories about their mistreatment further clarified the stakes of access to taverns and hotels. Frederick Douglass repeatedly articulated the links between public accommodations and the free exercise of mobility, economic opportunity, and political choice. In his *North Star* newspaper, Douglass explained the importance of his own travel: his lecture tours created opportunities to recruit new subscribers, whose money supported both his livelihood and his political work.[105] He also detailed the highly variable treatment that he and other Black travelers encountered. In describing the 1848 Colored National Convention in Cleveland, he noted that Black delegates suffered "a slight want of courtesy" from the barkeeper at the city's

New England Hotel. In contrast, at the American Hotel and at Durham House, "one of the most orderly and elegantly conducted hotels in the city," the staff treated Black delegates "with the respect and attention commonly paid to other travellers." First-class treatment at a first-class hotel implied a right to first-class citizenship. He noted further that delegates had come from New York, Ohio, Illinois, and Michigan to attend this "deliberative assembly" and would now "return to the various circles who sent them, and carry to them new zeal." In other words, whether hotels received them well or poorly, public accommodations undergirded Black Americans' ongoing political work, and that work included the local-to-national-to-local dynamics that white men also practiced.[106]

By the time of this convention, taverns were no longer as important to cultivating and claiming citizenship as they once had been. Political partisans, moderate reformers, and radicals alike could find other venues for their political gatherings. In most large towns and any city, they could lodge in private boarding houses instead of taverns or hotels. But as far as Black Americans were concerned, the proliferation of accommodations and gathering places had created additional sites of exclusion. Even the Marlboro' Hotel, friendly to temperance and antislavery, refused to treat Black performer Mary E. Webb "as a woman and a sister": the management did not allow her to dine alongside white patrons in the dining room or attend on-site religious services. As Frederick Douglass noted, free people of color were "excluded from equal accommodation in the use of steamboats—excluded from respectable hotels—excluded from Museums, Lyceums, Concerts, and many other places of popular and useful resort in this country." Douglass's list reflected the long history of improvement and stratification in public accommodations and entertainment, which in turn formed and reflected middling and elite preferences. Douglass returned multiple times to the question of access, linking it to the work of activism and to the political disability of living under "laws which we have had no voice in making." At midcentury, public accommodations remained tied to vernacular understandings of citizenship in ways both abstract and concrete.[107]

While the stakes of this struggle were perhaps most evident to Black activists, keepers had their own perspectives. After learning of Frederick Douglass's description of being ill-treated at the Forest City Hotel in Cincinnati in 1852, the hotel's clerk issued a rebuttal. J. B. Clarke insisted that Douglass had been "permitted" to lodge at the hotel "upon condition of having his meals sent to his room." When Douglass broke that agreement and appeared at the common breakfast table, he was allowed to remain only because "the presence of the ladies" prevented his forcible removal. Clarke maintained that a keeper's occupation required him "to accommodate himself to the wishes and tastes of the traveling community." "Permitting a person, of African extraction, to mingle in common with whites, at the ordinary public table," he continued, "violated" the "tastes and wishes" of that community. Clarke was probably correct about the views of most white American travelers at midcentury. He may even have believed that his stance had the color of tavern law.[108]

In his response, Frederick Douglass rejected Clarke's facts and his interpretation of the keeper's duty. In the process, he framed the public house itself as a temporary, contingent political community. A keeper could only know the "wishes and tastes of the traveling community" by canvassing the men and women at the "public table." For Douglass, whoever was in the room represented the community at that moment, a point others had made before him in disputes about political tavern meetings. In addition, this contingent, temporary community must itself respect limits, Douglass reasoned. Any traveler had an equal right to be served "as decently and attentively as others," according to the standard of service at a given hotel or tavern. No traveler had the right "to demand the removal of a tall man, a short man, a light man, or a dark man, a brown-haired man, or a red-haired man who shall take a seat at the same table." "For my part," Douglass concluded, "I'd rather be a wood-sawyer or a boot-black"—that is, perform manual or menial labor—"than to shrivell my soul into the dimensions" of an outwardly genteel but "soulless" man like Clarke.[109]

As Douglass and Clarke's debate showed, who had the right to use taverns and other public accommodations and how remained very much in question at midcentury. Both men believed that how they behaved and were treated in public accommodations was linked to their actual and desired status in the wider world. They agreed that the presence of ladies mattered, but they disagreed entirely about how: as a temporary and often unwelcome constraint on manly behavior for Clarke and as members of the political community for Douglass.[110] These questions of access and influence remained pressing not just in themselves, but because public accommodations, self-willed mobility, economic opportunities, and political self-determination remained so tightly connected in the maturing republic. They would remain entangled for a century and more as Americans continued to contest the formal and vernacular boundaries of citizenship.

ANY UNDERSTANDING OF TAVERNS' PLACE in early republican politics means reckoning with the fact that the nation's white men often exercised their political rights and did the practical work of collective governance in the very places where they took their right to socialize, conduct business, and drink for granted. That white men routinely used taverns in some or all of these ways did not make these spaces entirely safe or equitable even for them, however. Societies that met in taverns often fused deliberative forms and persuasive means, in no small part because of the layered social, economic, and other uses to which men put their taverns. Most obviously, from the republic's early decades, politically motivated interpersonal violence remained a potential risk. Early in the nineteenth century, Americans and foreigners noted the "astonishing" levels of political hostility, spontaneous violence, and formal dueling. J. B. Dunlop marveled that quarreling Quids, Tories, Democrats, and Federalists in Charleston opted to risk their lives "at 10 paces" with "alarming" frequency. Radical causes also inspired the threat and sometimes the reality of violence through midcentury and beyond.[111]

For white men, participating in formal, collective tavern politics entailed more subtle risks as well, most notably in heightening the visibility and significance of social, economic, political, and even life-cycle differences. Participating in collective political activity cost time and, directly or indirectly, money. Some associations kept members' costs to a minimum or used them for direct action. Others entailed conspicuous expenditures by gathering for business meetings in the most refined taverns available to dine on elaborate meals in elegantly furnished rooms. A man who attended costly events of this sort made a highly legible investment of his resources, particularly if he participated in several organizations that operated on this scale. Other men who gathered in the street outside, on the porch, or in the barroom could hardly help but notice the comings and goings of their better-off neighbors.

From another perspective, the practice of gathering in taverns to conduct collective politics slowly expanded the opportunities for active political participation. Doubts about whether associating for political ends violated the constitution or created illicit alternatives to duly elected government slowly yielded, and voluntary societies of all sorts proliferated. In turn, these varied forms of collective action made it increasingly clear that elections were not the only means for the people to shape their republic. While these opportunities were open almost exclusively to white men at first, white women and people of color created many vehicles for collective action both with white men and on their own. For many of them, the mantle of religion provided the greatest validation for their work, and so gathering in churches and meetinghouses became far more commonplace than in taverns or hotels.

Yet however normative or infrequent the practice, when anyone assembled *in taverns* to engage in collective political work, they aligned themselves with an institution that had great legal and popular significance. Through the mid-nineteenth century, taverns' legal existence hinged on the premise of serving the public good, specifically for travelers. In practice, taverns remained essential to local and long-distance mobility for many Americans. Lawmakers also harnessed taverns to policing public order and expanding representative government with real if incomplete success. In addition, certain people could indulge in tavern sociability and incorporate taverns into their strategies for making a livelihood for themselves and their households. As a result, taverns had more than functional importance. Because of the ways that ordinary people and legal authorities used and defined taverns, tavern gatherings came to represent communities in an informal, eminently disputable, and yet meaningful way. That representational understanding—or story or myth; all three words are appropriate—in turn helped legitimate what people gathered to do in taverns.

The tenets of middle-class respectability and morality that undergirded so much voluntarism in the early republic might have represented a categorical barrier to the expansion of collective tavern politics, had they developed independently of tavern improvements and temperance. As more tavern keepers separated barrooms from dining rooms, created bedrooms and parlors, and crafted explicit appeals to genteel travelers and families, they made taverns suitable for wider ranges of people, causes, and gatherings. In both their physical and symbolic dimensions, tavern politics encompassed an ongoing struggle to control the culture and significance of taverns. Tavern improvements were political in themselves and contributed to the dramatic increase in Americans' participation in collective action organized on representative principles from 1789 through the 1850s.

Conclusion

In 1800, many tavern keepers were generalists: they provided their patrons not only alcohol, meals, lodgings, and stabling but also sundries, groceries, credit, and spaces for social, commercial, and political activity. For some Americans, the day-to-day work and pleasure of tavern-going bolstered their exercise of political citizenship and opportunities for commercial and social self-advancement. The extent of and constraints on these opportunities in turn helped define what it could mean to be an American. At the same time, the regional variations that created possibilities for trade also generated both a need and a means to bind heterogeneous regions to each other, sometimes building and sometimes eroding the material and imagined foundations for national unity.

Changing experiences of and ideas about drinking in the generation that came of age from the 1820s through the 1840s, however, altered the playing field in important ways. One consequence was an accelerating interest in separating tavern patrons by their behaviors, including isolating travelers from local drinkers, and reducing or eliminating drinking. Keepers had reason to resist these changes: the loss of alcohol sales might be ruinous, while the possibility of encountering strangers and novelties had represented nearly as strong an inducement to tavern-going as alcohol itself. At the same time, hostility to alcohol did not emerge in a vacuum but overlapped with continuously developing ideas and practices around gentility, respectability, and improvement that a healthy fraction of keepers and patrons embraced. Improvements that made taverns more congenial for middling and wealthy travelers often made the same taverns useful to enterprising Americans who needed a place to transact, network, raise capital, display, teach, perform, or deliberate. These improvements also created new grounds for contention both among white men and between them and other types of patrons, especially those who mobilized respectability to make tavern spaces and opportunities more available to white women and people of color.

The dynamics of improvement had different implications according to place. In the white South, the very language of improvement began to sound like a betrayal and a threat, especially to enslavers. Travelers in the South still needed tavern services, however, and courthouse taverns continued to serve some southerners' social, political, and economic needs. Yet as many of the region's wealthiest and most powerful men hunkered down in defense of slavery, it became more and more difficult for anyone else to use taverns—or any other spaces—to mobilize competing opinions.[1] Taverns also faced challenges in the nation's rapidly growing cities, where more and more people needed lodgings, food, and entertainment and often had cash in hand to pay for them. By midcentury, city directories identified many entrepreneurs and businesses specializing in one or two elements in the broad array of goods, services, and spaces that leading taverns in small towns still offered: dedicated eateries such as oyster cellars, chop houses, refectories, victualling houses, and restaurants; sources of free or low-cost information, including libraries, reading rooms, and exchanges; and a wealth of commercial entertainment venues, from theaters and play houses to museums, galleries, exhibition rooms, music halls, and public gardens. In addition, urban real estate afforded men of business many alternatives for office and meeting space. Well before the 1850s in the nation's cities, taverns were no longer the distinctive locales for cultivating and claiming citizenship that they once had been. Formerly key nodes in transportation, economic, and political networks, taverns were supplemented and to some degree supplanted.[2]

Yet a place remained for taverns that served a variety of users and uses. East of the Mississippi River, in many corners of long-settled states, geography ensured a place for taverns as hubs for local community life and transportation. Even at the end of the nineteenth century, only one hundred miles beyond New York City, fifty-one stagecoach lines served the Catskills region, most of them operating on short routes of ten miles or less.[3] To the west, in the wake of the Civil War, continued American aggression against Indigenous peoples paved the way for renewed waves of migration and thus for founding towns and counties, each of which would need community gathering places, temporary premises for local government, and lodgings for newcomers and through-travelers.[4] Later generations would see the rise of the automobile and its roadside helpmeets. While interstate highways eventually whisked travelers past countless small towns, car travel also spurred the building of many types of motels. Some offered little more than food, fuel, and a bed to drivers in a hurry, while others provided an alternative to camping for leisure travelers or even promised a home away from home.[5] Meanwhile, the automobiles that seemed to promise Black Americans a respite from segregated public transportation offered instead, as Mia Bay has argued, "new and complex forms of traveling Black."[6]

While each of these patterns echoed developments from the early years of canals and railroads, later generations of taverns, hotels, and other public accommodations have been less likely to incubate interlocking cultural, economic, social, and political improvements than their predecessors did a century and more before. The temperance movement's renewed vigor in the late nineteenth and early twentieth centuries intensified the legal and moral policing of commercial public spaces.[7] Also contributing to the segmentation of civic life was the imperfect yet growing separation between businesses that catered to travelers, and eateries, entertainment venues, drinking spots, and gathering places that primarily served locals. For these and other reasons, in the late twentieth and early twenty-first centuries, scholars looking for sites of collective politics and community building have rarely had occasion to examine public accommodations and the hospitality industry, with the vital exception of the struggle against segregation.[8] Instead, in exploring the importance and the decline of community engagement, Ray Oldenberg and Robert Putnam explored local service and entertainment institutions such as barbershops, coffee shops, and bowling alleys. Others have noted that modern shopping malls created new opportunities for consumption, employment, sociability, and even physical activity. Taking the long view, one might argue that malls thus offered some of the layered functions that taverns once provided, and malls certainly resemble early national taverns in arousing conflict over who can use public places and how. Yet modern American malls provide limited scope for community-based collective action. They rarely offer public spaces appropriate to mass meetings, for starters, and owners of commercial property have imposed curfews on teenagers or denied access for grassroots political work such as petition campaigns and voter registration drives.[9]

In a very different echo of the early republic's taverns, early twenty-first-century speculators in commercial space insisted that the right kind of workspaces would "drive innovation" by promoting networking and eroding thought silos. These beneficial outcomes were certain, it was said, because "proximity between people and groups" encourages "planned and unplanned connectivity." In 2020, COVID-19 knocked such optimism on its heels, but the optimism itself is resilient. Ongoing urban planning efforts to promote blended commercial and residential development continue to suggest that individuals and interest groups see value in the ability to engage in multiple activities in one place.[10]

For anyone seeking models for both serendipitous and intentional connection, early republican taverns' ability to foster entrepreneurial ventures, organized sociability, and grassroots political activism might well prompt a touch of nostalgia. The multistranded work of improvement, networking, and innovation in small-town taverns might also interest anyone troubled by the urban-rural gaps in contemporary American politics, culture, social life, and economic opportunity. But the early republic's taverns operated at once as places of opportunity, zones of contestation, and sites of dominion. And to the limited extent that they became more welcoming to middle-class white women or Black Americans, they changed for white men, too, becoming both more and less useful depending on which men and which circumstances we consider.

Like those taverns, modern public accommodations as well as bowling alleys, coffee shops, and shopping malls have created much value for their primary users. As in the early republic, all that value remains inextricable from intrinsic and extrinsic factors such as corporate policies and patterns of work, property ownership, and infrastructural investment that ensure that different users and workers will have not only distinctly varied but also interdependent experiences of those spaces. Also at play are law enforcement, municipal government, and competing norms of appropriate behavior in any public space, business, or institution. Today, even noncommercial public institutions that make a strong commitment to serving the whole public remain subject to similar dynamics. Public libraries house books, provide internet access, host meetings, and help people solve individual and collective problems. Public libraries are also vulnerable to state, interest-group, and individual monitoring of the content they provide, the groups they host, the norms they foster, and the behaviors they tolerate. For Americans today, access to public spaces, be they nonprofit or commercial, still reflects and undergirds the freedom to move, pursue economic opportunity, and participate in collective self-determination. But what Americans think about the proper uses and users of public accommodations—and about who truly belongs in the republic and on what terms—remains as contested as ever.[11]

Notes

Abbreviations for Archives

APS	American Philosophical Society, Philadelphia, Pennsylvania
DU	David M. Rubenstein Rare Book & Manuscript Library, Duke University, Durham, North Carolina
HBS	Baker Library, Harvard Business School, Cambridge, Massachusetts
HSP	Historical Society of Pennsylvania, Philadelphia, Pennsylvania
NYHS	New-York Historical Society, New York, New York
NYPL	New York Public Library, New York, New York
NYSA	New York State Archives, Albany, New York
SHC	Southern Historical Collection, University of North Carolina, Chapel Hill, North Carolina
UGA	Hargrett Rare Book and Manuscript Library, University of Georgia Libraries, Athens, Georgia
VHS	Virginia Historical Society, Richmond, Virginia
WMC	Special Collections Research Center, William & Mary College, Williamsburg, Virginia

Abbreviations for Archival Collections

Adair Papers	William H. P. Adair Papers, 1836–1858, DU
Adams Papers	Samuel Adams Papers, 1758–1819, NYPL
Anonymous Diary	Unidentified Travel Diary (also known as Anonymous. Diary of a Tour through Pennsylvania and New York, 1836–1840), HSP
Antwerp Daybook	Hamlin, David. (Antwerp, NY) Daybook, 1822–1855 (bulk 1842–1855), NYHS
Bill Diary	Bill, John Wight. Diary/Account Book, 1835–1838, NYHS
Bourne Papers	Sylvanus Bourne Papers, 1799–1815, DU
Boykin & Lee Journal	Journal of the travels of Colonel John Boykin and Francis P. Lee from Morristown, New Jersey to Camden, South Carolina, August 15, 1833–September, 1833, APS
Brevard Diary	Joseph Brevard Travel Diary, 1791, in Brevard and McDowell Family Papers, 1754–1953, SHC
Brown Ledger	William Brown Ledger, 1776–1791, DU
Browne Papers	Martin Browne Papers, 1770–1830, SHC
Burroughs Papers	Richard D. Burroughs Papers, 1807–1889, DU
Chamberlain Diary	Thomas Chamberlain Diary, 1835–1860, NYPL

Clifford Diary   John Clifford Diary, 1804, Pemberton Papers, HSP

Clitherall Diary   James Clitherall Diary, 1776, SHC

Cocke Papers   Cocke Family Papers, VHS

Cumberland   Petitions for Tavern Licenses, 1802–1822. Cumberland County,
    License Petitions   in New Jersey boxes, 1700–1888, NYHS

Drew Diary   Drew, James. Diary, 1845 June–1846 July, NYHS

Dun & Company   R. G. Dun & Company records, 1841–1933, Dun & Bradstreet
    records   Corporation Records, HBS

Dunlop Diary   Dunlop, J. B. Diary, 1810–1811, NYHS

Eagle Tavern   Register, 1843–1844, Eagle Tavern (Watkinsville, GA), DU
    Register

Elkton Ledger   Elkton (Md) tavern keeper's ledger, 1806–1816, DU

Fisher Papers   Samuel Rowland Fisher Papers, HSP

Foulke Papers   William Parker Foulke Papers, 1840–1865, APS

Gibbons Journal   James Gibbons Journal, HSP

Grimball Diary   Diary, May–October 1835, John Berkley Grimball Diaries,
    1832–1883, SHC

Grotjahn Memoir   Peter Adolph Grotjahn Memoir, APS

Haines Papers   Hiram Haines Papers, 1826–1838, DU

Harriet Wiley   [Tavern] License No. [76] To the honorable the mayor . . .
    License Petition   The petition of Harriet Wiley. Philadelphia, 1827, NYHS

Hewitt Diary   Hewitt, "Journal of a Pedestrian Tour to the White Mountains,"
    Hewitt, Abram S. Diary and letterpress copybooks, 1843, 1876,
    1887–1888 (bulk 1887–1888), NYHS

Howland Diary   Howland, Sarah Hazard. Diaries and notebook, 1818–1822, NYHS

HSP Miscellaneous   Historical Society of Pennsylvania Miscellaneous Collection,
    1676–1937, HSP

HSP Road and   Historical Society of Pennsylvania Road and Travel Notes Collection,
    Travel Notes   1699–1885

Hunter Journals   George Hunter Journals, APS

Kirby Papers   Kirby, Samuel Tompkins. Papers, 1785–1807, DU

Kline Account   "Servant's Book of the Virginia House," Volume 1: Account book,
    Book   1841–1849, Jacob A. Kline Account Books and Letter, 1838–1849;
    1853, SHC

Lampi Collection   Lampi Collection of American Electoral Returns, 1788–1825.
    American Antiquarian Society, 2007, available at https://
    elections.lib.tufts.edu

Lester Diary   Lester, Andrew. Diary, 1836–1888, NYHS

Liebmann Tavern   Tavern Licenses. Liebmann Collection of American historical
    Licenses   documents relating to spiritous liquors , 1665–1910
    (bulk 1665–1865), NYPL

Loveland Diary   Loveland, Samuel. Diary, 1843 July–1843, September 16, NYHS

Lowrance   Tavern Account Book, 1749–1796, Alexander and John Lowrance
    Account Book   Papers, 1749–1796, DU

Marriner Daybook   Sarah Marriner daybook, 1812–1813, Lewes (Del.) collection, HSP

Mitchell Journal	Maria Mitchell, "Journal of a Trip to the West, 1857," Maria Mitchell papers, ca. 1825–1887, APS
Nevins Journal	Pim Nevins Journal, APS
Patterson Diary	Robert Patterson Diaries, HSP
Reed Memoir	Memoir of Mrs. John Reed, HSP
Schulling Diary	S. Schulling Diary, HSP
Southworth Diary	Southworth, Henry Clay. Diary, 1850–1851, NYHS
Stateburg Account Book	Tavern Account Book from Stateburg, South Carolina, 1837–1838, in Borough House Books, 1815–1910, SHC
Steele Papers	John Steele Papers, 1716–1846, SHC
Swaim Diary	Swaim, Curran. "Diary, 1852," in Swaim, Lyndon. Papers, 1844–1872, DU
Traveller's Rest Daybooks	Traveller's Rest Daybooks [Louisa County, VA, 1821–1822] (online), WMC
Vaux Diary	Roberts Vaux Diary, HSP
Vaux Papers	Vaux Family Papers, HSP
Virginia Merchant's Account Book	Virginia Merchant's Account Book, 1838–1839, DU
Warsaw Daybook	(Warsaw, New York) Daybook, 1830–1831, NYSA
Woodruff Journal	Robert Woodruff Journal. December 17, 1785–May 1, 1788, APS
Wyck Collection	Wyck Association Collection, APS

Introduction

1. *Salem Gazette*, October 8, 1833 (all quotations). I do not use "sic" to indicate misspellings.

2. The joke might run something like this: "What is the only kind of tavern that ever went out of business in the early United States? A temperance tavern!"

3. The alcohol content of the early republic's drinks varied: approximately 45 percent alcohol by volume (ABV) for spirits such as rum or whiskey, 10 percent in cider, 5 percent in beer, and less for householders' small beer. Rorabaugh, *Alcoholic Republic*, 11 ("'regular topers,'" "'confirmed drunkards'"), 230, 232–33, tables A.1.1–A.1.2.

4. Early republican citizenship was not the exclusive creation of the constitution or the federal government but was also composed of state law, local observances, and everyday pursuits. For abstract, concrete, and embodied dimensions of citizenship in this period, consider, for example, Kettner, *Development of American Citizenship*, especially 213–333; Brooke, *Columbia Rising*; Field, *Struggle for Equal Adulthood*; Berlant, "Citizenship"; Pryor, *Colored Travelers*; Fraser, "Expropriation and Exploitation"; Van Horn, *Power of Objects*, 342–401; Jones, *Birthright Citizens*; Mathisen, *Loyal Republic*, 13–37; O'Brassill-Kulfan, *Vagrants and Vagabonds*; Spires, *Practice of Citizenship*; Bonner, *Remaking the Republic*; O'Keefe, *Stranger Citizens*; Stanfield, *Rewriting Citizenship*. Historians have long recognized taverns' importance to infrastructure and community in the early republic. See, for example, A. Earle, *Stage-Coach and Tavern Days*; Coleman, *Stage-Coach Days in the Bluegrass*; Lathrop, *Early American Inns*; Holmes and Rohrbach, *Stagecoach East*; Garvin and Garvin, *On the Road North of Boston*; H. Cole, *Stagecoach and Tavern Tales*; Schoelwer, *Lions and Eagles and Bulls*; Criblez, "Tavernocracy."

5. Perhaps the best-known defense of rowdy masculinity from the period is Otter and Stott, *History of My Own Times*. For beliefs and behaviors related to early nineteenth-century taverns, consider Kaplan, "New York Tavern Violence"; Roberts, "Harry Jones and His Cronies"; Stott, *Jolly Fellows*; Dorsey, *Reforming Men and Women*, 90–135; Criblez, "Tavernocracy"; Roberts, *In Mixed Company*. For the colonial period, key interpretations include Conroy, *In Public Houses*; Thompson, *Rum Punch and Revolution*; Salinger, *Taverns and Drinking*; Scribner, *Inn Civility*. Oxford University recently investigated and upheld allegations of misconduct brought against Thompson. While the exact findings remain private, some complaints involved drinking. See, for example, Nidhi Bhaskar, "Debate over Professor Sanctioned for Sexual Harassment," *The Oxford Blue*, May 10, 2022. Thompson was one of my undergraduate preceptors (similar to a teaching assistant).

6. Emphases in the original. *Webster's 1828 American Dictionary*, 717 (all quotations), 362, 391, 741–42. For global scholarship on commercial drinking institutions, consider, for example, G. Berry, *Taverns and Tokens of Pepys' London*; Scardaville, "Alcohol Abuse and Tavern Reform"; Duis, *The Saloon*; Power, *Faces along the Bar*; Hanawalt, "The Host, the Law"; Cowell, *At Play in the Tavern*; Wamsley and Kossuth, "Fighting It Out"; Phillips, *Bolsheviks and the Bottle*; Roberts, "'A Mixed Assemblage of Persons'"; R. Campbell, *Sit Down and Drink Your Beer*; Lewicka, "Restaurants, Inns and Taverns"; Roberts, *In Mixed Company*; Sismondo, *America Walks into a Bar*; Barleen, *The Tavern*.

7. For public accommodations terminology, compare Scharf and Westcott, *History of Philadelphia*, 2:981; Thorp, "Taverns and Tavern Culture," 661–62n1; Criblez, "'Motley Array,'" 262. For boarding houses, see Gamber, *The Boardinghouse*.

8. For American whiskey and alternatives, see Rorabaugh, *Alcoholic Republic*, 61–122.

9. On domestic travel, consider Gassan, *Birth of American Tourism*; White, *Wet Britches*; Mackintosh, *Selling the Sights*. For the domestic implications of Americans' European travel, see Kilbride, *Being American*.

10. Salinger, *Taverns and Drinking*, 5 ("preserved"); Conroy, *In Public Houses*; Thompson, *Rum Punch and Revolution*; Carp, *Rebels Rising*; Sismondo, *America Walks into a Bar*; Scribner, *Inn Civility*. For taverns in the rural South, see Thorp, "Taverns and Tavern Culture."

11. Scribner, *Inn Civility*, 42–108; Lennon, "A Stage for Gentility"; DeGennaro, "From Civic to Social"; Shields, *Civil Tongues and Polite Letters*, 55–65; Bushman, *Refinement of America*, 160–64. For the lack of "clearly defined hierarchy" across rural taverns, see Conroy, *In Public Houses*, 148 ("clearly"); Rockman and Rothschild, "City Tavern, Country Tavern"; Burrow et al., *John Tweed's Log Tavern*, 7.1–7.3. See also Roberts, "Harry Jones and His Cronies," 6–8.

12. *Pennsylvania Gazette*, July 1, 1789 ("tippling-houses"); Barnes, *Connexion of Temperance with Republican Freedom*, 18 ("dram shops"); Cheves, *Cases at Law*, 230 ("groggeries").

13. Kaplan, "New York Tavern Violence," 598–99 and passim; Kaplan, "World of the B'Hoys," 10–12. For the colonial ratio of taverns to population, see Salinger, *Taverns and Drinking*, 185, table 6.1.

14. King, "First-Class Hotel"; Sandoval-Strausz, *Hotel*; Berger, *Hotel Dreams*. See also Roberts, "Harry Jones and His Cronies," 8. For the luxury hotel's historical significance, see Berger, *Hotel Dreams*, 9, 263n9. For nineteenth-century white American notions of culture and class, also consider Halttunen, *Confidence Men*; Levine, *Highbrow, Lowbrow*; Kasson, *Rudeness and Civility*; Grier, *Culture and Comfort*; C. Hemphill, *Bowing to Necessities*.

15. To understand public accommodations in the early republic, I argue that we must look beyond the nation's largest cities and not anticipate hotels' divergence from taverns. Cf. Sandoval-Strausz, *Hotel*, 3–4, 7, 9, 46–68, 77–99; Berger, *Hotel Dreams*, 7–10.

16. For population density and distribution, see Paullin and Wright, *Historical Geography of the United States*, plates 76B–77B, 80A. In 1860, approximately 22 percent of the U.S. population lived in towns and cities with populations of 2,500 or more. Wilkie, "United States Population by Race and Urban-Rural Residence," 143, table 2.

17. Cf. Roberts, *In Mixed Company*. My use of the words "improvements," "improved," and "improving" denotes not my own conclusion that certain changes in the early republic were necessarily for the better, but rather, a discourse and set of practices that advanced this message. At the same time, contemporaries had doubts and, sometimes, ferocious and even violent disagreements over certain activities that some people claimed as improvements.

18. Andrew Sandoval-Strausz argues that important hotel subtypes began to develop around the mid-nineteenth century. Sandoval-Strausz, *Hotel*, 81–99. Cf. Berger, *Hotel Dreams*, 263n9. In this study, I have avoided what Jack Blocker describes as historians' focus on urban drinking, but many small-town taverns contributed to what Richard Brown has framed as rural urban society. Blocker, "Tidy Pictures of Messy Behavior," 473; R. Brown, "Emergence of Urban Society."

19. Sandoval-Strausz makes a similar claim for hotels. Sandoval-Strausz, *Hotel*, 9.

20. For economic and political infrastructures, consider Watson, *Jacksonian Politics*; C. Clark, *Roots of Rural Capitalism*; Larson, *Internal Improvement*; Bruegel, *Farm, Shop, Landing*; A. Rothman, *Slave Country*; C. Clark, *Social Change in America*; D. Howe, *What Hath God Wrought*; Bremer, *A Store Almost in Sight*.

21. Welke, *Law and the Borders of Belonging*; Zelnick, "Self-Evident Walls," 12. Although some tavern companies had Habermasian elements, taverns were sites of business that projected state authority; see chapters 4 and 5 in the present book and Conroy, *In Public Houses*, 177–78, 180n38, 187–88; Thompson, *Rum Punch and Revolution*, 17; Salinger, *Taverns and Drinking*, 5; Scribner, *Inn Civility*, 185n38. See also Barnhurst and Nerone, *The Form of News*, 47; Berger, *Hotel Dreams*, 4–5; Brooke, *Columbia Rising*, 4–6.

22. For migration and early American citizenship, see Kettner, *Development of American Citizenship*, 9–10, 65–247; Seeley, *Race, Removal, and the Right to Remain*; O'Keefe, *Stranger Citizens*. For mobility and citizenship beyond the United States, consider L. Putnam, "Citizenship from the Margins"; Nyamnjoh, "Keynote Address"; Spinney, Aldred, and Brown, "Geographies of Citizenship."

23. For white mobility, migration, and travel, see Cashin, *Family Venture*; P. Cohen, "Safety and Danger"; Bolton, *Poor Whites*; P. Cohen, "Women at Large"; Imbarrato, "Ordinary Travel"; O'Brassill-Kulfan, *Vagrants and Vagabonds*.

24. For chosen and coerced mobility for Black Americans, consider Franklin and Schweninger, *Runaway Slaves*; Camp, *Closer to Freedom*; Deyle, *Carry Me Back*; Baptist, "'Stol' and Fetched Here'"; Pryor, *Colored Travelers*; Jones, *Birthright Citizens*. For an entrée into recent scholarship on Indigenous Americans, forced movement, and land, see Zelnick, "Self-Evident Walls," 19–21; Snyder, "Many Removals."

25. For free and legally dependent women's economic roles, consider Lebsock, *Free Women of Petersburg*; Jensen, *Loosening the Bonds*; Salmon, *Women and the Law of Property*; Ditz, *Property and Kinship*; Boydston, *Home and Work*; C. Clark, *Roots of Rural Capitalism*, 23–27, 274–79;

Osterud, *Bonds of Community*; Rosen, *Courts and Commerce*; Bruegel, *Farm, Shop, Landing*, 52–54, 114–25, 138–42; K. Wood, *Masterful Women*; Hartigan-O'Connor, *Ties That Buy*; Jones-Rogers, *They Were Her Property*; Moore, *Women before the Court*; Damiano, *To Her Credit*.

26. Berlin and Morgan, *The Slaves' Economy*; J. Campbell, "As 'a Kind of Freeman'"; Hudson, *To Have and to Hold*; J. D. Martin, *Divided Mastery*; Berry, "*Swing the Sickle*"; Zaborney, *Slaves for Hire*; Hilliard, *Masters, Slaves, and Exchange*; J. Edwards, *Unfree Markets*; L. Edwards, *Only the Clothes*, 21–38.

27. For immigrant servitude in the early republic, consider Fogleman, "From Slaves, Convicts, and Servants"; Grubb, *German Immigration*. For uneven opportunities in the early republic, consider Appleby, *Inheriting the Revolution*, 56–128. For the social construction of work and of adult white manhood, see, respectively, Boydston, *Home and Work*; Field, *Struggle for Equal Adulthood*, 12–19, 30–34, 55–60.

28. For speculation, consider Kamensky, *Exchange Artist*; J. Rothman, *Flush Times*; Baptist, *The Half Has Never Been Told*. For ambition within the "competency" framework, see Vickers, "Competency and Competition."

29. Ratcliffe, "Right to Vote," 246 ("could be"), 221–30, 236–48; Keyssar, *Right to Vote*, 7, appendix, tables A1–A6, A9; "Voter and Officeholder Qualifications"; Wilentz, *Rise of American Democracy*, 188, 805–6n37; O'Brassill-Kulfan, *Vagrants and Vagabonds*, 26–29.

30. For women's political influence through familial connections, see K. Wood, "'One Woman So Dangerous,'" 248–57; Allgor, *Parlor Politics*, 102–46 and passim. For alternative sources of female influence, consider Ginzberg, "'Moral Suasion Is Moral Balderdash'"; Ginzberg, *Women and the Work of Benevolence*; Isenberg, *Sex and Citizenship*; Varon, *We Mean to Be Counted*; Jeffrey, *Great Silent Army*; Hershberger, "Mobilizing Women"; Portnoy, "'Female Petitioners'"; Zaeske, *Signatures of Citizenship*. For nonpartisan voluntarism as compared to party politics, see Neem, "Two Approaches to Democratization."

31. For political endeavors in rural settings, consider A. Taylor, *Liberty Men*; Huston, *Land and Freedom*; Ginzberg, *Untidy Origins*; Bouton, *Taming Democracy*.

32. Works influencing my thinking here include Pasley, Robertson, and Waldstreicher, *Beyond the Founders*; Brooke, "Patriarchal Magistrates"; Peart and Smith, *Practicing Democracy*.

33. For improvement's varied meanings, consider Indenture, March 29, 1834, Burroughs Papers; Patterson Diary, September 11, 1835; Feller, "Market Revolution," 412–13; P. Johnson, *Early American Republic*, 65–67, 153; Majewski, "Who Financed the Transportation Revolution?" For the toll of claimed improvements, consider A. Taylor, *Liberty Men*; Saunt, *New Order of Things*; Huston, *Land and Freedom*; Baptist, *The Half Has Never Been Told*.

34. For the political and legal history of American speculation, consider Banner, *Speculation*. For speculative behavior and its consequences in the early republic, consider Wagner, "Composing Pioneers"; J. Rothman, *Flush Times*; Lepler, *Many Panics*; Baptist, *The Half Has Never Been Told*; Wagner, "Footloose Founders"; Wagner, "Location, Location, Location." For a useful review of early American political economy, see Norwood, "What Counts?"

35. My expansive take on improvements highlights commonalities that encouraged tavern-going and spanned partisan and religious divides, without ignoring related conflicts. See Watson, *Jacksonian Politics*; Sellers, *Market Revolution*; Martin, *Killing Time*; Larson, *Internal Improvement*; Shaw, *City Building on the Eastern Frontier*; Wells, *Origins of the Southern Middle Class*; D. Howe, *What Hath God Wrought*; Brooke, *Columbia Rising*; Larson,

Market Revolution; Brooke, "Patriarchal Magistrates." For the early American middle class, see, for example, P. Johnson, *Shopkeeper's Millennium*; Stansell, *City of Women*; Ryan, *Cradle of the Middle Class*; Blumin, *Emergence of the Middle Class*; Wells, *Origins of the Southern Middle Class*; Hart, *Building Charleston*; Goloboy, *Charleston and the Emergence of Middle-Class Culture*. See also Vinovskis, "Stalking the Elusive Middle Class."

36. For the "republican court," see the summer 2015 issue of the *Journal of the Early Republic*, especially Teute and Shields, "Jefferson in Washington."

37. Within the vast masculinities scholarship, topical contributions include Gorn, "'Gouge and Bite'"; Smith-Rosenberg, *Disorderly Conduct*; Ditz, "Shipwrecked"; Dorsey, *Reforming Men and Women*; Stott, *Jolly Fellows*; Foote, *Gentlemen and the Roughs*. Consider also Martin, *Killing Time*. For a critical take on masculinity studies, consider Ditz, "What's Love Got to Do with It"; Ditz, "New Men's History."

38. For midwestern taverns, see, for example, H. Cole, *Stagecoach and Tavern Tales*; Criblez, "Tavernocracy"; Criblez, "'Motley Array.'"

39. Waldstreicher, *In the Midst of Perpetual Fetes*; Pasley, "Tyranny of Printers"; Steffen, "Newspapers for Free"; Brooke, "Cultures of Nationalism"; Bonner, *Remaking the Republic*. For print and orality in early America, compare Gilmore, *Reading Becomes a Necessity of Life*; Zboray, *Fictive People*; Shields, *Civil Tongues and Polite Letters*; Kelley, *Learning to Stand and Speak*; Loughran, *Republic in Print*; Gustafson, "American Literature"; Eastman, *Nation of Speechifiers*; Spires, *Practice of Citizenship*, 79–120. See also the Viral Texts Project, http://viraltexts.org (accessed January 23, 2023).

40. Kerber, "Separate Spheres"; Ryan, *Women in Public*; Ingold, "Against Space."

41. B. Meyer, *History of Transportation*; G. Taylor, *Transportation Revolution*. Most early work on the U.S. transportation revolution focused on freight. For human travel, see Mackintosh, "'Ticketed Through'"; White, *Wet Britches*; Mackintosh, "Mechanical Aesthetics."

42. Bushman, *Refinement of America*; Kross, "Mansions, Men, Women"; Crowley, *The Invention of Comfort*; K. Brown, *Foul Bodies*; Kelly, *Republic of Taste*. Compare the urban and rural interpretations of space and power in Upton and Vlach, *Common Places*; Vlach, *Back of the Big House*; Herman, *Town House*.

43. For economic, social, and cultural change beyond the nation's largest cities, see C. Clark, *Roots of Rural Capitalism*; Tolbert, *Constructing Townscapes*; Wermuth, *Rip Van Winkle's Neighbors*; Bruegel, *Farm, Shop, Landing*; Wells, *Origins of the Southern Middle Class*; Shaw, *City Building on the Eastern Frontier*; Larson, *Market Revolution*. I also draw insight from Farber, "Practical Americans." My argument about feminization and women's presence in improving taverns re-evaluates a conclusion I reached in K. Wood, "'One Woman So Dangerous.'"

44. I borrow the term from Hart, *Trading Spaces*.

45. O. Williamson, "Economics of Organization"; Tadelis, "Tribute to Oliver Williamson." For the spectrum of economic activity, consider Luskey and Woloson, *Capitalism by Gaslight*; Lipartito and Jacobson, *Capitalism's Hidden Worlds*.

46. Neem, "Two Approaches to Democratization," 250 (all quotations).

47. For "governance as conduct," see Novak, *People's Welfare*, 8 ("governance"), 149–89; L. Edwards, *People and Their Peace*; Brooke, "Patriarchal Magistrates"; Bates, "Government by Improvisation." For an overview of taverns in colonial law, see Salinger, *Taverns and Drinking*, 83–181.

48. For "organized political action" within and beyond electoral politics, see Koschnik, "Fashioning a Federalist Self," 221 ("organized"); Neem, "Two Approaches to Democratization"; Peart and Smith, "Introduction"; Robertson, "Jeffersonian Parties, Politics, and Participation." On the problematics of associating, see Neem, *Creating a Nation of Joiners*; Butterfield, *Making of Tocqueville's America*. In the broad field of women's and Black citizenships, significant recent work includes Field, *Struggle for Equal Adulthood*; Manning, "Working for Citizenship"; Pryor, *Colored Travelers*; Gronningsater, "'Expressly Recognized'"; Spires, *Practice of Citizenship*; Bonner, *Remaking the Republic*; Gosse and Waldstreicher, *Revolutions and Reconstructions*; Foreman, Casey, and Patterson, *Colored Conventions Movement*; Gosse, *First Reconstruction*; Stanfield, *Rewriting Citizenship*.

49. Consider, for example, the idea of "meaningful access" under the Americans with Disabilities Act. Ameri et al., "No Room at the Inn"; Stout, "Meaningful Access."

Chapter One

1. Bill Diary, September 23, 1835 (all quotations).

2. For the transportation revolution, see B. Meyer, *Transportation in the United States*; G. Taylor, *Transportation Revolution*; Atack, "Transportation." For people as travelers, consider Mackintosh, "'Ticketed Through'"; White, *Wet Britches*; Mackintosh, "Mechanical Aesthetics." For the broad significance of transportation changes in this period, consider Pred, *Urban Growth and the Circulation of Information*; Pred, *Urban Growth and City-Systems*; Cronon, *Nature's Metropolis*; Rasmussen, *Ox Cart to Automobile*.

3. Cuming, *Sketches of a Tour*, 46–47 (all quotations).

4. More precisely, as I discuss in chapter 5, keepers faced penalties for selling alcohol to slaves, servants, and other legally subordinated people without their legal superiors' consent.

5. The Constitution granted Congress exclusive jurisdiction over interstate commerce, and in the late 1840s, the Supreme Court ruled that Congress had sole authority over immigration. See Freyer and Thomas, "Passenger Cases Reconsidered"; Freyer, *Passenger Cases*; Masur, "State Sovereignty and Migration before Reconstruction," 593–98. For immigration and citizenship, see O'Keefe, *Stranger Citizens*. For legal restrictions on Black mobility, consider Pryor, *Colored Travelers*, 46–51 and passim; Jones, *Birthright Citizens*, 96–99; Schoeppner, *Moral Contagion*; Schoeppner, "Black Migrants and Border Regulation."

6. For Indigenous mobility and removal, consider, for example, Bowes, *Land Too Good for Indians*; Seeley, *Race, Removal, and the Right to Remain*; Snyder, "Many Removals." For poverty and mobility, see O'Brassill-Kulfan, *Vagrants and Vagabonds*; Masur, "State Sovereignty and Migration before Reconstruction," 598–600.

7. For masculinity and travel, see Wagner, "Composing Pioneers," 118–19 and passim; Scribner, *Inn Civility*, 47–63; Goldsmith, *Masculinity and Danger*. For travel and white women or people of color, consider P. Cohen, "Safety and Danger"; P. Cohen, "Women at Large"; Imbarrato, "Ordinary Travel"; Richter, *Home on the Rails*; Imbarrato, *Traveling Women*; Walsh, "Gender in the History of Transportation Services"; Pryor, *Colored Travelers*. My thinking about gender and race owes much to E. Brown, "Polyrhythms and Improvization"; E. Brown, "What Has Happened Here"; Hewitt, "Compounding Difference"; Higginbotham, "African-American Women's History and the Metalanguage of Race."

8. For maps in early America, including decorative and travel maps, see Brückner, *Geographic Revolution*; Brückner, *Social Life of Maps*.

9. Mackintosh, "'Ticketed Through'"; Mackintosh, *Selling the Sights*, 23–83; Wagner, "Location, Location, Location," 127.

10. George, *Almanack, for the Year of Our Lord and Saviour, 1777*, n.p. ("Roads" and "Houses"); West and Callender, *Bickerstaff's Boston Almanack*; Andrews, *Poor Will's Pocket Almanack, for the Year 1771*. For early American almanacs, see Stowell, *American Almanacs*; Spero, "Revolution in Popular Publications"; McCarthy, *Accidental Diarist*, 11–53.

11. Tobler, *Georgia and South-Carolina Almanack*; *Osborne's New-Hampshire Register*; Andrews, *Virginia Almanack, for the Year of Our Lord, 1794*; *Camden (SC) Gazette and Mercantile Advertiser*, June 1, 1820. For the postal road network, see Paullin and Wright, *Historical Geography of the United States*, plates 138H–K, 139A–B.

12. George Hunter, "Journal to Upper Louisiana of G Hunter and G H Hunter, 1809," August 1, 1809 ("best Taverns"), Hunter Journals; "Routes to & from Charleston, 1815 & 1816" ("bad," "tole," and "good"), "Road from Philad. to Pittsburg recd from the Chief Justice Sep 27 1824," and similar items, Box 1, HSP Road and Travel Notes; Volume 1, p. 25, "From Widner's to Harris's," Browne Papers; Boykin & Lee Journal, n.d.

13. Chastellux, *Travels in North-America*, 1:5 ("alighted"), 1:24 ("obliged"); see also 1:4–25; I. Weld, *Travels*, 65, 105, 114–15.

14. On U.S. travel narratives, see Imbarrato, *Traveling Women*, 131–211; Gassan, *Birth of American Tourism*, 71–73. On travel writing more broadly, consider Brettell, "Introduction"; Pratt, *Imperial Eyes*; Haynes, *Unfinished Revolution*, 24–50; Kilbride, "Travel Writing as Evidence."

15. Temple, *American Tourist's Pocket Companion*, 79–82 (Albany to Niagara), 56 ("provide"), 12 ("either"). One reader used blank pages in Temple's guide for travel notes: see the LCP's copy. For binding extra pages into almanacs, see McCarthy, *Accidental Diarist*, 49.

16. Clitherall Diary, April 11, 1776 ("the ladies").

17. Gibbons Journal, 2 (all quotations), 1–2; Howland Diary.

18. W. Williams, *Appleton's Railroad and Steamboat Companion*, 23; Mackintosh, *Selling the Sights*, 54–83.

19. Vandewater, *The Tourist*; Mitchell, *Travellers' Guide*; *Benjamin's New Map of the Hudson River* ("principal Hotels"); W. Williams, *Appleton's Railroad and Steamboat Companion*, 39–41, 50; W. Williams, *Appleton's Northern and Eastern Travellers' Guide*, 249 ("upwards"); T. Richards, *Appleton's Companion, 1860*, 53–57, 73, 82, 88.

20. *(Philadelphia, PA) Dunlap's American Daily Advertiser*, August 23, 1793; *(Wilmington, DE) American Watchman*, July 10, 1811.

21. *(New Orleans) Daily Picayune*, March 27, 1839, September 20, 1838 ("sleep and refreshment"); *Richmond (VA) Enquirer*, October 10, 1837 ("good accommodations," "no travelling"); *Newport (RI) Mercury*, January 3, 1835.

22. Jane B. Haines to John A. Warder, [July 1, 1836] ("breakfast"), Ann Haines to Jane B. Haines, September 8, 1832, Wyck Collection; Lester Diary, October 19, 1836.

23. Accounts with "The Stage Holders," and Robert Wallace, Kirby Papers. For taverns and stage travel generally, see B. Meyer, *Transportation in the United States*, 122; K. Rice, *Early American Taverns*, 43–45; Garvin and Garvin, *On the Road North of Boston*, 74–76, 107–10; White, *Wet Britches*, 21–63. An account of broken stagecoach equipment appears in

the annotations in the LCP's copy of Temple, *American Tourist's Pocket Companion*. For changing stagecoach horses at a tavern, see Royall, *Mrs. Royall's Southern Tour*, 1:55.

24. *Baltimore Patriot*, March 21, 1831 (*"Tavern"*), May 12, 1831 ("easy"); *Richmond (VA) Enquirer*, December 8, 1837 ("Hacks"); *(Brattleboro, VT) Semi-Weekly Eagle*, January 14, 1850 ("within"); White, *American Railroad Passenger Car*, 313–14.

25. *Baltimore Patriot*, May 12, 1831, November 17, 1831; *Richmond (VA) Enquirer*, May 6, 1836; Maria Mitchell, "Journal of a Trip to the West, 1857," May [9], 1857 ("took"), Mitchell Papers; Houstoun, *Hesperos*, 1:34; *Railroad Hotel*. See also *Report of the Committee of Investigation of the Northern Railroad*, appendix; *Report of the Michigan Central Railroad*, 24; Grant, *Living in the Depot*, 7; Meeks, *Railroad Station*, 26–28, 48–55. On railroad building and investments, see B. Meyer, *Transportation in the United States*, 306–550; Majewski, "Who Financed the Transportation Revolution"; D. Meyer, *Roots of American Industrialization*, 157–58.

26. C. Adams, *Railroads*, 10, 20, 37–38; Stover, *History of the Baltimore and Ohio Railroad*, 33–34.

27. Hunter and Hunter, *Steamboats on the Western Rivers*, 264–66; Sheriff, *Artificial River*, 119, 147; Buchanan, *Black Life on the Mississippi*, 70–71; Sandoval-Strausz, *Hotel*, 50, 58–59, 78; Grivno, *Gleanings of Freedom*, 81–82; Bremer, *A Store Almost in Sight*, 116–17.

28. On travel dangers, see Ann Haines to Jane B. Haines, July 24, 1835, Wyck Collection; Bernhard, *Travels through North America*, 2:135; Kierner, *Inventing Disaster*, 166–200.

29. Temple, *American Tourist's Pocket Companion*, 13 ("occasional," "with the landlord's"); Gibbons Journal, 1 ("contemplated"); Willson, *Journey in 1836*, June 8, 1836 ("movers"), June 9, 1836, June 25, 1836; J. Alexander, *Transatlantic Sketches*, 261 ("interrogatories"), 264 ("improving"); T. Flint, *Recollections of the Last Ten Years*, 64. For men's travel writing and revising, see Wagner, "Composing Pioneers," 98–119.

30. Cuming, *Sketches of a Tour*, 80, 285; *(Augusta, GA) Southern Cultivator*, February 7, 1844; Stuart-Wortley, *Travels*, 99–102.

31. Waldstreicher, "Reading the Runaways," 252–54 and passim; O'Brassill-Kulfan, *Vagrants and Vagabonds*, 80–81, 94–95, and passim.

32. Temple, *American Tourist's Pocket Companion*, 10 ("expensive," "appear"); T. Richards, *Appleton's Companion, 1860*, 7 ("rude"); I. Weld, *Travels*, 58 ("consequence"). For clothing's meanings, consider Halttunen, *Confidence Men*, 56–91; Zakim, *Ready-Made Democracy*; Haulman, *Politics of Fashion*; L. Edwards, *Only the Clothes*.

33. James P. Parke to Roberts Vaux, December 26, 1804 (all quotations), Vaux Papers. I explore counterfeiting in chapter 4. For cultural concerns about confidence men, consider Halttunen, *Confidence Men*, 1–55. For young manhood, consider Kett, *Rites of Passage*, 31–37 and passim; Koschnik, "Young Federalists"; Hessinger, *Seduced, Abandoned, and Reborn*, 125–76.

34. Bill Diary, September 23, 1835 ("we have," "quite a"), November 26, 1835 ("supped," "his Lady"); "Hopkins Holsey," *Biographical Directory of the United States Congress*, https://bioguide.congress.gov/search/bio/H000744 (accessed December 12, 2022). On manly restraint around ladies, see, for example, Bederman, *Manliness & Civilization*, 11–12; C. Hemphill, *Bowing to Necessities*, 179–212.

35. Patterson Diary, June 23, 1835 ("seeing"); *Dictionary of American Biography* (Gale In Context online edition), s.v. "Robert Patterson." For masculinity and violence, see Flint,

Recollections of the Last Ten Years, 175; Gorn, "'Gouge and Bite'"; Smith-Rosenberg, *Disorderly Conduct*, 90–108; Kaplan, "New York Tavern Violence"; Parsons, "Risky Business"; Wamsley and Kossuth, "Fighting It Out"; Foote, *Gentlemen and the Roughs*. For rakishness, see Lyons, *Sex among the Rabble*, 137–51, 206–10, and passim; P. Cohen et al., *Flash Press*, 55–78, 131–32; Scribner, *Inn Civility*, 87–108.

36. Cuming, *Sketches of a Tour*, 56 ("politicks"); Vaux Diary, June 6, 1808 ("up to his"); Dunlop Diary, November 12, 1810; Appleby, *Inheriting the Revolution*, 40–43; Freeman, *Affairs of Honor*.

37. Emphasis in the original. Bill Diary, [September 22,] 1835 ("keep aloof"), November 14, 1835 ("not the one half"), December 20, 1835 ("trumpet-tongued," "designing," "disordered," "bold"), October 16, 1835, November 3, 1835. For the mid-1830s political context, see Freehling, *Road to Disunion*, 1:289–307; J. Rothman, *Flush Times*, 91–117; P. Breen, *The Land Shall Be Deluged in Blood*; Sinha, *Slave's Cause*, 235–36. For Bill's possible social context, consider Kelly, "'Well Bred Country People.'" For book distribution, see Zboray, "Transportation Revolution."

38. Hewitt Diary, August 9, 1843 (all quotations); Abram S. Hewitt, "The Hyphen," https://nyhistory.tumblr.com/post/163638027704/abram-s-hewitt-was-born-july-31-1822 (accessed February 2, 2023). For clothing, class, and masculinity, consider Zakim, *Ready-Made Democracy*; Luskey, "Jumping Counters in White Collars."

39. Temple, *American Tourist's Pocket Companion*, 9 ("recourse"); Dunlop Diary, [July 9, 1810]. For the public reading of newspapers, consider Henkin, *City Reading*, 109–10; Steffen, "Newspapers for Free," 413–14. For the possible significance of the child in Krimmel's painting, consider Breitenbach, "Sons of the Fathers."

40. Boykin & Lee Journal, August 15–17, 1833 (all quotations). For letter writing, see S. Stowe, *Intimacy and Power*, 3–4 and passim; Henkin, *Postal Age*, 10–11, 93–118; Dierks, *In My Power*; Wagner, "Composing Pioneers," 22–44 and passim. Colonel Boykin may have been John Boykin Sr., who enslaved twenty-seven people in 1830, or John Boykin Jr., who enslaved twelve. 1830 U.S. Census for Kershaw County, South Carolina, courtesy of Ancestry.com. Lee's relationship to the Boykins is unclear; the colonel could, perhaps, have been Lee's stepfather and Mrs. Boykin his second wife. Boykin & Lee Journal, August 5, 1833, September 5, 1833.

41. Brevard Diary, July 28, 1791 ("very pretty"); Hunter, *Quebec to Carolina*, 141 ("sweet"); Dunlop Diary, August 23, 1811 ("Beautiful," "invaluable"). For prostitution along new roads, canals, and railroad lines, see Grivno, *Gleanings of Freedom*, 177–78. For urban tavern prostitution, see K. Hemphill, *Bawdy City*, 38–39 and passim. Like Hemphill's Baltimore-centered study, much prostitution history is urban: see, for example, Walkowitz, *Prostitution and Victorian Society*; Stansell, *City of Women*, 171–92; Peiss, *Cheap Amusements*; Gilfoyle, "Strumpets and Misogynists"; Corbin, *Women for Hire*; Hill, *Their Sisters' Keepers*; J. Rothman, *Notorious in the Neighborhood*, 92–129.

42. Hiram Haines to Mary Ann Currie Philpotts, January 26, 1826 ("L-E-G-S" etc.); see also February 10, 1826, March 1, 1826, May 19, 1826, May 23, 1826, May 26, 1826, Hiram Haines to Mary Ann Haines, December 21, 1826 ("liking," "cocktail," "pretty," "looked"), Haines Papers; Boykin & Lee Journal, August 15, 1833 ("tingling"), August 23, 1833 ("spent," "succeeded"), September 3, 1833 ("usual," "best"); P. Cohen, "Women at Large," 47–48. For kissing and other intimacies, see E. Rothman, *Hands and Hearts*, 51–55; Jabour, *Scarlett's Sisters*, 146.

43. For leisure travel, migration, and missionary work, see Faragher and Stansell, "Women and Their Families"; Cashin, *Family Venture*; Jabour, "'Privations and Hardships'"; Imbarrato, "Ordinary Travel"; Lewis, *Ladies and Gentlemen on Display*; Chambers, *Drinking the Waters*; DeRogatis, *Moral Geography*; Imbarrato, *Traveling Women*, 53–88; Gassan, *Birth of American Tourism*.

44. P. Cohen, "Women at Large"; Welke, "When All the Women Were White," 268–72; Welke, *Recasting American Liberty*, 254–57; Richter, *Home on the Rails*, 93–107; Pryor, *Colored Travelers*, 60–102; M. Bay, *Traveling Black*, 21–33.

45. Dominant understandings of female innocence operated to exclude Black and working-class white women. Royall, *Letters from Alabama*, 23 (all quotations), 23–24; Stansell, *City of Women*, 23–30, 67–75; Smith-Rosenberg, *Disorderly Conduct*, 109–28; Kennedy, *Braided Relations*, 72–73; Manion, *Liberty's Prisoners*, 156–57.

46. Hannah Marshall Haines to [Esther] Garrigues, August 28, 1808 ("rudely," "detained," "lest," "Inhabitants," "trying," "very bigoted"), Hannah Marshall Haines to Patience Marshall, August 31, 1808 ("intirely"), Wyck Collection. For women's travel writing, consider Imbarrato, "Ordinary Travel," 167–211.

47. Jane B. Haines to John A. Warder, [July 1, 1836] ("dirty"), Wyck Collection; Howland Diary, July [4], 1818 ("foam"); other quotations in undated entries. For cleanliness and gentility, see K. Brown, *Foul Bodies*, 118–58. For Niagara Falls, consider Gassan, *Birth of American Tourism*, 92–104.

48. Howland Diary. Julia Roberts suggests that Harry Jones also paid very selective attention to the people he noticed in visiting his local taverns in and around Kingston in Upper Canada. Roberts, "Harry Jones and his Cronies," 15–16.

49. Schulling Diary, [July 1,] 1824 (all quotations); P. Cohen, "Safety and Danger," 114–16; Imbarrato, *Traveling Women*, 76–79. For aspects of urban sexual culture that may have informed Schulling's alarm, see Kaplan, "New York Tavern Violence"; Lyons, *Sex among the Rabble*. More politically astute than Schulling, Harriet Martineau acknowledged enslaved women's and children's prostitution in taverns and hotels. See Martineau, *Society in America*, 1:384–85.

50. Willson may have become more assertive as she traveled. Willson, *Journey in 1836*, May 15, 1836 ("rough unguarded"), June 18, 1836 ("much annoyed," "the landlord"), June 27, 1836 ("intoxicated," "of feeling," "knew his place"). For life cycle and female experience, see Boylan, "Timid Girls"; Premo, *Winter Friends*; Wilson, *Life after Death*; Conger, *Widows' Might*. For the eighteenth-century "man of feeling," see, for example, Barker-Benfield, *Culture of Sensibility*, 247–50.

51. Royall, *Mrs. Royall's Southern Tour*, 2:203 ("all," "infamous"), 3:206–7; Clapp, "'Virago-Errant,'" 208–9, 216, 228–29; Clapp, "Black Books and Southern Tours"; Clapp, *Notorious Woman*, 136, 148–52; Pottroff, "The Royall Coach."

52. Women's involvement caused tension and growth within the temperance movement. See, for example, Varon, *We Mean to Be Counted*, 30–39; Isenberg, *Sex and Citizenship*, 157–61; Fletcher, *Gender and Temperance*, 7–57.

53. For Black citizenship, see, for example, E. Ball, *To Live an Antislavery Life*; Pryor, *Colored Travelers*; Jones, *Birthright Citizens*; Spires, *Practice of Citizenship*; Bonner, *Remaking the Republic*; Foreman, Casey, and Patterson, *Colored Conventions Movement*.

54. Zylstra, "Whiteness, Freedom, and Technology"; Pryor, *Colored Travelers*, 60–102; M. Bay, *Traveling Black*, 13–14, 25–32. For Black travelers' use of private boarding houses, consider Williams-Forson, "Where Did They Eat?"

55. Hodgson, *Richard Potter*, 4, 125–36, 231–40.

56. Northup, *Twelve Years a Slave*, 24 ("high wages"), 20–38; Cox, *Traveling South*, 86–90. For the slave-trading business, see especially W. Johnson, *Soul by Soul*; J. Rothman, *Ledger and the Chain*. For Black steamboat workers, see, for example, Buchanan, *Black Life on the Mississippi*.

57. Aaron also recalled multiple occasions when antislavery people refused to shelter or help him. Aaron, *Aaron's History*, 27 ("comfortable," "pallet," "his customers"), 17 ("eight," "where"), 18 ("sell"); see also 4–6, 7, 13–14, 21. John Blassingame identified Aaron's narrative as "unreliable," but other scholars have developed frameworks for examining texts with narrative shifts and ambiguous or remarkable biographical details. Blassingame, "Using the Testimony of Ex-Slaves," 478n17; Yellin, "Written by Herself"; Anne Dowling Grulich, "Putting Charles Ball on the Map in Calvert County, Maryland," 2008, https://jefpat .maryland.gov/Documents/mac-lab/grulich-anne-dowling-putting-charles-ball-on-the -map-in-calvert-county-maryland.pdf; L. Cohen, *Fabrication of American Literature*, 101–32; Dahl, "Unfreedom and the Crises of Witnessing," 215, 217–18, 223–24; Chaney, "Digression, Slavery, and Failing to Return," 515.

58. *The Liberator*, October 11, 1839; *Frederick Douglass' (Rochester, NY) Paper*, February 11, 1853; Corrigan, "Imaginary Cruelties," 10–11; Heerman, "Reducing Free Men to Slavery"; Bell, *Stolen*; J. Rothman, *Ledger and the Chain*, 48, 88–96, 132.

59. *(New York, NY) Weekly Advocate*, February 25, 1837 (all quotations), January 7, 1837.

60. *(Rochester, NY) North Star*, September 15, 1848 (all quotations), June 15, 1849.

61. Armistead, *Tribute for the Negro*, 90 ("gentlewoman," "huts"), 89–90; *Frederick Douglass' (Rochester, NY) Paper*, June 15, 1855 ("public table"); Jeffrey, *Abolitionists Remember*, 125–26. On Black action against transportation discrimination in the early republic, see Pryor, *Colored Travelers*, 85–90, 95–99.

62. Jacobs, *Incidents in the Life*, 265–66 (all quotations), 264–67.

63. On the domestic slave trade, see Tadman, *Speculators and Slaves*; W. Johnson, *Soul by Soul*; Deyle, *Carry Me Back*; Baptist, "'Cuffy,' 'Fancy Maids' and 'One-Eyed Men'"; Baptist, "'Stol' and Fetched Here'"; J. Rothman, *Ledger and the Chain*.

64. T. Weld, *American Slavery*, 69; Henson, *Autobiography*, 45; Slaughter, *Bloody Dawn*, 44; Jeffrey, *Abolitionists Remember*, 126; J. Rothman, *Ledger and the Chain*, 44.

65. T. Weld, *American Slavery*, 69–70; Clarke and Clarke, *Narratives of Lewis and Milton Clarke*, 106 ("to pay"); J. Brown, *An American Bondman*, 27 ("affects," "kindness"). For enslaved suicide, consider Gomez, *Exchanging Our Country Marks*, 117–20; T. Snyder, "Suicide, Slavery, and Memory."

66. T. Weld, *American Slavery*, 100; H. Adams, *God's Image in Ebony*, 118 ("waylaid"), 117–19; Henson, *Life*, 14–18; C. Ball, *Slavery in the United States*, 128 ("toddy," "gentleman," "cut").

67. Slaughter, *Bloody Dawn*, 53–54; Lubet, *Fugitive Justice*, 57; Mainwaring, *Abandoned Tracks*; J. Rothman, *Ledger and the Chain*, 109–10 and passim; "Freedom on the Move," https://app.freedomonthemove.org/ (accessed February 2, 2023).

68. Northup, *Twelve Years a Slave*, 25 ("cherished"); C. Ball, *Fifty Years in Chains*, 103 ("the best means"); W. Craft, *Running a Thousand Miles*, 45, 51–52. On information networks and "pathways to freedom," see also Grivno, *Gleanings of Freedom*, 84 ("pathways").

69. Edward Said's "rival geography" and Houston Baker's "geography of containment," as quoted in Camp, *Closer to Freedom*, 6–7.

70. Robin D. G. Kelley's "moving theaters," as quoted in Pryor, *Colored Travelers*, 45.

Chapter Two

1. *Camden (SC) Gazette*, February 18, 1819 (all quotations); *Winyaw (SC) Intelligencer*, February 20, 1819.

2. For gentility and comfort in early America, see Bushman, *Refinement of America*; Kross, "Mansions, Men, Women"; Crowley, *Invention of Comfort*; K. Brown, *Foul Bodies*, 118–58. For a related argument about respectable men and Canadian public accommodations, that also suggests the greater possibilities for socioeconomic segmentation in urban as compared to rural settings, see Roberts, "Harry Jones and His Cronies"; Roberts, *In Mixed Company*, 11–38 and passim.

3. I discuss tavern licensing in chapter 5.

4. Bushman, *Refinement of America*, 160–64; Sandoval-Strausz, *Hotel*, 11–109; Berger, *Hotel Dreams*, 69–82; Lennon, "Stage for Gentility"; Scribner, *Inn Civility*, 3–11, 42–86. For the "republican court," see Teute and Shields, "Jefferson in Washington." For the nascent middle class, consider Ryan, *Cradle of the Middle Class*; Blumin, *Emergence of the Middle Class*; Goloboy, "Early American Middle Class"; Marshall, "Rural Experience and the Development of the Middle Class"; Hart, *Building Charleston*; Goloboy, *Charleston and the Emergence of Middle-Class Culture*. On early nineteenth-century resorts, see Lewis, *Ladies and Gentlemen on Display*; Sandoval-Strausz, *Hotel*, 81, 87–92; Gassan, *Birth of American Tourism*.

5. Bushman, *Refinement of America*, 399 ("intellectual geography"); see also 227–31, 376, 398–401, 420–25; Crowley, "Sensibility of Comfort," 780–82; Crowley, *Invention of Comfort*, 128–30, 147–49, 224–29; Herman, *Town House*, 193–259; Wenger, "Reading the Gemberling-Rex House," 74; A. Martin, *Buying into the World of Goods*, 121–27. For capital investments in luxury hotels, see Sandoval-Strausz, *Hotel*, 20–29, 68–72; Berger, *Hotel Dreams*, 26–27, 32–36, 90–92.

6. Crowley argues that eighteenth-century notions of comfort implied the "*discomfort* of previously acceptable facilities." Crowley, "The Sensibility of Comfort," 780 ("*discomfort*").

7. Martin points out that a log cabin could be well or roughly finished. A. Martin, *Buying into the World of Goods*, 118–19.

8. Cf. Sandoval-Strausz, *Hotel*, 34–36. For domesticity and citizenship, consider Stanfield, *Rewriting Citizenship*, especially 43–67.

9. For tavern signs, see Smith, *Tavern Signs of America*; Schoelwer, *Lions and Eagles and Bulls*.

10. On Krimmel, consider Naeve, *John Lewis Krimmel*; John and Leonard, "Illusion of the Ordinary."

11. I. Weld, *Travels*, 16 ("common," "all" "the family"); see also 17, 58, 65; Fearon, *Sketches of America*, 292 ("knowledge," emphasis included); see also 80, 82; Crowley, *Invention of*

Comfort, 221–23. For Americans' concerns about their cultural relationship to England and Europe, see, for example, Haynes, *Unfinished Revolution*; Yokota, *Unbecoming British*; Kilbride, *Being American in Europe*; Scribner, *Inn Civility.*

12. Reeves, "Lieutenant Enos Reeves," 248 ("not worthy"), 254–55; Bill Diary, December 19, 1835 ("too indolent," "improve"); Birkbeck, *Journey in America,* 15, 42–43.

13. Olmsted, *Cotton Kingdom,* 305 ("bullying"). For politicized northern views of the South in the 1850s, see, for example, Foner, *Free Soil,* 40–72.

14. Strickland, *Journal,* 74 ("a race"), 123 ("merest"); Nevins Journal, November 13, 1802 ("pay more"); Gilpin, *Pleasure and Business,* 18 "("Dutch").

15. Emphases in the originals. William Parker Foulke to Eleanor Foulke, January 17, 1848 ("badly," "merely"), February 22, 1848 (all other quotations), December 7, 1847, Foulke Papers; this collection also documents Foulke's reform commitments. For the eighteenth-century comfortable cottage, consider Crowley, *Invention of Comfort,* 203–29. In the early republic, the discourse of rural declension coexisted with a contrary idealization. See, famously, Jefferson, *Notes on the State of Virginia,* 240–41. Foulke suggested that civilization banished dirt; for views that perhaps shaped his own childhood, consider K. Brown, *Foul Bodies,* 233–50. For British and Anglo-American reactions to German food in a later period, see Waddington, "'We Don't Want Any German Sausages Here'"; Lobel, *Urban Appetites,* 186–88.

16. Clifford Diary, 292 (all quotations); K. Brown, *Foul Bodies,* 140, 145.

17. Gilpin, *Pleasure and Business,* 125–26 (all quotations). On staircases, see Bushman, *Refinement of America,* 114–20.

18. Martha Lewis Cocke to Caroline Lewis Cocke, November 19, 1810 (all quotations), Cocke Papers.

19. Royall, *Letters from Alabama,* 36–37 (all quotations).

20. *(Wilmington, DE) American Watchman,* October 20, 1810 ("superior," "repaired, "fitted up"); *Camden (SC) Gazette,* August 15, 1818 ("their establishment," "convenient").

21. *Camden (SC) Gazette,* January 30, 1817 ("improved"); *(Fredericksburg) Virginia Herald,* June 21, 1799 ("2 rooms," "new," "very commodious"), October 22, 1802; Herman, *Town House,* 250–52; Lennon, "Stage for Gentility," 43–55.

22. Sansom, "Travels in Lower Canada," 57 ("neat"); Cuming, *Sketches of a Tour,* 183 ("handsome"); *Bartgis's Federal Gazette, or the Frederick-Town (MD) and County, Weekly Advertiser,* June 9, 1796; *Potowmac Guardian, and (Martinsburg, VA) Berkeley Advertiser,* April 7, 1796; Dun & Company Records, Pennsylvania, 54:36; Herman, *Town House,* 115; Lennon, "Stage for Gentility," 56–61. On regional vernacular architecture, see Chappell and Richter, "Wealth and Houses"; Richie, Milner, and Huber, *Stone Houses;* A. Martin, *Buying into the World of Goods,* 113–21; Hubka, *Houses without Names.*

23. *(Fredericksburg) Virginia Herald,* July 19, 1803, September 14, 1816, January 25, 1823; T. Breen, "Horses and Gentlemen," 249; Isaac, *Transformation of Virginia,* 53, 99.

24. *Camden (SC) Gazette,* February 18, 1819 ("elegantly," "vacant," "faithful"); *(Lexington, KY) Western Monitor,* September 20, 1817 ("good"); Nevins Journal, October 19, 180[2] ("attentive"); *Washington Hotel.*

25. Stuart-Wortley, *Travels,* 42 ("covered," "narrow"); *Crawford House;* Morgan, *Cape Ann Pavilion;* Shurtleff, *Island House;* Packard, *Pequot House, New London, Conn.;* Flad, "Parlor in the Wilderness," 359.

26. *(Fredericksburg) Virginia Herald,* January 22, 1789, December 28, 1815, January 27, 1816; Cuming, *Sketches of a Tour,* 20; Bushman, *Refinement of America,* 261–62.

27. For bar cages, see figures 1.2 and 2.1 in the present book and Garvin and Garvin, *On the Road North of Boston,* 25; Meacham, "Keeping the Trade," 146, figure 2; Bergengren, "The Physical Thing Itself," 105, figure 16.

28. *(Fredericksburg) Virginia Herald,* January 27, 1816 ("front room"). For examples of men's barroom conduct, see Stott, *Jolly Fellows,* 10–26, 39–44.

29. *Tavern Rates, Established at Baltimore-County April Term, 1789* (all quotations). On wealth and drinking choices, see McDaid, "'Best Accustomed House,'" 167, 193–94. For ersatz imported wines, see Beastall, *Useful Guide,* 54–63.

30. *(New York) Royal Gazette,* July 1, 1780 ("best wines"), April 21, 1781 ("best liquors"); *(Cincinnati, OH) Centinel of the North-Western Territory,* November 14, 1795 ("best liquors"); *(Lenox, MA) Berkshire Journal,* September 30, 1830 ("finest flavour"); Rorabaugh, *Alcoholic Republic,* 82–83.

31. Dunlop Diary, February 13, 1811 ("crowded"); Steffen, "Newspapers for Free," 411–15.

32. Caldwell, *Tour through Part of Virginia,* 9 ("excellent"); Hannah Marshall Haines to "Brother and Sister" Garrigues, August 14, 1808 ("the Gentlemen"); Reuben Haines III to Jane B. Haines, August 22, 1830 ("papers"), Wyck Collection; William Parker Foulke to Eleanor Foulke, January 17, 1848 ("newspaper"), Foulke Papers; Boykin & Lee Journal, August 17, 1833 ("hardly possible"). For news, print, and mails, consider John, *Spreading the News*; Henkin, *City Reading*; Henkin, *Postal Age*; Loughran, *Republic in Print*; Pasley, *"Tyranny of Printers."*

33. Lennon, "Stage for Gentility," 3, 34, 70, 84–85, 100, 105; Scribner, *Inn Civility,* 28. For masculine authority over eighteenth-century domestic space, consider Kross, "Mansions, Men, Women"; Harvey, *Little Republic.*

34. "William Davis," Federal Writers' Project: Slave Narrative Project, 16:1, p. 291 ("'bout two miles," "hustle round"), https://www.loc.gov/resource/mesn.161/?sp=298 (accessed May 15, 2023); Martineau, *Western Travel,* 1:211 ("as many"); Hall, *Travels in North America,* 1:54 ("snatched," "in less").

35. Unknown, "Diary," n.d. (all quotations), Fisher Papers.

36. *(Fredericksburg) Virginia Herald,* June 21, 1799 ("commodious"); *Tavern Rates, 1809* ("common," "good"); New Jersey, *Hunterdon County Rates* ("extraordinary"); *Camden (SC) Gazette,* January 30, 1817 ("the best viands," "the best"). For the meanings of meals, consider Sandoval-Strausz, *Hotel,* 168–71; Bruegel, "'Acceptable Refreshment'"; Lobel, *Urban Appetites,* 103–67.

37. Grimball Diaries, July 2, 1835; Houstoun, *Hesperos,* 1:69, 2:67; Campbell, *Hotel Keepers,* viii. For the emergence of private dining in luxurious large hotels, see Nathan Levy to Sylvanus Bourne, December 27, 1802, Bourne Papers; Reuben Haines III to Jane B. Haines, August 22, 1830, Wyck Collection; Berger, *Hotel Dreams,* 101, 152.

38. *(Charleston, SC) City Gazette,* July 28, 1796 ("Gentlemen," "Societies," "PRIVATE"); *(Washington, DC) Daily National Intelligencer,* December 15, 1815 ("private," "Societies"); *(Wilmington, DE) American Watchman,* June 27, 1810; Sansom, "Travels in Lower Canada," 4, footnote; Thompson, *Rum Punch and Revolution,* 86–88; Lennon, "Stage for Gentility," 89–93. I discuss July Fourth entertainments and ladies in chapter 6.

39. American Independence Museum, Exeter, NH, personal observation; *(Fredericks-burg) Virginia Herald*, January 27, 1816 ("folding," "large"); November 22, 1823 ("three large," "either"); Kross, "Mansions, Men, Women," 395–96.

40. *Nashville (TE) Whig* as reprinted in *Camden (SC) Gazette*, February 21, 1818 (all quotations); Waldstreicher, *In the Midst of Perpetual Fetes*, 10–14, 18, and passim.

41. *(Charleston, SC) City Gazette*, September 3, 1806; *(Portsmouth) New-Hampshire Gazette*, July 25, 1820 ("GRAND Caravan"); Hewitt Diary, August 9, 1843 ("superlative" "factory girls"). For wax figures, see Benes, *For a Short Time Only*, 272–87; Kelly, *Republic of Taste*, 159–94.

42. For welcome and unwanted sounds, consider Attali, *Noise*; Smith, *Listening to Nineteenth-Century America*; Hegarty, *Noise/Music*; LaBelle, "Sharing Architecture," 179, 186.

43. Gibbs, "Taverns in Tidewater Virginia," 52–53; Bushman, *Refinement of America*, 109, 251–52.

44. Thomas Jefferson to Thomas Mann Randolph Jr., November 2, 1793 (all quotations), https://founders.archives.gov/documents/Jefferson/01-27-02-0264; see also Thomas Jefferson to James Madison, November 2, 1793, https://founders.archives.gov/documents/Madison/01-15-02-0086, both courtesy of Founders Online, National Archives (accessed February 2, 2023). For Jefferson's childhood home, see Historic American Buildings Survey, Tuckahoe Plantation, Library of Congress, https://www.loc.gov/item/va0490/ (accessed February 2, 2023). For the 1793 epidemic, consider Powell, *Bring out Your Dead*.

45. Woodruff Journal, October 27, 1786 ("very full"); Hannah Haines Diary, September 21, 1810 ("crowded," "it was"), Wyck Collection; Bernhard, *Travels Through North America*, 2:34 ("obliged"); William Parker Foulke to Eleanor Foulke, April 2, 1848 ("unadulterated"), Foulke Papers.

46. R. Hunter, *Quebec to Carolina*, 120, 177; J. Alexander, *Transatlantic Sketches*, 255–56 (all quotations). For concerns about crowded conditions and same-sex intimacies—but not in taverns—see Manion, *Liberty's Prisoners*, 171–78. Bruce Dorsey offers a thoughtful exploration of same-sex sexuality and prosecutorial evidence in a case involving temporary lodgings. Dorsey, "'Making Men What They Should Be.'"

47. *(Fredericksburg) Virginia Herald*, June 21, 1799 ("sundry," "convenient," "more privately"), January 27, 1816 ("handsome," "divided").

48. *Baltimore, January 1st, 1827* ("private," "as desirable"); *Richmond Enquirer*, October 23, 1828; Drew Diary, n.d. ("City Gentlemen," "generally," "more private").

49. Hall, *Travels in North America*, 2:183 ("during," "this amount"); Schulling Diary, July [1], 1824 ("main").

50. Gilpin, *Pleasure and Business*, 5 ("neat rooms"); Bernhard, *Travels through North America*, 1:65 ("wide," "fine," "necessary," "three"); K. Brown, *Foul Bodies*, 141, 146, 206, 266–69. For homespun, see Clitherall Diary, April 29, 1776; Melish, *Travels in the United States*, 1:110; William Parker Foulke to Eleanor Foulke, April 2, 1848, Foulke Papers; Hartigan-O'Connor, *Ties That Buy*, 165, 176–77; L. Edwards, *Only the Clothes*, 81–82.

51. Hickey et al., "The Lincolns' Globe Tavern," 650 ("Superior"), 648–51. See also Bushman, *Refinement of America*, 227–31.

52. Reuben Haines III to Hannah Marshall Haines, July 24, 1805 ("some"), Wyck Collection; *(Boston, MA) Columbian Centinel*, August 4, 1813 ("transient," "for those," "the

charges"). For hotel charges, see Sandoval-Strausz, *Hotel*, 85; Berger, *Hotel Dreams*, 119–21. On boarding versus housekeeping, see Gamber, *Boardinghouse*, 116–39.

53. Hall, *Travels in North America*, 2:183 ("matter of course," "travellers with families," "inconvenience"); Anonymous Diary, October 27, 1836 ("single rooms"). For white middle-class domesticity, consider the classic, Welter, "Cult of True Womanhood," and cf. Stansell, *City of Women*, Kerber, "Separate Spheres, Female Worlds"; Greenberg, *Advocating the Man*.

54. *Boston (MA) Patriot,* November 10, 1817 ("families"); *Camden (SC) Gazette,* March 4, 1819 ("entirely remote"), July 27, 1820 ("private," "Travelling Families"), August 11, 1817 ("Camp Houses"); Caldwell, *Tour through Part of Virginia,* 18 ("cabins," "log-houses"); Lewis, *Ladies and Gentlemen on Display,* 44–45; Gassan, *Birth of American Tourism,* 163n2.

55. *Camden (SC) Gazette,* January 20, 1820 ("his house"); *Alexandria (VA) Daily Gazette. Commercial & Political,* February 8, 1811 ("genteel boarders"); *Eastern Argus (Portland, ME),* January 26, 1819. For private genteel boarding, see Gamber, *Boardinghouse,* 39; Carr, "Marketing Gentility," 49.

56. Emphases in the original. *(Charleston, SC) City Gazette,* October 17, 1806 (all quotations). For slave sales' role in drawing planters to Charleston, especially before the international trade closed, see O'Malley, "Slavery's Converging Ground," 271–72, 276–82.

57. Morgan, *Cape Ann Pavilion* ("new"); *United States Hotel* ("single gentlemen"); *Sangamo (IL) Journal,* February 18, 1840, as reproduced in Hickey et al., "The Lincolns' Globe Tavern," 636 ("Ye strangers," "anxious," "choice," "beds"); Brown, *Arcade Hotel Guide,* 5 ("fullest wants"), 10 ("gentlemen," "*Ladies*"). For hotel categories, consider Sandoval-Strausz, *Hotel,* 81–99.

58. *(Fredericksburg) Virginia Herald,* June 21, 1799 ("privately," "convenient"), March 23, 1822 ("large," "great," "house"); Bernhard, *Travels through North America,* 1:65 ("gentleman"); Herman, *Town House,* 243–53; Bergengren, "Physical Thing Itself," 112–13.

59. McMurry, "City Parlor"; Bushman, *Refinement of America,* 264–67, 273–79, 361; Grier, *Culture and Comfort*; Kross, "Mansions, Men, Women," 396–97, 399, 402.

60. Memoir of Mrs. John Reed, 9 ("handsomely"); Trollope, *Domestic Manners,* 165 ("without asking," "literally"); Bernhard, *Travels through North America,* 1:65 ("separate sitting-room," "separate charge," "especially"); Pottroff, "Royall Coach," 132. For urban populations in 1830, see "Table 6. Population of the 90 Urban Places: 1830," https://www2.census.gov/library/working-papers/1998/demo/pop-twps0027/tab06.txt.

61. Loguen, *As a Slave and as a Freeman,* 288–89 (all quotations), 227–28, 232–36, 260–62; *(Rochester, NY) North Star,* July 20, 1849. After his self-emancipation, Loguen worked for a time in a hotel in Rochester, New York. Broyld, *Borderland Blacks,* 65.

62. Margaret Steele to Mary Steele, October 9, 1814 ("very well"), Steele Papers; Royall, *Mrs. Royall's Southern Tour,* 2:43; Berger, *Hotel Dreams,* 125–26. For a "hostile satire of the parlor ideal" amid the slave trade, see Baptist, "'Cuffy,' 'Fancy Maids' and 'One-Eyed Men,'" 1646.

63. Olmsted, *Cotton Kingdom,* 306 (all quotations). For navigating within and between different manly norms, consider Roberts, *In Mixed Company,* 134–37 and passim; Foote, *Gentlemen and the Roughs,* 41–65 and passim; Scribner, *Inn Civility,* 87–90, 98–99, 161–62.

64. Hannah Marshall Haines to [Uncle and Aunt] Charles Marshall, June 30, 1808 ("cott beds"), Wyck Collection; Cuming, *Sketches of a Tour,* 40 ("small," "breakfast"); Hall, *Travels in North America,* 1:311 ("cheerful), 2:178 ("smiling").

65. Bernhard, *Travels through North America*, 1:34 ("parlour"), 1:65 ("several sitting"); *Sangamo (IL) Journal*, May 28, 1846 ("four front"), as reproduced in Hickey et al., "The Lincolns' Globe Tavern," 637; see also 629, 638–40.

66. R. Van Branken as quoted in Drew, *North-Side View of Slavery*, 305 (all quotations).

67. Douglass, *My Bondage and My Freedom*, 370–71 (all quotations). For Black activists and middle-class respectability, see E. Ball, *To Live an Antislavery Life*, 1–61; Pryor, *Colored Travelers*, 36–38, 68–71; Blight, *Frederick Douglass*, 256–57. I return to Douglass's views on accommodations, labor, and citizenship in chapter 6.

68. Royall, *Mrs. Royall's Southern Tour*, 2:114 (all quotations).

69. Royall, *Mrs. Royall's Southern Tour*, 1:86–91 (all quotations); Clapp, "'Virago-Errant,'" 212, 216.

70. William Parker Foulke to Eleanor Foulke, February 13, 1848 (all quotations), Foulke Papers.

71. Royall, *Letters from Alabama*, 5 (all quotations).

72. Melish, *Travels in the United States*, 1:268 ("civil"); Royall, *Mrs. Royall's Southern Tour*, 1:121, 2:130; William Parker Foulke to Eleanor Foulke, April 2, 1848 ("attentive"), Foulke Papers; Cuming, *Sketches of a Tour*, 36; Campbell, *Hotel Keepers*, 26.

73. *Camden (SC) Gazette*, March 4, 1819 ("assiduous"); *Poughkeepsie (NY) American*, October 7, 1848 ("assiduous"); Sandoval-Strausz, *Hotel*, 179–84; Sandoval-Strausz and Wilk, "Princes and Maids"; Levinson Wilk, "Cliff Dwellers," 101. This section both draws on and revises conclusions I reached in K. Wood, "Making a Home in Public."

74. Fairfax, *Journey from Virginia*, 13 ("as few," "daughters," "make"); Cuming, *Sketches of a Tour*, 63 ("the business").

75. Hall, *Travels in North America*, 1:67 (all quotations).

76. Melish, *Travels in the United States*, 1:32 (all quotations).

77. Volume 4, October 1, [1803] (Minty Johnson mentioned), February 2, [1804] ("left"), Browne Papers.

78. *(New York) Packet*, May 16, 1788 ("good"); *Camden (SC) Gazette*, February 18, 1819 ("faithful"); *Richmond (VA) Enquirer*, December 23, 1828 ("competent"); Stansell, *City of Women*, 155–65; Dudden, *Serving Women*, 44–71; Boydston, *Home and Work*, 79–80; S. Cole, "Servants and Slaves," 205–14. Complaining about servants helped female keepers assert their status as ladies of the house. See, for example, Fairfax, *Journey from Virginia*, 22.

79. Emphases in the originals. Royall, *Mrs. Royall's Southern Tour*, 2:199 ("landlady," "she had"), 3:97 ("I am"); Royall, *Letters from Alabama*, 5–6 (*"consequentials," "'sanctum'"*).

80. Lester Diary, August 19, 1836 ("boys," "did not dare").

81. *The Eagle of Freedom; or, The Baltimore Town & Fell's Point Gazette*, July 15, 1796 ("assiduity"); *Potowmac (VA) Guardian, and Berkeley Advertiser*, September 23, 1793 ("attention," "minute"); *Charter and Directory of the City of Rochester*, n.p. ("spare no pains"); *Richmond (VA) Enquirer*, June 2, 1804 ("no exertion"). See also *The (Russellville, KY) Mirror*, August 15, 1807; *(Alexandria) Louisiana Herald*, September 30, 1820; *(Portland, ME) Eastern Argus*, August 31, 1827; Shurtleff, *Island House*; Simons, *Lake Dunmore House*.

82. *Wheeling (VA) Times and Advertiser*, April 29, 1841 (all quotations). For other Boniface references, see, for example, Strickland, *Journal*, 67; Northup, *Twelve Years a Slave*, 294. Used for a tavern keeper, the name comes from an eighteenth-century play. M. G. W. and H. W. L., "Archetypes in Literature," 90.

83. Kline Account Book; *Wheeling (VA) Times and Advertiser*, January 29, 1842 ("in some"). For staffing large public houses, see Campbell, *Hotel Keepers*; Sandoval-Strausz and Wilk, "Princes and Maids"; Levinson Wilk, "Cliff Dwellers."

84. Kline Account Book. After removing duplicate and illegible entries, I found that 35 percent of the workers were listed by first name only, described as Black or yellow, or both. If Kline listed any people of color by first and last name *without* racial signifiers, the proportion of Black workers could have been higher. On hotel and boarding-house labor in the border South, see S. Cole, "Servants and Slaves," 289, table A-2-7, 290, table A-5-10. For ethnicity among female domestic workers, see Dudden, *Serving Women*, 60–71. For the social and economic texture of the border region, consider also Salafia, *Slavery's Borderland*.

85. *(Rochester, NY) North Star*, June 13, 1850; Campbell, *Hotel Keepers*, 21; Buchanan, *Black Life on the Mississippi*, 62, 70.

86. Kline Account Book. Using first names as a proxy for sex and classifying all illegible entries as individual men suggests that the work force was at most 60 percent male. On female tavern cooks, see Meacham, "Keeping the Trade," 156; "Tom Randall," Federal Writers' Project: Slave Narrative Project, 8:57, https://www.loc.gov/resource/mesn.080/?sp=60&st=image (accessed May 15, 2023); Bibb, *Narrative*, 57. For hotel housekeepers, see *(Charleston, SC) City Gazette*, January 9, 1793; Campbell, *Hotel Keepers*, 32. On social status of later nineteenth-century tavern and hotel workers, see Sandoval-Strausz and Wilk, "Princes and Maids." On women's vulnerability to sexual violence in urban working-class taverns, consider Kaplan, "New York Tavern Violence."

87. Broyld, *Borderland Blacks*, 23, 46, 64–65; see also 121–24.

88. Browne, *Autobiography of a Female Slave*, 212 ("speak 'spectable"); Tubbee and Allen, *Life of Okah Tubbee*, 39; E. Davis and Hogan, *Barber of Natchez*; Zacek, *Kingdom for a Horse*. For Black barbers in other settings, see Fearon, *Sketches of America*, 60; Olmsted, *Cotton Kingdom*, 634–35; Buchanan, *Black Life on the Mississippi*, 67–68.

89. *Report of the Proceedings of the Colored National Convention*, 17 (all quotations); E. Ball, *To Live an Antislavery Life*, 42–43. For Black theorizing about "economic citizenship" in this period, see Spires, *Practice of Citizenship*, 121–28.

90. For making and contesting gendered boundaries in other contexts, see, for example, Stansell, *City of Women*; Ryan, *Women in Public*; Kennedy, *Braided Relations*.

91. Sandoval-Strausz, *Hotel*, 137–202; Shiring and Shiring, *Hotelkeepers Organize in Twentieth Century*; Diary, April 7, 1792, Adams Papers.

92. For the idea of liquor profits, see, for example, Barnes, *Immorality of the Traffic in Ardent Spirits*. For the emergent American middle class as a matter of cultural, social, and familial strategies and values as much as financial standing or occupation, see note 4 in the current chapter and Wells, *Origins of the Southern Middle Class*; Hart, "Work, Family."

93. Gilpin, *Pleasure and Business*, 5 (all quotations).

Chapter Three

1. Martin Browne to Luke Byrn[s], August 26, 1797 (all quotations), Folder 2, Browne Papers. Browne's spelling, or perhaps his handwriting, varied, and Burns was the more frequent version.

2. Keepers and other retailers used daybooks to record sales as they occurred, later transferring unpaid sales into ledgers organized by customer. For historians, daybooks may illuminate consumption and sociability better than ledgers, while ledgers can be better tools for understanding credit and payments. Archived tavern accounts rarely document keepers' running costs or capital investments. For Anglo-American bookkeeping, see Sampson, "American Accounting Education," 460–63; Coclanis, "Bookkeeping in the Eighteenth-Century South"; Poovey, *History of the Modern Fact*, 29–91; Lamoreaux, "Rethinking the Transition to Capitalism," 440–45. To understand tavern accounts, I transcribed thousands of lines of data and analyzed each set of records in multiple ways but did not construct a combined data set for quantitative analysis, largely because of the many discrepancies across keepers' records.

3. Volume 4, "Luke Barnes particular acct of Grogg, February 14, 1794–May 2, 1794," Luke Burns and George Kyner, March 21, 1794, Folder 12, miscellaneous accounts, Browne Papers; Wermuth, *Rip Van Winkle's Neighbors*, 93–103; Bruegel, *Farm, Shop, Landing*, 5, 97.

4. For tavern licensing, see chapter 5 in the present book.

5. For patterns in rural and small-town retailing and consumption, consider, Jaffee, "Peddlers of Progress"; Friend, "Merchants and Markethouses"; Bruegel, *Farm, Shop, Landing*, 159–86; Rainer, "The 'Sharper' Image"; Craig, *Backwoods Consumers*, 113–36, 199–220; Bremer, *Store Almost in Sight*, 115–58; MacMaster, "Philadelphia Merchants, Backcountry Shopkeepers, and Town-Making Fever." For consumption in Canada, see also McCalla, *Consumers in the Bush*.

6. C. Clark, *Roots of Rural Capitalism*, 220–27; Baxter, "Observations on Money," 132–37; Greenberg, *Bank Notes and Shinplasters*. For credit and its productive and destructive consequences, consider Mann, *Republic of Debtors*; Sandage, *Born Losers*, 99–128 and passim; Kamensky, *Exchange Artist*; Baptist, *The Half Has Never Been Told*.

7. In the historiography of the early republic, economic, social, and cultural change inspired overt and indirect political conflict as a function of geography, history, and interpretation. Compare, for example, Watson, *Jacksonian Politics*; A. Taylor, *Liberty Men*; Huston, *Land and Freedom*, with C. Clark, *Roots of Rural Capitalism*; Tolbert, *Constructing Townscapes*; Wermuth, *Rip Van Winkle's Neighbors*; Bruegel, *Farm, Shop, Landing*; Wells, *Origins of the Southern Middle Class*; Shaw, *City Building on the Eastern Frontier*.

8. Brown Ledger; *Independent Journal (New York, NY)*, March 24, 1784; *Pennsylvania Packet, and Daily Advertiser*, November 17, 1784; "Port Bath," *NCPedia*, https://www.ncpedia.org/port-bath.

9. In 1781, Brown was a port commissioner. Later accounts may reflect fees collected as a private actor. Brown Ledger, accounts of Richard Cogdell ("cawking the ship"), Captain John Cowper, Captain John Aldorson, Robert Loughead; W. Clark, *Laws 1777–1788*, 381.

10. Lowrance Account Book; Thorp, "Taverns and Tavern Culture," 666, 668–69, 674–75.

11. Cresson, *Diary of Caleb Cresson*, 12 ("stops"); Marriner Daybook. For Marriner's widowhood, see Scharf, *History of Delaware*, 2:1206 (cf. 1227). Figures for Marriner's tavern here and below refer only to the number of transactions because her daybook includes neither prices nor volumes. For female keepers, consider Conroy, *In Public Houses*, 128, table 2, 318; Thorp, "Taverns and Tavern Culture," 680–81; Salinger, *Taverns and Drinking*, 170–73, 181; Meacham, "Keeping the Trade."

12. L. Miller, *Charles Willson Peale*, 54–55 (all quotations).

13. Marriner Daybook; Scharf, *History of Delaware*, 1:285–89, 2:1236–37; Goldenberg, "Royal Navy's Blockade," 428.

14. I. Weld, *Travels*, 16–17; Ellicott, *Journal of Andrew Ellicott*, 1; "Rout from Philadelphia to Charleston SC by the Post Road," HSP Road and Travel Notes.

15. Elkton Ledger, accounts of stage drivers Jacob Evans, Samuel Lusher, and Roger Mc-Neal. My identification of Joshua Richardson is conjectural: Matthias Tyson also kept a stage tavern in Elkton. *Poulson's (Philadelphia) American Daily Advertiser*, January 13, 1812; *(Wilmington, DE) American Watchman*, June 25, 1811, December 9, 1815; 1810 U.S. Census for Cecil County, Maryland, courtesy of FamilySearch.org.

16. *(Wilmington, DE) American Watchman*, August 16, 1809, April 24, 1811; Elkton Ledger: for court and election expenses, see especially accounts of Phillip Thomas, Samuel Wilson Jr., Richard Bassett, George Alexander, and Andrew Peterson; Johnston, *History of Cecil County, Maryland*, 425. Percentages here, and other Elkton Tavern figures, are based on a one-in-four sample of the ledger.

17. Antwerp Daybook; Durant and Peirce, *History of Jefferson County*, 277–78; Ginzberg, *Untidy Origins*, 51–53.

18. From August 5, 1822 through November 4, 1822, the period examined here, the keeper made three entries for lodgings, fifteen for horse care, and eighteen for meals. Antwerp Daybook; Spafford, *Gazetteer of New York*, 31. For villages as local centers, and taverns therein, consider Rasmussen, *Ox Cart to Automobile*, 28–32.

19. In the Warsaw daybook, I examined December 1830, January 1831, and June 1831; figures here and below refer to roughly 350 entries made from mid-December to mid-January. Warsaw Daybook; Young, *History of the Town of Warsaw*, 23–24, 37, 45, 59, 61, 78, 80–81, 87.

20. F. Thomas, *Portrait of Historic Athens*, 33, 35, 117–18.

21. The figures are based on Eagle Tavern Register, January 1843–December 1844. This ledger includes almost no alcohol sales; perhaps a separate alcohol book once existed. Microfilmed Eagle Tavern ledgers cover other years but were not consulted for this chapter. For Georgia's temperance movement, consider Huebner, "Joseph Henry Lumpkin and Evangelical Reform," 260–61; F. Thomas, *Portrait of Historic Athens*, 68–69; Carlson, "'Drinks He to His Own Undoing,'" 667, map 2. For Richardson's improvements, see Eagle Tavern Floor Plan and Elevation, Thomas G. Little architectural drawings, UGA; "Eagle Tavern, Macon Road, Watkinsville, Oconee County, GA," Historic American Buildings Survey, Library of Congress, https://www.loc.gov/pictures/item/ga0353/ (accessed May 19, 2023); Historic Eagle Tavern, Watkinsville, Georgia, April 13, 1958, Atlanta Journal-Constitution Photographic Archives, Georgia State University Library, https://digitalcollections.library.gsu.edu/digital/collection/ajc/id/3729/ (accessed April 18, 2023). For a digital tour of the Eagle Tavern Museum, see https://visitoconee.com/portfolio-item/eagle-tavern/ (accessed February 2, 2023). For the eagle as a tavern sign, see Smith, *Tavern Signs of America*, 19–21.

22. For a man's reflections on his drinking, see, for example, Chamberlain Diaries, July 4–5, 1835. For sifting and mixing in the eighteenth century, see Scribner, *Inn Civility*; Thompson, *Rum Punch and Revolution*. On masculinity, drinking, and temperance, see Dorsey, *Reforming Men and Women*, 97–99, 113–31; Fletcher, *Gender and Temperance*, 7–29.

23. Traveller's Rest Daybooks, November 16, 1821 ("Pedlar" and "Mr. Gentleman"). For whiskey supplied with meals, see Knight, *Letters from the South and West*, 72, 126; Bernhard, *Travels through North America*, 1:66, 2:128. For manipulating money and signs of identity,

see Mihm, *Nation of Counterfeiters*, 228; Greenberg, *Bank Notes and Shinplasters*, 67. For clothes, consider Bushman, *Refinement of America*, 69–74, 400; Zakim, *Ready-Made Democracy*; Haulman, *Politics of Fashion*. For itinerancy, consider Jaffee, "Peddlers of Progress"; Rainer, "The 'Sharper' Image"; Gamble, "'For Lucre of Gain.'"

24. Grotjahn Memoir, 56 ("three"). For coffee house sociability, see Shields, *Civil Tongues and Polite Letters*, 62 and passim; Steffen, "Newspapers for Free," 412–13; Scribner, *Inn Civility*, 46.

25. Brown Ledger, accounts of Thomas Respess Sr., Thomas Respess Jr., Colonel James Bonner, Hen. Bonner, Captain Hoel, Phillip Reilly, Dr. Bryan McMahon, and others; 1790 U.S. Census for Beaufort County, North Carolina, courtesy of Genealogy Trails.com; Elkton Ledger, account of Dr. Thomas Rutter, December 24, 1807. For punch and similar drinks, see Beastall, *Useful Guide*, 261; K. Rice, *Early American Taverns*, 95; Garvin and Garvin, *On the Road North of Boston*, 157; Scribner, *Inn Civility*, 76–77. For colonial clubs, see Salinger, *Taverns and Drinking*, 76–82.

26. Marriner Daybook, see, for example, Dr. Willbank, April 27, 1813, Colonel A[rmwell] Long, June 1, 1813, Capt. Bell, April 21, 1813. Figures based on analysis of all legible entries in the daybook.

27. Elkton Ledger; Thompson, *Rum Punch and Revolution*, 71, 97. For sangaree, see J. Thomas, *How to Mix Drinks*, 55–56.

28. Warsaw Daybook, see, for example, December 16, 1830, December 31, 1831, January 8, 1831.

29. Barnes, *Immorality of the Traffic in Ardent Spirits*, 33 (all quotations).

30. Browne owned pint and half pint glasses. Volume 5, March 3, [1797], March 15, 1803, Browne Papers.

31. Adair often did not specify the volume of alcohol sold for multiples of $.06¼. Higher-value entries may reflect multiple glasses, larger-capacity vessels, or a mixture of both. Account Book, 1843–1844, Adair Papers. For fixed-price self-service from a decanter, see Fearon, *Sketches of America*, 249.

32. For toasting, see K. Rice, *Early American Taverns*, 98–100; Thompson, *Rum Punch and Revolution*, 192–93; Dorsey, *Reforming Men and Women*, 97; Salinger, *Taverns and Drinking*, 217–20; K. Wood, "'Join with Heart and Soul and Voice,'" 1099, 1111.

33. Account Book 1841–1843, October 3, 1842 ("Democrat Ticket"), Adair Papers; Dubin, *United States Congressional Elections, 1788–1997*, 126, 132.

34. Emphasis in the original. [Unknown], "Voyage to Charleston, SC and Georgia, 14th 1 mo. 1817," n.d. ("the man"), Fisher Papers; Alexander, *Transatlantic Sketches*, 279; Dupre, "Barbecues and Pledges"; Waldstreicher, *In the Midst of Perpetual Fetes*, 196–98; Bensel, *American Ballot Box*, 57–63; Robertson, "Voting Rites," 66.

35. Volume 4, n.d., "Luke Burns particular accot" ("Old Sam," "strange Cooper"), Volume 6, April 2, 1803 ("for Old Joe"), April 16, 1804, April 19, 1804, April 23, 1804, April 24, 1804, April 25, 1804, April 30, 1804, Browne Papers. For treating related to work, see Bernhard, *Travels through North America*, 2:23; Swaim Diary, 35, 37. For Virginia voting law, see Keyssar, *Right to Vote*, appendix, table A.2.

36. Elkton Ledger. For the evolution of moderation and total abstinence, see Tyrrell, *Sobering Up*, 33–224. For moderate tavern drinking, see also Roberts, "Harry Jones and His Cronies," 13.

37. *(Canal Dover) Ohio Democrat*, February 3, 1842 ("temperance tavern").

38. Warsaw Daybook. Whiskey's high alcohol content facilitates rapid ingestion and intoxication: one pint of 45% ABV (or ninety proof) whiskey has the same alcohol content as 2¼ quarts of 10% ABV cider or 4½ quarts of 5% ABV beer.

39. Account Book, 1841–1843, accounts of Henry Floyd, W. D. Alexander, James W. Anthony, Gibson H. Hill, and Levi M. Adams for August–November 1842 and August 1843, Account Book, 1845, accounts of Henry Floyd, Adair Papers.

40. For similar patterns, see A. Martin, *Buying into the World of Goods*; Wenger, *Country Storekeeper in Pennsylvania*.

41. See, for instance, Brown Ledger, accounts of Dr. William Savage and Captain John Cowper. For country store sales of food and food-related items, see A. Martin, *Buying into the World of Goods*, 82–85.

42. Cuming, *Sketches of a Tour*, 128 ("a store"); Lowrance Account Book Brown Ledger, accounts of Captain John Gladen, Samuel Garrett, Dr. William Savage, Phillip Reilly, Cossono Medice, William McCabe; Rorabaugh, *Alcoholic Republic*, 66.

43. Brown Ledger, accounts of Edward Rice and Thomas Respess Sr.; *Heads of Families at the First Census, 1790, North Carolina*, 125.

44. Brown Ledger, accounts of Samuel Garret and Richard Blackledge. For book debt—a form of unsecured credit—and its significance, see Mann, *Neighbors and Strangers*, 11–46, but note that book debt persisted (or reappeared) in early republican taverns alongside paper money and other financial instruments.

45. Volume 6, April 17, 1803 ("pocket Bottle"), and all calculable entries, see also Volumes 1, 3, and 4 for alcohol purchases, Browne Papers.

46. Volume 1, account of William Dalloway, Browne Papers. Here, the figures refer to sales in Volume 1 that can be categorized as either tavern or store goods, where alcohol in any quantity is considered a tavern good. For debt, credit, and buying patterns in a backcountry Virginia store around the same time, see A. Martin, *Buying into the World of Goods*, 72–93.

47. Volume 3, account with Betsy Duty ("two Linsey"), Folder 2, Edward Talbot to Mr. Hardy, December 30, 1803 ("the balance"), Browne Papers.

48. Figures based on Volume 1, Browne Papers.

49. Volume 1, account of Thomas Burns [February 1, 1796] (all quotations), Folder 2, Martin Browne to Thomas Stribling, February 25, 1803, see also Browne to John Danks, August 18, 1804, Browne Papers; Shepherd, *Statutes at Large of Virginia*, 1:145; J. Rice, "Old Appalachia's Path to Interdependency," 357. For banking in northern Virginia, see Crothers, "Banks and Economic Development."

50. Thorp, "Taverns and Tavern Culture," 667; Mann, "Law, Economy, and Society," 1874–75; Bruegel, *Farm, Shop, Landing*, 5–6 and passim. For the complexities of cash, see Greenberg, *Bank Notes and Shinplasters*.

51. Elkton Ledger; Johnston, *History of Cecil County, Maryland*, 425; Greenberg, *Bank Notes and Shinplasters*, 2 ("monetary knowledge"), 1–7, 115–32.

52. Antwerp Daybook; Warsaw Daybook; Spafford, *Gazetteer of New York*, 31, 545 ("considerable"); Gordon, *Gazetteer of the State of New York*, 461, 464, 466–67; Young, *History of the Town of Warsaw*, 24, 37, 59, 78; Durant and Peirce, *History of Jefferson County*, 277–78; Larkin, *Overcoming Niagara*; Ginzberg, *Untidy Origins*, 52; "The Genesee Valley Canal," Historical Markers Database, https://www.hmdb.org/m.asp?m=76061.

53. See, for example, Eagle Tavern Register, January 6, March 4, April 18, June 11, and June 22, 1844. See also F. Thomas, *Portrait of Historic Athens*, 35. Tavern owner Richard Richardson may not have run the tavern. His household included twenty enslaved and twelve white people in 1840, two of them listed as working in agriculture, and none in other occupations. 1840 U.S. Census for Clarke County, Georgia, courtesy of Family Search.org.

54. Account Book, 1841–1843, Account Book, 1843–1844, Account Book, 1845, Adair Papers.

55. For the coexistence and competition of taverns and stores in "frontier" towns, compare Harris, "General Store," 124 ("frontier"), 125; and Bremer, *Store Almost in Sight*.

56. Craft and Tingle, *Old Account Book Entries*, 63 ("merchandise"), 162; *Compendium of the Returns of the Sixth Census*, 58; A. Brown, *History of Newton County, Mississippi*, 40, 328. Craft and Tingle suggest that Ellis managed both store and tavern, although he appears as an account holder in the store's daybook and as the creditor in the tavern ledger. The 1840 census lists an S.C. Walker as the head of a small household of seven people, including two slaves. 1840 U.S. Census for Newton County, Mississippi, courtesy of FamilySearch.org. For meat rations in Louisiana around the same time, see Follett, *Sugar Masters*, 160. For the relationship between cotton and southern urbanization, consider Woodman, *King Cotton and His Retainers*; Goldfield, "The Urban South."

57. For a further comparison, consider Rorabaugh, *Alcoholic Republic*, 234–36, tables A.1.3–A.1.5.

58. The sixty payments derive from a one-in-three sample of the ledger. Virginia Merchant's Account Book.

59. Stateburg Account Book, accounts of Thomas W. Sanders, [John Hucherson,] and Joseph [Pail]. For the panic and its meanings for bank notes, consider Greenberg, *Bank Notes and Shinplasters*, 25–26, 30, 35–36, 64–65. On access to banks in and beyond the South, consider Schweikart, "Southern Banks and Economic Growth"; Wang, "Banks, Credit Markets, and Early American Development," 456–57; Lamoreaux, *Insider Lending*, 11–30. The price of agricultural commodities climbed before the panic and then collapsed, changing the incentives for accepting them in trade. See, for example, D. Adams, "Prices and Wages," 212–14, table 1: appendix.

60. Account Book, 1845, accounts of Rebecka Moffit, Mrs. Pennington, Green Fuller, Henly Simons, Hudson Burdishaw, John Benton, S. A. Breedlove, Henry Floyd, A. J. McWilliams, Jacob Williams, James [Swint], George B. Wright, Bishop Cone, Adair Papers.

61. For a pointed synthesis of the often-unintended consequences of economic improvements in the early republic, see Larson, *Market Revolution*, 92–140.

62. For female tavern patronage, consider Thorp, "Taverns and Tavern Culture," 680–82; Dorsey, *Reforming Men and Women*, 100–102. For women's purchases against their kinsmen's accounts, see, for example, Craft and Tingle, *Old Account Book Entries*, 13, 15. For the concept of "family credit," see Hartigan-O'Connor, *Ties That Buy*, 69–100. For white women's economic activity in and beyond coverture, see also Lebsock, *Free Women of Petersburg*; A. Martin, *Buying into the World of Goods*, 155–58, 164–67; Hartigan-O'Connor, "The Personal Is Political Economy"; Jones-Rogers, *They Were Her Property*; Damiano, *To Her Credit*; L. Edwards, *Only the Clothes*, 152–72 and passim. For enslaved people's consumption, consider Camp, *Closer to Freedom*, 79–80; A. Martin, *Buying into the World of*

Goods, 173–93; Hilliard, *Masters, Slaves, and Exchange*, 46–93; J. Edwards, *Unfree Markets*, 167–69; L. Edwards, *Only the Clothes*, 31–34.

63. Marriner Daybook, November 2, 1812 (Jack [Nicny]), January 30, 1813 (Moses Harris), and June 14, 1813 (Solomon Gibs); 1800 U.S. Census for Sussex County, Delaware, 1810 U.S. Census for Sussex and Kent Counties, Delaware, courtesy of Ancestry.com; *Aggregate Amount of Each Description of Persons, in the Year 1810*, 3:52–52a.

64. Marriner Daybook, May 22, 1813 ("Ladi[e]s" and "Gentleman"), Betty: July 11, July 31, August 5, August 13, August 15, August 18, September 12, and November 2, 1812.

65. Volume 6, April 17, 1803 ("Negro," "pocket"), Browne Papers.

66. Volume 6, December 31, 1803 ("for Coe's Isaac"), April 16, 1803, April 17, 1803, April 24, 1803 ("pr order"), May 25, 1803 ("Black Man"), February 3, 1804 ("free Black"), Volume 3, n.d., "Black Daniel," "Ball's Billy," "Black [Gile]," Browne Papers. The archive of Black people's patronage is thicker for urban taverns; see, for example, R. Johnson, "'Laissez les bons temps rouler!'"

67. *Heads of Families at the First Census, 1790, Virginia*, 9.

68. Volume 1, accounts of "Black Hercules," "Black Robbin," "Black Manuel," Browne Papers; Grivno, *Gleanings of Freedom*, 184–86.

69. Volume 3, p. 3 ("present"), Volume 1, accounts of Andrew Carnagy, David Conclyn, Volume 6, April 13, 1803, April 14, 1803, September 1, 1803, April 14, 1804, February 25, 1805, Browne Papers.

70. Volume 6, April 27, 1803 ("at night"), April 14, 1803 ("Herself"), April 17, 1803 ("her son Andy"), April 18, 1803, May 11, 1803, May 26, 1803, Browne Papers; Rorabaugh, *Alcoholic Republic*, 12–13; Dorsey, *Reforming Men and Women*, 100–102.

71. Traveller's Rest Daybooks, accounts of Katharine P. White, Lucy B. White, Anna Going, Mary Walker, Elizabeth Burnley, and Mary Anthony; Hartigan-O'Connor, *Ties That Buy*, 133, 138–40, 146. A Catherine White appears in the 1820 Louisa County census as the head of a household with seventeen enslaved people. 1820 U.S. Census for Louisa County, Virginia, courtesy of Ancestry.com.

72. William H. P. Adair in account with Jane D. McCardy, Widow Coleman, Sarah Coleman, Mrs. Rainey, Sarah [Jusey], Rebecka Moffitt, Anne A. Burge, Elizabeth & Mrs. Burge, Mrs. Elizabeth Ragland, Mrs. Pennington, Account Books, 1841–1843, 1843–1844, 1845, Adair Papers.

73. Warsaw Daybook, December 20, 1830, December 30, 1830; 1830 U.S. Census for Genesee County, New York, courtesy of Ancestry.com.

74. Craft and Tingle, *Old Account Book Entries*, 6, 35, 45, 49, 53, 82, 101, 107, 120–21, 141. For the importance of textiles and sewing items in country stores, consider A. Martin, *Buying into the World of Goods*, 76 (table 3.5), 78–82.

75. Gilpin noted that Mrs. Dickie attended to travelers while her husband and a partner dealt with other business that often took them away from the tavern. Gilpin, *Pleasure and Business*, 125.

76. Eagle Tavern floor plan, Thomas G. Little architectural drawings, UGA. At the historic Eagle Tavern Museum, the interior door that connects the store and tavern appears to be closer to the wall that fronts the street than Little's architectural drawings indicate. See https://visitoconee.com/portfolio-item/eagle-tavern/ (accessed February 2, 2023).

77. Account Book, 1845, Adair Papers; Hartigan-O'Connor, *Ties That Buy*, 129–60. For women in southern towns, see Tolbert, *Constructing Townscapes*, 123–52; Wells, *Origins of the Southern Middle Class*, 111–32. Adair had one customer who might have been Black, "Black Johnson," while at the Eagle, Richardson noted at least one occasion when a traveler paid for a meal for himself and three "negroes." Account Book, 1841–1843, October 31 and November 3, 1842 ("Black Johnson"), Adair Papers; Eagle Tavern Register, July 4, 1843 ("negroes").

78. I draw this insight about authorized illegality from J. Edwards, *Unfree Markets*.

79. For a similar argument, see MacMaster, "Philadelphia Merchants, Backcountry Shopkeepers, and Town-Making Fever."

Chapter Four

1. *Charter and Directory of the City of Rochester*, n.p. (all quotations). For Rochester's socioeconomic development, consider Shaw, *City Building on the Eastern Frontier*; P. Johnson, *Shopkeeper's Millennium*; N. Hewitt, *Women's Activism and Social Change*. For southern towns, see Wells, *Origins of the Southern Middle Class*; Tolbert, *Constructing Townscapes*.

2. *Agriculture of the United States in 1860*, viii–xxviii; Lebergott, "Labor Force and Employment," 118–20, tables 1–3; C. Clark, *Roots of Rural Capitalism*; Baptist, *The Half Has Never Been Told*; Olmstead and Rhode, "Agriculture," 159–67.

3. See, for example, "Lexington (KY) Directory, 1806, Taken for Charless' Almanack, for 1806," https://sites.rootsweb.com/~kyfayett/1806directory.htm (June 1999) (accessed May 15, 2023); *Pittsburgh Directory for 1815*; MacCabe, *Lexington Directory, 1838–39*; *Pittsburgh Directory, 1839*; *Harris's Business Directory of Pittsburgh, 1847*; C. Williams, *Lexington Directory, 1859–60*.

4. For the early nineteenth-century legal framework of American capitalism, consider Horwitz, *Transformation of American Law*; Novak, *People's Welfare*, 84–88; Hilt, "Early American Corporations and the State." For insightful analyses of the creative and brutal in the early republican economy, consider J. Rothman, *Flush Times*; W. Johnson, *River of Dark Dreams*; Luskey and Woloson, *Capitalism by Gaslight*; Berry, *Price for Their Pound of Flesh*.

5. D. Howe, *What Hath God Wrought*, 690–96 and passim. For railroads and their impacts on agriculture and cities beginning in the 1840s, see G. Taylor, *Transportation Revolution*, 74–103, 388–92; Pred, *Urban Growth and City Systems*, 44–49 and passim; Cronon, *Nature's Metropolis*.

6. Most widely associated with Oliver E. Williamson, the concept of "transaction costs" builds on the work of John R. Commons in the 1930s, while Ronald Coase apparently coined the term. Commons, "Institutional Economics"; Coase, "Nature of the Firm"; O. Williamson, "Economics of Organization"; Tadelis, "Tribute to Oliver Williamson." For management issues, see Chandler, *Visible Hand*; Majewski, "Who Financed the Transportation Revolution?" 780. For railroads in manufacturing growth, consider Atack, Haines, and Margo, "Railroads and the Rise of the Factory." My colleague Ken Lipartito made the helpful suggestion that I consider the transactions costs literature.

7. Although the number and variety of American corporations grew rapidly in the early republic, sole proprietors and small firms predominated and most corporations remained small by later standards. Chandler, *Visible Hand*; Blackford, "Small Business in America";

Sylla and Wright, "Corporation Formation," 651–58; Sylla, "How the American Corporation Evolved," 355–59; Hilt, "Business Organization," 261–70.

8. Mihm, *Nation of Counterfeiters*, 5–19; Luskey and Woloson, *Capitalism by Gaslight*, 1–9; B. Murphy, *Building the Empire State*, 9–16; Lipartito and Jacobson, *Capitalism's Hidden Worlds*, 1–4, 8–9.

9. For reputation, risk, trust, and other factors that complicated long-distance transactions, consider Lamoreaux, Raff, and Temin, "Beyond Markets and Hierarchies," 407–17; Ditz, "Shipwrecked," 55–58; Olegario, *A Culture of Credit*, 32–118; J. Rothman, "Hazards of the Flush Times"; S. Murphy, "Selecting Risks"; K. Cohen, "'Entreaties and Perswasions,'" 599–601, 606, 608–9; Levy, *Freaks of Fortune*, 3–20. For business failures, see Sandage, *Born Losers*, 1–188; Kamensky, *Exchange Artist*, 145–313.

10. For agency, consider S. Murphy, "Selecting Risks"; Marine-Street, "'Agents Wanted,'" 2–8, 11; Blevins, *Paper Trails*, 12–13. For alcoholic excess, its causes, and its immediate and long-range consequences in the early republic, consider P. Johnson, *Shopkeeper's Millennium*; Rorabaugh, *Alcoholic Republic*, 125–83; Dorsey, *Reforming Men and Women*, 90–135; Caric, "The Man with the Poker"; Osborn, "Detestable Shrine"; Osborn, *Rum Maniacs*, 80–105, 169–204.

11. Andrews, *The Virginia Almanack, for the Year of Our Lord, 1794* ("two doors"); Andrews, *The Virginia Almanack, for the Year of Our Lord, 1795* ("next door").

12. *(Lexington) Kentucky Gazette*, October 10, 1795 ("next door"); *(Charleston, SC) City Gazette*, September 3, 1806 ("opposite"); *Salem (MA) Gazette*, November 3, 1795 ("west of"); *Carthage (TN) Gazette; and Friend of the People*, March 6, 1809 ("Ladies Habit," "one door above"); *(Concord, NH) Daily Patriot*, June 6, 1847 ("two doors," emphasis omitted); *Charter and Directory of the City of Rochester*, n.p. ("central").

13. For executors' and sheriffs' responsibilities, see Leavitt, *Ohio Justices' Guide*; Iredell, *Law of Executors*; Ditz, *Property and Kinship*, 144–48.

14. A Gentleman of the law, *New Conductor Generalis*, 136 ("the usual"); Garvin and Garvin, *On the Road North of Boston*, 10.

15. Hartigan-O'Connor, "Public Sales," 759–66 and passim; A. Taylor, *William Cooper's Town*, 68–70.

16. *Boston Evening Post*, January 28, 1760; *(New York) Mercury*, November 10, 1766; *(Charleston) South-Carolina Weekly Gazette*, May 10, 1783; *(Fredericksburg) Virginia Herald*, November 22, 1815. For wholesale auctions, see J. Cohen, "'Right to Purchase.'"

17. *Berkshire (MA) Journal*, October 7, 1830 ("lunatick"), August 4, 1831; *Salem (MA) Gazette*, July 25, 1820; *(Keene) New-Hampshire Sentinel*, April 22, 1820; *(Concord) New Hampshire Patriot & State Gazette*, January 2, 1837; *Amherst (NH) Farmer's Cabinet*, March 22, 1849.

18. *(Lexington) Kentucky Gazette*, October 17, 1795; *(Charles Town, VA) Farmers' Repository*, January 5, 1820; *American Beacon and Norfolk & Portsmouth Daily (VA) Advertiser*, January 15, 1820.

19. Emphasis in the original. *(Easton) Maryland Herald and Eastern Shore Intelligencer*, November 3, 1795 ("annex"); *(Washington, DC) National Intelligencer*, February 6, 1818; *(Dedham, MA) Village Register and Norfolk County Advertiser*, October 3, 1823; *(Concord) New Hampshire Patriot and State Gazette*, October 31, 1825. On widows, probate, and property, consider Hoff, *Law, Gender, and Injustice*, 85–87; Ditz, *Property and Kinship*, 145–48; K. Wood, *Masterful Women*, 31–33; Hartigan-O'Connor, *Ties That Buy*, 91–93, 95.

20. *Richmond Enquirer*, December 24, 1836 ("young man," "excellent").

21. For Black families and property, see Berlin, *Slaves without Masters*, 62–64, 244–47, 344–45; Rael, *Black Identity and Black Protest*, 22–29, 40–44; Myers, *Forging Freedom*, 99–100, 113–46; Foy and Bradley, "African American Community," 141–42. For white mobs' destruction of Black property, consider Sinha, *Slave's Cause*, 207–9, 232–36, 363; Gosse, *First Reconstruction*, 119–24, 142–43, 200–1, 255.

22. Cogan, "The Look Within," 476–81; Keyssar, *Right to Vote*, tables A.1–A.3. For the significance of early nineteenth-century property qualifications, cf. Ratcliffe, "Right to Vote"; Bateman, "Democratization in the USA?"

23. For land speculation from white Americans' perspective, consider M. Jensen, "Cession of the Old Northwest"; Chappell, "Some Patterns of Land Speculation"; Hammes, "Land Transactions"; Kamensky, *Exchange Artist*, 263–67; J. Rothman, *Flush Times*, 6–7, 25–28, 178–79; Baptist, *The Half Has Never Been Told*, 18–21; Saunt, *Unworthy Republic*, 201–21, 299–300. For conflicts preceding speculative privatization, see, for example, Saunt, *New Order of Things*; Saler, *Settlers' Empire*; Bowes, *Land Too Good for Indians*; Blaakman, "'Haughty Republicans.'"

24. *(Boston) Continental Journal, and Weekly Advertiser*, January 26, 1786 ("other good"); *(Boston) Massachusetts Centinel*, August 8, 1787; *Boston Gazette, and the Country Journal*, November 12, 1787; *(Boston) Argus*, August 5, 1791; G. Wood, *Empire of Liberty*, 117. For the Bunch of Grapes, see Conroy, *In Public Houses*, 257–58.

25. Lombardi, *Jamestown, New York*, 4; Rasmussen, *Ox Cart to Automobile*, 40.

26. *Richmond Enquirer*, October 22, 1830 (all quotations), September 7, 1830, October 12, 1830; Wagner, "Location, Location, Location," 143; K. Cohen, *They Will Have Their Game*, 125; Natalie Zacek, personal communication, November 6, 2021.

27. John Campbell as quoted in Chappell, "Patterns of Land Speculation," 464 (all quotations), 470–72; T. Owen, *History of Alabama*, 1:368; Wagner, "Composing Pioneers"; Wagner, "Location, Location, Location," 125–26, 128–31.

28. For a fuller picture, see J. Rothman, *Flush Times*, 25–28. For removals (plural) in the early republic, see Bowes, *Land Too Good for Indians*; Pierce, *Making the White Man's West*; Seeley, *Race, Removal, and the Right to Remain*.

29. *Public Documents, Second Session, Twenty-Third Congress*, 2:22, p. 12 ("south room," "its existence"), 95 ("called,"), 83 ("company"), 11, 88, 99.

30. *Public Documents, Second Session, Twenty-Third Congress*, 2:22, p. 113 ("appeared"), 108 ("it had").

31. Seavoy, "Laws to Encourage Manufacturing," 85, 88–91; G. Wood, *Empire of Liberty*, 459–66; Hilt, "Early American Corporations and the State," 43–59.

32. Sylla, "How the American Corporation Evolved," 355–59; Hilt, "Business Organization," 264–67.

33. *(Boston) New-England Palladium*, May 23, 1806; *Index to the Laws of New Hampshire*, 323; Merrill and Merrill, *Gazetteer of New-Hampshire*, 134.

34. *(New York) Royal Gazette*, November 15, 1783; *New York Packet and the American Advertiser*, March 1, 1784, December 19, 1785; Colles, *Sir, Your Company Is Requested at the Coffee-House*; Majewski, "Who Financed the Transportation Revolution?" 765–75.

35. T. Miller, *Artisans and Merchants of Alexandria*, 1:131–32 ("friends"); *(Wilmington, DE) American Watchman*, December 31, 1814, May 3, 1815; Wright, "Governance and the Success of U.S. Community Banks," 15–20.

36. *Hudson (NY) Northern Whig,* May 18, 1813; *Columbia County at the End of the Century,* 1:49; *(New York, NY) American,* May 1, 1820; *North Star (Danville, VT),* March 2, 1824, March 9, 1824; *(Hartford) Connecticut Courant,* July 27, 1830; Majewski, "Who Financed the Transportation Revolution?" 766–67, 770–73; Wermuth, *Rip Van Winkle's Neighbors,* 52–62; Bruegel, *Farm, Shop, Landing,* 54–57.

37. Cutter, *History of Jaffrey,* 55–56; J. Davis, *Essays in the Earlier History of American Corporations,* 225; F. Wood, *Turnpikes of New England,* 219–20; Sylla and Wright, "Corporation Formation," 653.

38. *(Walpole, NH) Farmer's Weekly Museum,* March 17, 1801, February 14, 1806; *(Keene) New-Hampshire Sentinel,* October 10, 1801, February 4, 1804, February 6, 1813, January 29, 1814, July 24, 1819, July 20, 1822; Majewski, Baer, and Klein, "Responding to Relative Decline," 117–18; Majewski, "Who Financed the Transportation Revolution?" 773–75.

39. *(Keene) New-Hampshire Sentinel,* July 10, 1813, June 15, 1822 ("any other"), June 9, 1826, June 19, 1829; *Index to the Laws of New Hampshire,* 183; F. Wood, *Turnpikes of New England,* 220.

40. Wells, "Southern Middle Class," 657 (all quotations); *Acts Passed at a General Assembly of the Commonwealth of Virginia, 1819,* 61; T. Miller, *Artisans and Merchants of Alexandria,* 1:131; Majewski, "Who Financed the Transportation Revolution?"; Majewski, "Commerce and Continuity"; Debbie Robison, "Middle Turnpike and Leesburg Turnpike," Northern Virginia History Notes, http://www.novahistory.org/MiddleTurnpike/MiddleTurnpike.htm, February 21, 2015; Debbie Robison, "Wiley's Tavern, Built ca. 1790," Northern Virginia History Notes, http://www.novahistory.org/WileysTavern/WileysTavern.htm, March 5, 2015.

41. *The Seventeenth, Eighteenth and Nineteenth Annual Reports of the Board of Public Works to General Assembly of Virginia,* 7:16 and 156 ("tavern bills"), 18, 66, and 168; *(Amherst, NH) Farmer's Cabinet,* May 6, 1847.

42. For female investors, see L. Davis, "Stock Ownership," 215–16, 220–22, tables 3–8; Majewski, "Who Financed the Transportation Revolution?" 768; Wright, "Bank Ownership and Lending Patterns," 42, 44, 46, 47, 55; Crothers, "Banks and Economic Development," 20; Hartigan-O'Connor, "The Personal Is Political Economy," 338n5. For the near-gender parity among nineteenth-century savings bank depositors, see Wadhwani, "Citizen Savers," 394, table 3.2.

43. Callcott, *Mistress of Riversdale,* 198 ("giving"), 238 ("frequently," "which converge), 306 ("greatly decrease"); see also 218, 230, 237–39, 247–48, 251–53, 256–57, 276–77, 317–19, 322–23; *Baltimore Patriot,* June 15, 1818.

44. On productivity gains from intensified exploitation and division of labor, see Goldin and Sokoloff, "Women, Children, and Industrialization," 755, 773; Baptist, *The Half Has Never Been Told,* 111–44.

45. Sokoloff and Khan, "Democratization of Invention"; Lubar, "Antebellum Patent Law," 934–42; MacLeod, "Paradoxes of Patenting," 887; Khan, "Property Rights and Patent Litigation," 59–60, 78n35, 79n37; Lamoreaux and Sokoloff, "Market Trade in Patents"; Connors, *Ingenious Machinists;* Regele, "World's Best Carpets," 127–29.

46. *(Richmond) Enquirer,* July 18, 1804, December 10, 1808, October 24, 1809.

47. "Thomas Wells to Thomas Jefferson, 2 April 1817" (all quotations), Founders Online, National Archives, https://founders.archives.gov/documents/Jefferson/03-11-02-0202 (accessed December 20, 2022). For Jefferson and machines, consider Hodin, "Mechanisms of Monticello."

48. Emphases in the original. *(Hartford, CT) American Mercury,* July 6, 1813 (all quotations); *(Lexington, KY) Western Monitor,* July 28, 1815. For farm women's labor, consider J. Jensen, "'You May Depend'"; C. Clark, *Roots of Rural Capitalism,* 24–27, 96–98, 105–6, and passim; Osterud, *Bonds of Community,* 139–227; Borish, "'Another Domestic Beast of Burden.'" For machines invented by and for women, especially after 1860, see Khan, "'Not for Ornament.'"

49. Emphases in the original. *(Hartford, CT) American Mercury,* October 7, 1823 (all quotations); *Richmond Enquirer,* April 8, 1831; K. Brown, *Foul Bodies,* 215–19, 266–71.

50. *Baltimore Patriot,* January 9, 1834 (all quotations); Matchett, *Matchett's Baltimore Director, 1833,* 18, 145; Sandoval-Strausz, *Hotel,* 50–51; Berger, *Hotel Dreams,* 17–22. On the evolution of early American advertising, consider Hart, "British Atlantic World of Advertising"; Keyes, "History Prints"; Keyes, "Advertising."

51. Washington Irving's *Bracebridge Hall* as quoted in *(New Bern, NC) Carolina Centinel,* July 20, 1822 ("stand"). On gossipy inquisitiveness, see, for example, Graydon, *Memoirs of a Life,* 123; J. Flint, *Letters from America,* 286; Bill Diary, November 17, 1835.

52. I found no examples of keepers' objecting to outsiders and their inventions, but for later perceptions of machine technology as intrusive and destructive, see Marx, *Machine in the Garden.*

53. Delbourgo, *Scene of Wonders;* Kelly, *Republic of Taste,* 33–38, 63, 74–75, 84, 87–88, 163–64; Benes, *For a Short Time Only.*

54. Hanners, *"It Was Play or Starve,"* 97–99; Sherman, *Comedies Useful;* Nathans, *Early American Theatre,* 13–70, 139–40; O. Johnson, *Absence and Memory,* 17–92; Keller, *Dance and Its Music,* 402–3 and passim. For the relationship between transportation and women's ability to earn a living on the stage, see Mullenneaux, *Staging Family,* 80–119.

55. Emphasis omitted. *(Hartford, CT) American Mercury,* July 6, 1813; *(Hartford, CT) Times, and Weekly Adviser,* October 2, 1821 ("Grand"); *(Portsmouth) New Hampshire Gazette,* July 25, 1820; *Middlesex (CT) Gazette,* December 6, 1821; *Eastern (Portland, ME) Argus,* June 27, 1825; *Haverhill (MA) Gazette & Essex Patriot,* April 22, 1826; *Pittsfield (MA) Sun,* September 28, 1826; *Portsmouth (NH) Journal and Rockingham Gazette,* March 3, 1832; R. Flint, "Entrepreneurial and Cultural Aspects"; Benes, *For a Short Time Only,* 127–35.

56. *Haverhill (MA) Gazette,* April 10, 1824, August 14, 1824, August 21, 1824, September 18, 1824, June 25, 1825; P. Johnson, "Playing with Race," 269–70, 280–81; Hodgson, *Richard Potter,* 111–74, 231–40.

57. Emphasis in the original. *Der Readinger (Reading, PA) Adler,* July 20, 1802 (all quotations); Keller, *Dance and Its Music,* 156, 205.

58. *Albany (NY) Register,* January 5, 1813, December 28, 1813; Fry, *Albany Directory for 1813,* 24; *(Portland, ME) Eastern Argus,* June 27, 1825 (all quotations); Benes, *For a Short Time Only,* 145–48.

59. *Mr. Pool, the First American . . . Intends Performing; Elizabethtown New-Jersey Journal and Political Intelligencer,* August 31, 1791; *(Charleston) City Gazette,* February 9, 1793; *(Wilmington, DE) American Watchman,* September 8, 1810; *Hudson (NY) Northern Whig,* April 11, 1820; *Norwich (CT) Courier,* May 26, 1830.

60. On itinerancy, misrepresentation, and potential criminal conduct, see Benes, *For a Short Time Only,* 62–67; Berkin, "Antebellum Touring and the Culture of Deception." For midcentury theatrical cultures and content, including performances of *delirium tremens,*

consider Halttunen, *Confidence Men,* 153–90; Levine, *Highbrow, Lowbrow,* 13–104; Hughes, *Spectacles of Reform,* 46–85; Monod, *Soul of Pleasure;* Osborn, *Rum Maniacs,* 196–204; Mullenneaux, *Staging Family;* Lampert, "'Presence of Improper Females.'"

61. *Der Readinger (Reading, PA) Adler,* July 20, 1802 (*"for a few"*); *Albany (NY) Register,* February 9, 1813 ("lately arrived"); Keller, *Dance and Its Music,* 510–11, 617–25. For manipulating length of stays as a marketing strategy, see Benes, *For a Short Time Only,* 75–76.

62. *(Philadelphia) Pennsylvania Evening Post,* January 21, 1777 ("late Fencing Master"); *New-York Daily Advertiser,* September 29, 1792 ("at all courts"); *Albany (NY) Register,* February 9, 1813 ("lately arrived," "most fashionable"); Kelly, *Republic of Taste,* 31–35; Benes, *For a Short Time Only,* 35, table 1.2, 52–55.

63. *Der Readinger (Reading, PA) Adler,* July 20, 1802 ("those gentlemen"); *Middlesex (CT) Gazette,* March 12, 1828 ("several," "principles"). For balls in the early republic, see *Etiquette at Washington,* 55, 60; *Morrison's Stranger's Guide,* 56; Bushman, *Refinement of America,* 304, 376; A. Taylor, *William Cooper's Town,* 378; Kelly, *Republic of Taste,* 33; Key, "Aristocratic Pretension."

64. *Albany (NY) Register,* December 28, 1813 (*"FOR TWO NIGHTS,"* "Ladies," *"Philosophical"*); *Haverhill (MA) Gazette,* April 10, 1824 ("highly distinguished"); Benes, *For a Short Time Only,* 53, figure 3.1 ("in ample order"), 56–58; P. Johnson, "Playing with Race," 259–60, 265–67.

65. All emphases appear as quoted in Hodgson, *Richard Potter,* 146–50 (all quotations); see also 145–53; P. Johnson, "Playing with Race," 281–84.

66. F. J. Webb, "Biographical Sketch" (1856), Uncle Tom's Cabin & American Culture, http://utc.iath.virginia.edu/uncletom/xianslav/xsesfjwat.html (accessed February 2, 2023); S. Clark, "Solo Black Performance before the Civil War," 341–43, 346.

67. Lampert, "Black Swan/White Raven," 75 ("'no colored'"); Lott, *Love and Theft;* Black, "Abolitionism's Resonant Bodies"; Conlin, *Pleasure Garden;* K. Cohen, *They Will Have Their Game,* 121–27, 204–44; Zacek, *Kingdom for a Horse.* For consuming urban entertainments, see, for example, Southworth Diary, June 3–July 13, 1850.

68. *Der Readinger Adler,* July 20, 1802 (all quotations).

69. Emphasis in original. *American Beacon and Commercial Diary (Norfolk, VA),* October 7, 1816 ("bilks"); *(New York) Commercial Advertiser,* October 9, 1816; *Boston Daily Advertiser,* October 12, 1816; *Camden (SC) Gazette,* October 17, 1816; Benes, *For a Short Time Only,* 142–45.

70. John Hogg to John Steele, August 27, 1810 ("keep"), Steele Papers. On paper money, consider Mihm, *Nation of Counterfeiters,* 1–16; Kamensky, *Exchange Artist,* 14–70, 128–35, 139–64; B. Murphy, *Building the Empire State,* ix–xi; Greenberg, *Bank Notes and Shinplasters.*

71. For other examples of crime linked to mobility, consider Henderson et al., *Trials and Confessions;* Mackintosh, "Loomis Gang."

72. Mihm, *Nation of Counterfeiters,* 87 ("extensive network"), 88–89, 95–97, 145; Marin, "'Well Calculated and Intended to Deceive,'" 103–9.

73. *Baltimore Patriot,* August 12, 1815 ("tavern keepers"); "Counterfeit Notes" from the *Bedford Gazette,* as printed in *(Brownsville, PA) American Telegraph,* May 8, 1816 ("club," "noted gamblers"). See also *(Washington, KY) Union,* May 10, 1816; *Albany (NY) Advertiser,* May 10, 1816; *(Elizabethtown) New Jersey Journal,* May 14, 1816; *Portsmouth (NH) Oracle,* May 18, 1816.

74. Mihm, *Nation of Counterfeiters*, 210–11 ("shovers"), 228 ("counterfeited"); *(Norfolk, VA) American Beacon and Commercial Diary*, October 7, 1816 ("demeanor"); *(Brownsville, PA) American Telegraph*, May 8, 1816 ("genteel," "sandy whiskers," "brandy grog").

75. Trimble, "Autobiography," 16 (all quotations); Appleby, *Recollections of the Early Republic*, 186–88.

76. William Parker Foulke to Eleanor Foulke, January 17, 1848 (all quotations), Foulke Papers.

77. Loughran, *Republic in Print*, xix–xx, 5–24; D. Howe, *What Hath God Wrought*, 211–29. For the overlap of personal and business correspondence, see Callcott, *Mistress of Riversdale*; Henkin, *Postal Age*, 95–99. For orality and print in politics, see Waldstreicher, *In the Midst of Perpetual Fetes*, 225–28 and passim; Eastman, *Nation of Speechifiers*; Spires, *Practice of Citizenship*, 79–120, especially 79–82.

Chapter Five

1. "An Essay on the Means of Promoting Federal Sentiments in the United States, by a Foreign Spectator," *Pennsylvania Gazette*, September 5, 1787 (all quotations); T. Breen, *George Washington's Journey*, 73–78.

2. For authority to issue tavern licenses, see Watkins and Watkins, *Digest of the Laws of Georgia*, 405; A Gentleman of the law, *New Conductor Generalis*, 448; E. Bay, *Report of Cases Argued*, 2:316; Littell and Swigert, *Digest of the Statute Law of Kentucky*, 2:1187; Harriet Wiley License Petition; Barbour, *Reports of Cases in Law and Equity*, 54:311–19. For colonial licensing, see Conroy, *In Public Houses*, 62–64, 112–13, 135–37, 193–94; Thorp, "Taverns and Tavern Culture," 668–70; Thompson, *Rum Punch and Revolution*, 35–41; Salinger, *Taverns and Drinking*, 151–81; Meacham, "Keeping the Trade," 141–44, 159; Meacham, *Every Home a Distillery*, 68–74. For local versus state law, see L. Edwards, *The People and Their Peace*, 3–10, 299–300.

3. For licensing, anti-licensing, and prohibition campaigns in the early republic, consider Rorabaugh, "Rising Democratic Spirits"; Novak, *People's Welfare*, 171–89; Hampel, *Temperance and Prohibition in Massachusetts*, 61–182; Dannenbaum, *Drink and Disorder*, 69–179; Volk, "Perils of 'Pure Democracy.'" For the temperance movement, see Tyrrell, *Sobering Up*; Kett, "Temperance and Intemperance"; Hampel, *Temperance and Prohibition in Massachusetts*; Breitenbach, "Sons of the Fathers"; Dannenbaum, *Drink and Disorder*; R. Alexander, "'We Are Engaged as a Band of Sisters'"; Carlson, "'Drinks He to His Own Undoing'"; Dorsey, *Reforming Men and Women*, 90–135; Augst, "Temperance, Mass Culture, and the Romance of Experience"; Fletcher, *Gender and Temperance*; P. Anderson, "'By Legal or Moral Suasion Let Us Put It Away'"; S. Meyer, *We Are What We Drink*.

4. The legal nexus of tavern regulation, mobility, and race had local, state, and regional contours. In the Midwest, for example, tavern keepers and other retailers who traded with the Miamis and the Potawatomis sometimes opposed Indian removal efforts. See Bowes, *Land Too Good for Indians*, 72, 146–47, 150. For hopes and fears about the west as key to the sectional crisis, see Morrison, *Slavery and the American West*.

5. For Black citizenship, consider Bradburn, *Citizenship Revolution*, 235–71; Jones, *Birthright Citizens*; Gosse, *First Reconstruction*; Pryor, *Colored Travelers*; Spires, *Practice of Citizenship*; Bonner, *Remaking the Republic*.

6. Kent, *Commentaries on American Law* (1827), 2:445 ("bound"); James, *Digest of the Laws of South Carolina*, 529 ("without"); A Gentleman of the law, *New Conductor Generalis*, 453–54; *Public Acts of Maine*, 234.

7. See, for example, Hadden, *Slave Patrols*; O'Brassill-Kulfan, *Vagrants and Vagabonds*; Benes, *For a Short Time Only*, 254–55. As Jessica Choppin Roney argues, "settler-driven expansion . . . required the state" and involved a process with more actors and violence than this chapter explores. Roney, "1776, Viewed from the West," 698 ("settler-driven").

8. John, *Spreading the News*, 26 ("remarkably high"), 3–4, 26–27, 30–42; Pred, *Urban Growth and the Circulation of Information*, 58–61, 78–101; John and Leonard, "Illusion of the Ordinary," 89–90. For the post office in the later nineteenth-century West, see Blevins, *Paper Trails*.

9. John, *Spreading the News*, 169–205, 257–80; John and Leonard, "Illusion of the Ordinary," 91–92; Wosh, "Going Postal," 225–26; Loughran, *Republic in Print*, 303–440; Verhoeven, "Case for Sunday Mails." For the post office and Black mobility, consider Pottroff, "Circulation," 625–27.

10. Pred, *Urban Growth and the Circulation of Information*, 82–88; John, *Spreading the News*, 4, 28, 64, 90–100, 112–34; John and Leonard, "Illusion of the Ordinary."

11. A Gentleman of the law, *New Conductor Generalis*, 453.

12. *Laws of the Territory of Michigan*, 466 ("release," "hay"); *Public Acts of Maine*, 234 ("populous towns"); Burch, *Laws of Washington, D.C.*, 168; Hotchkiss, *Statute Law of Georgia*, 862.

13. A Gentleman of the law, *New Conductor Generalis*, 450 ("actually keep"); *Second Annual Report of the Society for the Prevention of Pauperism*, 50–51.

14. Grimké, *Laws of South-Carolina*, 384 ("clean"); *Laws of the Territory of Michigan*, 465–66 ("good").

15. Peter Thompson argues that the "collapse of controls on the maximum retail price of liquor" in Philadelphia after 1778 enabled tavern stratification. In many states, legislators continued to authorize or require local authorities to set tavern rates, and tavern improvements took place with and without rate-setting. Thompson, *Rum Punch and Revolution*, 78 ("collapse"), 146. Cf. Wenham (MA) and Fairfield, *Price Act of Wenham*; Groton (CT) Selectmen, *Civil Authority*; Salem (MA) and Britton, *List of Prices*; *Tavern Rates, Established at Baltimore-County April Term, 1789*; Watkins and Watkins, *Digest of the Laws of Georgia*, 453–54; Clayton, *Laws of Georgia*, 568; Brevard, *Law of South-Carolina*, 1:419; Littell and Swigert, *Digest of the Statute Law of Kentucky*, 2:1184; Prince, *Digest of the Laws of Georgia*, 839; *Revised Laws of Indiana, Adopted and Enacted by the General Assembly at Their Eighth Session*, 147, 407; New Jersey, *Hunterdon County Rates*; Hotchkiss, *Statute Law of Georgia*, 862; *Acts of Kentucky, November Session, 1851*, 43; Brightly, *Purdon's Digest*, 1:1021.

16. Petitions of Samuel Coombs, February 4, 1811 ("two spare"), William McCormick, February 7, 1811 ("two good," "in every way"), Jonathan Fithian Jr., February 24, 1806, Elias Rose, February 20, 1810, Cumberland License Petitions; *Laws of the Territory of Michigan*, 465–66 ("at least two").

17. Burch, *Laws of Washington, D.C.*, 168 ("at least" "two good").

18. A Gentleman of the law, *New Conductor Generalis*, 454 ("ready money"); O'Brassill-Kulfan, *Vagrants and Vagabonds*, 28 ("arrestable offense"), 17–35 and passim.

19. Hotchkiss, *Statute Law of Georgia*, 742 ("lewd"), 751; *Acts and Laws of the State of Connecticut*, 242 ("Persons"); Brevard, *Law of South-Carolina*, 1:421, 2:273 ("suffer," "abide," "ex-

cepting"); Prince, *Laws of Georgia to 1837*, 887; Cooley, *Laws of Michigan*, 1:499–500; Novak, *People's Welfare*, 156, 173. For colonial limits on Sunday sales and "ambulant vendors," see Salinger, *Taverns and Drinking*, 22 ("ambulant"), 31, 95, 98, 105, 116. For early republican anti-sabbatarianism, see Verhoeven, "Case for Sunday Mails."

20. Watkins and Watkins, *Digest of the Laws of Georgia*, 131 ("leave"); A Gentleman of the law, *New Conductor Generalis*, 452; *Revised Statutes of Mississippi*, 478; *Statutes of Wisconsin*, 124; Tomlins, "Subordination, Authority, Law," 70 ("authorized power"); Jones, *Birthright Citizens*, 50–58; O'Brassill-Kulfan, *Vagrants and Vagabonds*, 100–101, 158.

21. Wallace, *Rockdale*, 148–49; Galenson, "Rise and Fall of Indentured Servitude," 13–14; Steinfeld, *Invention of Free Labor*, 122–72; Fogleman, "From Slaves, Convicts, and Servants to Free Passengers," 61–66; Grubb, "Babes in Bondage," 1, 3–5, 9, 32; O'Brassill-Kulfan, *Vagrants and Vagabonds*, 16, 165, table A.1, and passim. For changes in white men's work, see also Rock, *Artisans of the New Republic*; Laurie, *Artisans into Workers*, 3–46; Roediger, *Wages of Whiteness*; Licht, *Industrializing America*; Tomlins, "Subordination, Authority, Law"; Wilentz, *Chants Democratic*, 23–142; Rockman, *Scraping By*, 45–74. For white male adulthood, see Field, *Equal Adulthood*, 13–18, 29–35. For age and birth certificates after the Civil War, see Pearson, "New Birth of Regulation"; Pearson, *Birth Certificate*.

22. As Douglas Bradburn argues, during the revolutionary era, many citizenship privileges were "still bound by custom, property, and place, not defined as 'rights.'" Over time, racialized mobility helped make white men's privileges look like natural rights even as immigration, religion, poverty, and physical ability complicated white manhood's boundaries. Bradburn, *Citizenship Revolution*, 12 ("still bound"), 235–71; O'Keefe, *Stranger Citizens*, 111–61; Hirota, *Expelling the Poor*, 41–128; Gosse, *First Reconstruction*, 29–37; Seeley, *Race, Removal, and the Right to Remain*, 196–97, 207, and passim; Welke, *Law and the Borders of Belonging*, 21–60.

23. For the 1793 Fugitive Slave Act and its legal aftermath, see, for example, Fehrenbacher, *Slaveholding Republic*, 211–25.

24. A Gentleman of the law, *New Conductor Generalis*, 452 ("reason"); *Index to the Laws of Pennsylvania*, 164 ("negro servants"). On gradual abolition in Pennsylvania and New York, see R. Newman, *Transformation of American Abolitionism*. On travel, racialized constraints, and economic opportunity, see Pryor, *Colored Travelers*, 44–75; Jones, *Birthright Citizens*, 68–70, 96–102; Seeley, *Race, Removal, and the Right to Remain*, 209–43 and passim. For legal efforts to establish freedom and citizenship for Black residents, consider Morris, *Free Men All*.

25. Between 1824 and 1836, Mississippi halved the maximum fines but preserved the 2:1 ratio. *Revised Code of the Laws of Mississippi*, 367; *Revised Statutes of Mississippi*, 478; *Statutes of Wisconsin*, 124–25; *Laws of the Territory of Michigan*, 496; Bowes, *Land Too Good for Indians*, 182–210.

26. *Revised Code of the Laws of Mississippi*, 367; J. Martin, "'Greatest Evil,'" 38–39 ("Indian country").

27. Bowes, *Land Too Good for Indians*, 67 (all quotations). For alcohol sales to Indigenous people, see also Toulmin, *Digest of the Laws of Alabama*, 729; *Statutes of Wisconsin*, 125; Critchfield, *Revised Statutes of Ohio*, 1:450; *Revised Statutes of Iowa*, 206; Middleton, *Black Laws in the Old Northwest*, 288. For Indigenous perspectives on alcohol and its regulation, consider Mancall, "Men, Women, and Alcohol"; Bontrager, "'From a Nation of Drunkards'"; Kramer, "'That She Shall Be Forever Banished.'"

28. The same Ohio law authorized the sale of medicinal alcohol to "temperate Indians." Curwen, *Public Statutes of Ohio*, 1:621 ("traveling," "temperate"); Bowes, *Land Too Good for Indians*, 146–47, 200–203. For white travelers' varied reactions to Indigenous settlements and travelers, see, for example, Hannah Marshall Haines to [Esther Garrigues], July 27, 1808, [Hannah Marshall Haines] to Esther Garrigues, August 9, 1808, Ann Haines to John Smith Haines, June 25, 1833, Wyck Collection; Howland Diary, July [4], 1818; Royall, *Letters from Alabama*, 76–79; Bill Diary, December 9, 1835; Loveland Diary, August 10, 1843.

29. For the use of "person" and "his" with no special attention to female guests (or keepers), see, for example, A Gentleman of the law, *New Conductor Generalis*, 448–58. On gendered norms and racial segregation in commercial transportation in this period, see P. Cohen, "Safety and Danger"; P. Cohen, "Women at Large"; Welke, "When All the Women Were White"; Welke, *Recasting American Liberty*; Richter, *Home on the Rails*, 93–107; Pryor, *Colored Travelers*, 44–102; M. Bay, *Traveling Black*, 21–33. For aspects of early republican legal thinking about women, marriage, and households, consider Isenberg, *Sex and Citizenship*, 155–90; L. Edwards, *People and Their Peace*, 172–86, 244–51.

30. My thinking here might be said to filter McCoy's *Elusive Republic* through more recent interpretations such as Baptist's *The Half Has Never Been Told*, Sachs's *Home Rule*, and Roney's "1776, Viewed from the West." For removal policies and pressures in and beyond Indigenous contexts, see, for example, Jones, *Birthright Citizens*; Hirota, *Expelling the Poor*; O'Brassill-Kulfan, *Vagrants and Vagabonds*; Saunt, *Unworthy Republic*; Seeley, *Race, Removal, and the Right to Remain*. For itinerancy and consumption, see Jaffee, "Peddlers of Progress"; Remer, "Preachers, Peddlers, and Publishers"; Rainer, "'Sharper' Image."

31. Novak, *People's Welfare*, 92 (all quotations); see also 9, 83–113.

32. *Revised Code of Virginia*, 1:561–71, especially 566; Yoder, "Tavern Regulation," 265–66; K. Cohen, "'Entreaties and Perswasions,'" 613–15; K. Cohen, *They Will Have Their Game*, 120–21. On the possible recovery of property loaned to a gambler, see E. Bay, *Report of Cases Argued*, 2:560–63. For leisure pursuits in and beyond colonial taverns, see also Struna, *People of Prowess*; Daniels, *Puritans at Play*; Martin, *Killing Time*.

33. *Statutes of Wisconsin*, 123; New York State, *Laws of the State of New York, 1848*, 125, 160, 260.

34. On the changing legal treatment of drunkenness, see, for example, Thacher, "How Law Shapes Policing."

35. Littell and Swigert, *Digest of the Statute Law of Kentucky*, 2:1183 ("scandalous," "any person"); Tate, *Digest of the Laws of Virginia*, 437 ("more than"); James, *Laws of South Carolina*, 270 ("idle and disorderly," "remain").

36. Brevard, *Law of South-Carolina*, 2:198 ("any seaman," "one hour"); Tate, *Digest of the Laws of Virginia*, 437–38; Salinger, *Taverns and Drinking*, 38–46. On rivermen, see Geyer, *Digest of the Laws of Missouri*, 97–101; Allen, *Western Rivermen*; Buchanan, *Black Life on the Mississippi*. For sailors under British law, see Lemisch, "Jack Tar in the Streets," 377–80.

37. Biggs and Mackoy, *History of Greenup County, Kentucky*, 27. Only tavern keepers could sell liquor by the small measure, often defined as less than one quart, but tavern licenses did not preclude selling larger volumes. See, for example, *Laws of the Territory of Michigan*, 465. For nonkeepers' carryout alcohol trade, see Thacher, "How Law Shapes Policing," 1176–77; Rorabaugh, *Alcoholic Republic*, tables A.1.4–A.1.5. On alcohol as reward, stimulant, or medicine, see Bernhard, *Travels through North America*, 2:23–24; Swaim Diary, 35, 37; Rorabaugh, *Alcoholic Republic*, 12–13.

38. Curwen, *Public Statutes of Ohio*, 1:548 ("common"); Elmer, *Laws of New Jersey*, 339 ("in one," "under," "entirely").

39. Hotchkiss, *Statute Law of Georgia*, 742 (all quotations); Gilfoyle, "Strumpets and Misogynists," 54–56; M. Hill, *Their Sisters' Keepers*; Hemphill, *Bawdy City*, 130.

40. For sexual culture in the early republic, best documented in cities, consider *Pocket Companion for the Fancy*; Kennedy, *Braided Relations*, 77–126; Lyons, *Sex among the Rabble*; P. Cohen et al., *Flash Press*, 55–76, 130–58; K. Hemphill, *Bawdy City*, 23–145; Nunley, *Threshold of Liberty*, 88–93, 129–31.

41. *Laws of the Territory of Michigan*, 488; Dawson, *Laws of Georgia*, 429; *Revised Statutes of Mississippi*, 453; New York State, *Laws of the State of New York, 1848*, 160; Benes, *For a Short Time Only*, 75, 188; Hodgson, *Richard Potter*, 151.

42. Hodgson, *Richard Potter*, 145–53. For the familial connections of Farnum and another keeper implicated in Potter's performances, see Steere, *History of the Town of Smithfield*, 61, 66, 190–91, 193–94, 202–4.

43. *Public Laws of Rhode Island, 1822*, 296; Gosse, *First Reconstruction*, 255. Richard Potter received a keeper's license in Andover, Massachusetts, but his biographer describes the venture as a mistake. See Hodgson, *Richard Potter*, 157–63. Female license holders were probably less common in the early republic than in the colonial period, but women sometimes managed taverns even if they did not hold the license. Cuming, *Sketches of a Tour*, 77; List of Licensees (Innholders and Retailers), Newburyport, September–October, 1813, Folder 13, Liebmann Tavern Licenses; Conroy, *In Public Houses*, 318; Salinger, *Taverns and Drinking*, 163, table 5.1.

44. Cheves, *Cases at Law*, 225 ("fit"); A Gentleman of the law, *New Conductor Generalis*, 449 ("good"); *Public Acts of Maine*, 232–33 ("sober"); Burch, *Laws of Washington, D.C.*, 168; *A Law; Regulating Tavern Licenses*, 6; *Laws of the Territory of Michigan*, 465, 467; Metcalf, *Laws of Massachusetts, 1822–1832*, 3:377; Barbour, *Reports of Cases in Law and Equity*, 316. For character witnesses and sureties, see petitions and licenses in HSP Miscellaneous; Liebmann Tavern Licenses; Cumberland License Petitions. For local connections and law's enforcement, consider also Conroy, *In Public Houses*, 112–14; Gamble, "'For Lucre of Gain,'" 845–46; Edwards, *People and Their Peace*, 3–10, 47–53; Meacham, *Every Home a Distillery*, 68–70; Mathisen, "'Know All Men By These Presents.'"

45. Cumberland License Petitions. For New Jersey's tavern history, see Boyer, *Old Inns and Taverns of West Jersey*; Van Hoesen, *Early Taverns*.

46. We should not, of course, overstate lawmakers' concern for ordinary people's access to government. For constraints on legal personhood, including age, ability, race, gender, and nationality, consider, for example, Welke, *Law and the Borders of Belonging*; Field, *Struggle for Equal Adulthood*; Blumenthal, *Law and the Modern Mind*. For scholarship on the early American state, consider Bates, "Government by Improvisation."

47. For so-called backcountry conflicts in which limited access to government aggravated economic grievances, consider Klein, *Unification of a Slave State*; A. Taylor, *Liberty Men*; Kars, *Breaking Loose Together*.

48. Gookins, "The History of Vigo County," 36 ("place"), 10–11, 38, 64, 85, bound with Beckwith, *History of Vigo and Parke Counties*; Bradsby, *History of Vigo County, Indiana*, 139; Oakley, *Greater Terre Haute*, 48, 67, 80–82, 92–93. For related examples from the Midwest, see H. Howe, *Historical Collections of Ohio*, 386; *History of Jefferson County, Wisconsin*, 466; Reifel, *History of Franklin County, Indiana*, 194.

49. Cincinnati (OH) City Council, *1802–1902 History of Council*, 16–17, [new pagination] 3–6; Greve, *History of Cincinnati*, 446–47.

50. McNamara, *From Tavern to Courthouse*; Lounsbury, *Courthouses of Early Virginia*. For a case involving jury sequestration in a tavern, see *Hare v. State*, 5 Miss. 187, 1839 Miss. LEXIS 70.

51. New York State, *Laws of the State of New York, 1840*, 16 ("lately occupied"); Roscoe, *Schoharie County*, 2:272; Meginness, *History of Lycoming County, Pennsylvania*, 274. For historical county boundaries, see "Atlas of Historical County Boundaries," Newberry Library, https://digital.newberry.org/ahcb/index.html (accessed February 2, 2023).

52. *Alexandria (VA) Daily Advertiser*, February 29, 1804; *Alexandria (VA) Herald*, February 9, 1814; *Alexandria (VA) Gazette*, March 4, 1820; T. Miller, *Artisans and Merchants of Alexandria*, 1:96, 1:306, 1:337, 2:173; Greve, *History of Cincinnati*, 446, 447. See also *(New York) Daily Advertiser*, April 27, 1803; *National Intelligencer and Washington Advertiser*, June 2, 1809; *(Richmond, VA) Enquirer*, March 10, 1809; *Blakeley (AL) Sun*, February 19, 1819; *New York Herald*, November 5, 1850.

53. *Village Record, or Chester & Delaware (PA) Federalist*, September 6, 1820; *State Gazette of South-Carolina*, July 9, 1794; *(Charleston, SC) City Gazette*, July 30, 1816, August 30, 1820; Altschuler and Blumin, *Rude Republic*, 73; Bensel, *American Ballot Box*, 9–14.

54. *(Charles Town, VA) Farmer's Repository*, October 21, 1808, December 7, 1815, March 28, 1816 ("house of"), September 11, 1816, December 10, 1817 ("Negroes"), December 23, 1818, March 31, 1819, December 27, 1820; Keyssar, *Right to Vote*, table A.2. For a prominent man influencing voters at the polls, see A. Taylor, *William Cooper's Town*, 174–76.

55. *Acts of the State of Ohio [1809]*, 7:216 (all quotations); *Laws of the Territory of Michigan*, 487; Neem, "Freedom of Association," 262. Indiana and Nebraska passed similar laws: *Revised Laws of Indiana, Fifteenth Session*, 193; G. Brown, *General Statutes of Nebraska, 1873*, 726. For similarities across state codes, see Funk and Mullen, "Spine of American Law." I am indebted to Cynthia Kierner for this reference.

56. *History of the English Settlement in Edwards County*, 129 ("no longer"). Cf. William Cooper's "commercial village," in A. Taylor, *William Cooper's Town*, 74.

57. Emphases omitted. *(Keene) New-Hampshire Sentinel*, February 18, 1846 ("temperance plan"); *Rhode Island American and (Providence) Gazette*, April 5, 1831; *(Haverhill, MA) Essex Gazette*, February 9, 1833; *(Brattleboro, VT) Independent Inquirer*, December 28, 1833; Garvin and Garvin, *On the Road North of Boston*, 160–64. For alcohol consumption over time, see Rorabaugh, *Alcoholic Republic*, appendix, table A.1.1–A1.2. This section's title nods to Anker, *Ugly Freedoms*. For the "local origins of prohibition," see Tyrrell, *Sobering Up*, 225–51; Hampel, *Temperance and Prohibition*. For archaeological evidence of middle- and working-class drinking, consider Reckner and Brighton, "'Free from All Vicious Habits.'"

58. For New York, see Cross, *Burned-over District*. For southern temperance, see Tyrrell, "Drink and Temperance in the Antebellum South"; Carlson, "'Drinks He to His Own Undoing'"; Varon, *We Mean to Be Counted*, 30–40; Stewart, "Select Men"; Stewart, "'Forces of Bacchus Are Fast Yielding'"; Willis, *Southern Prohibition*. For commissioners of roads and tavern licenses, see Brevard, *Law of South-Carolina*, 1:421.

59. The decision in *South Carolina vs. John Chamblyss* can be found in Cheves, *Cases at Law*, 220–28. The case had some impact beyond South Carolina: *Bonner v. Welborn*, 7 Ga. 296 (1849); *Clary v. Willey*, 49 Vt. 55 (1876); *Jensen v. State*, 60 Wis. 577 (1884); *In re Schnei-*

der, 11 Ore. 288 (1884); *Babb v. Lewis*, 244 Ore. 537 (1966); Story, *Law of Contracts*; Redfield, *Law of Carriers*. The three South Carolina judges I discuss were substantial slaveholders or members of planter families. 1830 and 1840 U.S. Census for Greenville and Darlington Counties, South Carolina, courtesy of Family History Library Film, Ancestry.com. For O'Neall, see also L. Edwards, *People and Their Peace*, 30, 34, 38.

60. O'Neall as paraphrased in Cheves, *Cases at Law*, 220 (all quotations).

61. Brooks, *South Carolina Bench and Bar*, 1:22 ("learned"), 1:24–26, 1:29–30; *Camden (SC) Journal*, September 26, 1849; *Sumter (SC) Banner*, September 26, 1849.

62. Evans as quoted in Cheves, *Cases at Law*, 221 ("popular," "clearly shewn," "a tavern"), 227 ("most"), 228 ("deep," "my duty," "interfere"). Evans served in the South Carolina legislature and the circuit court and, later, in the U.S. Senate as a Democrat. Onofrio, *South Carolina Biographical Dictionary*, 216.

63. O'Neall as quoted in Cheves, *Cases at Law*, 228 ("same point," "his Honour's"), 229 ("entitled," "great respect," "I regard"), 230 ("relief"). For other efforts to distinguish inns from taverns, see, for example, Judge Warner's dissent in *Bonner v. Welborn* (7 Ga. 296, 1849); *Statutes of New Jersey*, 577–89; Kent, *Commentaries on American Law*, 7th ed., 763–64, note b.

64. Emphases in the original. O'Neall as quoted in Cheves, *Cases at Law*, 220, 230 (all quotations), 229–32. For the state's conferral of local tavern licensing and rate-setting powers in South Carolina after 1840, see *Acts of the General Assembly of the State of South Carolina, Passed in December, 1849*, 594.

65. Gantt as quoted in Cheves, *Cases at Law*, 233 (all quotations). For Gantt, see *Nineteenth Century*, 867. For amalgamation fears, see, for example, Clytus, "'Keep It Before the People,'" 314–16. For amalgamation and travel, see Martineau, *Society in America*, 1:384–85; Pryor, *Colored Travelers*, 64–69.

66. Hedeen, "Road to Prohibition," 1; Cherrington, *Evolution of Prohibition*, 108, 111, 119–20, 121, 128, 129, 130, 146, 149; Rumbarger, *Profits, Power, and Prohibition*, 35. For 1830s prohibition agitation, see *Documentary History of the Maine Law*, 7–11.

67. *Statutes of New Jersey*, 577, 588; *Acts and Resolves of Vermont, October Session, 1846*, 22 ("suitable"), 18–23.

68. Clubb, *Maine Liquor Law*, 331–50; Tyrrell, *Sobering Up*, 252–89.

69. Clubb, *Maine Liquor Law*, 313–14 ("presumptive"), 300, 322; *Documentary History of the Maine Law*, 14 ("public amusement," "place"); Keyssar, *Right to Vote*, appendix, table A.4. Several states preserved a limited right for farmers to make and sell cider or wine. Clubb, *Maine Liquor Law*, 299, 318, 320.

70. Clubb, *Maine Liquor Law*, 199 (all quotations). In addition to prohibition, competition shaped tavern keepers' persistence in the trade. See, for example, Garvin and Garvin, *On the Road North of Boston*, 170–73; Lobel, "'Out to Eat'"; Lobel, *Urban Appetites*, 103–38.

71. *Bristol County (MA) Democrat, and Independent Gazette*, August 9, 1839; *Bunker-Hill (MA) Aurora and Boston Mirror*, April 29, 1843 ("course"); *Fitchburg (MA) Sentinel*, October 14, 1853.

72. Paullin and Wright, *Historical Geography of the United States*, 128–29; Tyrrell, *Sobering Up*, 290–315; Novak, *People's Welfare*, 171–89; Volk, "Perils of 'Pure Democracy.'"

73. My keyword search in the Lexis Nexis database suggests an increase in liability suits in the 1840s. Transportation accidents and statutory changes in torts likely contributed to

this growth. See, for example, Hunt, "Law, Business, and Politics"; Abraham, "Common Law Prohibition on Party Testimony."

74. In law, an agreement in which one person takes temporary custody of another's property for a particular purpose is a bailment. Mid-nineteenth-century legal authorities generally agreed that a tavern keeper, who received payment for housing guests and their property, had greater liability than a bailee. J. Story, *Law of Bailments*, 1–2, 303–17.

75. "Innkeeper's Liability," 468 ("according"), 467–69.

76. McDaniels v. Robinson, 26 Vt. 316, 1854 Vt. LEXIS 21, *1("business"), p. 333 ("other goods"); *McDaniels v. Robinson*, 28 Vt. 387 (1856); C. Williams, *Compiled Statutes of Vermont*, 505.

77. *Neal v. Wilcox*, 49 N.C. 146, 1856 N.C. LEXIS 48 *3 (all quotations). For hotels geared to commercial travelers, see Sandoval-Strausz, *Hotel*, 82–83.

78. McDaniels v. Robinson, 26 Vt. 316, 1854 Vt. LEXIS 21, p. 332 ("transitory," "mere"), 328 ("comes"), 329 ("superior"), 336 ("severe"), 339 ("indispensable"); Kent, *Commentaries on American Law*, 7th ed., 758–63.

79. *Richmond (VA) Daily Whig*, September 29, 1854; *Weekly (Saint Paul) Minnesotian*, October 21, 1854.

80. "Liability of Innkeepers"; "Innkeeper's Liability"; A. Davis, *Traveler's Legal Guide*, 83 ("sleigh-load"); "Steamboats Liable for Robbery," 592 ("great traveling"), 591 ("we have").

81. *Chamberlain & Co. v. Masterson*, 26 Ala. 371, 1855 Ala. Lexis 168 *4 (all quotations).

82. A. Davis, *Traveler's Legal Guide*, 81 (all quotations). Cf. A Gentleman of the law, *New Conductor Generalis*, 453; James, *Laws of South Carolina*, 519, 529. For disease and other urban public health concerns, see Novak, *People's Welfare*, 191–233; O'Brassill-Kulfan, *Vagrants and Vagabonds*, 142–55.

83. "Fugitive Slave Act, 1850," Sections 5, 7, 8, Avalon Project, https://avalon.law.yale.edu /19th_century/fugitive.asp (accessed January 19, 2023). On the Fugitive Slave Act's reception and consequences, see, for example, Sinha, *Slave's Cause*, 500–542; Carter Jackson, *Force and Freedom*, 48–79; Masur, *Until Justice Be Done*, 234–66; Holness, "Self-Emancipated Slaves."

84. McDaniels v. Robinson, 26 Vt. 316, 1854 Vt. LEXIS 21, p. 335 ("absurd," "no such right"); A. Davis, *Traveler's Legal Guide*, 84. A lifelong Democrat, Redfield may have aligned with most of his party in accepting slavery and the Fugitive Slave Act in the 1850s. Dartmouth College Alumni Association, *Memorials of Judges*, 98, 106.

85. Slaughter, *Bloody Dawn*, 53 ("Special"), 52–54, 57, 126; Carter Jackson, *Force and Freedom*, 54–57. For Black Americans' adopting the name of Venezuelan revolutionary Simón Bolívar, see Fitz, *Our Sister Republics*, 153–55.

86. For the aftermath of the 1857 Dred Scott decision, consider Pryor, *Colored Travelers*, 115–16, 122–25; Jones, *Birthright Citizens*, 128–45; Sinha, *Slave's Cause*, 570–72; Carter Jackson, *Force and Freedom*, 100–103; Bonner, *Remaking the Republic*, 133–48; Gosse, *First Reconstruction*, 216, 469.

87. *Journal of the Proceedings of the General Assembly of South Carolina*, 1839, 5–6, 28, 52, 55–56, 167; *Acts and Resolutions of South Carolina*, 1839, 68; *(Wilkes-Barre, PA) Republican Farmer, and Democratic Journal*, September 29, 1841; Cherrington, *Evolution of Prohibition*, 123.

88. New York State, *Laws of the State of New York*, 1848, 76, 108, 286, 416; *Revised Statutes of the State of Delaware*, 50–51; *(Concord) New Hampshire Patriot & State Gazette*, Febru-

ary 1, 1849; *Amherst (NH) Farmer's Cabinet*, March 22, 1849; *Pawtucket (RI) Gazette & Chronicle*, March 30, 1849.

89. Elmer, *Laws of New Jersey*, 339 (all quotations).

Chapter Six

1. *(Hartford) Connecticut Courant*, October 23, 1797 ("public house," "never speaks"); Swaim Diary, 34–35 ("shabbiness"); Thompson, *Rum Punch and Revolution*, 200–202. On the party tactics and anti-partisanship that likely informed Swaim's reaction, see Altschuler and Blumin, *Rude Republic*, 49–86, 110, and passim.

2. For an "expanded definition of politics and political culture," see Koschnik, "Fashioning a Federalist Self," 221 ("expanded"). Contributors to the C19: Dissent conference in 2020—especially Rosa Martinez, Lydia G. Fash, Lisa Vandenbossche, Scott Rice, Valerie Sirenko, Christy Pottroff, and Brandon Wild—informed my thinking here. The conference program is available at https://www.c19society.org (accessed February 2, 2023).

3. Conroy, *In Public Houses*, 157 ("organize"); Thompson, *Rum Punch and Revolution*, 119 ("political questions"); Salinger, *Taverns and Drinking*, 218–20. For the interplay of democratic and conservative influences in the Constitution's drafting, see Holton, *Unruly Americans*. For Federalist values and accomplishments, see Elkins and McKitrick, *Age of Federalism*.

4. On the rise of parties, consider Bradburn, "'Parties Are Unavoidable.'"

5. K. Owen, "Legitimacy, Localism." See also Robertson, "Voting Rites"; Brooke, "Consent, Civil Society, and the Public Sphere"; K. Cohen, *They Will Have Their Game*, 157–66.

6. For scholarship that refocuses on electoral politics and political organizing, following a generation of field-reshaping work on politics' sociocultural dimensions, see, for example, Pasley, Robertson, and Waldstreicher, *Beyond the Founders*; Wilentz, *Rise of American Democracy*; Avril and Neem, *Democracy, Participation and Contestation*; Peart and Smith, *Practicing Democracy*; te Velde and Janse, *Organizing Democracy*; Gosse, *First Reconstruction*; Shelden, "Most Available Man." My arguments may share some ground with Rachel Shelden and Erik Alexander's forthcoming "Dismantling the Party System."

7. Tocqueville, *Democracy in America*, 2:129 ("immense"). For political and legal issues related to associating, consider Neem, *Creating a Nation of Joiners*; Butterfield, *Making of Tocqueville's America*.

8. The monitoring impulse expressed fear of both insurgent subordinates and an expansive state that would constrain ordinary white men, while Brooke's improvers welcomed a broader range of actors and state action. Many voluntary societies had "Federalist, entrepreneurial Republican, or Whig partisan" tendencies, as Brooke observes, but I use improvements in a broader way that captures ideas and changes relevant to taverns. Brooke, "Patriarchal Magistrates, Associated Improvers," 179 ("monitoring"), 195 ("improving," "Federalist"); Brooke, *Columbia Rising*, 451–52. See also D. Howe, *What Hath God Wrought*, 243–84.

9. Jeffrey, *Great Silent Army*, 56–63; Neem, *Creating a Nation of Joiners*, 82, 89–90; Butterfield, *Making of Tocqueville's America*, 25–26 and passim. On persuasive and deliberative politics, see Brooke, "Consent, Civil Society, and the Public Sphere," 209–11; Brooke, *Columbia Rising*, 5–8. Cf. Robertson, "Voting Rites," 58–59. On voluntarism, popular politics,

and the translocal structure of many civic organizations, see Skocpol, *Diminished Democracy*, 20–43; Neem, *Creating a Nation of Joiners*, 90–113. On the rise of organized voluntarism, see R. Brown, "Emergence of Urban Society."

10. Van Gosse argues that free Black men were "not automatically excluded from the politics of voting and partisanship," but Black women usually operated in other arenas. Black women were also rare in collective tavern politics. Gosse, *First Reconstruction*, 23 ("not automatically"); Neem, "Two Approaches to Democratization," 252–60, 267; Butterfield, *Making of Tocqueville's America*, 25–37. Tavern-going "routines" helped manage the "liminal quality of events" and shaped political possibilities. Brooke, "Party, Nation, and Cultural Rupture," 76 (all quotations).

11. *(Hartford) Connecticut Courant*, October 23, 1797 (*"sovereign people"*); R. Newman, *Transformation of American Abolitionism*; Zaeske, *Signatures of Citizenship*; Brooke, "Consent, Civil Society, and the Public Sphere," 234–36; Neem, "Two Approaches to Democratization," 252–59; Foreman, Casey, and Patterson, *Colored Conventions Movement*.

12. A. Taylor, *Liberty Men*, 169–74, 184–85; P. Newman, "Fries's Rebellion," 54–58, 63–64; L. Richards, *Shays's Rebellion*, 5–9; Pfleger, "'Miserable Germans,'" 348, 353; P. Newman, *Fries's Rebellion*, 80, 89–108; Bouton, *Taming Democracy*, 158.

13. Waldstreicher, *In the Midst of Perpetual Fetes*; Pasley, "Tyranny of Printers," 5–10, 148; K. Wood, "'Join with Heart and Soul and Voice.'"

14. *Pennsylvania Gazette*, September 29, 1790 ("exert"); Pasley, "Tyranny of Printers," 8–9, 48–50; K. Owen, "Legitimacy, Localism," 176–77. For keeper Israel's business and civic activities, see *Dunlap's (Philadelphia) American Daily Advertiser*, November 3, 1791; *Claypoole's (Philadelphia) American Daily Advertiser*, May 29, 1797; Bric, "United Irishmen, International Republicanism," 95. For other examples of local political campaigning in or before the 1790s, consider A. Taylor, *William Cooper's Town*, 170–98; Carp, *Rebels Rising*, 62–98; Scribner, *Inn Civility*, 109–70. This section builds on Owen's work.

15. K. Owen, "Legitimacy, Localism," 178 (all quotations).

16. *Pennsylvania Gazette*, September 15, 1790 ("respectable," "strenuous"), September 22, 1790 ("dictate," "very numerous"), September 29, 1790 (*"select,"* "much more"); K. Owen, "Legitimacy, Localism," 177–80.

17. Bouton, *Taming Democracy*, 195–96. For Mifflin's and St. Clair's involvement in the 1790 Constitution, see *The Proceedings Relative to Calling the Conventions of 1776 and 1790*, 124, 139.

18. *(Philadelphia) Pennsylvania Packet, and Daily Advertiser*, September 23, 1790 (all quotations).

19. *Pennsylvania Gazette*, September 29, 1790 (all quotations); Futhey and Cope, *History of Chester County*, 213–14.

20. Elkins and McKitrick, *Age of Federalism*, 484 ("'self-created'"), 455–88; Waldstreicher, *In the Midst of Perpetual Fetes*, 132; Koschnik, "Democratic Societies of Philadelphia"; Butterfield, *Making of Tocqueville's America*, 45–47. For meeting notices in and beyond Philadelphia, see *Philadelphia Gazette*, January 16, 1794; *(Philadelphia) General Advertiser*, April 30, 1794, September 17, 1794, September 23, 1794; *Dunlap's American Daily Advertiser*, September 25, 1794; *Greenleaf's New York (NY) Journal and Patriotic Register*, May 31, 1794; *(Rutland, VT) Farmers' Library*, July 8, 1794.

21. Mifflin as quoted in Neem, "Freedom of Association," 274 ("Freemen," "obey," "remonstrate"), 264, 268–69, 273–78; Waldstreicher, *In the Midst of Perpetual Fetes*, 70 ("re-

vival"), 69–71. For Republican activities beyond tavern election meetings in the late 1790s, see Koschnik, "Democratic Societies of Philadelphia," 635–36.

22. R. Brown, "Emergence of Urban Society," 38–42; Neem, "Freedom of Association," 260–62; Butterfield, *Making of Tocqueville's America*, 9, 21–22; Scribner, "Inn Civility," 48–55.

23. *(New York) Packet*, July 8, 1788, December 5, 1788; *Pennsylvania Gazette*, November 28, 1787; *(Charleston) City Gazette*, January 8, 1793, July 2, 1793, November 11, 1793, November 14, 1793, November 16, 1793, November 25, 1793, December 4, 1793, February 10, 1796, March 14, 1796, May 4, 1796, July 1, 1806, July 3, 1806, July 8, 1806, September 2, 1806, October 10, 1806; Beath, *Historical Catalogue*, 2:6–18; Murray, "Music and Dance," 9.

24. Neem, *Creating a Nation of Joiners*, 30–43, 50–55; Neem, "Freedom of Association," 259–63, 273–75, 278; Butterfield, *Making of Tocqueville's America*, 49–56. For secretive masculine societies, see also Pflugrad-Jackisch, *Brothers of a Vow*; Carnes, *Secret Ritual*.

25. *Philadelphia Gazette*, October 8, 1794 (all quotations), October 7, 1795; *(Philadelphia) Gazette of the United States*, October 8, 1796, October 9, 1797, October 2, 1800, September 10, 1802; *Claypoole's (Philadelphia) American Daily Advertiser*, October 1, 1798, September 9, 1799. Partisan identifications here and below come from cited newspapers or the Lampi Collection.

26. K. Rice, *Early American Taverns*, 37–38; Murray, "Music and Dance," 9, 15, 17, 32; Thompson, *Rum Punch and Revolution*, 146–54, 172–73; Koschnik, *"Let a Common Interest,"* 102.

27. *Philadelphia Gazette*, October 7, 1797 ("respectable," "Democratic"), April 21, 1796 ("l'Hôtel François"), April 26, 1796. Fouquet's hosted at least one meeting of "the Citizens of Philadelphia" that nominated Federalists: *Claypoole's (Philadelphia) American Daily Advertiser*, August 31, 1798.

28. In Stafford's directory, some taverns received street addresses, such as George Lesher's stage tavern at 94 N 2nd Street. Stafford identified other taverns with less precision: for example, Rice's tavern in Southwark was on Swanton Street, below the Swedish Church. *Claypoole's (Philadelphia) Daily American Advertiser*, August 2, 1796; *(Philadelphia) General Advertiser*, January 10, 1794; Stafford, *Philadelphia Directory for 1799*, 20, 29, 47, 57, 85, 106, 116.

29. Bric, "United Irishmen, International Republicanism," 95–98.

30. *(Philadelphia) Gazette of the United States*, February 14, 1798 ("a number"). For Republican/Israel meetings, see *Philadelphia Gazette*, October 7, 1797, February 17, 1798; *Carey's (Philadelphia) U.S. Recorder*, February 15, 1798; *Claypoole's (Philadelphia) American Daily Advertiser*, February 21, 1798. For Federalist/Morgan meetings, see *(Philadelphia) Gazette of the United States*, October 9, 1797, February 14, 1798, February 15, 1798, February 17, 1798.

31. Thompson, *Rum Punch and Revolution*, 200 ("tavern demagogues").

32. Emphasis in the original. *(Philadelphia) Gazette of the United States*, February 17, 1798 (all quotations).

33. Grotjahn Memoir, 75 ("during"), 73–75; *(Philadelphia) Porcupine's Gazette*, September 13, 1798; *(New London) Connecticut Gazette*, October 10, 1798; S. Newman, *Parades and the Politics of the Street*, 152–85; Robertson, "Voting Rites," 72–73.

34. *Mercantile Advertiser (New York, NY)*, October 20, 1806; *People's Friend (New York, NY)*, November 14, 1806; *(New York, NY) Commercial Advertiser*, April 25, 1807; Longworth, *New York City Directory, 1086/07*, 266, 406, 409.

35. For political and social capital, consider Allgor, *Parlor Politics*; Boonshoft, "Litchfield Network."

36. Zagarri, *Revolutionary Backlash*, 27 ("elastic quality"), 11–45; Frey, *Water from the Rock*; K. Wood, *Masterful Women*, 23–24; Egerton, *Death or Liberty*; Sinha, *Slave's Cause*, 34–96. For Black Loyalists who left the United States, see Walker, *Black Loyalists*; Jasanoff, *Liberty's Exiles*.

37. *New-York Herald*, April 30, 1808 (all quotations); *(New York) Mercantile Advertiser*, November 6, 1807; *(New York) Spirit of '76*, April 25, 1809; Gronningsater, "'Expressly Recognized,'" 471–78; Gosse, *First Reconstruction*, 324–36.

38. *Federal Gazette and Philadelphia Daily Advertiser*, February 23, 1792 ("Daughters"); *(Washington, DC) National Intelligencer*, February 9, 1801 ("American Fair"); Allgor, *Parlor Politics*, 30–31, 48–146; Branson, *Fiery Frenchified Dames*, 125–42; Zagarri, *Revolutionary Backlash*, 11–45, 62–75; Winterer, *Mirror of Antiquity*, 68–101.

39. *(Elizabethtown) New-Jersey Journal and Political Intelligencer*, July 6, 1791 ("fair friends," "participation"); *(Newark, NJ) Centinel of Freedom*, June 24, 1800 ("fair daughters," "real republicans"); *Burlington (NJ) Advertiser, or Agricultural and Political Intelligencer*, July 13, 1790; *(Washington, DC) National Intelligencer*, February 9, 1801; *Columbian Museum and Savannah (GA) Advertiser*, August 9, 1799; *(Elizabeth, NJ) Federal Republican*, May 31, 1803; Waldstreicher, *In the Midst of Perpetual Fetes*, 166–73; Branson, *Fiery Frenchified Dames*, 85–87.

40. White women in the early republic very occasionally held appointive office, for example as post mistresses. John, *Spreading the News*, 138–40.

41. *Pennsylvania Gazette*, September 28, 1785, September 27, 1786, September 28, 1787, October 24, 1787, November 28, 1787, October 8, 1788, October 1, 1794, October 8, 1794, October 7, 1795; *(Philadelphia) Gazette of the United States*, October 8, 1796, October 9, 1797; Pennsylvania state senate election returns for District 1 in 1797, 1798 special, and 1798 elections, Lampi Collection.

42. *(Newark, NJ) Sentinel of Freedom*, October 7, 1806 (all quotations).

43. For persuasion as unfolding in "circumstances of inequality as measured by a command of economic, social, or cultural resources," see Brooke, "Consent, Civil Society, and the Public Sphere," 209 ("circumstances"), 226–27, 229–30.

44. Keyssar, *Right to Vote*, table A.4; Zagarri, *Revolutionary Backlash*, 115–80; Gronningsater, "'Expressly Recognized,'" 491–506; Gosse, *First Reconstruction*, 336–76. For nontavern venues, consider *(Newark, NJ) Centinel of Freedom*, April 26, 1803; *(Newburyport, MA) Political Calendar*, May 14, 1804, June 11, 1804; *Camden (SC) Gazette*, March 28, 1818. This section draws on Peart, "An 'Era of No Feelings'?"; Robertson, "Jeffersonian Parties, Politics, and Participation"; Huston, "Can 'the People' Speak?"

45. *(New York, NY) Commercial Advertiser*, November 8, 1813 ("*AFRICAN LIBERTY*," "General Committee," "friendly," "on business"); *New York Evening Post*, November 11, 1813 ("division," "respectable," "committee," "promote").

46. Gronningsater, "'Expressly Recognized,'" 494–95; Gosse, *First Reconstruction*, 346–48.

47. Klinghoffer and Elkis argue that competition among Republicans fueled the Essex courthouse fight. Klinghoffer and Elkis, "'The Petticoat Electors,'" 176 ("hotly"), 172–79, 186–89. Cf. Robertson, "Jeffersonian Parties, Politics, and Participation," 114–15. For tavern meetings and arguments, see, for example, *(Newark, NJ) Sentinel of Freedom*, January 13, 1807, January 20, 1807, February 10, 1807; *(Elizabethtown) New Jersey Journal*, January 27, 1807, February 3, 1807, March 17, 1807.

48. *(Newark, NJ) Sentinel of Freedom*, February 17, 1807 ("Manlius," "almost every," "improper"), April 21, 1807 ("some ladies"), January 20, 1807, January 27, 1807, February 10,

1807, March 3, 1807, May 26, 1807, November 17, 1807; *(Elizabethtown) New Jersey Journal*, January 27, 1807, February 24, 1807, March 3, 1807; Zagarri, *Revolutionary Backlash*, 30–37; L. Fisher, "Votes of the 'Privileged Fair,'" 56–58 and passim. For the Eagle tavern, see Atkinson, *History of Newark, New Jersey*, 144. Elsewhere, for women dressing as men to vote, see A. Cohen and Faulkner, "Enforcing Gender at the Polls."

49. Election returns from New Castle County, Delaware, 1809 House of Representatives, Lampi Collection. For Red Lion meetings, see *(Wilmington, DE) American Watchman*, August 26, 1809, May 26, 1810, June 6, 1810, September 1, 1810, September 5, 1810, September 19, 1810, September 29, 1810, August 24, 1811, May 30, 1812, August 19, 1812. For the Red Lion's location, see Scharf, *History of Delaware*, 2:853.

50. *(Wilmington, DE) American Watchman*, August 26, 1809 ("to agree"), June 6, 1810, September 5, 1810.

51. Emphasis omitted. *(Wilmington, DE) American Watchman*, September 8, 1810 ("Democratic Republican"), August 24, 1811 ("republican citizens"), May 30, 1812 ("democratic citizens"); Keyssar, *Right to Vote*, table A.2.

52. *(Wilmington, DE) American Watchman*, September 29, 1810 (all quotations); 1810 U.S. Census for New Castle County, Delaware, courtesy of FamilySearch.org; Scharf, *History of Delaware*, 2:939. For pseudonyms, see M. Warner, *Letters of the Republic*, 43, 67–68; Pasley, *"Tyranny of Printers,"* 34–36, 87; Loughran, *Republic in Print*, 131–41; Eastman, *Nation of Speechifiers*, 190.

53. *(Wilmington, DE) American Watchman*, October 27, 1810 (all quotations).

54. *(Wilmington, DE) American Watchman*, August 26, 1809, June 6, 1810, September 1, 1810, September 5, 1810, September 19, 1810; Koschnik, "Fashioning a Federalist Self," 223–25; Field, *Struggle for Equal Adulthood*, 31, 33.

55. *(Wilmington, DE) American Watchman*, September 29, 1810, October 27, 1810; Pasley, *"Tyranny of Printers,"* 204 (all quotations). For confidence men in politics, see Dupre, "Barbecues and Pledges," 509–10, and for sincerity with strangers, see Halttunen, *Confidence Men*, 50–55.

56. Emphases omitted. *Alexandria (VA) Gazette* as reprinted in *Alexandria (VA) Herald*, November 29, 1816 (all quotations). For impropriety of anonymity, see *(Norfolk, VA) American Beacon and Commercial Diary*, March 16, 1816. For sensibility in the early republic, see Knott, *Sensibility*, 195–327; Brooke, *Columbia Rising*, 7, 234–35, and passim.

57. *Alexandria (VA) Gazette, Commercial and Political*, November 25, 1815, January 3, 1816, June 28, 1816, August 5, 1816, March 13, 1817; *Alexandria (VA) Herald*, January 22, 1816, February 16, 1816, April 5, 1816, June 26, 1816.

58. For eighteenth- and early nineteenth-century militias, see Rosswurm, *Arms, Country, and Class*; Pitcavage, "Ropes of Sand"; Koschnik, "Fashioning a Federalist Self"; Laver, "Rethinking the Social Role of the Militia"; Kars, *Breaking Loose Together*; Koschnik, "Young Federalists"; Kerr-Ritchie, "Rehearsal for War"; Laver, *Citizens More than Soldiers*; Bonner, *Remaking the Republic*, 151–54; Holness, "Self-Emancipated Slaves."

59. J. Alexander, *Transatlantic Sketches*, 279 ("treating"); *Pennsylvania Gazette*, May 2, 1792; Hardie, *Philadelphia Directory*, 1793, 47, 79, 97, 107, 125; *Trenton (NJ) Federalist*, August 24, 1807; *(Lexington, KY) Western Monitor*, September 20, 1817; *(Newbern, NC) Carolina Centinel*, March 6, 1819.

60. Emphasis in the original. Hertell, *Expose of the Causes of Intemperate Drinking*, 36 (all quotations).

61. *Blakeley (AL) Sun*, December 22, 1818, February 19, 1819, March 2, 1819, April 27, 1819, April 30, 1819. For social and economic improvements in southern towns, see Tolbert, *Constructing Townscapes*; Wells, *Origins of the Southern Middle Class.*

62. *(Keene) New Hampshire Sentinel*, February 11, 1825 ("the place"), February 6, 1819, November 20, 1819, April 22, 1820, October 7, 1820, September 15, 1821, November 16, 1822, December 19, 1823, May 28, 1824, August 26, 1825, August 18, 1826, August 10, 1827. For anti-horse thief societies, see Szymanski, "Stop, Thief!"

63. *(Washington, DC) Daily National Intelligencer*, August 24, 1816 ("to frame"), October 18, 1814, December 14, 1814, February 11, 1815, April 25, 1815.

64. *Ballston Spa (NY) Gazette and Saratoga Farmer*, November 7, 1821, January 23, 1822; *Ballston Spa (NY) Gazette*, December 31, 1822, October 14, 1823, July 26, 1825; *Saratoga (NY) Sentinel*, January 6, 1824, January 13, 1824, February 10, 1824; Gassan, *Birth of American Tourism*, 4–5, 9, 29, 35.

65. Brooke, "Patriarchal Magistrates, Associated Improvers," 196–205; Butterfield, *Making of Tocqueville's America*, 229, 237–43. On reform and white women's gender roles, see, for example, Ginzberg, *Women and the Work of Benevolence*, 11–35; Jeffrey, *Great Silent Army*, 54–55 and passim; Dorsey, *Reforming Men and Women*, 90–135, especially 124–31; Fletcher, *Gender and Temperance*, 7–29; Stott, *Jolly Fellows*, 65–96.

66. Hertell, *Expose of the Causes of Intemperate Drinking*, 40 (all quotations).

67. Neem, *Creating a Nation of Joiners*, 82 ("ordinary people"); Neem, "Two Approaches to Democratization," 252–59.

68. Peart, "An 'Era of No Feelings'?" 132. On partisan conflict in and after the 1820s, compare, for example, Wilentz, *Rise of American Democracy*, 280–518; Huston, "Rethinking 1828"; Peck, "Was There a Second Party System?"; Huston, "Rethinking the Origins of Partisan Democracy"; Huston, "Can 'the People' Speak?"; Cheathem, *Coming of Democracy*; Shelden and Alexander, "Dismantling the Party System."

69. For petitioning among partly or wholly disfranchised people, see Van Broekhoven, "'Let Your Names Be Enrolled'"; Hershberger, "Mobilizing Women, Anticipating Abolition"; Zaeske, *Signatures of Citizenship*; Portnoy, "'Female Petitioners'"; Carpenter and Topich, "Contested Boundaries of Representation"; N. Wood, "A 'Class of Citizens'"; Blackhawk et al., "Congressional Representation by Petition." For a comparative perspective, see H. Miller, "Transformation of Petitioning." "For the electoral turn in American women's politicking, see Ginzberg, "'Moral Suasion Is Moral Balderdash.'"

70. I focus on the two major parties here, but diverse interests called forth multiple parties from the 1830s through the 1850s. Shelden, "'The Most Available Man.'" For the "infrastructure" of free Black communities, consider Stanfield, *Rewriting Citizenship*, 68 ("infrastructure"), 68–100; Harbour, *Organizing Freedom*, 29–52; Foreman, Casey, and Patterson, *Colored Conventions Movement*; Nunley, *At the Threshold of Liberty*, 95–127.

71. *Baltimore Patriot*, October 4, 1822 (all quotations). For the "symbiotic relationship between print and oratory," see Eastman, *Nation of Speechifiers*, 10 ("symbiotic") and passim.

72. Emphasis omitted. *Baltimore Patriot*, October 4, 1822, October 3, 1823 (all quotations).

73. *(Haverhill, MA) Gazette & Patriot*, September 18, 1824 (all quotations), April 10, 1824; 1820 U.S. Census for Essex County, Massachusetts, courtesy of FamilySearch.org. For Black

men's political standing in early 1820s Massachusetts, see Gosse, *First Reconstruction*, 195–204.

74. Emphasis omitted. *Baltimore Patriot*, July 31, 1824 ("friends"), January 7, 1824 ("Young American," "respectable," "patriotic," "attend"), March 29, 1819, February 4, 1820, February 23, 1824, March 12, 1824, October 22, 1824. For the Young America movement, see Wilentz, *Rise of American Democracy*, 562–64; Eyal, *Young America Movement*.

75. Emphases in the original. *Baltimore Patriot*, August 12, 1828 ("Friends"); *Matchett's Baltimore Director for 1827*, Maryland State Archives, 491:261, https://msa.maryland.gov /megafile/msa/speccol/sc2900/sc2908/000001/000491/html/am491--261.html (2002) (accessed May 15, 2023). The other locations included a pleasure garden, the Jackson Reading Room, and several that might also have been taverns.

76. *Richmond Enquirer*, January 26, 1828 ("friends"), January 10, 1828.

77. While the Democratic Party absorbed many city and country radicals, the Whigs developed their own popular style. See, for example, Huston, *Land and Freedom*; Wilentz, *Rise of American Democracy*, 282–87, 487–518.

78. *Baltimore Patriot*, August 18, 1818 ("very large"), September 17, 1822 ("Many Voters," "warmly"), October 1, 1819, February 4, 1820, August 19, 1822, September 27, 1822, October 4, 1822, October 3, 1823, February 23, 1824, September 6, 1824, October 5, 1824, October 16, 1824, October 22, 1824, August 26, 1826, August 31, 1826, September 15, 1826, September 19, 1826, September 22, 1826, September 26, 1826, October 16, 1830, October 17, 1834; *The Ordinances of the Mayor and City Council of Baltimore*, 522; Scharf, *History of Baltimore City and County*, 188, 192.

79. Cuming, *Sketches of a Tour*, 82 ("considerable influence"); *Biographical Directory of the United States Congress, 1774–2005*, 568, 577, 578, 590, 659, 806, 1029, 1177, 1202, 1227, 1296, 1377, 1406, 1508, 1512, 1829, 1875, 1921, 2032, 2144, 2154; Brooke, *Columbia Rising*, 14–15; Garvin and Garvin, *On the Road North of Boston*, 22; "Franklin Pierce Homestead," https://www.nps.gov/nr/travel/presidents/franklin_pierce_homestead.html (accessed January 21, 2023). For contrary perceptions of the political tavern keeper, consider Altschuler and Blumin, *Rude Republic*, 123, 125.

80. Growing Democratic enthusiasm for infrastructure did not automatically produce well-networked transportation systems. See Majewski, "Commerce and Continuity"; Majewski, "Who Financed the Transportation Revolution"; D. Howe, *What Hath God Wrought*, 829–30; Eyal, *Young America Movement*, 44–79. For earlier elite associationalism, consider Schreiber, "Bluebloods and Local Societies."

81. For the contrast between improving societies that Democrats endorsed and policy-centered Whiggish reform societies, consider Wells, *Origins of the Southern Middle Class*, 89–110, 136–46. For Whig ideas, consider D. Howe, *Political Culture of the American Whigs*. For the range of women's activism, consider N. Hewitt, *Women's Activism and Social Change*; Ginzberg, *Women and the Work of Benevolence*; Zboray and Zboray, "Whig Women, Politics, and Culture"; Jeffrey, *Great Silent Army*; Ginzberg, *Untidy Origins*; Varon, *We Mean to Be Counted*; Zboray and Zboray, *Voices Without Votes*. For women and partisan politics, see also Cheatham, *Coming of Democracy*, 32–34, 49–51, 87–90, 115–19, 164–69.

82. *Baltimore Patriot*, February 11, 1828 ("General Convention"), May 22, 1828 ("friends"), February 4, 1828, February 26, 1828, April 7, 1828, September 2, 1828, September 9, 1828. For National Republican tavern meetings, see also *Portsmouth (NH) Journal and Rockingham*

Gazette, January 12, 1828, *National Republican Ticket,* but note that venues such as court-houses and schools were equally or more common.

83. *Baltimore Patriot,* September 8, 1834 (all quotations), September 4, 1834, September 22, 1834, October 1, 1834.

84. *(Lenox, MA) Berkshire Journal,* December 3, 1829, April 22, 1830, April 28, 1831.

85. *(Lenox, MA) Berkshire Journal,* September 30, 1830 ("Champaigne"); *(Hartford, CT) American Mercury,* June 17, 1828 ("*intemperate,*" "moderate," "wine," "subservient"); *(Concord) New Hampshire Patriot and State Gazette,* January 14, 1822, June 20, 1825, June 2, 1828; *Ithaca (NY) Journal,* January 2, 1830; *(New London, CT) Morning News,* March 28, 1845; Osborn, *Rum Maniacs,* 119–36.

86. *(Amherst, NH) Farmer's Cabinet,* November 27, 1840 ("dispense"), December 4, 1840 ("intoxicating," "festival," "excellent"); *Portsmouth (NH) Journal of Literature and Politics,* December 26, 1840.

87. Emphasis omitted. *(Keene) New-Hampshire Sentinel,* July 1, 1846 (all quotations), February 18, 1846, February 25, 1846.

88. *The Liberator,* January 2, 1837, February 11, 1837, March 4, 1837, March 9, 1838, October 26, 1838, November 2, 1838, November 30, 1838, March 15, 1839, July 26, 1839.

89. *The Liberator,* February 11, 1837, November 2, 1838. The keeper of Wesson's hotel in 1838 may have been convicted of violating Massachusetts's liquor law in 1853, a possibility I am exploring for another project. See *Bristol County (MA) Democrat, and Independent Gazette,* August 9, 1839; *Bunker-Hill (MA) Aurora and Boston Mirror,* April 29, 1843; *Fitchburg (MA) Sentinel,* October 14, 1853; Hampel, *Temperance and Prohibition in Massachusetts,* 170, table 10.14, 180–181.

90. *The Liberator,* November 30, 1838 (all quotations), November 2, 1838.

91. *The Liberator,* March 9, 1838 ("large delegation"). For the abolitionist schism, consider Sinha, *Slave's Cause,* 256–98.

92. *The Liberator,* October 6, 1832 ("literally jammed,"), February 18, 1837 ("representatives").

93. *Southport (Wisconsin Territory) Telegraph,* September 1, 1848. For the Buffalo convention, compare Pierson, *Free Hearts and Free Homes,* 52–57; Earle, *Jacksonian Antislavery,* 160–63; Wilentz, *Rise of American Democracy,* 622–26.

94. *The Liberator,* February 11, 1837 ("to attract"); *(Rochester, NY) North Star,* June 29, 1849 ("[h]otels," "appropriated"), September 14, 1849. For August First celebrations, see Kachun, *Festivals of Freedom;* Kerr-Ritchie, *Rites of August First;* Schoolman, *Abolitionist Geographies,* 71–72, 84.

95. *Vincennes (IN) Gazette,* December 17, 1859 (all quotations); *Davenport (IA) Gazette,* January 9, 1851; *(Clinton, LA) American Patriot,* January 24, 1855; *Richmond (IN) Palladium,* March 17, 1859; Roberson, "Memphis Commercial Convention of 1853," 281–83.

96. *(Keene) New-Hampshire Sentinel,* March 9, 1837 ("of voters").

97. *(Portsmouth) New-Hampshire Journal of Literature and Politics,* January 13, 1838 ("every town"); *(NY) Hudson River Chronicle,* October 1, 1839.

98. *(Concord) New Hampshire Patriot and State Gazette,* January 18, 1850 ("credentials"), January 24, 1850, January 31, 1850.

99. *The Liberator,* October 6, 1837 (all quotations).

100. *(Washington, DC) National Era*, May 6, 1847 ("nothing," "many pleasant"); *The Liberator*, February 4, 1837 ("friends").

101. *(Rochester, NY) North Star*, February 4, 1848 ("active"), February 2, 1849 ("Anti-Slavery women"), September 14, 1849; *The Liberator*, March 4, 1837; *(Washington, DC) National Era*, March 20, 1851; Yellin and Van Horne, *Abolitionist Sisterhood*; Jeffrey, *Great Silent Army*, 53–133. For other female societies, see *(Baltimore) Republican or, Anti-Democrat*, February 22, 1802; *(Newburyport, MA) Political Calendar*, June 11, 1804; *(Charleston, SC) City Gazette and Daily Advertiser*, September 11, 1820. For agricultural fairs, see *(Keene) New Hampshire Sentinel*, October 30, 1819; *Ithaca (NY) American Journal*, December 6, 1820; *Springfield (MA) Gazette*, October 19, 1842; Kelly, "'The Consummation of Rural Prosperity,'" 578, 580–83.

102. *The Liberator*, February 28, 1835, December 5, 1836, November 17, 1837; Tomek, *Pennsylvania Hall*; Sinha, *Slave's Cause*, 207–8, 228, 231–39; Pryor, *Colored Travelers*, 67–69, 84; Masur, *Until Justice Be Done*, 99–100, 131–32, 190–91; Williams-Forson, "Where Did They Eat?".

103. *(Washington, DC) National Era*, June 17, 1847 ("to induce," "disorderly taverns"); *The Liberator*, March 11, 1837 ("brutal, senseless"); *(New York) Colored American*, August 11, 1838, March 20, 1841. For temperance and abolition, see also Masters and Young, "Power of Religious Activism." For women's public speaking, consider Kelley, *Learning to Stand and Speak*; Eastman, *Nation of Speechifiers*, 179–210.

104. *The Liberator*, March 11, 1837 ("riotous"), July 28, 1837 ("ruffians," "rum tavern"); D. Howe, *What Hath God Wrought*, 826–27; Wilentz, *Rise of American Democracy*, 679–85. Abolitionists recognized that temperate churchgoers could be hostile to antislavery, and middle-class people who deplored others' drinking sometimes excused their own. *(Rochester, NY) North Star*, October 5, 1849; Reckner and Brighton, "'Free from All Vicious Habits,'" 73, 81, 82.

105. *(Rochester, NY) North Star*, March 9, 1849, September 14, 1849.

106. *(Rochester, NY) North Star*, September 15, 1848 (all quotations). For "circulating citizenship" and Black convening, see Spires, *Practice of Citizenship*, 79–120; Bonner, *Remaking the Republic*, 50–68; Foreman, Casey, and Patterson, *Colored Conventions Movement*; Gosse, *First Reconstruction*, 86–91, 449–50, and passim. For radical respectability, see E. Ball, *To Live an Antislavery Life*; Pryor, *Colored Travelers*, 70–71, 76–102.

107. *Frederick Douglass' (Rochester, NY) Paper*, June 15, 1855 ("as a woman"); *(Rochester, NY) North Star*, December 14, 1849 ("excluded," "laws"), November 9, 1849; Williams-Forson, "Where Did They Eat?" For public amusements, commercial eateries, and their sifting functions, consider Stubbs, "Pleasure Gardens of America"; Lobel, *Urban Appetites*, 103–38, 186–88.

108. *Frederick Douglass' (Rochester, NY) Paper*, May 27, 1852 (all quotations).

109. *Frederick Douglass' (Rochester, NY) Paper*, May 27, 1852 (all quotations); *The Liberator*, June 11, 1852; Sandoval-Strausz, *Hotel*, 180–83. For competing ideas about occupations, dignity, and Black independence, consider *Report of the Proceedings of the Colored National Convention*, 6, 13; E. Ball, *To Live an Antislavery Life*, 40–45.

110. *Frederick Douglass' (Rochester, NY) Paper*, May 27, 1852; *Report of the Proceedings of the Colored National Convention*, 11–12; Fought, *Women in the World of Frederick Douglass*, 152–67; Blight, *Frederick Douglass*, 196–97.

111. Cuming, *Sketches of a Tour*, 56 ("astonishing"); Dunlop Diary, November 12, 1810 ("at 10 paces," "alarming"). On political dueling around the turn of the century, see Freeman, *Affairs of Honor*.

Conclusion

1. Freehling, *Road to Disunion*, vol. 2; Sinha, *Counterrevolution of Slavery*; Wells, *Origins of the Southern Middle Class*, 207–29. For political manipulation in the context of the secession conventions, consider McCurry, *Confederate Reckoning*, 38–84. My framing of shifting southern attitudes owes a debt to the rhetorical analysis in Varon, *Disunion*.

2. "Lexington (KY) Directory, 1806, Taken for Charless' Almanack, for 1806," https:// sites.rootsweb.com/~kyfayett/1806directory.htm (June 1999) (accessed May 15, 2023); *Pittsburgh Directory for 1815*; E. Matchett, *Baltimore Directory, 1816*; R. Matchett, *Matchett's Baltimore Director, 1833*; MacCabe, *Lexington Directory, 1838–39*; Harris' *Pittsburgh and Allegheny Directory, 1841*; C. Williams, *Lexington Directory, 1859–60*; Conlin, ed., *Pleasure Garden*; Lobel, *Urban Appetites*, 77–82, 103–38, 182–88.

3. White, *Wet Britches*, 55.

4. Pierce, *Making the White Man's West*, 144, 151–74, and passim; Hine et al., *American West*, 2nd ed.; Blevins, *Paper Trails*, 59–156.

5. Belasco, *Americans on the Road*, 129–73; Beecher, "The Motel"; Sculle, "Frank Redford's Wigwam Village Chain"; Sandoval-Strausz, *Hotel*, 133–35; Rodway, "Managing Quasi-Domesticity at the Roadside."

6. M. Bay, *Traveling Black*, 110 ("new"), 107–50.

7. Fletcher, *Gender and the American Temperance Movement*, 79–123; Willis, *Southern Prohibition*, 102–53.

8. M. Bay, *Traveling Black*, 230–305.

9. Oldenburg, *The Great Good Place*; R. Putnam, *Bowling Alone*; Skocpol, *Diminished Democracy*, 7–12; Voyce, "Shopping Malls in Australia"; Di Masso, "Grounding Citizenship"; "Do's and Don'ts of Petition Gathering," ACLU of Florida, https://www.aclufl.org /sites/default/files/field_documents/dos_and_donts_of_petition_collection_say_yes _to_second_chances_campaign.pdf (accessed May 24, 2023); Barrett, "Defining their Right to the City," 710–713. For examples of political speech's protection in malls, see, for example, Scott Bullock, "The Law: The Mall's in Their Court," *Reason: Free Minds and Free Markets*, https://reason.com/1995/08/01/the-malls-in-their-court/ (August/September 1995).

10. "How Does Space Drive Innovation?" (all quotations), Gensler: Research and Insight, https://www.gensler.com/research-insight/gensler-research-institute/framework-for -innovation-spaces (2012) (accessed January 22, 2023); Congress for the New Urbanism, https://www.cnu.org/resources/what-new-urbanism (accessed February 2, 2023); Clifton, "Coworking Spaces, Proximity, Innovation and the Fourth Space"; Zenkteler et al., "Distribution of Home-Based Work in Cities." For inclusion, sustainability, and New Urbanism, consider, for example, Rigolon and Németh, "Privately Owned Parks in New Urbanist Communities."

11. For space, mobility, and social and political movements, consider Castells, *The City and the Grassroots*; McLean, Schults, and Steger, *Social Capital*; Davenport, Soule, and Armstrong, "Protesting While Black"; Jefferson-Jones, "'Driving While Black'"; Stokols,

"From the Square to the Shopping Mall," 3–5. For examples of recent discussions around municipal government, policing, and travel, consider Aaron Leibowitz, "Miami Beach officials vote for a curfew and secured perimeter during spring break 2024," *Miami Herald*, March 27, 2023; Kyra Gurney, "What's Memorial Day weekend going to look like this year? Miami Beach has big plans," *Miami Herald*, April 6, 2018. For libraries, consider M. Williamson, "Social Exclusion and the Public Library"; Birdi, Wilson, and Cocker, "The Public Library, Exclusion and Empathy"; Gehner, "Libraries, Low-Income People, and Social Exclusion"; Robinson and Williamson, "Overcoming Social Exclusion in Public Library Services"; Kohlburn et al., "Public Libraries and COVID-19."

Bibliography

Manuscripts

Albany, New York
  New York State Archives
    Warsaw, New York Tavern Daybook, 1830–1831
Athens, Georgia
  Hargrett Rare Book and Manuscript Library, University of Georgia Libraries
    Thomas G. Little architectural drawings
Cambridge, Massachusetts
  Baker Library, Harvard Business School
    R. G. Dun & Company records, 1841–1933, Dun & Bradstreet Corporation Records
Chapel Hill, North Carolina
  Southern Historical Collection, University of North Carolina
    Borough House Books, 1815–1910
    Brevard and McDowell Family Papers, 1754–1953
    Jacob A. Kline Account Books and Letter, 1838–1849; 1853
    James Clitherall Diary, 1776
    John Berkley Grimball Diaries, 1832–1883
    John Steele Papers, 1716–1846
    Martin Browne Papers, 1770–1830
Durham, North Carolina
  David M. Rubenstein Rare Book & Manuscript Library, Duke University
    Alexander and John Lowrance Papers, 1749–1796
    Brown, William. Ledger, 1776–1791
    Burroughs, Richard D. Papers, 1807–1889
    Elkton (Md.) tavern keeper's ledger, 1806–1816
    Hiram Haines papers, 1826–1838
    Kirby, Samuel Tompkins. Papers, 1785–1807
    Register, 1843–1844, Eagle Tavern (Watkinsville, GA)
    Swaim, Lyndon. Papers, 1844–1872
    Sylvanus Bourne Papers, 1799–1815
    Virginia Merchant's Account Book, 1838–1839
    William H. P. Adair Papers, 1836–1858
New York, New York
  New-York Historical Society
    Bill, John Wight. Diary/Account Book, 1835–1838
    Drew, James. Diary, 1845 June–1846 July
    Dunlop, J. B. Diary, 1810–1811

Hamlin, David. Daybook, 1822–1855 (bulk 1842–1855)

Hewitt, Abram S. Diary and letterpress copybooks, 1843, 1876, 1887–1888
   (bulk 1887–1888)

Howland, Sarah Hazard. Diaries and notebook, 1818–1822

Lester, Andrew. Diary, 1836–1888

Loveland, Samuel. Diary, 1843 Jul.–1843, Sept. 16.

New Jersey boxes, 1700–1888

Southworth, Henry Clay. Diary, 1850–1851

[Tavern] License No. [76] To the honorable the mayor . . . The petition of Harriet
   Wiley. Philadelphia, 1827

New York Public Library

   Liebmann collection of American historical documents relating to spiritous
      liquors, 1665–1910 (bulk 1665–1865)

   Samuel Adams Papers, 1758–1819

   Thomas Chamberlain Diaries, 1835–1860

Philadelphia, Pennsylvania

   American Philosophical Society

      George Hunter Journals

      Journal of the travels of Colonel John Boykin and Francis P. Lee from Morristown,
         New Jersey to Camden, South Carolina, August 15, 1833–September, 1833

      Maria Mitchell papers, ca. 1825–1887

      Peter Adolph Grotjahn Memoir

      Pim Nevins Journal

      Robert Woodruff Journal. December 17, 1785–May 1, 1788

      William Parker Foulke Papers, 1840–1865

      Wyck Association Collection

   Historical Society of Pennsylvania

      Historical Society of Pennsylvania Miscellaneous Collection, 1676–1937

      Historical Society of Pennsylvania Road and Travel Notes Collection, 1699–1885

      James Gibbons Journal

      Lewes (Del.) collection

      Memoir of Mrs. John Reed

      Pemberton Papers

      Robert Patterson Diaries

      Roberts Vaux Diary

      S. Schulling Diary

      Samuel Rowland Fisher papers

      Unidentified Travel Diary

      Vaux Family Papers

Richmond, Virginia

   Virginia Historical Society

      Cocke Family Papers

Williamsburg, Virginia

   Special Collections Research Center, William & Mary College

      Traveller's Rest Daybooks

Published Primary Sources

A Gentleman of the law. *A New Conductor Generalis: Being a Summary of the Law Relative to the Duty and Office of Justices of the Peace.* Albany: O. & S. Whiting, 1803.

A Law; Regulating Tavern Licenses. New York: Van Pelt and Spear, 1823.

Aaron. *The Light and Truth of Slavery. Aaron's History.* Worcester, MA: The Author, 1845.

Acts and Laws of the State of Connecticut in America. New London: Timothy Green, 1784.

The Acts and Resolves Passed by the Legislature of the State of Vermont at Their October Session, 1846. Burlington: Chauncey Goodrich, 1846.

Acts and Resolutions of the General Assembly of the State of South Carolina, Passed in December, 1839. Columbia: A. H. Pemberton, 1839.

Acts of the General Assembly of the Commonwealth of Kentucky, Passed at November Session, 1851. Frankfort: A. G. Hodges, 1852.

Acts of the General Assembly of the State of South Carolina, Passed in December, 1849. Columbia: I. C. Morgan, 1849.

Acts Passed at a General Assembly of the Commonwealth of Virginia, Begun and Held at the Capitol, in the City of Richmond, on Monday, the Sixth Day of December, in the Year of Our Lord One Thousand Eight Hundred and Nineteen. Richmond: Thomas Ritchie, 1820.

Acts Passed at the First Session of the Seventh General Assembly of the State of Ohio. Chillicothe: J. S. Collins, 1809.

Adams, H. G., ed. *God's Image in Ebony: Being a Series of Biographical Sketches, Facts, Anecdotes, etc., Demonstrative of the Mental Powers and Intellectual Capacities of the Negro Race.* London: Partridge and Oakey, 1854.

Aggregate Amount of Each Description of Persons Within the United States of America, and the Territories Thereof, Agreeably to Actual Enumeration Made According to Law, in the Year 1810. New York: N. Ross, 1990.

Agriculture of the United States in 1860; Compiled from the Original Returns of the Eighth Census. Washington, DC: U.S. Government Printing Office, 1864.

Alexander, Captain J. E. *Transatlantic Sketches, Comprising Visits to the Most Interesting Scenes in North and South America, and the West Indies. With Notes on Negro Slavery and Canadian Emigration.* Philadelphia: Key and Biddle, 1833.

Andrews, Robert. *The Virginia Almanack, for the Year of Our Lord, 1794.* Richmond: Dixon, 1793.

———. *The Virginia Almanack, for the Year of Our Lord, 1794.* Richmond: T. Nicholson, 1793.

———. *The Virginia Almanack, for the Year of Our Lord, 1795.* Richmond: Samuel Pleasants, 1794.

Andrews, William. *Poor Will's Pocket Almanack, for the Year 1771 Fitted to the Use of Pennsylvania, and the Neighbouring Provinces.* Philadelphia: Printed and sold by Joseph Crukshank, 1770.

Armistead, Wilson. *A Tribute for the Negro: Being a Vindication of the Moral, Intellectual, and Religious Capabilities of the Colored Portion of Mankind; with Particular Reference to the African Race.* Manchester, UK: W. Irwin, 1848.

Ball, Charles. *Fifty Years in Chains; or, the Life of an American Slave.* New York: H. Dayton, 1859.

———. *Slavery in the United States: A Narrative of the Life and Adventures of Charles Ball, a Black Man, Who Lived Forty Years in Maryland, South Carolina and Georgia, as a Slave under Various Masters, and Was One Year in the Navy with Commodore Barney, during the Late War*. New York: John S. Taylor, 1837.

Barbour, Oliver L. *Reports of Cases in Law and Equity, Determined in the Supreme Court of the State of New York*. Vol. 54. Albany: W. C. Little, 1870.

Barnes, Albert. *The Connexion of Temperance with Republican Freedom: An Oration, Delivered on the 4th of July, 1835, before the Mechanics and Workingmens Temperance Society of the City and County of Philadelphia*. Philadelphia: Boyle & Benedict, 1835.

—. *The Immorality of the Traffic in Ardent Spirits: A Discourse*. In *Temperance Pamphlets*. Philadelphia: George, Latimer, 1834.

Bay, Elihu Hall. *Report of Cases Argued and Determined in the Superior Courts of Law in the State of South Carolina, since the Revolution*. Vol. 2. New York: Isaac Riley, 1811.

Beastall, William. *A Useful Guide for Grocers, Distillers, Hotel and Tavern-Keepers, and Wine and Spirit Dealers, of Every Denomination*. New York: The Author; C. Bartlett, printer, 1829.

Benjamin's New Map of the Hudson River. Troy, NY: Tuttle, 1845.

Bernhard, Duke of Saxe-Weimar-Eisenach. *Travels through North America, during the Years 1825 and 1826*. 2 Vols. Philadelphia: Carey, Lea and Carey, 1828.

Bibb, Henry. *Narrative of the Life and Adventures of Henry Bibb, an American Slave, Written by Himself. With an Introduction by Lucius C. Matlack*. New York: The Author, 1849.

Birkbeck, Morris. *Notes on a Journey in America, from the Coast of Virginia to the Territory of Illinois: With Proposals for the Establishment of a Colony of English*. Philadelphia: Caleb Richardson, 1817.

Brevard, Joseph. *An Alphabetical Digest of the Public Statute Law of South-Carolina, in Three Volumes*. Charleston: John Hoff, 1814.

Brown, Guy A. *The General Statutes of the State of Nebraska, Comprising All Laws of a General Nature in Force, September 1, 1873*. Lincoln: Journal Company, 1873.

Brown, J. D. *The Arcade Hotel Guide, for the Use of Strangers Visiting Philadelphia, Containing an Account of Places of Interest, Public Buildings, Churches, Places of Amusement, and with Directions for Visiting the Same*. Philadelphia: Inquirer Printing Office, 1856.

Brown, Josephine. *Biography of an American Bondman, by His Daughter*. Boston: R. F. Wallcut, 1856.

Browne, Martha. *Autobiography of a Female Slave*. New York: Redfield, 1857.

Burch, Samuel. *A Digest of the Laws of the Corporation of the City of Washington, to the First of June, 1823*. Washington, DC: James Wilson, 1823.

Caldwell, John Edwards. *A Tour through Part of Virginia, in the Summer of 1808, in a Series of Letters*. New York: H. C. Southwick, 1809.

Callcott, Margaret Law, ed. *Mistress of Riversdale: The Plantation Letters of Rosalie Stier Calvert, 1795–1821*. Baltimore: Johns Hopkins University Press, 1991.

Campbell, Tunis G. *Never Let People Be Kept Waiting: A Textbook on Hotel Management. A Reprint of Tunis G. Campbell's Hotel Keepers, Head Waiters, and Housekeepers' Guide*. Edited with an introduction by Doris Elizabeth King. Raleigh: King Reprints in Hospitality History, 1973.

Charter and Directory of the City of Rochester: Also Statistics, Population, Publick Buildings, Institutions, Fire Department, &c. &c. Rochester, NY: C. & M. Morse, 1834.

Chastellux, François Jean, Marquis de. *Travels in North-America, in the Years 1780, 1781, and 1782*. Translated from the French by an English Gentleman. London: G. G. J. & J. Robinson, 1787.

Cheves, Langdon. *Cases at Law, Argued and Determined in the Court of Appeals of South Carolina.* Columbia: A. S. Johnston, 1840.

Clark, Walter, ed. and comp. *Laws 1777–1788,* Vol. 24 in *The State Records of North Carolina.* Goldsboro, NC: Nash Brothers, 1905.

Clarke, Lewis Garrard, and Milton Clarke. *Narratives of the Sufferings of Lewis and Milton Clarke, Sons of a Soldier of the Revolution, during a Captivity of More than Twenty Years among the Slaveholders of Kentucky, One of the So-Called Christian States of North America.* Boston: Published by Bela Marsh, 1846.

Clayton, Augustin Smith. *A Compilation of the Laws of the State of Georgia Passed by the Legislature since the Political Year 1800, to the Year 1810, inclusive.* Augusta: Adams & Duyckinck, 1813.

Colles, Christopher. *Sir, Your Company Is Requested at the Coffee-House.* New York: n.p., 1785.

Compendium of the Enumeration of the Inhabitants and Statistics of the United States as Obtained at the Department of State from the Returns of the Sixth Census, by Counties and Principal Towns. Washington, DC: T. Allen, 1841.

Cooley, Thomas M. *The Compiled Laws of the State of Michigan.* Vol. 1. Lansing: Hosmer & Kerr, 1857.

Craft, Myrtis, and Melvin Tingle. *Old Account Book Entries, 1837–1841, Decatur, Newton County, Mississippi.* Carrollton, MS: Pioneer Publishing, 2001.

Craft, William. *Running a Thousand Miles for Freedom; or, the Escape of William and Ellen Craft from Slavery.* London: William Tweedle, 1860.

Crawford House. White Mountains, N.H. Boston: Dutton & Wentworth, 1851.

Cresson, Caleb. *Diary of Caleb Cresson, 1791–1792.* Philadelphia: Ezra Townsend Cresson and Charles Caleb Cresson, 1877.

Critchfield, Leander J. *Revised Statutes of the State of Ohio, of a General Nature.* 2 Vols. Cincinnati: Robert Clarke, 1870.

Cuming, Fortescue. *Sketches of a Tour to the Western Country: Through the States of Ohio and Kentucky; a Voyage Down the Ohio and Mississippi Rivers, and a Trip through the Mississippi Territory, and Part of West Florida. Commenced at Philadelphia in the Winter of 1807, and Concluded in 1809.* Pittsburgh: Cramer, Spear & Eichbaum, 1810.

Curwen, Maskell E., ed. *The Public Statutes at Large of the State of Ohio: From the Close of Chase's Statutes, February, 1833, to the Present Time.* 3 Vols. Cincinnati: The Author, 1853.

Davis, Alexander S. *The Traveler's Legal Guide and Business Men's Directory.* Rochester, NY: D. M. Dewey, 1855.

Dawson, William C. *A Compilation of the Laws of the State of Georgia, Passed by the General Assembly since the Year 1819 to the Year 1829, inclusive.* Milledgeville: Grantland and Orme, 1831.

Documentary History of the Maine Law, Comprising the Original Maine Law, the New-York Prohibitory Liquor Law, Legislative Debates, Arguments, Judicial Decisions, Statistics, Important Correspondence. New York: Hall & Brother, 1855.

Douglass, Frederick. *My Bondage and My Freedom. Part I. Life as a Slave. Part II. Life as a Freeman.* New York: Miller, Ortin & Milligan, 1855.

Drew, Benjamin. *A North-Side View of Slavery. The Refugee: Or the Narratives of Fugitive Slaves in Canada.* Boston: John P. Jewett, 1856.

Ellicott, Andrew. *The Journal of Andrew Ellicott, Late Commissioner on Behalf of the United States during part of the year 1796, the years 1797, 1798, 1799, and part of the year 1800.* Philadelphia: Budd & Bertram, for Thomas Dobson, 1803.

Elmer, Lucius, ed. *Digest of the Laws of New Jersey.* 2nd ed. Philadelphia: J. B. Lippincott, 1855.

Etiquette at Washington; Together with the Customs Adopted by the Polite Society in the Other Cities of the United States. 2nd ed. Washington, DC: Taylor & Maury, 1850.

Fairfax, Thomas. *Journey from Virginia to Salem, Massachusetts, 1799.* London: Printed for private circulation, 1936.

Fearon, Henry Bradshaw. *Sketches of America: A Narrative of a Journey of Five Thousand Miles through the Eastern and Western States of America.* London: Longman, Hurst, Rees, Orme, and Brown, 1818.

Flint, James. *Letters from America, Containing Observations on the Climate and Agriculture of the Western States.* Edinburgh: W. & C. Tait, 1822.

Flint, Timothy, ed. *Recollections of the Last Ten Years: Passed in Occasional Residences and Journeyings in the Valley of the Mississippi, from Pittsburg and the Missouri to the Gulf of Mexico, and from Florida to the Spanish Frontier: In a Series of Letters to the Rev. James Flint.* Boston: Cummings, Hilliard, and Company, 1826.

Fry, J., comp. *The Albany Directory, Containing about Two Thousand Names, Arranged in Alphabetical Order.* Albany: Websters and Skinners, 1813.

General Index to the Laws of Pennsylvania in Five Volumes. From the Year 1700, to the Thirty-First of March, Inclusive. Philadelphia: John Bioren, 1812.

George, Daniel. *An Almanack, for the Year of Our Lord and Saviour, 1777. Being First after Leap Year, Calculated for the Meridian of Boston.* [Boston] Massachusetts-Bay: Draper and Phillips, 1776.

Geyer, Henry S. *A Digest of the Laws of Missouri Territory.* Saint Louis: Joseph Charless, 1818.

Gilpin, Joshua. *Pleasure and Business in Western Pennsylvania: The Journal of Joshua Gilpin, 1809.* Edited by Joseph E. Walker. Harrisburg: Pennsylvania Historical and Museum Commission, 1975.

Gordon, Thomas F. *Gazetteer of the State of New York.* New York: Printed for the Author, 1836.

Graydon, Alexander. *Memoirs of a Life, Chiefly Passed in Pennsylvania, within the Last Sixty Years; with Occasional Remarks upon the General Occurrences, Character and Spirit of That Eventful Period.* Harrisburg: John Wyeth, 1811.

Grimké, John Faucheraud. *The Public Laws of the State of South-Carolina, From Its First Establishment as a British Province down to the Year, 1790, Inclusive.* Philadelphia: R. Aitken & Son, 1790.

Groton (Connecticut) Selectmen. *The Civil Authority and Select-Men of the Town of Groton.* [New London, CT]: Timothy Green, 1778.

Guide to the Stranger, or, Pocket Companion for the Fancy: Containing a List of the Gay Houses and Ladies of Pleasure in the City of Brotherly Love and Sisterly Affection. Philadelphia: [n.p., 1849].

Hall, Basil. *Travels in North America, in the Years 1827 and 1828.* 2 Vols. Philadelphia: Carey, Lea & Carey, 1829.

Hardie, James. *The Philadelphia Directory and Register: Containing the Names, Occupations and Places of Abode of the Citizens, Arranged in Alphabetical Order.* Philadelphia: T. Dobson, 1793.

Harris' General Business Directory, of the Cities of Pittsburgh & Allegheny. Pittsburgh: A. A. Anderson, 1841.

Harris's General Business Directory of the Cities of Pittsburgh & Allegheny: With the Environs. Pittsburgh: A. A. Anderson, 1847.

Harris' Pittsburgh & Allegheny Directory, with the Environs, &c. Pittsburgh: A. A. Anderson, 1839.

Heads of Families at the First Census of the United States Taken in the Year 1790, North Carolina. Washington, D.C.: U.S. Government Printing Office, 1908.

Heads of Families at the First Census of the United States Taken in the Year 1790, Virginia. Washington: U.S. Government Printing Office, 1908.

Henderson, Madison, Alfred Amos Warrick, James W. Seward, and Charles Brown. *Trials and Confessions of Madison Henderson, Alias Blanchard, Alfred Amos Warrick, James W. Seward, and Charles Brown, Murderers of Jesse Baker and Jacob Weaver, as Given by Themselves; and a Likeness of Each, Taken in Jail Shortly after Their Arrest.* Saint Louis: Printed by Chambers & Knapp–Republican Office, 1841.

Henson, Josiah. *An Autobiography of Rev. Josiah Henson.* London: Schuyler, Smith, 1881.

———. *The Life of Josiah Henson, Formerly a Slave, Now an Inhabitant of Canada, as Narrated by Himself.* Boston: A. D. Phelps, 1849.

Hertell, Thomas. *An Expose of the Causes of Intemperate Drinking, and the Means by which It May Be Obviated.* New York: E. Conrad, 1820.

History of the English Settlement in Edwards County, Illinois, Founded in 1817 and 1818, by Morris Birkbeck and George Flower. Chicago: Fergus Printing Company, 1882.

Hotchkiss, William A. *A Codification of the Statute Law of Georgia.* Savannah: John M. Cooper, 1845.

Houstoun, Mrs. (Matilda Charlotte). *Hesperos: Or, Travels in the West.* London: J. W. Parker, 1850.

Hunter, Robert. *Quebec to Carolina in 1785–1786, Being the Travel Diary and Observations of Robert Hunter, Jr., a Young Merchant of London.* Edited by Louis B. Wright and Marion Tinling. San Marino, CA: Huntington Library, 1943.

Index to the Laws of New Hampshire: Recorded in the Office of the Secretary of State, 1679–1883. Manchester: John B. Clarke, 1886.

"Innkeeper's Liability. Evidence. Testimony of Plaintiff." *Livingston's Monthly Law Magazine* 3, no. 7 (July 1855): 467–69.

Iredell, James. *A Treatise on the Law of Executors and Administrators in North Carolina.* Raleigh: North Carolina Institution for the Deaf and Dumb and the Blind, 1851.

Jacobs, Harriet A. *Incidents in the Life of a Slave Girl. Written by Herself.* Boston: Published for the Author, 1861.

James, Benjamin. *A Digest of the Laws of South-Carolina, Containing the Public Statute Law of the State Down to the Year 1822.* Columbia: Telescope Press, 1822.

Jefferson, Thomas. *Notes on the State of Virginia.* 2nd American ed. Philadelphia: H. C. Carey & L. Lea, 1825.

Journal of the Proceedings of the Senate and House of Representatives of the General Assembly of South Carolina, at Its Regular Session of 1839. Columbia: A. H. Pemberton, 1839.

Kent, James. *Commentaries on American Law.* New York: O. Halstead, 1827.

———. *Commentaries on American Law.* 7th ed. New York: William Kent, 1851.

Knight, Henry C. (Henry Cogswell). *Letters from the South and West, by Arthur Singleton, Esq.* Boston: Richardson and Lord, 1824.

Lampi Collection of American Electoral Returns, 1788–1825. American Antiquarian Society, 2007.

Laws of the Territory of Michigan: Comprising the Acts, of a Public Nature, Revised by Commissioners Appointed by the First Legislative Council and Passed by the Second Council. Detroit: Sheldon & Wells, 1827.

Leavitt, Humphrey Howe. *The Ohio Officer and Justices' Guide: Embracing the Duties of Justices of the Peace, Constables, and Other Township Officers.* Steubenville, OH: James Turnbull, 1843.

"Liability of Innkeepers." *Livingston's Monthly Law Magazine* 3, no. 1 (January 1855): 1–5.

Littell, William, and Jacob Swigert. *A Digest of the Statute Law of Kentucky.* Frankfort: Kendall and Russell, 1822.

Loguen, J[ermain] W[esley]. *The Rev. J. W. Loguen, as a Slave and as a Freeman. A Narrative of Real Life.* Syracuse: J. G. K. Truair, 1859.

Longworth, David. *New-York Register and City Directory for the thirty-first year of American independence.* New York: David Longworth, 1806.

MacCabe, Julius P. Bolivar. *Directory of the City of Lexington and County of Fayette for 1838 & '39.* Lexington, KY: J. C. Noble, 1838.

Martineau, Harriet. *Retrospect of Western Travel.* 3 Vols. London: Saunders and Otley, 1838.

———. *Society in America, in Two Volumes.* London: Saunders and Otley, 1837.

Matchett, Edward. *The Baltimore Directory and Register, for the Year 1816: Containing the Names, Residence and Occupation of the Citizens.* Baltimore: Wanderer Office, 1816.

Matchett, Richard J. *Matchett's Baltimore Director, Corrected up to May 1833.* Baltimore: n.p., 1833.

Melish, John. *Travels in the United States of America, in the Years 1806 & 1807, and 1809, 1810, & 1811.* 2 Vols. Philadelphia: Printed for the Author, 1812.

Merrill, Eliphalet, and Phinehas Merrill. *Gazetteer of the State of New-Hampshire, in Three Parts.* Exeter: C. Norris, 1817.

Metcalf, Theron. *The General Laws of Massachusetts, from June 1822 to November, 1832.* Boston: Hilliard, Gray, Little, and Wilkins, 1832.

Miller, Lillian B., ed. *Charles Willson Peale: The Artist as Museum Keeper, 1791–1810.* Vol. 2. The Selected Papers of Charles Willson Peale and His Family. New Haven: Yale University Press, 1988.

Mitchell, S. Augustus. *Mitchell's Travellers Guide through the United States: A Map of the Roads, Distances, Steam Boat & Canal Routes &c.* Philadelphia: S. Augustus Mitchell, 1832.

Morgan, Albert. *Cape Ann Pavilion; The Gloucester House.* [Gloucester, MA]: n.p., 1849.

Morrison's Stranger's Guide and Etiquette, for Washington City and Its Vicinity. Washington, DC: W. H. and O. H. Morrison, 1860.

Mr. Pool, the First American That Ever Exhibited the Following Equestrian Feats of Horsemanship on the Continent, Intends Performing on Saturday Afternoon Next, Near the Powder-House. Providence: Printed by John Carter, 1786.

National Republican Ticket. For Congress, Luther Bradish. For Assembly, Gideon Hammond. For County Clerk, Leonard Stow. Essex County, NY: n.p., 1830.

New Jersey, Court of General Quarter Sessions of the Peace, Hunterdon County. *State of New-Jersey. At a Court of General Quarter Sessions of the Peace held at Flemington, in and for the county of Hunterdon, the first Tuesday in May, A.D. eighteen hundred and twenty [nine] the following rates & prices of the several liquors, meat and entertainment for man, and also for provender, stabling, and pasture for horse, to be taken by every licensed inn-holder and tavern-keeper in the county aforesaid, were ascertained* . . . Hunterdon County: n.p., 1829.

New York State. *Laws of the State of New York: Passed at the Seventy-First Session of the Legislature.* Albany: Charles Van Benthuysen, 1848.

———. *Laws of the State of New York: Passed at the Sixty-Third Session of the Legislature.* Albany: Thurlow Weed, 1840.

Northup, Solomon. *Twelve Years a Slave: Narrative of Solomon Northup, a Citizen of New-York, Kidnapped in Washington City in 1841, and Rescued in 1853.* Auburn [NY]: Derby and Miller, 1853.

Olmsted, Frederick Law. *The Cotton Kingdom: A Traveller's Observations on Cotton and Slavery in the American Slave States.* Edited by Arthur M. Schlesinger Sr. New York: Modern Library, 1984.

The Ordinances of the Mayor and City Council of Baltimore. Baltimore: John D. Toy, 1838.

Osborne, J. M. *Railroad Hotel at the Rail-Road Depot, Geneva.* [Geneva, NY]: n.p., 1850.

Osborne's New-Hampshire Register: With an Almanack for . . . 1788. Portsmouth, NH: George Jerry Osbourne, 1787.

Otter, William. *History of My Own Times; or, the Life and Adventures of William Otter, Sen. Comprising a Series of Events, and Musical Incidents Altogether Original.* Edited by Richard B. Stott. Ithaca: Cornell University Press, 1995.

Packard, J. G. *Pequot House, New London, Conn.* New London, CT: Taylor & Adams, engraver, 1859.

Petigru, J. L. *Portion of the Code of Statute Law of South Carolina, Submitted to the General Assembly.* Charleston: Evans & Cogswell, 1861.

The Pittsburgh Directory for 1815, Comprising the Names, Professions, and Residence of the Heads of Familys and Persons in Business, in the Borough of Pittsburgh with an Appendix Containing a Variety of Useful Information. Pittsburgh: Colonial Trust Company, 1905.

Prince, Oliver H. *A Digest of the Laws of the State of Georgia Containing All Statutes and the Substance of All Resolutions of a General and Public Nature, and Now in Force, which Have Been Passed in this State, Previous to the Session of the General Assembly of December, 1820.* Milledgeville: Grantland & Orme, 1822.

———. *A Digest of the Laws of the State of Georgia Containing All Statutes and the Substance of All Resolutions of a General and Public Nature, and Now in Force, which Have Been Passed in this State, Previous to the Session of the General Assembly of Dec. 1837.* 2nd ed. Athens: The Author, 1837.

The Proceedings Relative to Calling the Conventions of 1776 and 1790. Harrisburg, PA: John S. Wiestling, 1825.

Public Acts of the State of Maine, from 1832 to 1839 Inclusive. Augusta: William R. Smith, 1842.

Public Documents, Printed by Order of the Senate of the United States, Second Session of the Twenty-Third Congress. Washington, DC: Duff Green, 1834.

Redfield, Isaac Fletcher. *The Law of Carriers of Goods and Passengers, Private and Public, Inland and Foreign, by Railway, Steamboat, and Other Modes of Transportation.* Cambridge, MA: H. O. Houghton, 1869.

Reeves, John B., comp. "Extracts from the Letter-Books of Lieutenant Enos Reeves, of the Pennsylvania Line." *Pennsylvania Magazine of History and Biography* 21, nos. 1–4 (1897): 72–85, 235–56, 376–91, 466–76.

Report of the Committee of Investigation of the Northern Railroad to the Stockholders, May, 1850. Concord, NH: Asa McFarland, 1850.

Report of the Directors of the Michigan Central Railroad Company to the Stockholders. Boston: Wright & Potter, 1865.

Report of the Proceedings of the Colored National Convention, Held at Cleveland, Ohio. Rochester, NY: John Dick, 1848.

The Revised Code of the Laws of Mississippi in which Are Comprised All Such Acts of the General Assembly of a Public Nature as Were in Force at the End of the Year 1823. Natchez: Francis Baker, 1824.

The Revised Code of the Laws of Virginia: Being a Collection of All Such Acts of the General Assembly, of a Public and Permanent Nature as Are Now in Force; with a General Index. Vol. 1. Richmond: Thomas Ritchie, 1819.

Revised Laws of Indiana, Adopted and Enacted by the General Assembly at Their Eighth Session. Corydon, IN: Carpenter and Douglass, 1824.

Revised Laws of Indiana, in which Are Comprised All Such Acts of a General Nature as Are in the Force in the Said State; Adopted and Enacted by the General Assembly at Their Fifteenth Session. Indianapolis: Douglass and Maguire, 1831.

Revised Statutes of the State of Delaware, to the Year of Our Lord One Thousand Eight Hundred and Fifty-Two, Inclusive. Dover, DE: Samuel Kimmey, 1852.

Revised Statutes of the State of Mississippi. Jackson: G. R. & J. S. Fall, 1836.

Revised Statutes of the Territory of Iowa. Iowa City: Hughes & Williams, 1843.

Richards, T. Addison, ed. *Appletons' Companion Hand-Book of Travel: Containing a Full Description of the Principal Cities, Towns, and Places of Interest, Together with Hotels and Routes of Travel through the United States and the Canadas.* New York: Appleton, 1860.

Royall, Anne Newport. *Letters from Alabama on Various Subjects: To which is Added, an Appendix, Containing Remarks on Sundry Members of the 20th & 21st Congress, and Other High Characters, &c. &c. at the Seat of Government.* Washington, DC: n.p., 1830.

———. *Mrs. Royall's Southern Tour, or, Second Series of the Black Book.* 3 Vols. Washington, DC: n.p., 1831.

Salem (Massachusetts), and David Britton. *List of Prices for the Town of Salem.* Danvers, [MA]: E. Russell, 1779.

Sansom, Joseph. "Travels in Lower Canada, with the Author's Recollections of the Soil, and Aspect; the Morals, Habits, and Religious Institutions, of That Country." In *New Voyages and Travels; Consisting of Originals and Translations,* vol. 3, no. 1, edited and compiled by Richard Phillips. London: Sir Richard Phillips, 1819–1823.

Second Annual Report of the Managers of the Society for the Prevention of Pauperism in the City of New-York. New York: E. Conrad, 1820.

The Seventeenth, Eighteenth and Nineteenth Annual Reports of the Board of Public Works to General Assembly of Virginia. Vol. 7. Richmond: Samuel Shepherd, 1835.

Shepherd, Samuel. *Statutes at Large of Virginia, from October Session 1792, to December Session 1806, Inclusive, in Three Volumes.* Richmond: Samuel Shepherd, 1835.

Shurtleff, R. *Island House, Bellows Falls Vt.* [Bellows Falls, VT]: n.p., 1855.

Simons, James A. *Circular. Lake Dunmore House.* Salisbury, VT: n.p., 1857.

Spafford, Horatio Gates. *A Gazetteer of the State of New York.* Albany: B. D. Packard, 1824.

Stafford, Cornelius William. *The Philadelphia Directory for 1799.* Philadelphia: William W. Woodward, 1799.

Statutes of the State of New Jersey. Trenton: Phillips & Boswell, 1847.

Statutes of the Territory of Wisconsin, Passed by the Legislative Assembly Thereof, at a Session Commencing in November 1838, and at an Adjourned Session Commencing in January, 1839. Albany, NY: Packard, Van Benthuysen, 1839.

"Steamboats Liable for Robbery." *Hunt's Merchants' Magazine and Commercial Review* 33, no. 5 (November 1855): 590–92.

Story, Joseph. *Commentaries on the Law of Bailments, with Illustrations from the Civil and the Foreign Law.* London: John Richards, 1839.

Story, William W. *A Treatise on the Law of Contracts.* Boston: Little, Brown, 1856.

Strickland, William. *Journal of a Tour in the United States of America, 1794–1795.* New York: New-York Historical Society, 1971.

Stuart-Wortley, Lady Emmeline Charlotte Elizabeth (Manners). *Travels in the United States, Etc., during 1849 and 1850.* London: R. Bentley, 1851.

Tate, Joseph. *A Digest of the Laws of Virginia: Which Are of a Permanent Character and General Operation.* Richmond: Shepherd and Pollard, 1823.

Tavern Rates, as Fixed by the Court of General Quarter Sessions of the Peace, at New Brunswick in and for the County of Middlesex of the Term of March, One Thousand, Eight Hundred and Nine, n.p., 1809.

Tavern Rates, Established at Baltimore-County April Term, 1789. [Baltimore: John Hayes], 1789.

Temple, George. *The American Tourist's Pocket Companion, or, a Guide to the Springs, and Trip to the Lakes.* New York: D. Longworth, 1812.

Thomas, Jerry. *How to Mix Drinks, or The Bon-Vivant's Companion.* New York: Dick & Fitzgerald, 1862.

Tobler, John. *The Georgia and South-Carolina Almanack, for the Year of Our Lord 1774.* Charleston: Wells for Johnson in Savannah, 1773.

Tocqueville, Alexis de. *Democracy in America.* Translated by Francis Bowen. 2 Vols. Cambridge: Sever and Francis, 1862.

Toulmin, Harry, comp. *Digest of the Laws of the State of Alabama: Containing the Statutes and Resolutions in Force at the End of the General Assembly in January, 1823.* New York: Ginn & Curtis, 1823.

Trimble, Allen. "Autobiography of Allen Trimble." *The "Old Northwest" Genealogical Quarterly* 10, no. 1 (January 1907): 1–48.

Trollope, Frances. *Domestic Manners of the Americans.* London: Whittacher, Treacher, 1832.

Tubbee, Okah, and Rev. L[ewis] L[eonidas] Allen. *A Thrilling Sketch of the Life of the Distinguished Chief Okah Tubbee Alias, Wm. Chubbee, Son of the Head Chief, Mosholeh Tubbee, of the Choctaw Nation of Indians.* New York: n.p., 1848.

United States Hotel. *United States Hotel, Boston. By Spooner & Silsby.* Boston: n.p., 1850.

Vandewater, Robert J. *The Tourist, or Pocket Manual for Travellers on the Hudson River, the Western Canal, and Stage Road, to Niagara Falls.* New York: J. & J. Harper, 1830.

Washington Hotel. Timothy Boston, has the pleasure to inform his friends and the public generally, that he has recently enlarged his establishment. [Portland: ME], 1819.

Watkins, Robert, and George Watkins. *A Digest of the Laws of the State of Georgia.* Philadelphia: R. Aitken, 1800.

Webster's 1828 American Dictionary. Compact ed. West Valley City, UT: Waking Lion Press, 2010.

Weld, Isaac, Jr. *Travels through the States of North America and the Provinces of Upper and Lower Canada, during the Years 1795, 1796, and 1797.* London: John Stockdale, 1799.

Weld, Theodore Dwight. *American Slavery as It Is: Testimony of a Thousand Witnesses.* New York: American Anti-Slavery Society, 1839.

Wenham (Massachusetts), and Josiah Fairfield. *The Price Act: Or, the List of the Prices Now in Force in the Town of Wenham, for the Prevention of Monopoly and Oppression.* Danvers, MA: E. Russell, 1777.

West, Benjamin, and Joseph Callender. *Bickerstaff's Boston Almanack, for the Year of Our Redemption, 1774.* Boston: Mills and Hicks, 1773.

Williams, C. S. *Williams' Lexington Directory, City Guide, and Business Mirror.* Lexington, KY: Hitchcock & Searles, 1859.

Williams, Charles L., comp. *The Compiled Statutes of the State of Vermont Being Such of the Revised Statutes, and of the Public Acts and Laws Passed since, as Are Now in Force.* Burlington: Chauncey Goodrich, 1851.

Williams, W. *Appleton's Northern and Eastern Travellers' Guide.* New York: Appleton, 1850.

———. *Appleton's Railroad and Steamboat Companion: Being a Traveller's Guide through New England and the Middle States, with Routes in the Southern and Western States, and Also in Canada.* New York: D. Appleton, 1847.

Willson, Elizabeth Lundy. *A Journey in 1836 from New Jersey to Ohio, Being the Diary of Elizabeth Lundy Willson.* Edited by William C. Armstrong. Morrison, IL: Shawver Publishing, 1929.

Secondary Sources

Abraham, Kenneth S. "The Common Law Prohibition on Party Testimony and the Development of Tort Liability." *Virginia Law Review* 95, no. 3 (May 2009): 489–515.

Adams, Charles Francis, Jr. *Railroads: Their Origin and Problems.* New York: Putnam, 1879.

Adams, Donald R., Jr. "Prices and Wages in Antebellum America: The West Virginia Experience." *Journal of Economic History* 52, no. 1 (March 1992): 206–16.

Alexander, Ruth M. "'We Are Engaged as a Band of Sisters': Class and Domesticity in the Washingtonian Temperance Movement, 1840–1850." *Journal of American History* 75, no. 3 (December 1988): 763–85.

Allen, Michael. *Western Rivermen, 1763–1861: Ohio and Mississippi Boatmen and the Myth of the Alligator Horse.* Baton Rouge: Louisiana State University Press, 1990.

Allgor, Catherine. *Parlor Politics: In which the Ladies of Washington Help Build a City and a Government.* Charlottesville: University Press of Virginia, 2000.

Altschuler, Glenn C., and Stuart M. Blumin. *Rude Republic: Americans and Their Politics in the Nineteenth Century.* Princeton: Princeton University Press, 2000.

Ameri, Mason, Sean Edmund Rogers, Lisa Schur, and Douglas Kruse. "No Room at the Inn? Disability Access in the New Sharing Economy." *Academy and Management Discoveries* 6, no. 2 (2020): 176–205.

Anderson, Patricia Dockman. "'By Legal or Moral Suasion Let Us Put It Away': Temperance in Baltimore, 1829–1870." PhD diss., University of Delaware, 2008.

Anker, Elisabeth R. *Ugly Freedoms*. Durham, NC: Duke University Press, 2022.

Appleby, Joyce. *Inheriting the Revolution: The First Generation of Americans*. Cambridge, MA: Belknap, 2000.

———., ed. *Recollections of the Early Republic: Selected Autobiographies*. Boston: Northeastern University Press, 1997.

Atack, Jeremy. "Transportation in American Economic History." In *The Oxford Handbook of American Economic History*, edited by Louis Cain, Price V. Fishback, and Paul D. Rhode, 2:23–53. New York: Oxford University Press, 2018.

Atack, Jeremy, Michael Haines, and Robert A. Margo. "Railroads and the Rise of the Factory: Evidence for the United States, 1850–1870." In *Economic Evolution and Revolution in Historical Time*, edited by Paul W. Rhode, Joshua L. Rosenbloom, and David F. Weiman, 162–79. Stanford: Stanford University Press, 2011.

Atkinson, Joseph. *History of Newark, New Jersey*. Newark: William B. Guild, 1878.

Attali, Jacques. *Noise: The Political Economy of Music*. Minneapolis: University of Minnesota Press, 1985.

Augst, Thomas. "Temperance, Mass Culture, and the Romance of Experience." *American Literary History* 19, no. 2 (Summer 2007): 297–323.

Avril, Emmanuelle, and Johann N. Neem, eds. *Democracy, Participation and Contestation: Civil Society, Governance and the Future of Liberal Democracy*. New York: Routledge, 2014.

Ball, Erica L. *To Live an Antislavery Life: Personal Politics and the Antebellum Black Middle Class*. Athens: University of Georgia Press, 2012.

Banner, Stuart. *Speculation: A History of the Fine Line between Gambling and Investing*. New York: Oxford University Press, 2017.

Baptist, Edward E. "'Cuffy,' 'Fancy Maids,' and 'One-Eyed Men': Rape, Commodification, and the Domestic Slave Trade in the United States." *American Historical Review* 106 (December 2001): 1619–50.

———. *The Half Has Never Been Told: Slavery and the Making of American Capitalism*. New York: Basic Books, 2014.

———. "'Stol' and Fetched Here': Enslaved Migration, Ex-Slave Narratives, and Vernacular History." In *New Studies in the History of American Slavery*, edited by Edward E. Baptist and Stephanie M. H. Camp, 243–74. Athens: University of Georgia Press, 2006.

Barker-Benfield, G. J. *The Culture of Sensibility: Sex and Society in Eighteenth-Century Britain*. Chicago: University of Chicago Press, 1992.

Barleen, Steven D. *The Tavern: A Social History of Drinking and Conviviality*. Santa Barbara: Greenwood, 2019.

Barnhurst, Kevin G., and John Nerone. *The Form of News: A History*. New York: Guilford, 2001.

Barrett, Edith J. "Defining Their Right to the City: Perspectives from Lower-Income Youth." *Urban Affairs Review* 57, no. 3 (May 2019): 709–30.

Bateman, David A. "Democratization in the USA? The Impact of Antebellum Suffrage Qualifications on Politics and Policy." Working paper, Yale University, New Haven, 2020.

Bates, R. M. "Government by Improvisation? Towards a New History of the Nineteenth-Century American State." *Journal of Policy History* 33, no. 3 (2021): 287–316.

Baxter, William T. "Observations on Money, Barter and Bookkeeping." *Accounting Historians Journal* 31, no. 1 (June 2004): 129–39.

Bay, Mia. *Traveling Black: A Story of Race and Resistance.* Cambridge, MA: Belknap, 2021.

Beath, Robert B., comp. *An Historical Catalogue of the St. Andrew's Society of Philadelphia.* 2 Vols. Philadelphia: J. P. Lippincott, 1913.

Beckwith, Hiram Williams. *History of Vigo and Parke Counties, Together with Historic Notes on the Wabash Valley.* Chicago: H. H. Hill and N. Iddings, 1880.

Bederman, Gail. *Manliness and Civilization: A Cultural History of Gender and Race in the United States, 1880–1917.* Chicago: University of Chicago Press, 1995.

Beecher, Mary Anne. "The Motel in Builder's Literature and Architectural Publications." In *Roadside America: The Automobile in Design and Culture,* edited by Jan Jennings, 115–24. Ames: Iowa State University Press, 1990.

Belasco, Warren James. *Americans on the Road: From Autocamp to Motel, 1910–1945.* Baltimore: Johns Hopkins University Press, 1979.

Bell, Richard. *Stolen: Five Free Boys Kidnapped into Slavery and Their Astonishing Odyssey Home.* New York: Simon & Schuster, 2019.

Benes, Peter. *For a Short Time Only: Itinerants and the Resurgence of Popular Culture in Early America.* Amherst: University of Massachusetts Press, 2016.

Bensel, Richard Franklin. *The American Ballot Box in the Mid-Nineteenth Century.* Cambridge: Cambridge University Press, 2004.

Bergengren, Charles. "The Physical Thing Itself: Architectural/Stylistic/Material Aspects of the Gemberling-Rex Tavern/House, Schaefferstown." *Pennsylvania History: A Journal of Mid-Atlantic Studies* 75, no. 1 (Winter 2008): 91–118.

Berger, Molly W. *Hotel Dreams: Luxury, Technology, and Urban Ambition in America, 1829–1929.* Baltimore: Johns Hopkins University Press, 2011.

Berkin, Nicole. "Antebellum Touring and the Culture of Deception: The Case of Master Diamond." *Theatre History Studies* 34, no. 1 (2005): 39–58.

Berlant, Lauren. "Citizenship." In *Keywords for American Cultural Studies,* edited by Bruce Burgett and Glenn Hendler, 41–45. 2nd ed. New York: New York University Press, 2014.

Berlin, Ira. *Slaves without Masters: The Free Negro in the Antebellum South.* New York: Pantheon, 1974.

Berlin, Ira, and Philip D. Morgan. *The Slaves' Economy: Independent Production by Slaves in the Americas.* London: Frank Cass, 1991.

Berry, Daina Ramey. *The Price for Their Pound of Flesh: The Value of the Enslaved from Womb to Grave in the Building of a Nation.* Boston: Beacon, 2017.

———. *"Swing the Sickle for the Harvest Is Ripe": Gender and Slavery in Antebellum Georgia.* Urbana: University of Illinois Press, 2007.

Berry, George. *Taverns and Tokens of Pepys' London.* London: Seaby, 1978.

Biggs, Nina Mitchell, and Mabel Lee Mackoy. *History of Greenup County, Kentucky.* Evansville, IN: Unigraphic, 1975.

Biographical Directory of the United States Congress, 1774–2005. Washington, DC: United States Government Printing Office, 2005.

Birdi, Briony, Kerry Wilson, and Joanne Cocker. "The Public Library, Exclusion and Empathy: A Literature Review." *Library Review* 57, no. 8 (2008): 576–92.

Blaakman, Michael A. "'Haughty Republicans,' Native Land, and the Promise of Preemption." *William and Mary Quarterly* 78, no. 2 (April 2021): 243–50.

Black, Alex W. "Abolitionism's Resonant Bodies: The Realization of African American Performance." *American Quarterly* 63, no. 3 (September 2011): 619–39.

Blackford, Mansel G. "Small Business in America: A Historiographic Survey." *Business History Review* 65, no. 1 (1991): 1–26.

Blassingame, John W. "Using the Testimony of Ex-Slaves: Approaches and Problems." *Journal of Southern History* 41, no. 4 (November 1975): 473–92.

Blevins, Cameron. *Paper Trails: The US Post and the Making of the American West.* New York: Oxford University Press, 2021.

Blight, David W. *Frederick Douglass: Prophet of Freedom.* New York: Simon & Schuster, 2018.

Blocker, Jack S., Jr. "Tidy Pictures of Messy Behavior." *Journal of Urban History* 29, no. 4 (May 2003): 472–82.

Blumenthal, Susanna L. *Law and the Modern Mind: Consciousness and Responsibility in American Legal Culture.* Cambridge, MA: Harvard University Press, 2016.

Blumin, Stuart M. *The Emergence of the Middle Class: Social Experience in the American City, 1760–1900.* Cambridge: Cambridge University Press, 1989.

Bolton, Charles C. *Poor Whites of the Antebellum South: Tenants and Laborers in Central North Carolina and Northeast Mississippi.* Durham, NC: Duke University Press, 1994.

Bonner, Christopher James. *Remaking the Republic: Black Politics and the Creation of American Citizenship.* Philadelphia: University of Pennsylvania Press, 2020.

Bontrager, Shannon. "'From a Nation of Drunkards, We Have Become a Sober People': The Wyandot Experience in the Ohio Valley during the Early Republic." *Journal of the Early Republic* 32, no. 4 (Winter 2012): 603–32.

Boonshoft, Mark. "The Litchfield Network: Education, Social Capital, and the Rise and Fall of a Political Dynasty, 1784–1833." *Journal of the Early Republic* 34, no. 4 (Winter 2014): 561–95.

Borish, Linda J. "'Another Domestic Beast of Burden': New England Farm Women's Work and Well-Being in the 19th Century." *Journal of American Culture* 18, no. 3 (1995): 83–100.

Bouton, Terry. *Taming Democracy: "The People," the Founders, and the Troubled Ending of the American Revolution.* New York: Oxford University Press, 2007.

Bowes, John P. *Land Too Good for Indians: Northern Indian Removal.* Norman: University of Oklahoma Press, 2016.

Boydston, Jeanne. *Home and Work: Housework, Wages, and the Ideology of Labor in the Early Republic.* New York: Oxford University Press, 1990.

Boyer, Charles S. *Old Inns and Taverns of West Jersey.* Camden, NJ: Camden County Historical Society, 1962.

Boylan, Anne M. "Timid Girls, Venerable Widows and Dignified Matrons: Life Cycle Patterns among Organized Women in New York and Boston, 1797–1840." *American Quarterly* 38, no. 5 (Winter 1986): 779–97.

Bradburn, Douglas. *The Citizenship Revolution: Politics and the Creation of the American Union, 1774–1804.* Charlottesville: University of Virginia Press, 2009.

———. "'Parties Are Unavoidable': Path Dependence and the Origins of Party Politics in the United States." In *Practicing Democracy: Popular Politics in the United States from the Constitution to the Civil War,* edited by Daniel Peart and Adam I. P. Smith, 23–45. Charlottesville: University of Virginia Press, 2015.

Bradsby, Henry C. *History of Vigo County, Indiana.* Chicago: S. B. Nelson, 1891.

Branson, Susan. *These Fiery Frenchified Dames: Women and Political Culture in Early National Philadelphia.* Philadelphia: University of Pennsylvania Press, 2001.

Breen, Patrick. *The Land Shall Be Deluged in Blood: A New History of the Nat Turner Revolt.* Oxford: Oxford University Press, 2015.

Breen, T. H. *George Washington's Journey: The President Forges a New Nation.* New York: Simon & Schuster, 2016.

———. "Horses and Gentlemen: The Cultural Significance of Gambling among the Gentry of Virginia." *William and Mary Quarterly* 34, no. 2 (April 1977): 239–57.

Breitenbach, William. "Sons of the Fathers: Temperance Reformers and the Legacy of the American Revolution." *Journal of the Early Republic* 3, no. 1 (Spring 1983): 69–82.

Bremer, Jeff. *A Store Almost in Sight: The Economic Transformation of Missouri from the Louisiana Purchase to the Civil War.* Ames: University of Iowa Press, 2014.

Brettell, Caroline B. "Introduction: Travel Literature, Ethnography, and Ethnohistory." *Ethnohistory* 33, no. 2 (Spring 1986): 127–38.

Bric, Maurice J. "The United Irishmen, International Republicanism and the Definition of the Polity in the United States of America, 1791–1800." *Proceedings of the Royal Irish Academy: Archaeology, Culture, History, Literature* 104C, no. 4 (2004): 81–106.

Brightly, Frederick C. *Purdon's Digest: A Digest of the Laws of Pennsylvania.* 8th ed. Philadelphia: Kay & Brother, 1857.

Brooke, John L. *Columbia Rising: Civil Life on the Upper Hudson from the Revolution to the Age of Jackson.* Chapel Hill: University of North Carolina Press, 2010.

———. "Consent, Civil Society, and the Public Sphere in the Age of Revolution and the Early American Republic." In *Beyond the Founders: New Approaches to the Political History of the Early American Republic,* edited by Jeffrey L. Pasley, Andrew W. Robertson, and David Waldstreicher, 207–50. Chapel Hill: University of North Carolina Press, 2004.

———. "Cultures of Nationalism, Movements of Reform, and the Composite-Federal Polity: From Revolutionary Settlement to Antebellum Crisis." *Journal of the Early Republic* 29, no. 1 (Spring 2009): 1–33.

———. "Party, Nation, and Cultural Rupture: The Crisis of the American Civil War." In *Practicing Democracy: Popular Politics in the United States from the Constitution to the Civil War,* edited by Daniel Peart and Adam I. P. Smith, 72–95. Charlottesville: University of Virginia Press, 2015.

———. "Patriarchal Magistrates, Associated Improvers, and Monitoring Militias: Visions of Self-Government in the Early American Republic, 1760–1840." In *State and Citizen: British America and the Early United States,* edited by Peter Thompson and Peter S. Onuf, 178–217. Charlottesville: University of Virginia Press, 2013.

Brooks, Ulysses Robert. *South Carolina Bench and Bar.* Columbia, SC: State Company, 1908.

Brown, Alfred John. *History of Newton County, Mississippi: From 1834 to 1894.* Jackson: Clarion-Ledger, 1894.

Brown, Elsa Barkley. "Polyrhythms and Improvisation: Lessons for Women's History." *History Workshop* 31 (Spring 1991): 85–90.

———. "'What Has Happened Here': The Politics of Difference in Women's History and Feminist Politics." *Feminist Studies* 18, no. 2 (Summer 1992): 295–312.

Brown, Kathleen M. *Foul Bodies: Cleanliness in Early America.* New Haven: Yale University Press, 2009.

Brown, Richard D. "The Emergence of Urban Society in Rural Massachusetts, 1760–1820." *Journal of American History* 61, no. 1 (June 1974): 29–51.

Broyld, dann j. *Borderland Blacks: Two Cities in the Niagara Region during the Final Decades of Slavery.* Baton Rouge: Louisiana State University Press, 2022.

Brückner, Martin. *The Geographic Revolution in Early America: Maps, Literacy, and National Identity.* Chapel Hill: University of North Carolina Press, 2006.

———. *The Social Life of Maps in America, 1750–1860.* Chapel Hill: University of North Carolina Press, 2017.

Bruegel, Martin. "'An Acceptable Refreshment': The Meaning of Food and Drink in the Hudson Valley, 1780–1860." *Journal of Social History* 44, no. 4 (Summer 2011): 1157–71.

———. *Farm, Shop, Landing: The Rise of a Market Society in the Hudson Valley, 1780–1860.* Durham, NC: Duke University Press, 2002.

Buchanan, Thomas C. *Black Life on the Mississippi: Slaves, Free Blacks, and the Western Steamboat World.* Chapel Hill: University of North Carolina Press, 2004.

Burrow, Ian, William Liebeknecht, Damon Tvaryanas, Douglas Scott, Nadine Sergejeff, and Rebecca White. *John Tweed's Log Tavern: The Archaeology, History, and Architecture of the Guthrie-Giacomelli House (Tweed's Tavern), CRS-#N-1101 and Tweed's Tavern Archaeological Site, 7NC-A-18, Mill Creek Hundred, New Castle County, Delaware.* Dover: Delaware Department of Transportation, 2003.

Bushman, Richard L. *The Refinement of America: Persons, Houses, Cities.* New York: Vintage, 1993.

Butterfield, Kevin. *The Making of Tocqueville's America: Law and Association in the Early United States.* Chicago: University of Chicago Press, 2015.

Camp, Stephanie M. H. *Closer to Freedom: Enslaved Women and Everyday Resistance in the Plantation South.* Chapel Hill: University of North Carolina Press, 2004.

Campbell, John. "As 'a Kind of Freeman'? Slaves' Market-Related Activities in the South Carolina Upcountry, 1800–1860." *Slavery and Abolition* 12, no. 1 (1991): 131–69.

Campbell, Robert A. *Sit Down and Drink Your Beer: Regulating Vancouver's Beer Parlours, 1925–1954.* Toronto: University of Toronto Press, 2001.

Caric, Ric N. "The Man with the Poker Enters the Room: *Delirium Tremens* and Popular Culture in Philadelphia, 1828–1850." *Pennsylvania History: A Journal of Mid-Atlantic Studies* 74, no. 4 (Autumn 2007): 452–91.

Carlson, Douglas W. "'Drinks He to His Own Undoing': Temperance Ideology in the Deep South." *Journal of the Early Republic* 18, no. 4 (Winter 1998): 659–91.

Carnes, Mark C. *Secret Ritual and Manhood in Victorian America*. New Haven: Yale University Press, 1989.

Carp, Benjamin. *Rebels Rising: Cities and the American Revolution*. New York: Oxford University Press, 2007.

Carpenter, Daniel, and Nicole Topich. "Contested Boundaries of Representation: Patterns of Transformation in Black Petitioning in Massachusetts, 1770–1850." In *Democracy, Participation and Contestation: Civil Society, Governance and the Future of Liberal Democracy*, edited by Emmanuelle Avril and Johann N. Neem, 201–22. New York: Taylor & Francis, 2015.

Carr, Jacqueline Barbara. "Marketing Gentility: Boston's Businesswomen, 1780–1830." *New England Quarterly* 82, no. 1 (March 2009): 25–55.

Carter Jackson, Kellie. *Force and Freedom: Black Abolitionists and the Politics of Violence*. Philadelphia: University of Pennsylvania Press, 2019.

Cashin, Joan E. *A Family Venture: Men and Women on the Southern Frontier*. New York: Oxford University Press, 1991.

Castells, Manuel. *The City and the Grassroots: A Cross-Cultural Theory of Urban Social Movements*. London: E. Arnold, 1983.

Chambers, Thomas. *Drinking the Waters: Creating an American Leisure Class at Nineteenth-Century Mineral Springs*. Washington, DC: Smithsonian Institute Press, 2002.

Chandler, Alfred. *The Visible Hand: The Managerial Revolution in American Business*. Cambridge, MA: Harvard University Press, 1977.

Chaney, Michael A. "Digression, Slavery, and Failing to Return in the 'Narrative of the Sufferings of Lewis Clarke.'" *Biography* 39, no. 4 (Fall 2016): 511–34.

Chappell, Edward A., and Julie Richter. "Wealth and Houses in Post-Revolutionary Virginia." In *Exploring Everyday Landscapes: Perspectives in Vernacular Architecture*, edited by Annemarie Adams and Sally McMurry, 3–22. Knoxville: University of Tennessee Press, 1997.

Chappell, Gordon T. "Some Patterns of Land Speculation in the Old Southwest." *Journal of Southern History* 15, no. 4 (November 1949): 463–77.

Cheathem, Mark. *The Coming of Democracy: Presidential Campaigning in the Age of Jackson*. Baltimore: Johns Hopkins University Press, 2018.

Cheever, Susan. *Drinking in America: Our Secret History*. New York: Twelve, 2015.

Cherrington, Ernest H. *The Evolution of Prohibition in the United States of America*. Westerville, OH: American Issue Press, 1920.

Cincinnati (Ohio) City Council. *1802–1902 History of Council*. [Cincinnati]: Printed by order of the Board of Legislation, 1902.

Clapp, Elizabeth J. "Black Books and Southern Tours: Tone and Perspective in the Travel Writing of Mrs. Anne Royall." *Yearbook of English Studies* 34 (2004): 61–73.

———. "'A Virago-Errant in Enchanted Armor'? Anne Royall's 1829 Trial as a Common Scold." *Journal of the Early Republic* 23, no. 2 (Summer 2003): 207–32.

———. *A Notorious Woman: Anne Royall in Jacksonian America*. Charlottesville: University of Virginia Press, 2016.

Clark, Christopher. *The Roots of Rural Capitalism: Western Massachusetts, 1780–1860*. Ithaca: Cornell University Press, 1990.

———. *Social Change in America: From the Revolution through the Civil War*. Chicago: Ivan R. Dee, 2006.

Clark, Susan F. "Solo Black Performance before the Civil War: Mrs. Stowe, Mrs. Webb, and 'The Christian Slave.'" *New Theatre Quarterly* 13, no. 52 (November 1997): 339–48.

Clifton, Nick. "Coworking Spaces, Proximity, Innovation and the Fourth Space." *Proceedings* 81, no. 153 (2022): 1–5.

Clubb, Henry Stephen. *The Maine Liquor Law: Its Origin, History, and Results.* New York: Fowler & Wells, 1856.

Clytus, Radiclani. "'Keep It Before the People': The Pictorialization of American Abolitionism." *Early African American Print Culture,* edited by Lara Langer Cohen and Jordan Alexander Stein, 290–317. Philadelphia: University of Pennsylvania Press, 2012.

Coase, Ronald. "The Nature of the Firm." *Economica* 4, no. 16 (November 1937): 386–405.

Coclanis, Peter A. "Bookkeeping in the Eighteenth-Century South: Evidence from Newspaper Advertisements." *South Carolina Historical Magazine* 91, no. 1 (January 1990): 23–31.

Cogan, Jacob Katz. "The Look Within: Property, Capacity, and Suffrage in Nineteenth-Century America." *Yale Law Journal* 107, no. 2 (November 1997): 473–98.

Cohen, Andrew Wender, and Carol Faulkner. "Enforcing Gender at the Polls: Transing Voters and Women's Suffrage Before the American Civil War." *Journal of Social History* 56, no. 2 (Winter 2022): 386–410.

Cohen, Joanna. "'The Right to Purchase Is as Free as the Right to Sell': Defining Consumers as Citizens in the Auction-House Conflicts of the Early Republic." *Journal of the Early Republic* 30, no. 1 (Spring 2010): 25–62.

Cohen, Kenneth. "'The Entreaties and Perswasions of Our Acquaintance': Gambling and Networks in Early America." *Journal of the Early Republic* 31, no. 4 (Winter 2011): 599–638.

———. *They Will Have Their Game: Sporting Culture and the Making of the Early American Republic.* Ithaca: Cornell University Press, 2017.

Cohen, Laura Langer. *The Fabrication of American Literature: Fraudulence and Antebellum Print Culture.* Philadelphia: University of Pennsylvania Press, 2012.

Cohen, Patricia Cline. "Safety and Danger: Women on American Public Transport, 1750–1850." In *Gendered Domains: Rethinking Public and Private in Women's History: Essays from the Seventh Berkshire Conference on the History of Women,* edited by Dorothy O. Helly, 109–22. Ithaca: Cornell University Press, 1992.

———. "Women at Large: Travel in Antebellum America." *History Today* 44, no. 12 (1994): 44–50.

Cohen, Patricia Cline, Timothy J. Gilfoyle, Helen Lefkowitz Horowitz, and the American Antiquarian Society. *The Flash Press: Sporting Male Weeklies in 1840s New York.* Chicago: University of Chicago Press, 2008.

Cole, Harry Ellsworth. *Stagecoach and Tavern Tales of the Old Northwest.* Edited by Louise Phelps Kellogg. Carbondale: Southern Illinois University Press, 1997.

Cole, Stephanie. "Servants and Slaves: Domestic Service in the Border Cities, 1800–1850." PhD diss., University of Florida, 1994.

Coleman, J. Winston, Jr. *Stage-Coach Days in the Bluegrass; Being an Account of Stage-Coach Travel and Tavern Days in Lexington and Central Kentucky, 1800–1900.* Louisville, KY: Standard Press, 1935.

Columbia County at the End of the Century: A Historical Record of its Formation and Settlement, its Resources, its Institutions, its Industries, and its People. Hudson, NY: Record Printing and Publishing, 1900.

Commons, John R. "Institutional Economics." *American Economic Review* 26, no. 1 (March 1936): 237–49.

Conger, Vivian Bruce. *The Widows' Might: Widowhood and Gender in Early British America.* New York: New York University Press, 2009.

Conlin, Jonathan, ed. *The Pleasure Garden, from Vauxhall to Coney Island.* Philadelphia: University of Pennsylvania Press, 2013.

Connors, Anthony J. *Ingenious Machinists: Two Inventive Lives from the American Industrial Revolution.* Albany: State University of New York Press, 2014.

Conroy, David W. *In Public Houses: Drink and the Revolution of Authority in Colonial Massachusetts.* Chapel Hill: University of North Carolina Press, 1995.

Corbin, Alain. *Women for Hire: Prostitution and Sexuality in France after 1850.* Cambridge, MA: Harvard University Press, 1990.

Corrigan, Mary Beth. "Imaginary Cruelties? A History of the Slave Trade in Washington, D.C." *Washington History* 13, no. 2 (Fall/Winter 2001/2002): 4–27.

Cowell, Andrew. *At Play in the Tavern: Signs, Coins, and Bodies in the Middle Ages.* Ann Arbor: University of Michigan Press, 1999.

Cox, John D. *Traveling South: Travel Narratives and the Construction of American Identity.* Athens: University of Georgia Press, 2005.

Craig, Béatrice. *Backwoods Consumers and Homespun Capitalists: The Rise of a Market Culture in Eastern Canada.* Toronto: University of Toronto Press, 2009.

Criblez, Adam. "From Grog-Punch to Hard Cider: Tavern Culture on Ohio's Western Reserve, 1796–1840." M.A. thesis, Kent State University, 2003.

———. "'A Motley Array': Changing Perceptions of Chicago Taverns, 1833–1871." *Journal of Illinois History* 8 (Winter 2005): 262–80.

———. "Tavernocracy: Tavern Culture in Ohio's Western Reserve." *Northeast Ohio Journal of History* 2, no. 2 (Summer 2004): 60–83.

Cronon, William. *Nature's Metropolis: Chicago and the Great West.* New York: Norton, 1992.

Cross, Whitney R. *The Burned-over District; the Social and Intellectual History of Enthusiastic Religion in Western New York, 1800–1850.* Ithaca: Cornell University Press, 1950.

Crothers, Glenn A. "Banks and Economic Development in Post-revolutionary Northern Virginia, 1790–1812." *Business History Review* 73, no. 1 (Spring 1999): 1–39.

Crowley, John E. *The Invention of Comfort: Sensibilities and Design in Early Modern Britain and Early America.* Baltimore: Johns Hopkins University Press, 2001.

———. "The Sensibility of Comfort." *American Historical Review* 104, no. 3 (June 1999): 749–82.

Cutter, Daniel B. *History of the Town of Jaffrey, New Hampshire.* Concord, NH: Republican Press, 1881.

Dahl, Christian. "Unfreedom and the Crises of Witnessing: A Republican Perspective on the African American Slave Narratives." In *To Be Unfree: Republicanism and Unfreedom in History, Literature, and Philosophy,* edited by Christian Dahl and Tue Andersen Nexö, 213–28. Bielefeld, Germany: Transcript Verlag, 2014.

Damiano, Sara. *To Her Credit: Women, Finance, and the Law in Eighteenth-Century New England Cities*. Baltimore: Johns Hopkins University Press, 2021.

Daniels, Bruce C. *Puritans at Play: Leisure and Recreation in Colonial New England*. New York: Palgrave Macmillan, 2005.

Dannenbaum, Jed. *Drink and Disorder: Temperance Reform in Cincinnati from the Washingtonian Revival to the WCTU*. Urbana: University of Illinois Press, 1983.

Dartmouth College Alumni Association. *Memorials of Judges Recently Deceased, Graduates of Dartmouth College. 1880*. Concord, NH: Republican Press, 1881.

Davenport, Christian, Sarah A. Soule, and David A. Armstrong. "Protesting While Black? The Differential Policing of American Activism, 1960 to 1990." *American Sociological Review* 76, no. 1 (February 2011): 152–78.

Davis, Edwin Adams, and William Ransom Hogan. *The Barber of Natchez: wherein a slave is freed and rises to a very high standing; wherein the former slave writes a two-thousand-page journal about his town and himself; wherein the free Negro diarist is appraised in terms of his friends, his code, and his community's reaction to his wanton murder*. Baton Rouge: Louisiana State University Press, 1954.

Davis, Joseph Stancliffe. *Essays in the Earlier History of American Corporations*. Cambridge, MA: Harvard University Press, 1917.

Davis, Lance Edwin. "Stock Ownership in the Early New England Textile Industry." *Business History Review* 32, no. 2 (Summer 1958): 204–22.

DeGennaro, Jeremiah J. "From Civic to Social: New York's Taverns, Inside and Outside the Political Sphere." MA thesis, University of North Carolina at Greensboro, 2008.

Delbourgo, James. *A Most Amazing Scene of Wonders: Electricity and Enlightenment in Early America*. Cambridge, MA: Harvard University Press, 2006.

DeRogatis, Amy. *Moral Geography: Maps, Missionaries, and the American Frontier*. New York: Columbia University Press, 2003.

Deyle, Steven. *Carry Me Back: The Domestic Slave Trade in American Life*. New York: Oxford University Press, 2005.

Dictionary of American Biography. New York: Scribner, 1936.

Di Masso, Andrés. "Grounding Citizenship: Toward a Political Psychology of Public Space." *Political Psychology* 33, no. 1 (February 2012): 123–43.

Dierks, Konstantin. *In My Power: Letter Writing and Communications in Early America*. Philadelphia: University of Pennsylvania Press, 2009.

Ditz, Toby L. "The New Men's History and the Peculiar Absence of Gendered Power: Some Remedies from Early American Gender History." *Gender & History* 16, no. 1 (April 2004): 1–35.

———. *Property and Kinship: Inheritance in Early Connecticut, 1750–1820*. Princeton: Princeton University Press, 1986.

———. "Shipwrecked; or, Masculinity Imperiled: Mercantile Representations of Failure and the Gendered Self in Eighteenth-Century Philadelphia." *Journal of American History* 81, no. 1 (June 1994): 51–80.

———. "What's Love Got to Do with It? The History of Men, the History of Gender in the 1990s." *Reviews in American History* 28 (June 2000): 167–80.

Dorsey, Bruce. "'Making Men What They Should Be': Male Same-Sex Intimacy and Evangelical Religion in Early Nineteenth-Century New England." *Journal of the History of Sexuality* 24, no. 3 (September 2015): 347–77.

———. *Reforming Men and Women: Gender in the Antebellum City.* Ithaca: Cornell University Press, 2002.

Dubin, Michael J. *United States Congressional Elections, 1788–1997: The Official Results of the Elections of the 1st through 105th Congresses.* Jefferson, NC: McFarland, 1998.

Dudden, Faye E. *Serving Women: Household Service in Nineteenth-Century America.* Middletown, CT: Wesleyan University Press, 1983.

Duis, Perry R. *The Saloon: Public Drinking in Chicago and Boston, 1880–1920.* Urbana: University of Illinois Press, 1983.

Dupre, Daniel. "Barbecues and Pledges: Electioneering and the Rise of Democratic Politics in Antebellum Alabama." *Journal of Southern History* 60, no. 3 (August 1994): 479–512.

Durant, Samuel W., and Henry B. Peirce. *History of Jefferson County, New York, with Illustrations and Biographical Sketches of Some of Its Prominent Men and Pioneers.* Philadelphia: L. H. Everts, 1878.

Earle, Alice Morse. *Stage-Coach and Tavern Days.* New York: Macmillan, 1900.

Earle, Jonathan H. *Jacksonian Antislavery and the Politics of Free Soil, 1824–1854.* Chapel Hill: University of North Carolina Press, 2004.

Edwards, Justene Hill. *Unfree Markets: The Slaves' Economy and the Rise of Capitalism in South Carolina.* New York: Columbia University Press, 2021.

Edwards, Laura F. *Only the Clothes on Her Back: Clothing and the Hidden History of Power in the Nineteenth-Century United States.* New York: Oxford University Press, 2022.

———. *The People and Their Peace: Legal Culture and the Transformation of Inequality in the Post-Revolutionary South.* Chapel Hill: University of North Carolina Press, 2009.

Egerton, Douglas R. *Death or Liberty: African Americans and Revolutionary America.* New York: Oxford University Press, 2009.

Elkins, Stanley, and Eric McKitrick. *The Age of Federalism.* New York: Oxford University Press, 1993.

Eyal, Yonatan. *The Young America Movement and the Transformation of the Democratic Party, 1828–1861.* New York: Cambridge University Press, 2007.

Faragher, Johnny, and Christine Stansell. "Women and Their Families on the Overland Trail to California and Oregon, 1842–1867." *Feminist Studies* 2, no. 2/3 (1975): 150–66.

Farber, Hannah. "Practical Americans." *William and Mary Quarterly* 78, no. 2 (April 2021): 339–57.

Fehrenbacher, Don E. *The Slaveholding Republic: An Account of the United States Government's Relations to Slavery.* Edited by Ward M. McAfee. New York: Oxford University Press, 2001.

Feller, Daniel. "The Market Revolution Ate My Homework." *Reviews in American History* 25, no. 3 (September 1997): 408–15.

Field, Corinne T. *The Struggle for Equal Adulthood: Gender, Race, Age, and the Fight for Citizenship in Antebellum America.* Chapel Hill: University of North Carolina Press, 2014.

Fisher, Louis. "The Votes of the 'Privileged Fair': Women's Suffrage in New Jersey, 1776–1807." BA thesis, Columbia University, 2011.

Fitz, Caitlin. *Our Sister Republics: The United States in an Age of American Revolutions.* New York: Liveright, 2016.

Flad, Harvey K. "The Parlor in the Wilderness: Domesticating an Iconic American Landscape." *Geographical Review* 99, no. 3 (July 2009): 356–76.

Fletcher, Holly Berkley. *Gender and the American Temperance Movement of the Nineteenth Century.* New York: Routledge, 2008.

Flint, Richard W. "Entrepreneurial and Cultural Aspects of the Early-Nineteenth Century Circus and Menagerie Business." In *Itinerancy in New England and New York*, edited by Peter Benes, 131–49. Boston: Boston University Press, 1986.

Fogleman, Aaron S. "From Slaves, Convicts, and Servants to Free Passengers: The Transformation of Immigration in the Era of the American Revolution." *Journal of American History* 85, no. 1 (June 1998): 43–76.

Follett, Richard. *The Sugar Masters: Planters and Slaves in Louisiana's Cane World, 1820–1860.* Baton Rouge: Louisiana State University Press, 2005.

Foner, Eric. *Free Soil, Free Labor, Free Men: The Ideology of the Republican Party before the Civil War.* New York: Oxford University Press, 1970.

Foote, Lorien. *The Gentlemen and the Roughs: Violence, Honor, and Manhood in the Union Army.* New York: New York University Press, 2010.

Foreman, P. Gabrielle, Jim Casey, and Sarah Lynn Patterson, eds. *The Colored Conventions Movement: Black Organizing in the Nineteenth Century.* Chapel Hill: University of North Carolina Press, 2021.

Fought, Leigh. *Women in the World of Frederick Douglass.* New York: Oxford University Press, 2017.

Foy, Charles R., and Michael I. Bradley. "The African American Community in Brushy Fork, Illinois, 1818–1861." *Journal of the Illinois State Historical Society* 112, no. 2 (Summer 2019): 129–62.

Franklin, John Hope, and Loren Schweninger. *Runaway Slaves: Rebels on the Plantation.* New York: Oxford University Press, 1999.

Fraser, Nancy. "Expropriation and Exploitation in Racialized Capitalism: A Reply to Michael Dawson." *Critical Historical Studies* 3, no. 1 (Spring 2016): 163–78.

Freehling, William W. *The Road to Disunion: Secessionists at Bay, 1776–1854.* New York: Oxford University Press, 1990.

———. *The Road to Disunion: Secessionists Triumphant, 1854–1861.* New York: Oxford University Press, 2008.

Freeman, Joanne B. *Affairs of Honor: National Politics in the New Republic.* New Haven: Yale University Press, 2002.

Frey, Sylvia R. *Water from the Rock: Black Resistance in a Revolutionary Age.* Princeton: Princeton University Press, 1991.

Freyer, Tony A. *The Passenger Cases and the Commerce Clause: Immigrants, Blacks, and States' Rights in Antebellum America.* Lawrence: University of Kansas Press, 2015.

Freyer, Tony A., and Daniel Thomas. "The Passenger Cases Reconsidered in Transatlantic Commerce Clause History." *Journal of Supreme Court History* 36, no. 3 (2011): 216–35.

Friend, Craig T. "Merchants and Markethouses: Reflections on Moral Economy in Early Kentucky." *Journal of the Early Republic* 17, no. 4 (Winter 1997): 553–74.

Funk, Kellen, and Lincoln A. Mullen. "The Spine of American Law: Digital Text Analysis and U.S. Legal Practice." *American Historical Review* 123, no. 1 (February 2018): 132–64.

Futhey, J. Smith, and Gilbert Cope. *History of Chester County, Pennsylvania, with Genealogical and Biographical Sketches.* Philadelphia: Louis H. Everts, 1881.

Galenson, David W. "The Rise and Fall of Indentured Servitude in the Americas: An Economic Analysis." *Journal of Economic History* 44, no. 1 (March 1984): 1–26.

Gamber, Wendy. *The Boardinghouse in Nineteenth-Century America.* Baltimore: Johns Hopkins University Press, 2007.

Gamble, Robert J. "'For Lucre of Gain and in Contempt of the Laws': Itinerant Traders and the Politics of Mobility in the Eighteenth-Century Mid-Atlantic." *Early American Studies* 13, no. 4 (Fall 2015): 836–55.

Garvin, Donna-Belle, and James L. Garvin. *On the Road North of Boston: New Hampshire Taverns and Turnpikes, 1700–1900.* Hanover, NH: University Press of New England, 1988.

Gassan, Richard H. *The Birth of American Tourism: New York, the Hudson Valley, and American Culture, 1790–1830.* Amherst: University of Massachusetts Press, 2008.

Gehner, John. "Libraries, Low-Income People, and Social Exclusion." *Public Library Quarterly* 29, no. 1 (2010): 39–47.

Gibbs, Patricia Ann. "Taverns in Tidewater Virginia, 1700–1770." MA thesis, College of William and Mary, 1968.

Gilfoyle, Timothy J. "Strumpets and Misogynists: Brothel 'Riots' and the Transformation of Prostitution in Antebellum New York City." *New York History* 68, no. 1 (January 1987): 44–65.

Gilmore, William J. *Reading Becomes a Necessity of Life: Material and Cultural Life in Rural New England, 1780–1835.* Knoxville: University of Tennessee Press, 1989.

Ginzberg, Lori D. "'Moral Suasion Is Moral Balderdash': Women, Politics, and Social Activism in the 1850s." *Journal of American History* 73, no. 3 (December 1986): 601–22.

———. *Untidy Origins: A Story of Woman's Rights in Antebellum New York.* Chapel Hill: University of North Carolina Press, 2005.

———. *Women and the Work of Benevolence: Morality, Politics and Class in the Nineteenth-Century United States.* New Haven: Yale University Press, 1990.

Goldenberg, Joseph A. "The Royal Navy's Blockade in New England Waters, 1812–1815." *International History Review* 6, no. 3 (August 1984): 424–39.

Goldfield, David. "The Urban South: A Regional Framework." *American Historical Review* 86, no. 5 (December 1981): 1009–34.

Goldin, Claudia, and Kenneth Sokoloff. "Women, Children, and Industrialization in the Early Republic: Evidence from the Manufacturing Censuses." *Journal of Economic History* 42, no. 4 (December 1982): 741–74.

Goldsmith, Sarah. *Masculinity and Danger on the Eighteenth-Century Grand Tour.* London: University of London Press, 2020.

Goloboy, Jennifer L. *Charleston and the Emergence of Middle-Class Culture in the Revolutionary Era.* Athens: University of Georgia Press, 2016.

———. "The Early American Middle Class." *Journal of the Early Republic* 25, no. 4 (Winter 2005): 537–45.

Gomez, Michael. *Exchanging Our Country Marks: The Transformation of African Identities in the Colonial and Antebellum South.* Chapel Hill: University of North Carolina Press, 1998.

Gorn, Elliot. "'Gouge and Bite, Pull Hair and Scratch': The Social Significance of Fighting in the Southern Backcountry." *American Historical Review* 90, no. 1 (February 1985): 18–43.

Gosse, Van. *The First Reconstruction: Black Politics in America from the Revolution to the Civil War*. Chapel Hill: University of North Carolina Press, 2021.

Gosse, Van, and David Waldstreicher, eds. *Revolutions and Reconstructions: Black Politics in the Long Nineteenth Century*. Philadelphia: University of Pennsylvania Press, 2020.

Grant, H. Roger. *Living in the Depot: The Two-Story Railroad Station*. Iowa City: University of Iowa Press, 1993.

Greenberg, Joshua R. *Bank Notes and Shinplasters: The Rage for Paper Money in the Early Republic*. Philadelphia: University of Pennsylvania Press, 2020.

Greve, Charles Theodore. *Centennial History of Cincinnati and Representative Citizens*. Chicago: Biographical Publishing, 1904.

Grier, Katherine C. *Culture and Comfort: Parlor Making and Middle-Class Identity, 1850–1930*. Washington, DC: Smithsonian Institution Press, 1997.

Grivno, Max. *Gleanings of Freedom: Free and Slave Labor along the Mason-Dixon Line, 1790–1860*. Urbana: University of Illinois Press, 2011.

Gronningsater, Sarah L. H. "'Expressly Recognized by Our Election Laws': Certificates of Freedom and the Multiple Fates of Black Citizenship in the Early Republic." *William and Mary Quarterly* 75, no. 3 (July 2018): 465–506.

Grubb, Farley. "Babes in Bondage? Debt Shifting by German Immigrants in Early America." *Journal of Interdisciplinary History* 37, no. 1 (Summer 2006): 1–34.

———. *German Immigration and Servitude in America, 1709–1920*. London: Routledge, 2011.

Gustafson, Sandra M. "American Literature and the Public Sphere." *American Literary History* 20, no. 3 (Fall 2008): 465–78.

Hadden, Sally E. *Slave Patrols: Law and Violence in Virginia and the Carolinas*. Cambridge, MA: Harvard University Press, 2001.

Halttunen, Karen. *Confidence Men and Painted Women: A Study of Middle-Class Culture in America, 1830–1870*. New Haven: Yale University Press, 1982.

Hammes, Raymond H. "Land Transactions in Illinois prior to the Sale of Public Domain." *Journal of the Illinois State Historical Society* 77, no. 2 (Summer 1984): 101–14.

Hampel, Robert L. *Temperance and Prohibition in Massachusetts, 1813–1852*. Ann Arbor: UMI Research Press, 1982.

Hanawalt, Barbara A. "The Host, the Law, and the Ambiguous Space of Medieval London Taverns." In *Medieval Crime and Social Control*, edited by Barbara A. Hanawalt and David Wallace, 204–23. Minneapolis: University of Minnesota Press, 1999.

Hanners, John. *"It Was Play or Starve": Acting in the Nineteenth-Century American Popular Theatre*. Bowling Green, OH: Bowling Green State University Popular Press, 1993.

Harbour, Jennifer R. *Organizing Freedom: Black Emancipation Activism in the Civil War Midwest*. Carbondale: Southern Illinois University Press, 2020.

Harris, Michael H. "The General Store as an Outlet for Books on the Southern Frontier, 1800–1850." *Journal of Library History, Philosophy, and Comparative Librarianship* 8, no. 3/4 (July–October 1973): 124–32.

Hart, Emma. "A British Atlantic World of Advertising? Colonial American 'For Sale' Notices in Comparative Context." *American Periodicals: A Journal of History & Criticism* 24, no. 2 (2014): 110–27.

———. *Building Charleston: Town and Society in the Eighteenth-Century British Atlantic World.* Charlottesville: University of Virginia Press, 2010.

———. *Trading Spaces: The Colonial Marketplace and the Foundations of American Capitalism.* Chicago: University of Chicago Press, 2019.

———. "Work, Family, and the Eighteenth-Century History of a Middle Class in the American South." *Journal of Southern History* 78, no. 3 (August 2012): 551–78.

Hartigan-O'Connor, Ellen. "The Personal Is Political Economy." *Journal of the Early Republic* 36, no. 2 (Summer 2016): 335–41.

———. "Public Sales and Public Values in Eighteenth-Century North America." *Early American Studies* 13, no. 4 (Fall 2015): 749–73.

———. *The Ties That Buy: Women and Commerce in Revolutionary America.* Philadelphia: University of Pennsylvania Press, 2009.

Harvey, Karen. *The Little Republic: Masculinity and Domestic Authority in Eighteenth-Century Britain.* Oxford: Oxford University Press, 2012.

Haulman, Kate. *The Politics of Fashion in Eighteenth-Century America.* Chapel Hill: University of North Carolina Press, 2011.

Haynes, Sam W. *Unfinished Revolution: The Early American Republic in a British World.* Charlottesville: University of Virginia Press, 2010.

Hedeen, Jane. *The Road to Prohibition in Indiana.* Indianapolis: Indiana Historical Society, 2011.

Heerman, M. Scott. "Reducing Free Men to Slavery: Black Kidnapping, the 'Slave Power,' and the Politics of Abolition in Antebellum Illinois, 1830–1860." *Journal of the Early Republic* 38, no. 2 (Summer 2018): 261–91.

Hegarty, Paul. *Noise/Music: A History.* New York: Continuum, 2009.

Hemphill, C. Dallett. *Bowing to Necessities: A History of Manners in America, 1620–1860.* New York: Oxford University Press, 1999.

Hemphill, Katie M. *Bawdy City: Commercial Sex and Regulation in Baltimore, 1790–1915.* Cambridge: Cambridge University Press, 2020.

Henkin, David M. *City Reading: Written Words and Public Spaces in Antebellum New York.* New York: Columbia University Press, 1998.

———. *The Postal Age: The Emergence of Modern Communications in Nineteenth-Century America.* Chicago: University of Chicago Press, 2006.

Herman, Bernard L. *Town House: Architecture and Material Life in the Early American City, 1780–1830.* Chapel Hill: University of North Carolina Press, 2005.

Hershberger, Mary. "Mobilizing Women, Anticipating Abolition: The Struggle against Indian Removal in the 1830s." *Journal of American History* 86, no. 1 (June 1999): 15–40.

Hessinger, Rodney. *Seduced, Abandoned, and Reborn: Visions of Youth in Middle-Class America, 1780–1850.* Philadelphia: University of Pennsylvania Press, 2005.

Hewitt, Nancy A. "Compounding Differences." *Feminist Studies* 18, no. 2 (Summer 1992): 313–26.

———. *Women's Activism and Social Change: Rochester, New York, 1822–1872.* Ithaca: Cornell University Press, 1984.

Hickey, James T., George W. Spotswood, C. G. Saunders, and Sarah Beck. "The Lincolns' Globe Tavern: A Study in Tracing the History of a Nineteenth-Century Building."

Journal of the Illinois State Historical Society (1908–1984) 56, no. 4 (Winter 1963): 629–53.

Higginbotham, Evelyn Brooks. "African-American Women's History and the Metalanguage of Race." *Signs* 17, no. 2 (Winter 1992): 251–74.

Hill, Marilyn Wood. *Their Sisters' Keepers: Prostitution in New York City, 1830–1870*. Berkeley: University of California Press, 1993.

Hilliard, Kathleen. *Masters, Slaves, and Exchange: Power's Purchase in the Old South*. Cambridge: Cambridge University Press, 2014.

Hilt, Eric. "Business Organization in American Economic History." In *The Oxford Handbook of American Economic History*, edited by Louis Cain, Price V. Fishback, and Paul D. Rhode, 1:261–87. New York: Oxford University Press, 2018.

———. "Early American Corporations and the State." In *Corporations and American Democracy*, edited by Naomi Lamoreaux and William Novak, 37–73. Cambridge, MA: Harvard University Press, 2017.

Hine, Robert V., John Mack Faragher and Jon T. Coleman. *The American West: A New Interpretive History*. 2nd ed. New Haven, CT: Yale University Press, 2017.

Hirota, Hidetaka. *Expelling the Poor: Atlantic Seaboard States and the Nineteenth-Century Origins of American Immigration Policy*. New York: Oxford University Press, 2017.

The History of Jefferson County, Wisconsin. Chicago: Western Historical, 1879.

Hodgson, John A. *Richard Potter: America's First Black Celebrity*. Charlottesville: University of Virginia Press, 2018.

Hodin, Stephen B. "The Mechanisms of Monticello: Saving Labor in Jefferson's America." *Journal of the Early Republic* 26, no. 3 (Fall 2006): 377–418.

Hoff, Joan. *Law, Gender, and Injustice: A Legal History of U.S. Women*. Rev. ed. New York: New York University Press, 1991.

Holmes, Oliver W., and Peter T. Rohrbach. *Stagecoach East: Stagecoach Days in the East from the Colonial Period to the Civil War*. Washington, DC: Smithsonian Institution Press, 1983.

Holness, Lucien. "Self-Emancipated Slaves, Black Militias, and Reimagining the Long Political Armed Struggle for Emancipation." Paper presented at the annual meeting of the Southern Historical Association, Baltimore, Maryland, 2022.

Holton, Woody. *Unruly Americans and the Origins of the Constitution*. New York: Hill and Wang, 2007.

Horwitz, Morton J. *The Transformation of American Law, 1780–1860*. Cambridge, MA: Harvard University Press, 1977.

Howe, Daniel Walker. *Political Culture of the American Whigs*. Chicago: University of Chicago Press, 1979.

———. *What Hath God Wrought: The Transformation of America, 1815–1848*. New York: Oxford University Press, 2007.

Howe, Henry. *Historical Collections of Ohio; Containing a Collection of the Most Interesting Facts, Traditions, Biographical Sketches, Anecdotes, etc.* Cincinnati: Bradley & Anthony, 1850.

Hubka, Thomas C. *Houses without Names: Architectural Nomenclature and the Classification of America's Common Houses*. Knoxville: University of Tennessee Press, 2013.

Hudson, Larry E. *To Have and to Hold: Slave Work and Family Life in Antebellum South Carolina.* Athens: University of Georgia Press, 1997.

Huebner, Timothy S. "Joseph Henry Lumpkin and Evangelical Reform in Georgia: Temperance, Education, and Industrialization, 1830–1860." *Georgia Historical Quarterly* 75, no. 2 (Summer 1991): 254–74.

Hughes, Amy E. *Spectacles of Reform: Theater and Activism in Nineteenth-Century America.* Ann Arbor: University of Michigan Press, 2012.

Hunt, James L. "Law, Business, and Politics: Liability for Accidents in Georgia, 1846–1880." *Georgia Historical Quarterly* 84, no. 2 (Summer 2000): 254–82.

Hunter, Louis C., and Beatrice Jones Hunter. *Steamboats on the Western Rivers: An Economic and Technological History.* New York: Dover, 1993.

Huston, Reeve. "Can 'the People' Speak? Popular Meetings and the Ambiguities of Popular Sovereignty in the United States, 1816–1828." In *Organizing Democracy: Reflections on the Rise of Political Organizations in the Nineteenth Century*, edited by Henk te Velde and Maartje Janse, 63–83. New York: Palgrave Macmillan, 2017.

———. *Land and Freedom: Rural Society, Popular Protest, and Party Politics in Antebellum New York.* New York: Oxford University Press, 2000.

———. "Rethinking 1828: The Emergence of Competing Democracies in the United States." In *Democracy, Participation and Contestation: Civil Society, Governance and the Future of Liberal Democracy*, edited by Emmanuelle Avril and Johann N. Neem, 13–24. New York: Routledge, 2014.

———. "Rethinking the Origins of Partisan Democracy in the United States, 1795–1840." In *Practicing Democracy: Popular Politics in the United States from the Constitution to the Civil War*, edited by Daniel Peart and Adam I. P. Smith, 46–71. Charlottesville: University of Virginia Press, 2015.

Imbarrato, Susan Clair. "Ordinary Travel: Tavern Life and Female Accommodation in Early America and the New Republic." *Women's Studies* 28, no. 1 (1998): 29–57.

———. *Traveling Women: Narrative Visions of Early America.* Athens: Ohio University Press, 2006.

Ingold, Tim. "Against Space: Place, Movement, Knowledge." In *Boundless Worlds: An Anthropological Approach to Movement*, edited by Peter Wynn Kirby, 29–43. New York: Berghahn, 2011.

Isaac, Rhys. *The Transformation of Virginia, 1740–1790.* New York: Norton, 1982.

Isenberg, Nancy. *Sex and Citizenship in Antebellum America.* Chapel Hill: University of North Carolina Press, 1998.

Jabour, Anya. "'The Privations and Hardships of a New Country': Southern Women and Southern Hospitality on the Florida Frontier." *Florida Historical Quarterly* 75, no. 3 (Winter 1997): 259–75.

———. *Scarlett's Sisters: Young Women in the Old South.* Chapel Hill: University of North Carolina Press, 2007.

Jaffee, David. "Peddlers of Progress and the Transformation of the Rural North, 1760–1860." *Journal of American History* 78, no. 2 (September 1991): 511–35.

Jasanoff, Maya. *Liberty's Exiles: American Loyalists in the Revolutionary World.* New York: Knopf, 2011.

Jefferson-Jones, Jamila. "'Driving while Black' as 'Living while Black.'" *Iowa Law Review* 106, no. 5 (2021): 2281–302.

Jeffrey, Julie Roy. *Abolitionists Remember: Antislavery Autobiographies and the Unfinished Work of Emancipation*. Chapel Hill: University of North Carolina Press, 2008.

———. *The Great Silent Army of Abolitionism: Ordinary Women in the Antislavery Movement*. Chapel Hill: University of North Carolina Press, 1998.

Jensen, Joan M. *Loosening the Bonds: Mid-Atlantic Farm Women, 1750–1850*. New Haven: Yale University Press, 1986.

———. "'You May Depend She Does Not Eat Much Idle Bread': Mid-Atlantic Farm Women and Their Historians." *Agricultural History* 61, no. 1 (Winter 1987): 29–46.

Jensen, Merrill. "The Cession of the Old Northwest." *Mississippi Valley Historical Review* 23, no. 1 (June 1936): 27–48.

John, Richard. *Spreading the News: The American Postal System from Franklin to Morse*. Cambridge, MA: Harvard University Press, 1995.

John, Richard R., and Thomas C. Leonard. "The Illusion of the Ordinary: John Lewis Krimmel's *Village Tavern* and the Democratization of Public Life in America." *Pennsylvania History* 65, no. 1 (Winter 1998): 87–96.

Johnson, Odai. *Absence and Memory in Colonial American Theatre: Fiorelli's Plaster*. New York: Palgrave Macmillan, 2006.

Johnson, Paul E. *The Early American Republic, 1789–1829*. New York: Oxford University Press, 2007.

———. "Playing with Race in the Early Republic: Mr. Potter, the Ventriloquist." *New England Quarterly* 89, no. 2 (June 2016): 257–85.

———. *A Shopkeeper's Millennium: Society and Revivals in Rochester, New York, 1815–1837*. New York: Hill and Wang, 1978.

Johnson, Rashauna. "'Laissez les bons temps rouler!' and Other Concealments: Households, Taverns, and Irregular Intimacies in Antebellum New Orleans." In *Interconnections: Gender and Race in American History*, edited by Carol Faulkner and Alison M. Parker, 51–74. Rochester, NY: University of Rochester Press, 2012.

Johnson, Walter. *River of Dark Dreams: Slavery and Empire in the Cotton Kingdom*. Cambridge, MA: Belknap, 2013.

———. *Soul by Soul: Life inside the Antebellum Slave Market*. Cambridge, MA: Harvard University Press, 1999.

Johnston, George. *History of Cecil County, Maryland*. Baltimore: Genealogical Publishing, 1998.

Jones, Martha S. *Birthright Citizens: A History of Race and Rights in Antebellum America*. New York: Cambridge University Press, 2018.

Jones-Rogers, Stephanie. *They Were Her Property: White Women as Slave Owners in the American South*. New Haven: Yale University Press, 2019.

Kachun, Mitch. *Festivals of Freedom: Memory and Meaning in African American Emancipation Celebrations, 1808–1915*. Amherst: University of Massachusetts Press, 2003.

Kamensky, Jane. *The Exchange Artist: A Tale of High-Flying Speculation and America's First Banking Collapse*. New York: Viking, 2008.

Kaplan, Michael. "New York Tavern Violence and the Creation of a Male Working-Class Identity." *Journal of the Early Republic* 15, no. 4 (Winter 1995): 592–617.

———. "The World of the B'Hoys: Urban Violence and the Political Culture of Antebellum New York City, 1825–1860." PhD diss., New York University, 1996.

Kars, Marjoleine. *Breaking Loose Together: The Regulator Rebellion in Pre-revolutionary North Carolina*. Chapel Hill: University of North Carolina Press, 2002.

Kasson, John F. *Rudeness and Civility: Manners in Nineteenth-Century Urban America*. New York: Hill and Wang, 1990.

Keller, Kate Van Winkle. *Dance and Its Music in America, 1528–1789*. Hilldale, NY: Pendragon, 2007.

Kelley, Mary. *Learning to Stand and Speak: Women, Education, and Public Life in America's Republic*. Chapel Hill: University of North Carolina Press, 2006.

Kelly, Catherine E. "'The Consummation of Rural Prosperity and Happiness': New England Agricultural Fairs and the Construction of Class and Gender, 1810–1860." *American Quarterly* 49, no. 3 (September 1997): 574–602.

———. *Republic of Taste: Art, Politics, and Everyday Life in Early America*. Philadelphia: University of Pennsylvania Press, 2016.

———. "'Well Bred Country People': Sociability, Social Networks, and the Creation of a Provincial Middle Class, 1820–1860." *Journal of the Early Republic* 19, no. 3 (Autumn 1999): 451–79.

Kennedy, Cynthia M. *Braided Relations, Entwined Lives: The Women of Charleston's Urban Slave Society*. Bloomington: Indiana University Press, 2005.

Kerber, Linda K. "Separate Spheres, Female Worlds, Woman's Place: The Rhetoric of Women's History." *Journal of American History* 75, no. 1 (June 1988): 9–39.

Kerr-Ritchie, Jeffrey R. "Rehearsal for War: Black Militias in the Atlantic World." *Slavery & Abolition* 26, no. 1 (2005): 1–34.

———. *Rites of August First: Emancipation Day in the Black Atlantic World*. Baton Rouge: Louisiana State University Press, 2007.

Kett, Joseph F. *Rites of Passage: Adolescence in America, 1790 to the Present*. New York: Basic Books, 1977.

———. "Temperance and Intemperance as Historical Problems." *Journal of American History* 67, no. 4 (March 1981): 878–85.

Kettner, James H. *The Development of American Citizenship, 1608–1870*. Chapel Hill: University of North Carolina Press, 1978.

Key, Samantha Sing. "Aristocratic Pretension in Republican Ballrooms: Dance, Etiquette, and Identity in Washington City, 1804." *Early American Studies: An Interdisciplinary Journal* 16, no. 3 (Summer 2018): 460–88.

Keyes, Carl Robert. "Advertising." In *U.S. Popular Print Culture to 1860*, edited by Ronald J. Zboray and Mary Saracino Zboray, 311–26. New York: Oxford University Press, 2019.

———. "History Prints, Newspaper Advertisements, and Cultivating Citizen Consumers: Patriotism and Partisanship in Marketing Campaigns in the Era of the Revolution." *American Periodicals: A Journal of History & Criticism* 24, no. 2 (2014): 145–85.

Keyssar, Alexander. *The Right to Vote: The Contested History of Democracy in the United States*. New York: Basic Books, 2000.

Khan, B. Zorina. "'Not for Ornament': Patenting Activity by Nineteenth-Century Women Inventors." *Journal of Interdisciplinary History* 31, no. 2 (Autumn 2000): 159–95.

———. "Property Rights and Patent Litigation in Early Nineteenth-Century America." *Journal of Economic History* 55, no. 1 (March 1995): 58–97.

Kierner, Cynthia. *Inventing Disaster: The Culture of Calamity from the Jamestown Colony to the Johnstown Flood*. Chapel Hill: University of North Carolina Press, 2019.

Kilbride, Daniel P. *Being American in Europe, 1750–1850*. Baltimore: Johns Hopkins University Press, 2013.

———. "Travel Writing as Evidence with Special Attention to Nineteenth-Century Anglo-America." *History Compass* 9, no. 4 (2011): 339–50.

King, Doris Elizabeth. "The First-Class Hotel and the Age of the Common Man." *Journal of Southern History* 23, no. 2 (May 1957): 173–88.

Klein, Rachel N. "Ordering the Backcountry: The South Carolina Regulation." *William and Mary Quarterly* 38, no. 4 (October 1981): 661–80.

———. *Unification of a Slave State: The Rise of the Planter Class in the South Carolina Backcountry*. Chapel Hill: University of North Carolina Press, 1990.

Klinghoffer, Judith Apter, and Lois Elkis. "'The Petticoat Electors': Women's Suffrage in New Jersey, 1776–1807." *Journal of the Early Republic* 12, no. 2 (Summer 1992): 159–93.

Knott, Sarah. *Sensibility and the American Revolution*. Chapel Hill: University of North Carolina Press, 2009.

Kohlburn, Joe, Jenny Bossaller, Hyerim Cho, Heather Moulaison-Sandy, and Denice Adkins. "Public Libraries and COVID-19: Perceptions and Politics in the United States." *Library Quarterly* 93, no. 1 (January 2023): 7–25.

Koschnik, Albrecht. "The Democratic Societies of Philadelphia and the Limits of the American Public Sphere, circa 1793–1795." *William and Mary Quarterly* 58, no. 3 (July 2001): 615–36.

———. "Fashioning a Federalist Self: Young Men and Voluntary Association in Early Nineteenth-Century Philadelphia." *Explorations in Early American Culture* 4 (2000): 220–57.

———. *"Let a Common Interest Bind Us Together": Associations, Partisanship, and Culture in Philadelphia, 1775–1840*. Charlottesville: University of Virginia Press, 2007.

———. "Young Federalists, Masculinity, and Partisanship during the War of 1812." In *Beyond the Founders: New Approaches to the Political History of the Early Republic*, edited by Jeffrey L. Pasley, Andrew W. Robertson, and David Waldstreicher, 159–79. Chapel Hill: University of North Carolina Press, 2004.

Kramer, Erin. "'That She Shall Be Forever Banished from This Country': Alcohol, Sovereignty, and Social Segregation in New Netherland." *Early American Studies* 20, no. 1 (Winter 2022): 3–42.

Kross, Jessica. "Mansions, Men, Women, and the Creation of Multiple Publics in Eighteenth-Century British North America." *Journal of Social History* 33, no. 2 (Winter 1999): 385–408.

LaBelle, Brandon. "Sharing Architecture: Space, Time and the Aesthetics of Pressure." *Journal of Visual Culture* 10, no. 2 (August 2011): 177–88.

Lamoreaux, Naomi R. *Insider Lending: Banks, Personal Connections, and Economic Development in Industrial New England*. Cambridge: Cambridge University Press, 1994.

———. "Rethinking the Transition to Capitalism in the Early American Northeast." *Journal of American History* 90, no. 2 (September 2003): 437–61.

Lamoreaux, Naomi R., Daniel M. G. Raff, and Peter Temin. "Beyond Markets and Hierarchies: Toward a New Synthesis of American Business History." *American Historical Review* 108, no. 2 (April 2003): 404–33.

Lamoreaux, Naomi R., and Kenneth L. Sokoloff. "Market Trade in Patents and the Rise of a Class of Specialized Inventors in the 19th Century United States." *American Economic Review* 91, no. 2 (May 2001): 39–44.

Lampert, Sara E. "Black Swan/White Raven: The Racial Politics of Elizabeth Greenfield's American Concert Career, 1851–1855." *American Nineteenth Century History* 17, no. 1 (2016): 75–102.

———. "'The Presence of Improper Females': Reforming Theater in Boston and Providence, 1820s–1840s." *New England Quarterly* 94, no. 3 (September 2021): 394–430.

Larkin, Janet Dorothy. *Overcoming Niagara: Canals, Commerce, and Tourism in the Niagara–Great Lakes Borderland Region, 1792–1837*. Albany: State University of New York Press, 2018.

Larson, John Lauritz. *Internal Improvement: National Public Works and the Promise of Popular Government in the Early United States*. Chapel Hill: University of North Carolina Press, 2001.

———. *The Market Revolution in America: Liberty, Ambition, and the Eclipse of the Common Good*. Cambridge: Cambridge University Press, 2010.

Lathrop, Elise. *Early American Inns and Taverns*. New York: Tudor Publishing, 1935.

Laurie, Bruce. *Artisans into Workers: Labor in Nineteenth-Century America*. New York: Noonday Press, 1989.

Laver, Harry S. *Citizens More than Soldiers: The Kentucky Militia and Society in the Early Republic*. Lincoln: University of Nebraska Press, 2007.

———. "Rethinking the Social Role of the Militia: Community-Building in Antebellum Kentucky." *Journal of Southern History* 68, no. 4 (November 2002): 777–816.

Lebergott, Stanley. "Labor Force and Employment, 1800–1860." In *Output, Employment, and Productivity in the United States after 1800*, edited by Dorothy S. Brady, 117–204. Cambridge, MA: National Bureau of Economic Research, 1966.

Lebsock, Suzanne. *The Free Women of Petersburg: Status and Culture in a Southern Town, 1784–1860*. New York: Norton, 1984.

Lemisch, Jesse. "Jack Tar in the Streets: Merchant Seamen in the Politics of Revolutionary America." *William and Mary Quarterly* 25, no. 3 (July 1968): 371–407.

Lennon, Heather Nicole. "A Stage for Gentility and the Performance of the Republican Gentleman: Taverns in Richmond, Virginia, 1780 to 1820." MA thesis, Virginia Polytechnic Institute and State University, 2013.

Lepler, Jessica. *The Many Panics of 1837: People, Politics, and the Creation of a Transatlantic Financial Crisis*. New York: Cambridge University Press, 2013.

Levine, Lawrence W. *Highbrow, Lowbrow: The Emergence of Cultural Hierarchy in America*. Cambridge, MA: Harvard University Press, 1988.

Levinson Wilk, Daniel. "Cliff Dwellers: Modern Service in New York City, 1800–1945." PhD diss., Duke University, 2005.

Levy, Jonathan. *Freaks of Fortune: The Emerging World of Capitalism and Risk in America*. Cambridge, MA: Harvard University Press, 2012.

Lewicka, Paulina B. "Restaurants, Inns and Taverns That Never Were: Some Reflections on Public Consumption in Medieval Cairo." *Journal of the Economic and Social History of the Orient* 48, no. 1 (2005): 40–91.

Lewis, Charlene M. Boyer. *Ladies and Gentlemen on Display: Planter Society at the Virginia Springs, 1790–1860.* Charlottesville: University of Virginia Press, 2001.

Licht, Walter. *Industrializing America: The Nineteenth Century.* Baltimore: Johns Hopkins University Press, 1995.

Lipartito, Kenneth, and Lisa Jacobson, eds. *Capitalism's Hidden Worlds.* Philadelphia: University of Pennsylvania Press, 2020.

Lobel, Cindy R. "'Out to Eat': The Emergence and Evolution of the Restaurant in Nineteenth-Century New York City." *Winterthur Portfolio* 44, no. 2/3 (Summer/Autumn 2010): 193–220.

———. *Urban Appetites: Food and Culture in Nineteenth-Century New York.* Chicago: University of Chicago Press, 2014.

Lombardi, Peter A. *Jamestown, New York: A Guide to the City and Its Urban Landscape.* Albany: State University of New York Press, 2014.

Lott, Eric. *Love and Theft: Blackface Minstrelsy and the American Working Class.* New York: Oxford University Press, 1993.

Loughran, Trish. *The Republic in Print: Print Culture in the Age of U.S. Nation Building, 1770–1870.* New York: Columbia University Press, 2007.

Lounsbury, Carl R. *The Courthouses of Early Virginia: An Architectural History.* Charlottesville: University of Virginia Press, 2005.

Lubar, Steven. "The Transformation of Antebellum Patent Law." *Technology and Culture* 32, no. 4 (October 1991): 932–59.

Lubet, Steven. *Fugitive Justice: Runaways, Rescuers, and Slavery on Trial.* Cambridge, MA: Harvard University Press, 2010.

Luskey, Brian P. "Jumping Counters in White Collars: Manliness, Respectability, and Work in the Antebellum City." *Journal of the Early Republic* 26, no. 2 (Summer 2006): 173–219.

Luskey, Brian P., and Wendy A. Woloson, eds. *Capitalism by Gaslight: Illuminating the Economy of Nineteenth-Century America.* Philadelphia: University of Pennsylvania Press, 2015.

Lyons, Clare A. *Sex among the Rabble: An Intimate History of Gender.* Chapel Hill: University of North Carolina Press, 2006.

M. G. W. and H. W. L. "Archetypes in Literature." *Yale University Library Gazette* 31, no. 2 (October 1956): 90–91.

Mackintosh, Will B. "The Loomis Gang's Market Revolution." In *Capitalism by Gaslight: Illuminating the Economy of Nineteenth-Century America,* edited by Brian P. Luskey and Wendy A. Woloson, 10–30. Philadelphia: University of Pennsylvania Press, 2015.

———. "Mechanical Aesthetics: Picturesque Tourism and the Transportation Revolution in Pennsylvania." *Pennsylvania History: A Journal of Mid-Atlantic Studies* 81, no. 1 (Winter 2014): 88–105.

———. *Selling the Sights: The Invention of the Tourist in American Culture.* New York: New York University Press, 2019.

———. "'Ticketed Through': The Commodification of Travel in the Nineteenth Century." *Journal of the Early Republic* 32, no. 1 (Spring 2012): 61–89.

MacLeod, Christine. "The Paradoxes of Patenting: Invention and Its Diffusion in 18th- and 19th-Century Britain, France, and North America." *Technology and Culture* 32, no. 4 (October 1991): 885–910.

MacMaster, Richard K. "Philadelphia Merchants, Backcountry Shopkeepers, and Town-Making Fever." *Pennsylvania History* 81, no. 3 (Summer 2014): 342–63.

Mainwaring, W. Thomas. *Abandoned Tracks: The Underground Railroad in Washington County, Pennsylvania*. Notre Dame, IN: University of Notre Dame Press, 2018.

Majewski, John. "Commerce and Continuity: Internal Improvements in Virginia and Pennsylvania, 1790–1860." *Journal of Economic History* 56, no. 2 (June 1996): 467–69.

———. "Who Financed the Transportation Revolution? Regional Divergence and Internal Improvements in Antebellum Pennsylvania and Virginia." *Journal of Economic History* 56, no. 4 (December 1996): 763–88.

Majewski, John, Christopher Baer, and Daniel B. Klein. "Responding to Relative Decline: The Plank Road Boom of Antebellum New York." *Journal of Economic History* 53, no. 1 (March 1993): 106–22.

Mancall, Peter C. "Men, Women, and Alcohol in Indian Villages in the Great Lakes Region in the Early Republic." *Journal of the Early Republic* 15, no. 3 (Autumn 1995): 425–48.

Manion, Jen. *Liberty's Prisoners: Carceral Culture in Early America*. Philadelphia: University of Pennsylvania Press, 2015.

Mann, Bruce H. "Law, Economy, and Society in Early New England." *Yale Law Journal* 111, no. 7 (May 2002): 1869–80.

———. *Neighbors and Strangers: Law and Community in Early Connecticut*. Chapel Hill: University of North Carolina Press, 1987.

———. *Republic of Debtors: Bankruptcy in the Age of American Independence*. Cambridge, MA: Harvard University Press, 2002.

Manning, Chandra. "Working for Citizenship in Civil War Contraband Camps." *Journal of the Civil War Era* 4, no. 2 (June 2014): 172–204.

Marin, Joseph. "'Well Calculated and Intended to Deceive': Counterfeiters, Counterfeiting, and the Antebellum South." PhD diss., Florida International University, 2020.

Marine-Street, Natalie. "'Agents Wanted': Sales, Gender, and the Making of Consumer Markets in America, 1830–1930." PhD diss., Stanford University, 2016.

Marshall, Nicholas. "Rural Experience and the Development of the Middle Class: The Power of Culture and Tangible Improvements." *American Nineteenth Century History* 8, no. 1 (March 2007): 1–25.

Martin, Ann Smart. *Buying into the World of Goods: Early Consumers in Backcountry Virginia*. Baltimore: Johns Hopkins University Press, 2008.

Martin, Jill E. "'The Greatest Evil': Interpretations of Indian Prohibition Laws, 1832–1953." *Great Plains Quarterly* 23, no. 1 (Winter 2003): 35–53.

Martin, Jonathan D. *Divided Mastery: Slave Hiring in the American South*. Jefferson, NC: McFarland, 2004.

Martin, Scott C. *Killing Time: Leisure and Culture in Southwestern Pennsylvania, 1800–1850*. Pittsburgh, PA: University of Pittsburgh Press, 1995.

Marx, Leo. *The Machine in the Garden: Technology and the Pastoral Ideal in America.*
New York: Oxford University Press, 1964.

Masur, Kate. "State Sovereignty and Migration before Reconstruction." *Journal of the Civil War Era* 9, no. 4 (December 2019): 588–611.

———. *Until Justice Be Done: America's First Civil Rights Movement, from the Revolution to Reconstruction.* New York: Norton, 2021.

Mathisen, Erik. "'Know All Men By These Presents': Bonds, Localism, and Politics in Early Republican Mississippi." *Journal of the Early Republic* 33, no. 4 (Winter 2013): 727–50.

———. *The Loyal Republic: Traitors, Slaves, and the Remaking of Citizenship in Civil War America.* Chapel Hill: University of North Carolina Press, 2018.

McCalla, Douglas. *Consumers in the Bush: Shopping in Rural Upper Canada.* Montreal: McGill-Queen's University Press, 2015.

McCarthy, Molly. *The Accidental Diarist: A History of the Daily Planner in America.* Chicago: University of Chicago Press, 2013.

McCoy, Drew R. *The Elusive Republic: Political Economy in Jeffersonian America.* Chapel Hill: University of North Carolina Press, 1980.

McCurry, Stephanie. *Confederate Reckoning: Power and Politics in the Civil War South.* Cambridge, MA: Harvard University Press, 2010.

McDaid, Christopher L. "'The Best Accustomed House in Town': Taverns as a Reflection of Elite Consumer Behavior in Eighteenth-Century Hampton and Elizabeth City County, Virginia." PhD diss., University of Leicester, 2013.

McLean, Scott L., David A. Schults, and Manfred B. Steger, eds. *Social Capital: Critical Perspectives on Community and "Bowling Alone."* New York: New York University Press, 2002.

McMurry, Sally. "City Parlor, Country Sitting Room: Rural Vernacular Design and the American Parlor, 1840–1900." *Winterthur Portfolio* 20, no. 4 (Winter 1985): 261–80.

McNamara, Martha J. *From Tavern to Courthouse: Architecture and Ritual in American Law, 1658–1860.* Baltimore: Johns Hopkins University Press, 2004.

Meacham, Sarah Hand. *Every Home a Distillery: Alcohol, Gender, and Technology in the Colonial Chesapeake.* Baltimore: Johns Hopkins University Press, 2009.

———. "Keeping the Trade: The Persistence of Tavernkeeping among Middling Women in Colonial Virginia." *Early American Studies* 3, no. 1 (Spring 2005): 140–63.

Meeks, Carroll L. V. *The Railroad Station: An Architectural History.* New York: Dover, 1995.

Meginness, John F., ed. *History of Lycoming County, Pennsylvania.* Chicago: Brown, Runk, 1892.

Meyer, Balthasar Henry, comp. *History of Transportation in the United States before 1860.* Washington, DC: Peter Smith, 1948.

Meyer, David R. *The Roots of American Industrialization.* Baltimore: Johns Hopkins University Press, 2003.

Meyer, Sabine N. *We Are What We Drink: The Temperance Battle in Minnesota.* Champaign: University of Illinois Press, 2015.

Middleton, Stephen. *The Black Laws in the Old Northwest: A Documentary History.* Westport, CT: Greenwood, 1993.

Mihm, Stephen. *A Nation of Counterfeiters: Capitalists, Con Men, and the Making of the United States.* Cambridge, MA: Harvard University Press, 2007.

Miller, T. Michael. *Artisans and Merchants of Alexandria, Virginia, 1780–1820.* 2 Vols. Westminster, MD: Heritage Books, 1991, 1992.

Monod, David. *The Soul of Pleasure: Sentiment and Sensation in Nineteenth-Century American Mass Entertainment.* Ithaca: Cornell University Press, 2016.

Moore, Lindsey R. *Women before the Court: Law and Patriarchy in the Anglo-American World, 1600–1800.* Manchester: Manchester University Press, 2019.

Morris, Thomas D. *Free Men All: The Personal Liberty Laws of the North, 1780–1861.* Union, NJ: Lawbook Exchange, 2001.

Morrison, Michael A. *Slavery and the American West: The Eclipse of Manifest Destiny and the Coming of the Civil War.* Chapel Hill: University of North Carolina Press, 1999.

Mullenneaux, Nan. *Staging Family: Domestic Deceptions of Mid-Nineteenth-Century American Actresses.* Lincoln: University of Nebraska Press, 2018.

Murphy, Brian Phillips. *Building the Empire State: Political Economy in the Early Republic.* Philadelphia: University of Pennsylvania Press, 2015.

Murphy, Sharon Ann. "Selecting Risks in an Anonymous World: The Agency System for Life Insurance in Antebellum America." *Business History Review* 82, no. 1 (Spring 2008): 1–30.

Murray, Sterling E. "Music and Dance in Philadelphia's City Tavern." In *American Musical Life in Context and Practice to 1865,* edited by James R. Heintze, 3–47. New York: Garland, 1994.

Myers, Amrita Chakrabarti. *Forging Freedom: Black Women and the Pursuit of Liberty in Antebellum Charleston.* Chapel Hill: University of North Carolina Press, 2011.

Naeve, Milo M. *John Lewis Krimmel: An Artist in Federal America.* Cranbury, NJ: Associated University Presses, 1987.

Nathans, Heather. *Early American Theatre from the Revolution to Thomas Jefferson: Into the Hands of the People.* New York: Cambridge University Press, 2003.

Neem, Johann N. *Creating a Nation of Joiners: Democracy and Civil Society in Early National Massachusetts.* Cambridge, MA: Harvard University Press, 2008.

———. "Freedom of Association in the Early Republic: The Republican Party, the Whiskey Rebellion, and the Philadelphia and New York Cordwainers' Cases." *Pennsylvania Magazine of History and Biography* 127, no. 3 (July 2003): 259–90.

———. "Two Approaches to Democratization: Engagement versus Capability." In *Practicing Democracy: Popular Politics in the United States from the Constitution to the Civil War,* edited by Daniel Peart and Adam I. P. Smith, 247–80. Charlottesville: University of Virginia Press, 2015.

Newman, Paul Douglas. *Fries's Rebellion: The Enduring Struggle for the American Revolution.* Philadelphia: University of Pennsylvania Press, 2004.

———. "Fries's Rebellion and American Political Culture, 1798–1800." *Pennsylvania Magazine of History and Biography* 119, no. 1/2 (January–April 1995): 37–73.

Newman, Richard S. *The Transformation of American Abolitionism: Fighting Slavery in the Early Republic.* Chapel Hill: University of North Carolina Press, 2002.

The Nineteenth Century. Charleston: XIX Century Publication, 1870.

Norwood, Dael A. "What Counts? Political Economy, or Ways to Make Early America Add Up." *Journal of the Early Republic* 36, no. 4 (Winter 2016): 753–82.

Novak, William J. *The People's Welfare: Law and Regulation in Nineteenth-Century America.* Chapel Hill: University of North Carolina Press, 1996.

Nunley, Tamika Y. *At the Threshold of Liberty: Women, Slavery, and Shifting Identities in Washington, D.C.* Chapel Hill: University of North Carolina Press, 2021.

Nyamnjoh, Francis B. "Keynote Address: Mobility, Globalisation, and the Policing of Citizenship and Belonging in the Twenty-First Century." *South African Historical Journal* 73, no. 2 (2021): 241–56.

Oakley, C. C. *Greater Terre Haute and Vigo County: Closing the First Century's History of City and County.* Vol. 1. Chicago: Lewis Publishing, 1908.

O'Brassill-Kulfan, Kristin. *Vagrants and Vagabonds: Poverty and Mobility in the Early American Republic.* New York: New York University Press, 2019.

O'Keefe, John McNelis. *Stranger Citizens: Migrant Influence and National Power in the Early American Republic.* Ithaca: Cornell University Press, 2021.

O'Malley, Gregory E. "Slavery's Converging Ground: Charleston's Slave Trade as the Black Heart of the Lowcountry." *William and Mary Quarterly* 74, no. 2 (April 2017): 271–302.

Oldenburg, Ray. *The Great Good Place: Cafés, Coffee Shops, Community Centers, Beauty Parlors, General Stores, Bars, Hangouts, and How They Get You through the Day.* New York: Paragon House, 1989.

Olegario, Rowena. *A Culture of Credit: Embedding Trust and Transparency in American Business.* Cambridge, MA: Harvard University Press, 2006.

Olmstead, Alan H., and Paul W. Rhode. "Agriculture in American Economic History." In *The Oxford Handbook of American Economic History*, edited by Louis Cain, Price V. Fishback, and Paul D. Rhode, 1:159–82. New York: Oxford University Press, 2018.

Onofrio, Jan. *South Carolina Biographical Dictionary.* 2nd ed. St. Clair Shores, MI: Somerset Publishers, 2000.

Osborn, Matthew Warner. "A Detestable Shrine: Alcohol Abuse in Antebellum Philadelphia." *Journal of the Early Republic* 29, no. 1 (Spring 2009): 101–32.

———. *Rum Maniacs: Alcoholic Insanity in the Early American Republic.* Chicago: University of Chicago Press, 2014.

Osterud, Nancy Grey. *Bonds of Community: The Lives of Farm Women in Nineteenth-Century New York.* Ithaca: Cornell University Press, 1991.

Owen, Kenneth. "Legitimacy, Localism, and the First Party System." In *Practicing Democracy: Popular Politics in the United States from the Constitution to the Civil War*, edited by Daniel Peart and Adam I. P. Smith, 173–95. Charlottesville: University of Virginia Press, 2015.

Owen, Thomas McAdory. *History of Alabama and Dictionary of Alabama Biography.* Chicago: S. J. Clarke, 1921.

Parsons, Elaine Frantz. "Risky Business: The Uncertain Boundaries of Manhood in the Midwestern Saloon." *Journal of Social History* 34, no. 2 (Winter 2000): 283–307.

Pasley, Jeffrey L. *"The Tyranny of Printers": Newspaper Politics in the Early American Republic.* Charlottesville: University of Virginia Press, 2001.

Pasley, Jeffrey L., Andrew W. Robertson, and David Waldstreicher, eds. *Beyond the Founders: New Approaches to the Political History of the Early American Republic.* Chapel Hill: University of North Carolina Press, 2004.

Patterson, Mark W., Nancy Hoalst-Pullen, and Sam Batzli. "Migration and the Evolving Landscape of U.S. Beer Geographies." In *Fermented Landscapes: Lively Processes of Socio-environmental Transformation*, edited by Colleen C. Myles, 127–52. Lincoln: University of Nebraska Press, 2020.

Paullin, Charles O., and John K. Wright, eds. *Atlas of the Historical Geography of the United States*. Washington, DC: Carnegie Institution of Washington and the American Geographical Society of New York, 1932.

Pearson, Susan J. *The Birth Certificate: An American History*. Chapel Hill: University of North Carolina Press, 2021.

———. "A New Birth of Regulation: The State of the State after the Civil War." *Journal of the Civil War Era* 5, no. 3 (September 2015): 422–39.

Peart, Daniel. "An 'Era of No Feelings'? Rethinking the Relationship between Political Parties and Popular Participation in the Early United States." In *Practicing Democracy: Popular Politics in the United States from the Constitution to the Civil War*, edited by Daniel Peart and Adam I. P. Smith, 123–44. Charlottesville: University of Virginia Press, 2015.

Peart, Daniel, and Adam I. P. Smith, eds. *Practicing Democracy: Popular Politics in the United States from the Constitution to the Civil War*. Charlottesville: University of Virginia Press, 2015.

Peck, Graham A. "Was There a Second Party System? Illinois as a Case Study in Antebellum Politics." In *Practicing Democracy: Popular Politics in the United States from the Constitution to the Civil War*, edited by Daniel Peart and Adam I. P. Smith, 145–69. Charlottesville: University of Virginia Press, 2015.

Peiss, Kathy. *Cheap Amusements: Working Women and Leisure in Turn-of-the-Century New York*. Philadelphia: Temple University Press, 1986.

Pfleger, Birte. "'Miserable Germans' and Fries's Rebellion: Language, Ethnicity, and Citizenship in the Early Republic." *Early American Studies* 2, no. 2 (Fall 2004): 343–61.

Pflugrad-Jackisch, Ami. *Brothers of a Vow: Secret Fraternal Orders and the Transformation of White Male Culture in Antebellum Virginia*. Athens: University of Georgia Press, 2010.

Phillips, Laura L. *Bolsheviks and the Bottle: Drink and Worker Culture in St. Petersburg, 1900–1929*. DeKalb: Northern Illinois University Press, 2000.

Pierce, Jason E. *Making the White Man's West: Whiteness and the Creation of the American West*. Boulder: University Press of Colorado, 2016.

Pierson, Michael. *Free Hearts and Free Homes: Gender and American Antislavery Politics*. Chapel Hill: University of North Carolina Press, 2003.

Pitcavage, Mark. "Ropes of Sand: Territorial Militias, 1801–1812." *Journal of the Early Republic* 13, no. 4 (Winter 1993): 481–500.

Poovey, Mary. *A History of the Modern Fact: Problems of Knowledge in the Sciences of Wealth and Society*. Chicago: University of Chicago Press, 1998.

Portnoy, Alisse. "'Female Petitioners Can Lawfully Be Heard': Female Decorum, U.S. Politics, and Political Agency, 1829–1831." *Journal of the Early Republic* 23, no. 4 (Winter 2003): 573–610.

Pottroff, Christy L. "Circulation." *Early American Studies* 16, no. 4 (Fall 2018): 621–27.

———. "The Royall Coach." *Early American Literature* 53, no. 1 (2018): 127–52.

Powell, J. H. *Bring out Your Dead: The Great Plague of Yellow Fever in Philadelphia in 1793.* Philadelphia: University of Pennsylvania Press, 1949.

Power, Madelon. *Faces along the Bar: Lore and Order in the Workingman's Saloon, 1870–1920.* Chicago: University of Chicago Press, 1998.

Pratt, Mary Louise. *Imperial Eyes: Travel Writing and Transculturation.* New York: Routledge, 2008.

Pred, Allan R. *Urban Growth and the Circulation of Information: The United States System of Cities, 1790–1840.* Cambridge, MA: Harvard University Press, 1973.

———. *Urban Growth and City-Systems in the United States, 1840–1860.* Cambridge, MA: Harvard University Press, 1980.

Premo, Terri L. *Winter Friends: Women Growing Old in the New Republic, 1785–1835.* Urbana: University of Illinois Press, 1990.

Pryor, Elizabeth Stordeur. *Colored Travelers: Mobility and the Fight for Citizenship before the Civil War.* Chapel Hill: University of North Carolina Press, 2016.

Putnam, Lara. "Citizenship from the Margins: Vernacular Theories of Rights and the State from the Interwar Caribbean." *Journal of British Studies* 53 (January 2014): 162–91.

Putnam, Robert D. *Bowling Alone: The Collapse and Revival of American Community.* New York: Simon & Schuster, 2000.

Rael, Patrick. *Black Identity and Black Protest in the Antebellum North.* Chapel Hill: University of North Carolina Press, 2002.

Rainer, Joseph T. "The 'Sharper' Image: Yankee Peddlers, Southern Consumers, and the Market Revolution." In *Cultural Change and the Market Revolution in America, 1789–1860,* edited by Scott C. Martin, 89–110. Lanham, MD: Rowman & Littlefield, 2005.

Rasmussen, Thomas. *Ox Cart to Automobile: Social Change in Western New York.* Lanham, MD: University Press of America, 2009.

Ratcliffe, Donald. "The Right to Vote and the Rise of Democracy, 1787–1828." *Journal of the Early Republic* 33, no. 2 (Summer 2013): 219–54.

Reckner, Paul E., and Stephen A. Brighton. "'Free from All Vicious Habits': Archaeological Perspectives on Class Conflict and the Rhetoric of Temperance." *Historical Archaeology* 33, no. 1 (1999): 63–86.

Regele, Lindsay Schakenbach. "The World's Best Carpets: Erastus Bigelow and the Financing of Antebellum Innovation." *Technology and Culture* 59, no. 1 (January 2018): 126–51.

Reifel, August Jacob. *History of Franklin County, Indiana: Her People, Industries, and Institutions.* Indianapolis: B. F. Bowen, 1915.

Remer, Rosalind. "Preachers, Peddlers, and Publishers: Philadelphia's Backcountry Book Trade, 1800–1830." *Journal of the Early Republic* 14, no. 4 (Winter 1994): 497–522.

Rice, James D. "Old Appalachia's Path to Interdependency: Economic Development and the Creation of Community in Western Maryland, 1730–1850." *Appalachian Journal* 22, no. 4 (Summer 1995): 348–74.

Rice, Kym S. *Early American Taverns: For the Entertainment of Friends and Strangers.* Chicago: Regnery Gateway, 1983.

Richards, Leonard L. *Shays's Rebellion: The American Revolution's Final Battle.* Philadelphia: University of Pennsylvania Press, 2002.

Richie, Margaret Bye, John D. Milner, and Gregory D. Huber. *Stone Houses: Traditional Homes of Pennsylvania's Bucks County and Brandywine Valley*. New York: Rizzoli, 2005.

Richter, Amy G. *Home on the Rails: Women, the Railroad, and the Rise of Public Domesticity*. Chapel Hill: University of North Carolina Press, 2005.

Rigolon, Alessandro, and Jeremy Németh. "Privately Owned Parks in New Urbanist Communities: A Study of Environmental Privilege, Equity, and Inclusion." *Journal of Urban Affairs* 40, no. 4 (2018): 543–59.

Roberson, Jere W. "The Memphis Commercial Convention of 1853: Southern Dreams and 'Young America.'" *Tennessee Historical Quarterly* 33, no. 3 (Fall 1974): 279–96.

Roberts, Julia. "Harry Jones and His Cronies in the Taverns of Kingston, Canada West." *Ontario History* 95, no. 1 (Spring 2003): 1–21.

———. "'A Mixed Assemblage of Persons': Race and Tavern Space in Upper Canada." *Canadian Historical Review* 83, no. 1 (March 2002): 1–28.

———. *In Mixed Company: Taverns and Public Life in Upper Canada*. Vancouver: UBC Press, 2009.

Robertson, Andrew W. "Jeffersonian Parties, Politics, and Participation: The Tortuous Trajectory of American Democracy." In *Practicing Democracy: Popular Politics in the United States from the Constitution to the Civil War*, edited by Daniel Peart and Adam I. P. Smith, 99–122. Charlottesville: University of Virginia Press, 2015.

———. "Voting Rites and Voting Acts: Electioneering Ritual, 1790–1820." In *Beyond the Founders: New Approaches to the Political History of the Early American Republic*, edited by Jeffrey L. Pasley, Andrew W. Robertson, and David Waldstreicher, 57–78. Chapel Hill: University of North Carolina Press, 2004.

Robinson, Tracy. "Overcoming Social Exclusion in Public Library Services to LGBTQ and Gender Variant Youth." *Public Library Quarterly* 35, no. 3 (2016): 161–74.

Rock, Howard B. *Artisans of the New Republic: The Tradesmen of New York City in the Age of Jefferson*. New York: New York University Press, 1979.

Rockman, Diana Diz, and Nan A. Rothschild. "City Tavern, Country Tavern: An Analysis of Four Colonial Sites." *Historical Archaeology* 18, no. 2 (1984): 112–21.

Rockman, Seth. *Scraping By: Wage Labor, Slavery, and Survival in Early Baltimore*. Baltimore: Johns Hopkins University Press, 2009.

Rodway, Cara. "Managing Quasi-Domesticity at the Roadside: Postwar Female Moteliers and the Space of Reinvention." *Women's Studies* 40, no. 8 (2011): 1030–51.

Roediger, David. *Wages of Whiteness: Race and the Making of the American Working Class*. New York: Verso, 1991.

Roney, Jessica Choppin. "1776, Viewed from the West." *Journal of the Early Republic* 37, no. 4 (Winter 2017): 655–700.

Rorabaugh, W. J. *The Alcoholic Republic: An American Tradition*. New York: Oxford University Press, 1979.

———. "Rising Democratic Spirits: Immigrants, Temperance, and Tammany Hall, 1854–1860." *Civil War History* 22, no. 2 (June 1976): 138–57.

Roscoe, William E. *History of Schoharie County, New York, 1713–1882*. Westminster, MD: Heritage Books, 1882.

Rosen, Deborah A. *Courts and Commerce: Gender, Law, and the Market Economy in Colonial New York*. Columbus: Ohio State University Press, 1997.

Rosswurm, Steven. *Arms, Country, and Class: The Philadelphia Militia and the "Lower Sort" during the American Revolution, 1775–1783*. New Brunswick, NJ: Rutgers University Press, 1987.

Rothman, Adam. *Slave Country: American Expansion and the Origins of the Deep South*. Cambridge, MA: Harvard University Press, 2005.

Rothman, Ellen K. *Hands and Hearts: A History of Courtship in America*. Cambridge, MA: Harvard University Press, 1987.

Rothman, Joshua D. *Flush Times and Fever Dreams: A Story of Capitalism and Slavery in the Age of Jackson*. Athens: University of Georgia Press, 2012.

———. "The Hazards of the Flush Times: Gambling, Mob Violence, and the Anxieties of America's Market Revolution." *Journal of American History* 95, no. 3 (December 2008): 651–77.

———. *The Ledger and the Chain: How Domestic Slave Traders Shaped America*. New York: Basic Books, 2021.

———. *Notorious in the Neighborhood: Sex and Families across the Color Line in Virginia, 1787–1861*. Chapel Hill: University of North Carolina Press, 2003.

Rumbarger, John J. *Profits, Power, and Prohibition: American Alcohol Reform and the Industrializing of America, 1800–1930*. Albany: State University of New York Press, 1989.

Ryan, Mary P. *Cradle of the Middle Class: The Family in Oneida County, New York, 1790–1865*. Cambridge: Cambridge University Press, 1981.

———. *Women in Public: Between Banners and Ballots, 1825–1880*. Baltimore: Johns Hopkins University Press, 1990.

Sachs, Honor. *Home Rule: Households, Manhood, and National Expansion on the Eighteenth-Century Kentucky Frontier*. New Haven: Yale University Press, 2015.

Salafia, Matthew. *Slavery's Borderland: Freedom and Bondage along the Ohio River*. Philadelphia: University of Pennsylvania Press, 2013.

Saler, Bethel. *The Settlers' Empire: Colonialism and State Formation in America's Old Northwest*. Philadelphia: University of Pennsylvania Press, 2015.

Salinger, Sharon V. *Taverns and Drinking in Early America*. Baltimore: Johns Hopkins University Press, 2002.

Salmon, Marylynn. *Women and the Law of Property in Early America*. Chapel Hill: University of North Carolina Press, 1986.

Sampson, Roy J. "American Accounting Education, Textbooks and Public Practice Prior to 1900." *Business History Review* 34, no. 4 (Winter 1960): 459–66.

Sandage, Scott A. *Born Losers: A History of Failure in America*. Cambridge, MA: Harvard University Press, 2005.

Sandoval-Strausz, A. K., and Daniel Levinson Wilk. "Princes and Maids of the City Hotel: The Cultural Politics of Commercial Hospitality in America." *Journal of Decorative and Propaganda Arts* 25 (2005): 160–85.

Sandoval-Strausz, Andrew K. *Hotel: An American History*. New Haven: Yale University Press, 2007.

Saunt, Claudio. *A New Order of Things: Property, Power, and the Transformation of the Creek Indians, 1733–1816*. Cambridge: Cambridge University Press, 1999.

———. *Unworthy Republic: The Dispossession of Native Americans and the Road to Indian Territory*. New York: Norton, 2020.

Scardaville, Michael C. "Alcohol Abuse and Tavern Reform in Late Colonial Mexico City." *Hispanic American Historical Review* 60, no. 4 (November 1980): 643–71.

Scharf, J. Thomas. *History of Baltimore City and County*. Philadelphia: Louis H. Everts, 1881.

———. *History of Delaware, 1609–1888*. 2 Vols. Philadelphia: L. J. Richards, 1888.

Scharf, J. Thomas, and Thompson Westcott. *History of Philadelphia, 1609–1884*. 3 Vols. Philadelphia: L. H. Everts, 1884.

Schoelwer, Susan P., ed. *Lions and Eagles and Bulls: Early American Tavern and Inn Signs*. Hartford: Connecticut Historical Society, 2000.

Schoeppner, Michael A. "Black Migrants and Border Regulation in the Early United States." *Journal of the Civil War Era* 11, no. 3 (September 2021): 317–39.

———. *Moral Contagion: Black Atlantic Sailors, Citizenship, and Diplomacy in Antebellum America*. Cambridge: Cambridge University Press, 2019.

Schoolman, Martha. *Abolitionist Geographies*. Minneapolis: University of Minnesota Press, 2014.

Schreiber, Lee L. "Bluebloods and Local Societies: A Philadelphia Microcosm." *Pennsylvania History* 48, no. 3 (July 1981): 251–66.

Schweikart, Larry. "Southern Banks and Economic Growth in the Antebellum Period: A Reassessment." *Journal of Southern History* 53, no. 1 (February 1987): 19–36.

Scribner, Vaughn. *Inn Civility: Urban Taverns and Early American Civil Society*. New York: New York University Press, 2019.

Sculle, Keith A. "Frank Redford's Wigwam Village Chain." In *Roadside America: The Automobile in Design and Culture*, edited by Jan Jennings, 125–35. Ames: Iowa State University Press, 1990.

Seavoy, Ronald E. "Laws to Encourage Manufacturing: New York Policy and the 1811 General Incorporation Statute." *Business History Review* 46, no. 1 (Spring 1972): 85–95.

Seeley, Samantha. *Race, Removal, and the Right to Remain: Migration and the Making of the United States*. Chapel Hill: University of North Carolina Press, 2021.

Sellers, Charles. *The Market Revolution: Jacksonian America, 1815–1846*. New York: Oxford University Press, 1991.

Shaw, Diane. *City Building on the Eastern Frontier: Sorting the New Nineteenth-Century City*. Baltimore: Johns Hopkins University Press, 2004.

Shelden, Rachel A. "'The Most Available Man': John McLean and the Antislavery Partisan Political Movement." Paper presented at the annual meeting of the Southern Historical Association, Baltimore, Maryland, 2022.

Shelden, Rachel A., and Erik Alexander. "Dismantling the Party System: Party Fluidity and the Mechanisms of Nineteenth-Century U.S. Politics." *Journal of American History* (forthcoming).

Sheriff, Carol. *The Artificial River: The Erie Canal and the Paradox of Progress*. New York: Hill and Wang, 1996.

Sherman, Susanne K. *Comedies Useful: A History of American Theatre in the South, 1775–1812*. Edited by Lucy B. Pilkinton. Williamsburg, VA: Celest Press, 1998.

Shields, David S. *Civil Tongues and Polite Letters in British America*. Chapel Hill: University of North Carolina Press, 1997.

Shiring, Stephen B., and Elizabeth J. Shiring. "Hotelkeepers Organize in Twentieth Century to Legitimize and Advance Profession in American Society." *Journal of Hospitality & Tourism Research* 45, no. 5 (June 2021): 862–73.

Sinha, Manisha. *The Counterrevolution of Slavery: Politics and Ideology in Antebellum South Carolina*. Chapel Hill: University of North Carolina Press, 2000.

———. *The Slave's Cause: A History of Abolition*. New Haven: Yale University Press, 2016.

Sismondo, Christine. *America Walks into a Bar: A Spirited History of Taverns and Saloons, Speakeasies, and Grog Shops*. New York: Oxford University Press, 2011.

Skocpol, Theda. *Diminished Democracy: From Membership to Management in American Civic Life*. Norman: University of Oklahoma Press, 2003.

Slaughter, Thomas P. *Bloody Dawn: The Christiana Riot and Racial Violence in the Antebellum North*. New York: Oxford University Press, 1991.

Smith, Helene. *Tavern Signs of America*. Greensburg, PA: McDonald/Sward Publishing Company, 1989.

Smith, Mark M. *Listening to Nineteenth-Century America*. Chapel Hill: University of North Carolina Press, 2001.

Smith-Rosenberg, Carroll. *Disorderly Conduct: Visions of Gender in Victorian America*. New York: Oxford University Press, 1986.

Snyder, Christina. "Many Removals: Re-evaluating the Arc of Indigenous Dispossession." *Journal of the Early Republic* 41, no. 4 (Winter 2021): 623–50.

Snyder, Terri L. "Suicide, Slavery, and Memory in North America." *Journal of American History* 97, no. 1 (June 2010): 39–62.

Sokoloff, Kenneth L., and B. Zorina Khan. "The Democratization of Invention during Early Industrialization: Evidence from the United States, 1790–1846." *Journal of Economic History* 50, no. 2 (June 1990): 363–78.

Spero, Patrick. "The Revolution in Popular Publications: The Almanac and New England Primer, 1750–1800." *Early American Studies* 8, no. 1 (Winter 2010): 41–74.

Spinney, Justin, Rachel Aldred, and Katrina Brown. "Geographies of Citizenship and Everyday (Im)mobility." *Geoforum* 64 (August 2015): 325–32.

Spires, Derrick R. "Imagining a State of Fellow Citizens: Early African American Politics of Publicity in the Black State Conventions." In *Early African American Print Culture*, edited by Lara Langer Cohen and Jordan Alexander Stein, 274–89. Philadelphia: University of Pennsylvania Press, 2012.

———. *The Practice of Citizenship: Black Politics and Print Culture in the Early United States*. Philadelphia: University of Pennsylvania Press, 2019.

Stanfield, Susan J. *Rewriting Citizenship: Women, Race, and Nineteenth-Century Print Culture*. Athens: University of Georgia Press, 2022.

Stansell, Christine. *City of Women: Sex and Class in New York, 1789–1860*. Urbana: University of Illinois Press, 1982.

Steere, Thomas. *History of the Town of Smithfield [RI] from Its Organization, in 1730–1, to Its Division, in 1871*. Providence: E. L. Freeman, 1881.

Steffen, Charles G. "Newspapers for Free: The Economies of Newspaper Circulation in the Early Republic." *Journal of the Early Republic* 23 (2003): 381–419.

Steinfeld, Robert J. *The Invention of Free Labor: The Employment Relation in English and American Law and Culture, 1350–1870*. Chapel Hill: University of North Carolina Press, 1991.

Stewart, Bruce E. "'The Forces of Bacchus Are Fast Yielding': The Rise and Fall of Anti-Alcohol Reform in Antebellum Rowan County, North Carolina." *North Carolina Historical Review* 87, no. 3 (July 2010): 310–38.

————. "Select Men of Sober and Industrious Habits: Alcohol Reform and Social Conflicts in Antebellum Appalachia." *Journal of Southern History* 73, no. 2 (May 2007): 289–322.

Stokols, Andrew. "From the Square to the Shopping Mall: New Social Media, State Surveillance, and the Evolving Geographies of Urban Protest." *Urban Geography* (2022): 1–26.

Stott, Richard. *Jolly Fellows: Male Milieus in Nineteenth-Century America.* Baltimore: Johns Hopkins University Press, 2009.

Stout, Mackenzie L. "Meaningful Access: True Equality or Frightening Reality?" *Missouri Law Review* 86, no. 2 (2021): 675–91.

Stover, John F. *History of the Baltimore and Ohio Railroad.* West Lafayette, IN: Purdue University Press, 1987.

Stowe, Steven M. *Intimacy and Power in the Old South: Ritual in the Lives of the Planters.* Baltimore: Johns Hopkins University Press, 1987.

Stowell, Marion Barber. *American Almanacs: The Colonial Weekday Bible.* New York: Burt Franklin, 1977.

Struna, Nancy L. *People of Prowess: Sport, Leisure, and Labor in Early Anglo-America.* Urbana: University of Illinois Press, 1996.

Stubbs, Naomi. "Pleasure Gardens of America: Anxieties of National Identity." In *The Pleasure Garden, from Vauxhall to Coney Island,* edited by Jonathan Conlin, 127–49. Philadelphia: University of Pennsylvania Press, 2013.

Sylla, Richard. "How the American Corporation Evolved over Two Centuries." *Proceedings of the American Philosophical Society* 158, no. 4 (December 2014): 354–63.

Sylla, Richard, and Robert E. Wright. "Corporation Formation in the Antebellum United States in Comparative Context." *Business History* 55, no. 4 (2013): 650–66.

Szymanski, Ann-Marie. "Stop, Thief! Private Protective Societies in Nineteenth-Century New England." *The New England Quarterly* 78, no. 3 (September 2005): 407–39.

Tadelis, Steven. "A Tribute to Oliver Williamson: Williamson's Contribution and Its Relevance to 21st Century Capitalism." *California Management Review* 52, no. 2 (Winter 2010): 159–66.

Tadman, Michael. *Speculators and Slaves: Masters, Traders, and Slaves in the Old South.* Madison: University of Wisconsin Press, 1989.

Taylor, Alan. *Liberty Men and Great Proprietors: The Revolutionary Settlement on the Maine Frontier, 1760–1820.* Chapel Hill: University of North Carolina Press, 1990.

————. *William Cooper's Town: Power and Persuasion on the Frontier of the Early American Republic.* New York: Vintage, 1995.

Taylor, George Rogers. *The Transportation Revolution, 1815–1860.* New York: Rinehart, 1951.

Teute, Fredrika J., and David S. Shields. "Jefferson in Washington: Domesticating Manners in the Republican Court." *Journal of the Early Republic* 35, no. 2 (Summer 2015): 237–59.

te Velde, Henk, and Maartje Janse, eds. *Organizing Democracy: Reflections on the Rise of Political Organizations in the Nineteenth Century.* New York: Palgrave Macmillan, 2017.

Thacher, David. "How Law Shapes Policing: The Regulation of Alcohol in the U.S., 1750–1860." *Policing and Society: An International Journal of Research and Policy* 30, no. 10 (2019): 1171–90.

Thomas, Frances Taliaferro. *A Portrait of Historic Athens and Clarke County.* 2nd ed. Athens: University of Georgia Press, 2009.

Thompson, Peter. *Rum Punch and Revolution: Taverngoing and Public Life in Eighteenth-Century Philadelphia*. Philadelphia: University of Pennsylvania Press, 1999.

Thorp, Daniel B. "Taverns and Tavern Culture on the Southern Colonial Frontier: Rowan County, North Carolina, 1753–1776." *Journal of Southern History* 62 (November 1996): 661–88.

Tolbert, Lisa. *Constructing Townscapes: Space and Society in Antebellum Tennessee*. Chapel Hill: University of North Carolina Press, 1999.

Tomek, Beverly C. *Pennsylvania Hall: A "Legal Lynching" in the Shadow of the Liberty Bell*. New York: Oxford University Press, 2014.

Tomlins, Christopher. "Subordination, Authority, Law: Subjects in Labor History." *International Labor and Working-Class History* 47 (Spring 1995): 56–90.

Tyrrell, Ian R. "Drink and Temperance in the Antebellum South: An Overview and Interpretation." *Journal of Southern History* 48, no. 4 (November 1982): 485–510.

———. *Sobering Up: From Temperance to Prohibition in Antebellum America, 1800–1860*. Westport, CT: Greenwood, 1979.

Upton, Dell, and John Michael Vlach, eds. *Common Places: Readings in American Vernacular Architecture*. Athens: University of Georgia Press, 1986.

Van Broekhoven, Deborah Bingham. "'Let Your Names Be Enrolled': Method and Ideology in Women's Antislavery Petitioning." In *The Abolitionist Sisterhood: Women's Political Culture in Antebellum America*, edited by Jean Fagan Yellin and John C. Van Horne, 179–200. Ithaca: Cornell University Press, 1994.

Van Hoesen, Walter H. *Early Taverns and Stagecoach Days in New Jersey*. Rutherford, NJ: Fairleigh Dickinson University Press, 1976.

Van Horn, Jennifer. *Power of Objects in Eighteenth-Century British America*. Chapel Hill: University of North Carolina Press, 2017.

Varon, Elizabeth R. *Disunion! The Coming of the American Civil War, 1789–1859*. Chapel Hill: University of North Carolina Press, 2008.

———. *We Mean to Be Counted: White Women and Politics in Antebellum Virginia*. Chapel Hill: University of North Carolina Press, 1998.

Verhoeven, Tim. "The Case for Sunday Mails: Sabbath Laws and the Separation of Church and State in Jacksonian America." *Journal of Church and State* 55, no. 1 (Winter 2013): 71–91.

Vickers, Daniel. "Competency and Competition: Economic Culture in Early America." *William and Mary Quarterly* 47, no. 1 (January 1990): 3–29.

Vinovskis, Maris A. "Stalking the Elusive Middle Class in Nineteenth-Century America. A Review Article." *Comparative Studies in Society and History* 33, no. 3 (July 1991): 582–87.

Vlach, John Michael. *Back of the Big House: The Architecture of Plantation Slavery*. Chapel Hill: University of North Carolina Press, 1993.

Volk, Kyle G. "The Perils of 'Pure Democracy': Minority Rights, Liquor Politics, and Popular Sovereignty in Antebellum America." *Journal of the Early Republic* 29, no. 4 (Winter 2009): 641–79.

"Voter and Officeholder Qualifications." *Harvard Law Review* 119, no. 7 (May 2006): 2230–51.

Voyce, Malcolm. "Shopping Malls in Australia: The End of Public Space and the Rise of 'Consumerist Citizenship'?" *Journal of Sociology* 42, no. 3 (2006): 269–86.

Waddington, Keir. "'We Don't Want Any German Sausages Here!' Food, Fear, and the German Nation in Victorian and Edwardian Britain." *Journal of British Studies* 52, no. 4 (October 2013): 1017–42.

Wadhwani, Rohit Daniel. "Citizen Savers: The Family Economy, Financial Institutions, and Social Policy in the Northeastern U.S. from the Market Revolution to the Great Depression." PhD diss., University of Pennsylvania, 2002.

Wagner, William. "Composing Pioneers: Personal Writing and the Making of Frontier Opportunity in Nineteenth-Century America." PhD diss., University of California, Berkeley, 2011.

———. "Footloose Founders: Young Men, Booster Culture, and Restless Mobility in the Antebellum West." Paper presented at the annual meeting of the Society for Historians of the Early American Republic, Raleigh, North Carolina, 2015.

———. "Location, Location, Location: Boosterism, Mobility, and the Market for Community in the Antebellum West." *Early American Studies* 17, no. 1 (Winter 2019): 120–46.

Waldstreicher, David. *In the Midst of Perpetual Fetes: The Making of American Nationalism, 1776–1820.* Chapel Hill: University of North Carolina Press, 1997.

———. "Reading the Runaways: Self-Fashioning, Print Culture, and Confidence in Slavery in the Eighteenth-Century Mid-Atlantic." *William and Mary Quarterly* 56, no. 2 (April 1999): 243–72.

Walker, James W. St. G. *The Black Loyalists: The Search for a Promised Land in Nova Scotia and Sierra Leone, 1783–1870.* Toronto: University of Toronto Press, 1992.

Walkowitz, Judith R. *Prostitution and Victorian Society: Women, Class, and the State.* Cambridge: Cambridge University Press, 1980.

Wallace, Anthony F. C. *Rockdale: The Growth of an American Village in the Early Industrial Revolution.* New York: Knopf, 1978.

Walsh, Margaret. "Gender in the History of Transportation Services: A Historiographical Perspective." *Business History Review* 81, no. 3 (Autumn 2007): 545–62.

Wamsley, Kevin B., and Robert S. Kossuth. "Fighting It Out in Nineteenth-Century Upper Canada/Canada West: Masculinities and Physical Challenges in the Tavern." *Journal of Sport History* 27, no. 3 (Fall 2000): 405–30.

Wang, Ta-Chen. "Banks, Credit Markets, and Early American Development: A Case Study of Entry and Competition." *Journal of Economic History* 68, no. 2 (June 2008): 438–61.

Warner, Michael. *The Letters of the Republic: Publication and the Public Sphere in Eighteenth-Century America.* Cambridge, MA: Harvard University Press, 1990.

Warner, Nicholas O. *Spirits of America: Intoxication in Nineteenth-Century American Literature.* Norman: University of Oklahoma Press, 1997.

Watson, Harry L. *Jacksonian Politics and Community Conflict: The Emergence of the Second American Party System in Cumberland County, North Carolina.* Baton Rouge: Louisiana State University Press, 1981.

Welke, Barbara Y. *Law and the Borders of Belonging in the Long Nineteenth-Century United States.* New York: Cambridge University Press, 2010.

———. *Recasting American Liberty: Gender, Race, Law, and the Railroad Revolution, 1865–1920.* Cambridge: Cambridge University Press, 2001.

———. "When All the Women Were White, and All the Blacks Were Men: Gender, Class, Race, and the Road to Plessy, 1855–1914." *Law and History Review* 13, no. 2 (Autumn 1995): 261–316.

Wells, Jonathan D. *The Origins of the Southern Middle Class, 1800–1861.* Chapel Hill: University of North Carolina Press, 2004.

———. "The Southern Middle Class." *Journal of Southern History* 75, no. 3 (August 2009): 651–62.

Welter, Barbara. "The Cult of True Womanhood: 1820–1860." *American Quarterly* 18 (Summer 1966): 151–74.

Wenger, Diane E. *A Country Storekeeper in Pennsylvania: Creating Economic Networks in Early America, 1790–1807.* University Park: Pennsylvania State University Press, 2008.

———. "Reading the Gemberling-Rex House: The Historical Evidence." *Pennsylvania History: A Journal of Mid-Atlantic Studies* 75, no. 1 (Winter 2008): 67–85.

Wermuth, Thomas S. *Rip Van Winkle's Neighbors: The Transformation of Rural Society in the Hudson River Valley, 1720–1850.* Albany: State University of New York Press, 2001.

White, John H., Jr. *The American Railroad Passenger Car.* Baltimore: Johns Hopkins University Press, 1978.

———. *Wet Britches and Muddy Boots: A History of Travel in Victorian America.* Bloomington: Indiana University Press, 2013.

Wilentz, Sean. *Chants Democratic: New York City and the Rise of the American Working Class, 1788–1850.* New York: Oxford University Press, 1984.

———. *The Rise of American Democracy: Jefferson to Lincoln.* New York: Norton, 2005.

Wilkie, Jane Riblett. "The United States Population by Race and Urban-Rural Residence 1790–1860: Reference Tables." *Demography* 13, no. 1 (February 1976): 139–48.

Williams-Forson, Psyche. "Where Did They Eat? Where Did They Stay? Interpreting the Material Culture of Black Women's Domesticity in the Context of the Colored Conventions." In *The Colored Conventions Movement: Black Organizing in the Nineteenth Century*, edited by P. Gabrielle Foreman, Jim Casey, and Sarah Lynn Patterson, 86–104. Chapel Hill: University of North Carolina Press, 2021.

Williamson, Matthew. "Social Exclusion and the Public Library: A Habermasian Insight." *Journal of Librarianship and Information Science* 32, no. 4 (2000): 178–86.

Williamson, Oliver. "The Economics of Organization: The Transaction Cost Approach." *American Journal of Sociology* 87, no. 3 (November 1981): 548–77.

Willis, Lee L. *Southern Prohibition: Race, Reform, and Public Life in Middle Florida, 1821–1920.* Athens: University of Georgia Press, 2011.

Wilson, Lisa. *Life after Death: Widows in Pennsylvania, 1750–1850.* Philadelphia: Temple University Press, 1992.

Winterer, Caroline. *The Mirror of Antiquity: American Women and the Classical Tradition, 1750–1900.* Ithaca: Cornell University Press, 2007.

Wood, Frederic J. *The Turnpikes of New England and Evolution of the Same through England, Virginia, and Maryland.* Boston: Marshall Jones, 1919.

Wood, Gordon S. *Empire of Liberty: A History of the Early Republic, 1789–1815.* New York: Oxford University Press, 2009.

Wood, Kirsten E. "'Join with Heart and Soul and Voice': Music, Harmony, and Politics in the Early American Republic." *American Historical Review* 119, no. 2 (October 2014): 1083–116.

———. "Making a Home in Public: Domesticity, Authority, and Family in the Old South's Public Houses." In *Family Values in the Old South*, edited by Craig Thompson Friend and Anya Jabour, 158–85. Gainesville: University Press of Florida, 2010.

———. *Masterful Women: Slaveholding Widows from the American Revolution through the Civil War*. Chapel Hill: University of North Carolina Press, 2004.

———. "'One Woman So Dangerous to Public Morals': Gender and Power in the Eaton Affair." *Journal of the Early Republic* 17, no. 2 (Summer 1997): 237–75.

Wood, Nicholas P. "A 'Class of Citizens': The Earliest Black Petitioners to Congress and Their Quaker Allies." *William and Mary Quarterly* 74, no. 1 (January 2017): 109–44.

Woodman, Harold D. *King Cotton and His Retainers; Financing and Marketing the Cotton Crop of the South, 1800–1925*. Lexington: University of Kentucky Press, 1968.

Wosh, Peter J. "Going Postal." *American Archivist* 61, no. 1 (Spring 1998): 220–39.

Wright, Robert E. "Bank Ownership and Lending Patterns in New York and Pennsylvania, 1781–1831." *Business History Review* 73, no. 1 (Spring 1999): 40–60.

———. "Governance and the Success of U.S. Community Banks, 1790–2010: Mutual Savings Banks, Local Commercial Banks, and the Merchants (National) Bank of New Bedford, Massachusetts." *Business and Economic History On-line* 9 (2011): 1–34.

Yellin, Jean Fagan. "Written by Herself: Harriet Jacobs' Slave Narrative." *American Literature* 53, no. 3 (November 1981): 479–86.

Yellin, Jean Fagan, and John C. Van Horne, eds. *The Abolitionist Sisterhood: Women's Political Culture in Antebellum America*. Ithaca: Cornell University Press, 1994.

Yoder, Paton. "Tavern Regulation in Virginia: Rationale and Reality." *Virginia Magazine of History and Biography* 87, no. 3 (July 1979): 259–78.

Yokota, Kariann Akemi. *Unbecoming British: How Revolutionary America Became a Postcolonial Nation*. New York: Oxford University Press, 2011.

Young, Andrew W. *History of the Town of Warsaw, New York, from Its First Settlement to the Present Time*. Buffalo: Sage, 1869.

Zaborney, John J. *Slaves for Hire: Renting Enslaved Laborers in Antebellum Virginia*. Baton Rouge: Louisiana State University Press, 2012.

Zacek, Natalie. *A Kingdom for a Horse: Making Self, Region, and Nation at the American Racetrack, 1791–1900*. Louisana State University Press, Baton Rouge, forthcoming 2024.

Zaeske, Susan. *Signatures of Citizenship: Petitioning, Antislavery, and Women's Political Identity*. Chapel Hill: University of North Carolina Press, 2003.

Zagarri, Rosemarie. *Revolutionary Backlash: Women and Politics in the Early American Republic*. Philadelphia: University of Pennsylvania Press, 2007.

Zakim, Michael. *Ready-Made Democracy: A History of Men's Dress in the American Republic, 1760–1860*. Chicago: University of Chicago Press, 2003.

Zboray, Ronald J. *A Fictive People: Antebellum Economic Development and the American Reading Public*. New York: Oxford University Press, 1993.

———. "The Transportation Revolution and Antebellum Book Distribution Reconsidered." *American Quarterly* 38, no. 1 (Spring 1986): 53–71.

Zboray, Ronald J., and Mary Saracino Zboray. "Whig Women, Politics, and Culture in the Campaign of 1840: Three Perspectives from Massachusetts." *Journal of the Early Republic* 17, no. 2 (Summer 1997): 277–315.

Zelnick, Eran. "Self-Evident Walls: Reckoning with Recent Histories of Race and Nation." *Journal of the Early Republic* 41, no. 1 (Spring 2021): 1–38.

Zenkteler, Matthew, Greg Hearn, Marcus Foth, and Marion McCutcheon. "Distribution of Home-Based Work in Cities: Implications for Planning and Policy in the Pandemic Era." *Journal of Urban and Regional Analysis* 14, no. 2 (2022): 187–210.

Zylstra, Geoff D. "Whiteness, Freedom, and Technology: The Racial Struggle over Philadelphia's Streetcars, 1859–1867." *Technology and Culture* 52, no. 4 (October 2011): 678–702.

Index

Page numbers in italics refer to figures. Page numbers followed by 't' refer to tables.

9 781469 675541